THE
FRENCH
POLITY

COMPARATIVE STUDIES OF POLITICAL LIFE

SERIES EDITOR: **Martin O. Heisler**

THE FRENCH POLITY

WILLIAM SAFRAN
University of Colorado

LONGMAN
New York and London

For Marian, Gabriella, and Joshua

THE FRENCH POLITY

Longman Inc., New York
Associated companies, branches, and representatives
throughout the world.

COPYRIGHT © 1977 BY LONGMAN INC.

MANUFACTURED IN THE UNITED STATES OF AMERICA

Printed:J I H G F E D
Year: 8 7 6 5 4 3 2 1

Library of Congress Cataloging in Publication Data

Safran, William.
    The French polity.

    (Comparative studies of political life)
    Bibliography: p.
    Includes index.
    1. France—Politics and government—1958–
I. Title.
JN2594.2.S23   1979   320.9'44'083   79-15019
ISBN 0-582-28102-4

NOTE ON THE SECOND IMPRESSION

In this second impression the main body of the text, which was completed in the late summer of 1976, remains largely unchanged, except for the correction of some errors that critics had kindly called to my attention, and a few additions and clarifications. The last part of chapter 13 has been recast, however. It now includes the results of the parliamentary elections of March 1978 and a discussion of developments in the party system that have occurred in the past two years.

W.S.
Boulder, Colorado
August 1978

PREFACE

This study of French politics is oriented around a number of themes, among them the following: institutional innovation within the context of constitutional continuity; the importance of both old and new decision-making structures, and the conflict between them; the persistence of administrative centralism; and democratic forms of elite selection modified by the durability of a political class.

In exploring these and other themes, I have tried to combine "modern" and "traditional" approaches. I have discussed a variety of models, without necessarily following any of them. Nevertheless, this work deliberately shows an institutionalist bias, owing to my conviction that the decision-making environment cannot be fully understood without sufficiently detailed treatment of parliaments, executives, bureaucracies, and other formal structures that have some meaning in France. Moreover, I have made frequent—and, I hope, judicious—references to earlier French regimes, in the belief that many institutional and sociological aspects of present-day France cannot be properly appreciated without such references. I have devoted a separate chapter (chapter 4) to the French Constitution and its background, because in France basic legal norms determine, and reflect, much of the contemporary political reality, and because it is a major theme of this book that the Fifth Republic does not constitute a clean break with the past.

In the awareness that bare facts do not speak for themselves, I have freely resorted to examples, explanations, and interpretations, some of which are doubtlessly controversial. While critical of certain aspects of French political behavior, I have been unable to accept the dichotomization of the "French-continental" and the "Anglo-American" culture models that has been in vogue in this country for several years and has served, incidentally, as a means of ethnocentric self-congratulation. Despite elements of fragmentation and dissensus, French political culture has been no more "dysfunctional," insofar as stability and policy outputs are concerned, than Anglo-American culture. For that reason, although I have frequently referred to the May Events of 1968, I have underemphasized their significance—in contrast to their customary overromanticization. The shifting emphasis of positive and negative aspects of French social and economic life and the frequent juxtaposition of "favorable" and "unfavorable" aggregate data (chapter 2) reflect my belief that France is neither hopelessly backward or "blocked" nor at the threshold of a "postindustrial" era. Moreover, it is argued (in chapter 3) that the incompleteness of institutional "Americanization" and the persistence of premodern patterns are not necessarily detrimental to system cohesion or democracy.

I have dealt with the historic background of political parties in order to show how they, like other institutions, are the captives of history; but at the same time, I subscribe neither to the "absolute-value" interpretation of French party ideology nor to its opposite: the currently fashionable exaggerations concerning the "end of ideology." The theme of a functional autonomy of ideology—e.g., the coexistence of behavioral conservatism with a widespread commitment to egalitarian and other progressive ideals—is taken up in chapters 2, 3, and 5. While I accept the evidence about recent trends in the bipolarization of parties, I also stress the survival of centrism as a distinct orientation, as well as the continuation of multipartisanship.

In each of the chapters dealing with institutions (chapters 7 to 10) an attempt was made to deal with them from various—and sometimes clashing—perspectives: on the one hand, to show how—if at all—these institutions have departed from their origins; on the other, to discuss the individuals who run the institutions, both in terms of recruitment and role perceptions. While fully acknowledging the predominance of the executive, I have provided a detailed treatment of Parliament, because that body has not been so permanently devalued as to be dismissed in a few paragraphs.

There is a separate chapter on economic planning (chapter 11), not only because that enterprise is of intrinsic intellectual interest, but also because it has spawned new decision-making institutions and new patterns of intergroup discourse that contribute to an incremental pluralism. Conversely, local and regional governments are subsumed under the general category of "Administration" (chapter 10) because French decision making is essentially national-bureaucratic and because "regionalization" has been more a matter of declaratory commitment than institutional reality.

The final chapter (chapter 13) addresses itself to the general question whether the "original" Fifth Republic still exists; in a summary overview of the evolution of politics under three Presidents, it tries to determine to what extent Gaullism has been transcended under President Giscard d'Estaing.

This study evolved from several years of teaching courses on French and Western European politics, and from perceptions gathered from discussions with academicians, politicians, and other people during three extended visits in France. In addition to the books listed in the Bibliography, I have relied heavily on periodical literature, much of it cited in the footnotes. After much agonizing, I have eliminated numerous source references, generally retaining those relating to material that is fugitive or contentious.

I wish to express my thanks to Henry Ehrmann, Maurice Fiskus, Alain Lancelot, Mme. Marie Meller, Jean-François Petitbon, Mme. Françoise Praderie, André Rossi, and Claude Salem—some for reading parts of the manuscript; others for supplying important information, correcting misapprehensions, and helping me to understand some of the intricacies of French political life that cannot always be gleaned from the existing literature—and all of them for numerous personal kindnesses. I also want to thank my colleagues George Codding, James Scarritt, Richard Wilson and W. A. E. Skurnik for acting as critical sounding boards and helping me clarify some of my ideas. My thanks also go to Edward Artinian for his encouragement and suggestions, and for obtaining several critical readings of an earlier draft. I wish in particular to mention with appreciation two anonymous reviewers for their thorough reading of the manuscript, and for their valuable suggestions, most of which I have incorporated in the final version. Finally, I want to express my gratitude to those to whom this book is dedicated: my wife, Marian, for having shared with me the excitement of Parisian life and the discomfitures of French inflation, for having read every line, and for having unstintingly contributed her critical judgment and editorial skills; and my children, for tolerating all-too-frequent deprivations of paternal attention. None of them, of course, shares my responsibility for any errors of fact or interpretation.

CONTENTS

TABLES

FIGURES

ABBREVIATIONS

CD	Centre démocrate
CDP	Centre de la démocratie et du progrès
CDS	Centre des démocrates sociaux
CERES	Centre d'Etudes, de Recherche et d'Education Socialistes
CFDT	Confédération française démocratique du travail
CFT	Confédération française de travail
CFTC	Confédération française de travailleurs chrétiens
CGC	Confédération générale des cadres
CGP	Commissariat général au Plan
CGPME	Confédération générale des petites et moyennes entreprises
CGT	Confédération générale du travail
CID-UNATI	Comité d'information et de défense-union nationale des artisans et travailleurs indépendants
CIR	Convention des institutions républicaines
CNEJ	Centre Nationale d'Etudes Judiciaires
CNIP	Centre national des indépendants et paysans
CNJA	Centre national des jeunes agriculteurs
CNPF	Conseil national du patronat français
CODER	Commission de développement économique régional
CSM	Confédération des syndicats médicaux
DATAR	Délégation à l'aménagement du térritoire et à l'action régionale
ENA	Ecole Nationale d'Administration
FEN	Fédération d'éducation nationale
FGDS	Fédération de la gauche démocratique et socialiste
FNOSS	Fédération nationale des organisations de sécurité sociale
FNSEA	Fédération nationale des syndicats des exploitants agricoles
FO	Force Ouvrière
HLM	Habitations à loyer modéré
IDI	Institut de développement industriel
IFOP .	Institut français d'opinion publique

INSEE	Institut national de la statistique et des études économiques
JAC	Jeunesse agricole chrétienne
LGDJ	Librairie Générale de Droit et de Jurisprudence
MODEF	Mouvement de coordination et de défense des exploitants agricoles familiales
MRP	Mouvement républicain populaire
OAS	Organisation armée sécrète
ORTF	Office de radiodiffusion-télévision françaises
PCF	Parti communiste français
PDM	Progrès et démocratie moderne
PR	Parti républicain
PRL	Parti républicain de la liberté
PS	Parti socialiste
PSA	Parti socialiste autonome
PSU	Parti socialiste unifié
PUF	Presses Universitaires de France
RFSP	Revue française de science politique
RGR	Rassemblement de gauche républicaine
RI	Républicains indépendants
RPF	Rassemblement du peuple français
RPR	Rassemblement du peuple pour la République
SFIO	Section française d'Internationale Ouvrière
SMIC	Salaire minimum industriel garanti
SMIG	Salaire minimum industriel de croissance
SOFRES	Société française d'enquêtes par sondages
TVA	Taxe sur valeur ajoutée
UDCA	Union pour la défense des commerçants et des artisans
UDF	Union pour la démocratie française
UDR	Union démocratique pour la République
UDSR	Union démocratique et socialiste de la Résistance
UDT	Union démocratique de travail
UEC	Union nationale des étudiants communistes de France
UER	Unité d'enseignement et de recherche
UFF	Union et fraternité française
UGSD	Union de la gauche socialiste et démocrate
UNEF	Union nationale des étudiants de France
UNR	Union pour la nouvelle République
URP	Union des républicains de progrès pour le soutien du Président

THE
FRENCH
POLITY

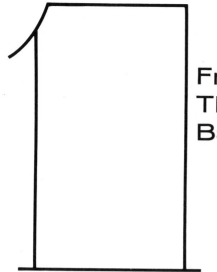

France:
The Historical
Background

"I have never appreciated, as I do here and now, how beautiful is France, how great, and how generous."

General de Gaulle in Algiers, June 1958

"We are an old country, and we are a new country. Everything demonstrates this fact. Every time the world outside is in contact with French ability, French technique, and French values, it is subjected to a kind of universal astonishment."

General de Gaulle in Saint-Chamond, June 1959

A Frenchman would never ask why his countrymen, or civilized people elsewhere, should study France, for he believes that her grandeur is self-evident. Such a point of view is not merely the result of indoctrination or patriotism, but derives from the fact that France is indeed unique among modern countries. The historical importance of France, the prestige of her language and culture, her diplomatic accomplishments, and the influence of her institutions—all these have been widely acknowledged.

France is the largest country in continental Europe (after Russia), her boundaries having been more or less fixed some two centuries ago. She achieved national unity earlier than did Germany or Italy; she was the first important European country to produce a revolution, to commit herself to republican rule, and to export her political ideals to foreign countries. Her great natural wealth, once measured in agricultural terms, led to relative economic self-sufficiency and inward-looking tendencies,

3

while her universal principles and her military power contributed to her international outlook. France is a country in which revolutionary mythologies have persisted alongside social and economic traditionalism, and in which the apparent disorder in politics has contrasted with the orderly and rigid patterns of culture in general: the geometric layout of Paris and other cities, the neoclassical architecture, the formal gardens, the stylized drama, a strictly codified etiquette, uniform school curricula, and the continuing attempts by the authorities to exert formal control over the purity of the French language.[1] Despite her changes of regime, which have occurred with disconcerting regularity, France is a country of uniform values, a highly developed national identity, and a centralized government. But she is also a country of remarkable diversity of cultural outlooks.

Historically, France owes much to Julius Caesar. Survivals of the Roman conquest are obvious: the Romance language, the Roman law, the mixed racial stock (Latin grafted onto the indigenous Celtic and Germanic), and the French toleration of differing races (a toleration that exists at least on the philosophical level). The movement toward centralization of the various autonomous provinces was gradual, and occurred essentially from about A.D. 1000 to the sixteenth century.

Physically, France is far from a uniform country. There are mountainous areas of the Alps, the Jura and the Vosges in the east, the Pyrenees in the south, and the Auvergne (Massif Central). In the south there is the subtropical vegetation typical of the Mediterranean; in the Paris area, there are forested regions and extensive wheat fields; in the west, there is the flat coastal Vendée fronting on the Atlantic Ocean; and there are the flatlands of the northwest spilling over into Belgian Flanders.[2] The French like to point out these diverse features, as well as the moderate climate and the fertility of the soil, and to relate them to the development of national pride, the economic and social self-sufficiency of their country, the hexagonal symmetry of her map, and the peculiar mix of national and local orientations.

Despite her relatively small size, France is at least as complex as the United States, and as culturally and geographically diverse; and it is noteworthy how many features the two countries share, regardless of differences in historical development. To name just a few common traits: (1) the belief that a constitution does not "evolve" organically, but rather is the result of rational choice; (2) the principle of popular

---

1. See Raymond Rudorff, *The Myth of France* (New York: Coward-McCann, 1970), pp. 183–87.
2. A. Ferre, "La terre et les paysages de France," in *La France d'aujourd'hui* (Paris: Librairie Hatier, 1960), pp. 28–42.

sovereignty, that is, the axiom that governmental powers are derived from the people; (3) a commitment to the principle of equal rights for all; (4) the occasional ahistoricism of political discourse: in the United States, the belief of the Founding Fathers that a political experiment could be started from scratch, and that previous political formulas could be rejected in toto; and in France, the politics, culture, and even religion of "reason" that, shortly after the Revolution of 1789, led to the temporary "abolition" of God, of the Christian calendar, and of traditional social institutions; (5) the rejection of "intermediaries" between the decision makers and the "general will"—embodied in the United States in Federalist Paper No. 10 and in France in the *Loi le Chapelier*; (6) the persistent localism in politics and the lack of discipline (found in some French parties), as well as the high degree of "personalism" in legislative behavior.

There are, in addition, similar political commitments to equal representation, to separation of church and state, and to economic modernization. Republicanism has characterized five of France's eleven political systems since 1789; each republic has given her new institutions and patterns, which were at least in part incorporated in succeeding regimes. The First Republic, from 1792 to 1799, proclaimed the notion of popular sovereignty, produced the Declaration of the Rights of Man and the Citizen, reduced the power of the church and inaugurated the secular age in politics. During the Second Republic, from 1848 to 1852, universal male suffrage was introduced, and a plebiscitarian element—the direct election of the President by popular vote—was injected into French political life. During the Third Republic, from 1875 to 1940, the church was formally disestablished, the executive was weakened and made responsible to a Parliament that asserted its supremacy, and the French nation, it seemed, was decisively converted to republicanism.

But republicanism is also a myth and, as such, has had to compete with prerepublican and antirepublican myths and political patterns. Many innovations introduced in the *ancien régime* have in fact persisted to the present day, and have been uneasily combined with republican rule. The monarchical centralization of administration, introduced by Cardinal Richelieu, Mazarin, and Colbert during the seventeenth century, has continued to the present day with only minor modifications; and the preeminence of Paris, secured by the Bourbon kings, still informs French public, commercial, industrial, and cultural life. The old social and legal distinctions between the nobility and the middle class that had characterized the *ancien régime* have given way, but they have been replaced by distinctions, almost equally pronounced, between the bourgeoisie and the working class. The French republic, whatever its latest constitutional expression, has continued to be adorned with several monarchist glosses: the glorification of French kings and of the royal and martial tradition in the history books, the châteaus and museums; the refurbishing—in the name of art or cultural continuity—of old buildings and neighborhoods; the retention of prerepublican codes of social intercourse; and the nostalgia or craving for a national hero.

Just as popular dissatisfactions with existing monarchies expressed themselves in periodic uprisings that culminated in republican experiments, these latter were inevitably overlaid and modified with reactionary or monarchist institutions, patterns, and ideologies. Thus the attempt in 1789 to moderate the absolute rule of the Bourbon dynasty ended with its abolition. The revolutionary republic that replaced it was in turn replaced by a Reign of Terror, a Directory and, finally, a Consulate. This last gave way to the First Empire of Napoleon Bonaparte (who had been first consul) in 1804. When that empire collapsed, largely from external causes, the French regime returned to Bourbon rule with the accession of Louis XVIII to the throne in 1814. That regime retained, at least in theory, some of Napoleon's accomplishments: the establishment of a merit-based bureaucracy, the abolition of feudal tax obligations, and a system of codified laws. Moreover, it looked as if the Charter of 1814 provided an auspicious framework for a constitutional monarchy on the English model. The Charter called for religious freedom, the sanctity of property, procedural safeguards against arrest, equality of all before the law, and some limited participation in the legislative process by a bicameral Parliament. But when Charles X assumed the throne in 1824, monarchic rule became increasingly arbitrary. The subsequent replacement of the Bourbon king by Louis Philippe (of the House of Orleans) after the Revolution of 1830 was intended to provide a better opportunity for the development of constitutional rule. As if to underline its republican spirit, the "July Monarchy" used as its symbol not the fleur-de-lis of the Bourbons, but the tricolor flag of the Revolution. Censorship was abolished; equality before the law was guaranteed; extraordinary courts were forbidden; trial by jury was instituted; and the Parliament was given more significant legislative responsibilities. But that regime too, was a disappointment, for Parliament continued to be disregarded, opposition leaders were arrested, and political liberty did not flourish. In 1848, the French revolted again, and instituted the Second Republic. The Constitution of (November) 1848 was a remarkably democratic and modern document, especially since its "social" provisions foreshadowed the programmatic constitutions of twentieth-century welfare states. The one plebiscitarian feature

of the Constitution—the provision for direct election of the President—
was soon injudiciously used by the French people when they voted for
Louis Napoleon, the nephew of the great emperor, as President, and
elected an Assembly with a monarchist majority; and when, three years
later, they acquiesced in the establishment of a Second Empire under
Napoleon III.

The Second Empire was, in theory, a republican or "popular" empire in the sense that it was inaugurated by a plebiscite. The Constitution of January 1852, on which it was based, confirmed "the great
principles proclaimed in 1789." The chief executive was "responsible to
the French people" (rather than to God), and "legislative power" was to
be exercised collectively by the President,[3] the Senate, and the Chamber
of Deputies. The Senate was appointed by Napoleon III, but the Chamber was elected on the basis of universal manhood suffrage. However,
legislative initiative rested with the President (later Emperor) and ministers were responsible to him rather than to Parliament. Moreover,
ministers were forbidden to be members of Parliament. The republican
features of the Constitution were progressively subverted by imperial
interference in legislative elections, by the persecution of opposition
candidates, and by the requirement of an oath of imperial support and
allegiance for all deputies. To counteract growing popular disenchantment—perhaps boredom—with the regime after 1860, Napoleon III
made halfhearted attempts to liberalize it by increasing the power of
the Parliament, which even obtained the right of legislative initiative
and interpellation. But it was too late, because the defeat of France at
the hands of the Prussians in 1870 completely discredited and disorganized the Second Empire, and a rebellion in Paris provided its
coup de grâce.

The regime that followed the Second Empire was a republic by de-
fault. The National Assembly that was hurriedly elected in 1871 to
provide a government capable of negotiating peace with Bismarck's
Germany did not want a republic at all: more than 400 of its 650 deputies were monarchists. But since the Assembly could not agree on which
of the three dynasties (Bourbon, Orleans, Bonaparte) should be called
upon to provide a king, the precise nature of the regime was left in
abeyance. The Assembly adopted a skeleton constitution that dealt
merely with the "organization of the public powers"—the executive and
legislature—and the relationship between them. This constitution contained neither a preamble nor a Bill of Rights. The first provisional

3. According to the Constitution of January 1852, Napoleon was to be President for
   a ten-year period. He was proclaimed emperor in December of that year.

president, Adolphe Thiers, who had served as a minister in several preceding monarchical regimes, had become convinced that "a Republic divides us least." His successor, Marshal MacMahon, was a conservative, a clericalist, and a monarchist. The question of the regime was tentatively and surreptitiously settled in 1875 when the Parliament accepted—by a one-vote majority—an amendment providing that "the President of the Republic shall be elected by a plurality of votes of the Senate and the Chamber of Deputies meeting in joint session."[4]

The "provisional" Third Republic was to last sixty-five years, and the political patterns established in it were to influence succeeding republican regimes. There was a popularly elected Chamber of Deputies, juxtaposed to a Senate dominated by indirectly elected, relatively aged, conservative representatives of rural communes. The cabinet, though appointed by the President, was collectively responsible to Parliament, which could oust it by a vote of no-confidence. The President, elected for seven years, was "irresponsible" in that his acts had to be countersigned by a minister. But he did have the power to dissolve the Chamber (upon the advice of the Senate).

The conflict between the legislature and the executive was never completely resolved, at least in formal constitutional terms, and was to lead to several crises. The first and most important of these was the episode of May 16, 1877, when President MacMahon dissolved the Assembly because he did not get along with the (by then "Radical") majority of the Chamber, and appointed a cabinet that did not enjoy the confidence of the latter. Following MacMahon's resignation in 1879, almost all succeeding Presidents of the Republic, from Jules Grévy onward, were deliberately selected on the basis of their lack of ambition. The presidential dissolution power atrophied, and the Chief of State became a figurehead, like an English monarch, rather than an active political decision maker. In fact, of the fourteen Presidents of the Third Republic, only six served full seven-year terms. Of the remaining chiefs of state, one died in office; two were assassinated; one resigned after six months in office because of his alleged involvement in scandals; one relinquished his position because of insanity; and four were prematurely forced out by the Chamber of Deputies. The Third Republic became a parliamentary regime that proved durable but very unstable, with the legislature recklessly overturning cabinets at an average rate of once every eight months.

While in Britain a gradually evolving democracy and parliamentary supremacy could accommodate itself easily to the retention of traditional

4. These sessions were usually held at the royal palace in Versailles.

institutions and patterns, such as the Crown, the House of Lords, the Established Church, and the acceptance of a deferential and hierarchical social order, the French, with their Cartesian intellectualism, were unable to compromise clashing political norms. For the moment, "republicanism" was grudgingly accepted, but its precise meaning was subject to disagreement. Its dominant form was Jacobinism, which could be traced back to the belief, espoused by Rousseau as well as the men of the Reign of Terror, in a direct democracy that excluded all intermediaries; in egalitarianism, anticlericalism, and the supremacy of the state as the embodiment of the "general will." And yet the Paris Commune of 1871, the first French egalitarian (or "socialist") uprising, was mercilessly crushed by the bourgeoisie that led the new Republic. Moreover, despite the distrust of institutions that would interpose themselves between people and government, the role of the Senate, an indirectly elected body, became very important. A commitment to the Republic did not necessarily mean the acceptance of a particular manifestation of it: the government was hated, while the state was depended upon by various sectors of society that expected protection and subvention.

Nor did the commitment to the Republic resolve a deep-seated dissensus about basic political values. This dissensus, which preceded and succeeded the Third Republic and must be considered one of the "hereditary factors"[5] of the French polity, stems from the confusion of three strains coexisting uneasily in French political culture: rationalism, historicism, and hero worship. The rationalistic spirit has been reflected in recurrent attempts to elevate a particular set of abstract principles and to construct a "logical" political system on their basis.[6] This attitude was personified by Abbé Sieyès, who, after the Revolution of 1789, wrote several draft constitutions based on his principles of an "indivisible popular sovereignty" and a "just representation"—principles first embodied in the Constitution of 1791. Historicism implies the belief that a political system cannot be constructed from logical blueprints; rather, it is a reaction to, and an evolution from, a nation's collective experiences, which are not always rational. In order to "explain" their political positions, many French citizens refer, without more specific identification, to "the 18th Brumaire" (in 1799, when Napoleon instituted his *coup d'état*); "the July Monarchy"; "the Affair of May 16"; "the episode of May 13" (the revolt of the Algerian officers in 1958); and "the May Events" (of 1968)—as if the references were clearly un-

5. Dorothy Pickles, *The Fifth French Republic* (3rd ed.; New York: Praeger, 1966), p. 3.
6. Charles Morazé, *The French and the Republic* (Ithaca, N.Y.: Cornell University Press, 1958), pp. 20–31.

derstood by all French school children. Moreover, all French political attitudes are said to be shaped by the Revolution of 1789. The republicans have considered themselves the true heirs of the Revolution, because they trace their own commitments to a secular parliamentary government to the years following that great event. The moderates believed that the Revolution established, once and for all, the political ascendancy of the bourgeoisie. The Left considered it their task to "complete" the revolution by adding economic rights to the political rights already gained, thereby achieving "liberty, equality, and fraternity"; while the Right considered the Revolution a mistake that must be rectified. The hero-worshiping French are essentially antirationalist and historicist. The belief that institutions are run by people and are therefore corruptible is coupled with the belief that there are individuals who are untainted by corruption and who must be called upon to rectify the evils of the "system" and to advance national unity. The French have always had numerous historical models for such heroes.

The memory of such heroes and the revolt against reason explain why the Third Republic was confronted by repeated irruptions of traditionalism, Bonapartism, monarchism, and fascism. In 1886, General Boulanger, a "man on horseback," was encouraged by antirepublican and clericalist forces to institute a *coup d'état*, and he might have succeeded had he not lost his nerve. In the 1890s the Dreyfus Affair, in which militarism, monarchism, clericalism, and anti-Semitism colluded in the pressing of trumped-up charges of espionage against a Jewish military officer, divided France into two hostile camps and almost destroyed the Republic. In the 1920s and 1930s, the *Action française*, the *Croix de Feu*, and other extreme nationalist and clericalist movements challenged the legitimacy and efficacy of the regime. Yet the Third Republic survived all these challenges. In the first decade of the twentieth century, the church was separated from the state; and the regime was on solid enough foundations to emerge intact from the experience of World War I. Parliament had asserted its supremacy, at least in theory; and despite chronic instability and legislative immobilism, it seemed that the egalitarian aspect of republicanism would finally be taken into account when the Popular Front, a left-wing coalition under Léon Blum in 1936, instituted far-reaching social reforms.

The Third Republic—the longest-lasting since 1789—ended with the fall of Paris to the invading German armies in the summer of 1940. Whether the Vichy regime that followed was constituted legally or not; whether the Republic could have survived if France had not been defeated; or whether the political institutions had been so subverted from within by apathy, defeatism, or antidemocratic sentiment as to weaken

France's power to fight Germany effectively—all these are questions not susceptible to clear answers. (France has only gradually been freeing herself from a Vichy guilt complex—stemming from the collaborationist behavior of many of her citizens—and has begun to reexamine the Occupation period objectively in both fiction and nonfiction, as well as in films.)

When France was liberated in 1944, monarchism was dead. A new spirit of unity had been forged during the Resistance, and there was general agreement that the Republic should be continued or renewed. The Catholics had become republican, and their party, the MRP, emerged from the Resistance as the largest party; the Communist party, too, was considered respectable and patriotic. An unprecedented leftist majority, composed of Christian Democrats, Socialists, and Communists, participated in the first postwar (tripartite) government coalition, and agreed on the desirability of instituting a progressive welfare state.

Nevertheless, disagreement arose about the form the new Republic should take. The Communists and Socialists favored a strong unicameral legislature and a weak executive. The first draft constitution that embodied these ideas was, however, not approved in the popular referendum held in May 1946. A second draft constitution provided for bicameralism. This constitution, which inaugurated the Fourth Republic, was ratified by a bare plurality of the French people. The Communists remained unenthusiastic about it, for they opposed the Second Chamber, even in its weakened form. And Charles de Gaulle, who, as leader of the Free French during World War II, had, in his opinion and that of many French people, incarnated republican legitimacy and who had been the President of the provisional government, started a vigorous campaign against the Fourth Republic Constitution, for he favored a strong presidency that would be independent of Parliament. This opposition to the constitution was reflected in the rise of the RPF (Rally of the French People)—the first Gaullist mass movement.

The Fourth Republic has been much maligned, and its accomplishments are often minimized. Nevertheless, it instituted the first "indicative" modernization plan for the economy and thereby helped bring prosperity to France. It initiated extensive social legislation. It started France on the road to decolonization and committed the nation to participation in the Schuman Plan and the Common Market. The Radical-Socialist party, the MRP, the SFIO, and other "pro-system" parties managed, by means of shifting coalitions, to preserve the Republic for twelve years. But these parties, because of internal ideological cleavages, were unable to accomplish much-needed domestic reforms. Especially after the collapse of the tripartite coalition in 1947, the French Parliament was unable to reform the tax system; to resolve the question of Algeria; to provide France with a stable, coherent executive that would possess international and domestic credibility; or to reduce the irresponsibility of a Parliament composed of ambitious deputies.

The Economic
and Social Context

ECONOMIC DEVELOPMENT

Political development and economic progress are widely thought to be
causally related. Certainly, the contradictions in French politics have
their economic corollaries: just as French political culture is characterized
by a tug of war between liberty and authority, and between tradition
and innovation, so the French economy has experienced cycles of liberalism and interventionism (*dirigisme*), protectionism and competition,
stagnation and growth. The French industrial revolution began during
the era of Louis Philippe in the 1830s, that is, somewhat later than in
England and somewhat earlier than in Germany. Its development in
France, as elsewhere, was spurred on both by "Manchester liberalism"
(or the philosophy of laisser-faire, which was popularized in France by
Jean-Baptiste Say) and by protectionism. French tariffs in the nineteenth
and twentieth centuries were among the highest in Europe. Domestically,
industrial expansion was impressive: production doubled between 1852
and 1870; tripled between 1870 and 1914; and slackened only after
World War I and the onset of the world depression.[1]

France, however, was not as rapidly and thoroughly industrialized
as England or Germany. Some scholars have cited the lack of resources—
in particular coal—as an impediment to industrialization; but probably

1. See Gordon Wright, *France in Modern Times* (Chicago: Rand McNally, 1960),
pp. 343–53.

more important has been the French distaste for bigness, essentially rural outlook, fear of competition, and Malthusian ideology—the notion that resources are necessarily limited and cannot be enlarged, and hence that everyone ought to be conservative and parsimonious and at the same time be entitled to a governmental guarantee of his share of the economic pie.[2] The French had little enthusiasm for domestic investment; they were reluctant to buy industrial shares and even to open savings accounts, and the economy suffered from periodic flights of capital to other European countries. Still another reason for the inadequate pace of industrial development and the underdeveloped mass consumption ethos was the distribution bottleneck: many items produced in the provinces returned to the provincial markets only after having passed through the hands of middlemen in Paris.[3] The economic dependence of the provinces upon the national capital has paralleled the political, cultural, and administrative dependence on Paris. Even today, most decisions affecting the provinces are channeled through Paris, just as the railway and road networks radiate outward from the capital.

Among the most important impediments to industrialization and to the growth of mass production was the rather insufficient domestic market. This in turn was due to the demographic stagnation resulting from the many wars in which France was embroiled, and as a result of which lost much of her productive manpower. In 1789 France, with 26 million inhabitants, was the most populous country in Europe apart from Russia; in 1973, when the French population reached 52 million, it had long been surpassed by that of Germany, Britain, and Italy.

French governments have tried to counteract demographic stagnation by a system of income supplements to families with more than one child (allocations familiales), as well as by fairly liberal immigration policies. Between 1946 and 1964, nearly 1.5 million immigrants entered France, in addition to about 1.0 million repatriates from the former French colonies in North Africa. These figures have been augmented by large numbers of "guest workers" from Spain, Portugal, Italy, and elsewhere, now manning French factories. Precisely what effect this population influx has had—and will have—on the French economy is unclear. On the one hand, it has contributed to the growth of the internal market; on the other, it has tended to keep industrial wages lower than they might have been, thus possibly reducing the pressure for industrial modernization.

2. On French Malthusianism, see Charles Morazé, *The French and the Republic* (Ithaca, N.Y.: Cornell University Press, 1958), pp. 49–62.
3. Herbert Luethy, *France Against Herself* (New York: Meridian, 1957), pp. 21–24.

By all measures France is one of the most industrialized nations in the world today. Spurred on by the French experiment in indicative economic planning inaugurated in 1946, her rate of growth, averaging close to 5 percent annually, has been much higher than that of the United States or Great Britain. Some of her industries, notably aeronautics and electronics, are among the most modern in the world. Her railway system, renovated in the late 1940s, is one of the best in Europe. Recently, certain other manifestations of economic modernization—often called "Americanization"—have been in evidence. The mass ownership of television sets and other durable goods, the proliferation of the supermarket throughout France, and the highest per capita ownership of automobiles in Europe (unfortunately coexisting with an inadequate network of superhighways) all attest to France's economic dynamism.

The growth of the national product in the past twenty-five years has been impressive, and is reflected in statistics indicating that, by 1968, the per capita income of the French had surpassed that of Britons and, temporarily, West Germans, and that by 1973, it was the fourth highest in Western Europe. Between 1959 and 1972, the purchasing power of the French doubled, consumption grew by 58 percent and the wages of workers by 63 percent (cf. table 1). This increase, nearly half of which was obtained as a consequence of the rebellions of May 1968, was partly nullified by inflation, so that the increase in real income amounted to only 28 percent. But such statistics hide the relative inequality of income distribution. In 1962, the top decile of the population received 36.8 percent of the net income and the bottom decile 0.5 percent (as compared to 34.1 percent and 0.7 percent, respectively, in 1956).

Table 1
Comparative Growth Figures, 1973
(1963 = 100)

	France	Germany	Italy	Great Britain	United States
Industrial production	185	170.6	168.3	139	164.2
Salaries	244	—	248.6	235	164.2
Retail prices	156.4	144	157.6	172.7	144.4

SOURCE: *L'Année politique 1973* (Paris: Presses Universitaires de France [hereafter cited as PUF], 1974), p. 319. Figures are for June 1973.

Or, to view the distribution somewhat differently, in 1958 the poorest 30 percent received 6.2 percent of the national income, and in 1968, only 4.8 percent. The most recent situation is illustrated in even more graphic terms: according to a report issued in 1974, the gap between the highest and the lowest deciles of earners was more than 8:1 (as compared to about 3:1 in Britain and 4:1 in Germany). There is little question that the real income of French workers has steadily declined in relation to the total output and that it has been overtaken in neighboring countries (notably West Germany); while the legal maximum work week, which in 1938 had been 40 hours, has been progressively increased, so that in 1971, at 44 hours, it was among the longest in Western Europe.[4]

France's economic growth was for many years impeded by an unbalanced distribution of her population. She is still a country of small towns and tiny rural communes, Paris being the only city with a population of over one million. The agricultural sector in France, which in 1945 accounted for a third of the labor force, has been reduced to 12 percent (in 1974), but it is still larger than in Britain, West Germany, and the United States. The majority of Frenchmen are recently—if at all—urbanized, and their cultural and emotional roots are in the provinces. The French succeeded for a long time in keeping the economy dominated by small farms and family firms producing for a limited market. Beginning with the Méline legislation of 1892, which imposed high tariffs on imported wheat, the French farmer has been accustomed to governmental protection against foreign competition. Indeed, many of the great political parties of the Third and Fourth republics, aware of their dependence on the votes of the provincial farmer and shopkeeper, embraced a protectionist ideology or policy, and thereby helped to perpetuate in France what has been called a "peasant republic."[5]

4. For samples of (sometimes conflicting) statistics, see "Comment va la France?" *L'Express,* special issue, Spring 1970, p. 18; ibid., 22–28 June 1970, p. 34; Michel Praderie, "Héritage social et chances d'ascension," in *Partage des bénéfices: expansion et inégalités en France* (Pàris: Editions de Minuit, 1969), pp. 76–78; and Karl Deutsch, *Politics and Government* (Boston: Houghton Mifflin, 1970), pp. 92–93. See also *Rapport du Centre d'études des revenus et des coûts* [CERC] (February 1974) cited in *Le Monde,* 1 June 1974. See also Gilbert Mathieu, "France, Where the Rich Are Richer," *Le Monde Weekly,* 10 June 1970; and *Annuaire statistique de la France 78,* n.s. 20 (1973): 65.
5. Gordon Wright, *Rural Revolution in France: The Peasantry in the Twentieth Century* (Stanford: Stanford University Press, 1964), p. 1. See also Yves Tavernier et al., *L'univers politique des paysans dans la France contemporaine* (Paris: Colin, 1972), pp. 12 f.

However, in the past twenty years there has been a "silent revolution" in agriculture,[6] marked by the abandonment of about 700,000 farms and the consolidation of farmland, the modernization of agricultural production, and the reduction of farm subsidies. At the same time, the government made credit more easily available for the purchase of farm machinery, so that the number of tractors increased nearly twentyfold between 1945 and 1970. The many farmers who left the land sought employment in industry and added to the growth of new urban agglomerations, especially in the environs of Paris, Lille, and Lyons. Yet despite growing urbanization, certain vestiges of rural domination in politics are still to be found. In the Third and Fourth republics the rural element—largely owing to the electoral system—dominated the Senate, and that element dominates the Senate today; many right-of-center parties reflected, and continue to reflect, the rural sector's preoccupation with smallness.

The postwar modernization of the French economy has inevitably contributed both to a consolidation of industries and to the rise of the tertiary (i.e., service and white-collar) sector. But although in the past two decades more than 150,000 independent tradesmen went out of business, the small-enterprise sector remains important socially, economically, and politically. In 1970, there were still 900,000 shopkeepers —and even in 1974 four-fifths of French businesses were family firms without outside employees. These shopkeepers continue, as in the past, to support the Radical Socialists and other non-Gaullist parties, and to fight, by means of the ballot or by spontaneous uprisings, any government that has embraced a policy of too abrupt economic modernization. Thus in 1970, CID-UNATI,[7] a radical association of small shopkeepers and artisans led by Gérard Nicoud, kidnapped policemen and destroyed local tax offices in an attempt to fight the takeover of commerce and industry by the "techno-capitalist" class.[8] It must be pointed out, however, that the techno-capitalist class is not excessively dynamic or technocratic: in 1970, 70 percent of the members of the boards of the forty largest companies were over sixty years of age; and many of the directors (présidents-directeurs-généraux—PDGs) of enterprises have attained their positions not via a business school but by virtue of their descent from the upper bourgeoisie.

6. Wright, *Rural Revolution*, pp. 143 ff.
7. CID-UNATI=*Comité d'information et de défence-Union nationale des artisans et travailleurs indépendants.*
8. *Le Monde*, 8 July 1972.

SOCIAL CLASSES AND MOBILITY

Historically, the social system of France is much like that of any other Western European country that experienced feudalism and inherited a division of society into classes of nobles, clergy, townsmen (bourgeoisie), and peasants. This division was reflected toward the end of the *ancien régime* in the "estate" representation of the old Parliament. Since that time, the bourgeoisie has gained in political and economic power; much of the landed aristocracy has disappeared or lost its importance because of revolutions, expulsions, and the impact of the guillotine. The independent farmers rose in number because of the parcellization of land among all the sons of the landowner; and in the nineteenth century, with the rise of the factory system, the industrial working class (the proletariat) made its appearance. Today it is still possible to talk about French society as being divided into the following social groups: (1) the upper class, including the graduates of the prestigious national universities, the upper echelons of the civil service, the directors of large and successful enterprises, and bankers; (2) the bourgeoisie, including members of the liberal professions, university and *lycée* professors, engineers and *cadres* (upper-echelon technical and administrative personnel), and owners of medium-sized shops and family firms; (3) the middle and lower middle class (*classe moyenne*), including white-collar employees, petty shopkeepers, lower-echelon civil servants, elementary school teachers, and, possibly, artisans; and finally (4) the lower classes (*classes populaires*), comprising in the main industrial workers and small farmers.[9] There is in France, as elsewhere in Western Europe, a correlation between class and ideology: thus membership in the working class usually implies membership in the socialist "ideological family." There is also a correlation between social status and access to economic benefits.

But such correlations are simplistic and of uncertain reliability. Ideological and class cleavages tend to overlap in complex industrial societies; in France (as in Italy) there are workers who are revolutionary, reformist, Catholic, or apathetic.[10] The perceived status of a unionized factory worker may be enhanced by the presence of foreign workers; the economic insecurity of a bourgeois may be compensated by his becoming a Knight in the Legion of Honor; and the diminishing purchas-

---

9. See David Granick, *The European Executive* (Garden City, N.Y.: Doubleday Anchor, 1964), pp. 19f. and passim.
10. Mattei Dogan, "Political Cleavage and Social Stratification in France and Italy," in *Party Systems and Voter Alignments*, ed. S. M. Lipset and S. Rokkan (New York: Free Press, 1967), pp. 175–77.

ing power of a *lycée* professor may be made up in part by the "psychic income" of his academic prestige. There are, in addition, geographical variables. There is still a status differential between residence in Paris as against the provinces; according to its former Director of Studies, the National School of Administration (ENA), which for the past twenty-five years has been training virtually all higher civil servants, is "practically closed not only to certain social classes, but also, by and large, to the provinces."[11] The social mobility that exists has been lateral rather than upward; recent statistics indicate that the majority of the various elites were descended from fathers who were themselves in elite positions (see table 2).

Between 1959 and 1964, 158,000 Frenchmen passed from salaried-worker status or from agriculture to positions of self-employment. At the same time, 68 percent of the sons of workers remained workers.[12] This lack of upward mobility (which is not decidedly different in France from that in Italy, Japan, Sweden, and even the United States),[13] fortified by a continuing inequality of educational opportunity, housing conditions, and tax loopholes for the rich—accompanied by the existence of a pronounced lower-class life style—has sharpened the self-perception of the working classes as a deprived segment.

To some extent, class cleavages and working-class consciousness have been moderated by the gradual democratization of primary and secondary education (or at least by a public commitment to the *principle* of such democratization), and the somewhat enhanced possibilities of the recruitment of the children of working-class and lower-middle-class parents to the lower echelons of the national civil service. These class cleavages have been reduced also by the expansion of the welfare state and the introduction specifically of such features as paid vacations and the statutory medical-care system. However, the worker has had to

11. *L'Express*, 27 July–2 August 1970, p. 15. See also chap. 9, p. 210.
12. Daniel Bertaux, "Mobilité sociale biographique: une critique de l'approche transversale," *Revue française de sociologie* 15 (July–September 1974): 329–60. According to an official source (INSEE no. 83, February 1973), the proportion of blue-collar workers in the total population has risen in the past two decades: it was 33.8% in 1954, 36.7% in 1962, and 37.4% in 1972. In that year, 46.4% of the active *male* population worked in factories. On the "mythology" of the tertiary sector, see André Glucksmann, "Nous ne sommes pas tous prolétaires," *Temps Modernes*, January 1974, pp. 1133–58.
13. Maurice Garnier and Lawrence Hazelrigg, "La mobilité professionnelle en France comparée à celle d'autres pays," *Revue française de sociologie* 15 (July–September 1974): 363–78. In the 1959–64 period, 36.5% went from agriculture to unskilled worker status in France, as against 55.2% in the United States. In both countries, less than 1% went from the working class to the elite. See also Raymond Boudon, *L'inegalité des chances* (Paris: Colin, 1973), for an exhaustive discussion of social mobility.

Table 2
Social Background, Education, and Elite Recruitment
(in percent)

	Justice	Business and Finance	Adminis- tration	Education	Total
Sons of industrialists	23	41	12	14	28
Sons of profes- sionals (cadre supérieur)	69	41	67	55	48
Sons of middle class	8	18	20	32	24
Postgraduate educa- tion	6	30	25	76	29
Higher education	88	48	72	20	53
No higher education	6	22	2	3	17
Lives in Paris	55	71	79	74	71
Lives in provinces	45	29	21	26	29
Born in Paris	26	37	29	22	32
Lives in one of the three wealthiest Parisian arrondissements	27	41	39	27	34

SOURCE: Olgierd Lewandowski, "Différentiation et méchanismes d'intégration de la classe dirigeante," *Revue française de sociologie* 15 (January–March 1974): 43–73. Based on INSEE sample study for 1968.

finance social security protection by means of ever-increasing payroll deductions. While paid vacations of four weeks are guaranteed by law to virtually all employed categories, a sizable proportion of industrial and agricultural workers do not take advantage of them. Family allowances are less effective than they might be as a means of encouraging the growth of the birthrate; many Frenchmen delay their marriages and procreation because of the difficulty of finding adequate housing. A large number of French families—and the vast majority of the working class—lives in substandard apartments lacking many modern facilities. Nearly half of all apartments existing in France today were built before 1914. Of course rents are low as a result of rent controls, but these have been abolished for all units constructed by private builders since the end of World War II. Since 1966, the government has provided a modest rent subsidy for some low-income families who cannot afford the inflated rents for the modern high-rises built by speculators.[14] In recent years, the government has undertaken the construction of housing projects for low- and middle-income families (habitations à loyer modéré— HLMs) in the center and the periphery of Paris and other cities. But many HLMs are in fact inhabited not by poor workers but by petit-bourgeois Frenchmen who have found means of bribing housing officials —a situation that has not contributed to an easing of interclass resentments.

After the accession of de Gaulle, co-management boards and profit-sharing schemes were introduced in order to "associate" the working class with industrial entrepreneurs and reduce proletarian resentments. In addition, interclass resentments were channeled into nationalistic (and often anti-American) sentiments, which were widespread and were counted upon to unite various socioeconomic sectors. With the partial disintegration of Gaullism that was reflected in the election of President Giscard d'Estaing in 1974, the resentments of the disprivileged have had to be resolved in a more concrete fashion. Despite the decline in economic output induced by the petroleum crisis, Giscard has allocated generous amounts of money for increases in unemployment and pension payments, and has even initiated measures aimed at the democratization of the tax system. However, such measures cannot immediately reverse the fiscally conservative policies introduced earlier in the Fifth Republic. Among these policies were the reduction of social security benefits and the introduction of the regressive value-added tax system (TVA).[15] Moreover, spurts of inflation and devaluations of the franc could rarely be compensated for by sufficient wage increases, because the fragmented trade-union movement had been in a very poor position to bargain col-

14. See J. T. Carroll, The French: How They Live and Work (New York: Praeger, 1969).
15. In 1968, France, compared to other Common Market countries, collected the lowest proportion of its total revenues from corporate taxes (8.1%) and the highest from indirect taxes (70.6%). European Community, no. 4 (April 1971): 32.

lectively, and because the officially determined minimum wage (the SMIG or the SMIC)[16] seldom made up for increases in the cost of living. Finally, the decline of the role of Parliament—in which the working classes, via Socialist and Communist parties, always had reasonably effective representation—and the corresponding enhancement of the position of the higher civil service since 1958, had greatly weakened the access of the working classes to decision-making organs.

For many years, the gap between the white collar (*salariat*) and the blue collar (*prolétariat*) in France remained one of the largest in Western Europe.[17] The radical trade unions (including the Communist-dominated CGT), despite their verbal commitment to egalitarianism, were hesitant about closing this gap because they hoped to recruit and retain as members the very status-conscious white-collar and *cadre* elements. Moreover, some leaders of political movements most given to egalitarian rhetoric, particularly the Socialist party and the PSU, were professors and others of upper-middle class or middle-class descent and status, and they did not wish to lose their social and economic privileges as a result of a precipitate policy of social leveling.

During the past two decades, the salary and status gaps between blue- and white-collar employees have been narrowed. In 1954, the median income of the white-collar employee was 13 percent higher than that of the industrial worker; in 1974, the differential had been reduced to 4 percent. This salary convergence may be interpreted as a sign that France has entered the "postindustrial" stage and as proof of the corollary proposition regarding the *embourgeoisement* of the masses, the weakening of the class struggle, and the "end of ideology" (see chapters 3 and 5).[18] Nevertheless, white-collar employees, too, have routinized jobs and low pay, experience unemployment, and resent the inequities of the tax system. Occasionally, industrial and white-collar workers discover that they have interests in common with intellectuals and students—the present and future members of the elite—as when,

16. SMIG—*salaire minimum industriel garanti*, the ordinary minimum wage; SMIC—*salaire minimum industriel de croissance*, a minimum wage dependent upon productivity growth.
17. Roger Prioret, "Les nouveaux pouvoirs," *L'Express*, special issue, Spring 1970, p. 26.
18. The gap between both categories of wage earners and the upper classes has not been reduced: between 1954 and 1974, the middle-level executive earned twice as much, and the top executive four times as much, as the individuals in the two above categories. Report of *CERC*, cited by Gilbert Mathieu, "Wage differentials: a steady narrowing since '68," *Guardian* (Weekly), 16 May 1976, p. 13. On the meaning of "postindustrial society," see Todd La Porte and C. J. Abrams, "Alternative Patterns of Postindustria," in *Politics and the Future of Industrial Society*, ed. Leon N. Lindberg (New York: McKay, 1976), pp. 21–24.

during the May Events of 1968, these social groups attempted (or pretended) to support each other in public demonstrations against the Gaullist system. But such camaraderie is at best tenuous, largely because of the history of mutual distrust, the different backgrounds, and the divergent concerns of these groups. Even after the May Events, the Parisian "mandarins" (the Sorbonne professors), no matter how far to the left, still live in their spacious apartments in the bourgeois neighborhoods of Paris, while the workers continue to live in the suburban slums, the "Red Belt," around the capital.

RELIGION AND CULTURE

France is, constitutionally, a secular country. The Catholic church was disestablished two generations ago; public education, even in the provinces, is consciously and officially nonreligious; and many political parties, and a large percentage of the parliamentary deputies from the Third Republic to the present, have had a decidedly anticlerical ideology. In the view of the Radical Socialists, Catholicism was incompatible with republicanism, and the Socialists held religion in general to be incompatible with social and economic progressivism. As if to advertise its commitment to laicism in public life, the Third Republic after the 1880s accorded few chances to practicing Catholics to serve as cabinet ministers. With the outbreak of World War II, Catholicism "reestablished" itself as a positive political force when many priests joined the Resistance; after the war a new Catholic party, the MRP, emerged with the fullest republican credentials. In the immediate postwar years France was, nevertheless, considered a "mission" country by the Vatican, which encouraged priests to mingle with workers and to live with them. But such identification went too far; after priests joined unions, participated in strikes, and even left the priesthood, the Vatican suspended the "worker-priest" movement in 1953. (It was revived on a modest scale in the mid-1960s.)

Despite the lessening of attacks upon religion by left-wing political parties, especially in the course of the past decade, the "convergence" between Catholicism and the working-class outlook remains incomplete, because many workers continue to identify the church with the system of economic privilege. In 1970, 46 percent of French workers considered themselves nonpracticing Catholics. To the extent that France is urbanized, it is largely "de-Christianized"; little more than a third of all Frenchmen (and only 8 percent of workers) regularly attend mass.[19]

19. François A. Isambert, "Les ouvriers et l'Eglise Catholique," *Revue française de sociologie* 15 (October–December 1974): 529–51.

Even in the provinces (where church attendance is predominantly a matter for women) there are now many small communes from which the priest has departed, and in which churches are in a state of disrepair.

There are, however, signs of a revival of religion. In Paris and its surroundings, for example, forty-four new parish churches were established between 1966 and 1972.[20] The parochial (mainly Catholic) schools are maintaining their enrollments, which in the late 1960s embraced 15–20 percent of all French schoolchildren from kindergarten through secondary school. There are several possible explanations for the survival of this aspect of religious culture. Undoubtedly, the Debré laws of 1959, under which Catholic schools obtain public funds after "contracting" with the national Ministry of Education to include state-approved subject matter in their curricula, have helped to sustain the Catholic school system. Moreover, indications are that in some of the less developed provinces—e.g., Brittany, where Catholic school enrollment is very high—parochial education is frequently viewed as a means of asserting the regions' cultural uniqueness. Even in the cities, parents may consider parochial schools a means of preserving many traditional moral values that are threatened by industrialization and other social changes.

In many respects France, "the eldest daughter of the church," manages to be a thoroughly Catholic country. The town cathedral remains in subtle ways the focal point of French culture. Most public holidays (except for May 1, the international Labor Day, and July 14, Bastille Day) are Catholic holidays, and public institutions are shut down. There is relatively little commerce on Sundays, and the major newspapers do not appear on that day. Until recently, the list of officially sanctioned first names for children born in France was based largely on the calendar of saints. These and other manifestations of Roman Catholicism are either ignored by avowedly secularist intellectuals, or rationalized as being a part of French history and hence thoroughly interwoven with the national culture.

Non-Catholics enjoy full religious, civil, and political liberties—and many of the 1 million Protestants and 550,000 Jews occupy prestigious positions in the political and economic systems. The Nazi holocaust decimated the Jewish community, but its remnants were augmented by refugees from Eastern Europe during the immediate postwar years. Jewish religious life was revitalized in the early 1960s with the influx of repatriates from North Africa, who now constitute about half of the

20. "Les bâtisseurs d'églises de la région parisienne n'ont pas ralenti le rythme de leurs activités," Le Monde, 30 June 1972. See also Michel Brion, La réligion vécue des Français (Paris: Le Cerf, 1972).

total Jewish population. Like their Protestant compatriots, Jews have not only consistently supported republicans (as against monarchists, who were traditionally identified with Catholicism), but they have also shown a preference for Radical and (since World War II) Socialist politicians. Jews are fully (and often self-consciously) French, and have participated prominently in French cultural life. Yet anti-Semitism, sometimes theologically inspired, is never far below the surface; and after the Arab-Israeli war of 1967 it received a new respectability as a result of a number of pronouncements by de Gaulle (and Pompidou) that were widely construed as anti-Jewish.

It is of course possible to exaggerate the extent to which anti-Semitism exists in France. If, as has been suggested, anti-Semitism is one of the constant—though often latent—factors of French sociopolitical thinking that pervades the bourgeois and the working classes, it cannot always be clearly separated from negative attitudes toward "out-groups" in general.[21] During the height of the Dreyfus affair, most anti-Semites were also anti-Protestant, anti-Masonic, and anti-foreigner.[22] Many Frenchmen then viewed—and view today—French culture as the embodiment of civilization generally: as a culture thoroughly bound up with Catholicism—although often in a somewhat secularized form—and with the idea of an organic evolution of Gallic tribes rooted in the soil of France. Like most European countries, France has tended to base citizenship upon *ius sanguinis*, as opposed to *ius solis*, that is, the fact of French parentage rather than birth in France. The same foreign immigrants whom France has traditionally welcomed have found it difficult to overcome the cultural xenophobia of her citizens and to find acceptance in the community of Frenchmen. Naturalization is permitted, but under strictly defined conditions, including the requirement that the applicant "speak French fluently; only a slight accent can be tolerated"; and that he submit proof that his circle of acquaintances is not based "on a narrow sector of [his] ethnic group."[23]

21. D. W. Brogan, *The Development of Modern France* (London: Hamish Hamilton, 1940), pp. 329–56.
22. Anti-Semitism was a component of the "integral nationalism" of ultra-conservative thinkers like Charles Maurras, who disliked Jews because they were not Catholics; and Maurice Barrès, who disliked Jews because they were "different." J. S. McClelland, ed., *The French Right* (London: Jonathan Cape, 1970), pp. 25–32. For instances of survival of small-town, petit-bourgeois anti-Semitism, see Edgar Morin, *Rumor in Orléans* (New York: Random House, 1971), esp. pp. 11–79. Cf. the series of articles by Jean Lacouture, "Les Français sont-ils racistes?" *Le Monde*, 20, 21, 22–23 March 1970.
23. Paul Marabuto, *Partis politiques et mouvements sociaux sous la IVe République* (Paris: Sirey, 1948), pp. 408–9. It should be noted, however, that 1.3 million out of 52 million Frenchmen are naturalized citizens; and that in 1974 alone, 24,000 foreigners were naturalized.

The notion of France as the center of Western civilization was inculcated in even the most backward and socially disadvantaged elements of the provinces.[24] According to one scholar, this notion ceased to be popular some decades ago except among the extreme right wing of the political spectrum[25]—but there is reason to believe that this view has revived. Since the end of World War II, with the rise of American power, the relative weakening of the French economic and international position, the inroads of the English language, and the emergence of a new internationally minded technocracy that appears to threaten the position of the traditional, humanistically educated elite, there has been a noticeable resurgence of cultural chauvinism among the educated Parisians even with leftist leanings—perhaps as a symptom of status overcompensation. French intellectuals are fiercely concerned about preserving the French language from corruptive foreign influences; there are a number of associations "for the defense of the French language," and Paris spends a great deal of money in order to spread knowledge of French to African and other countries.

This cultural chauvinism has been directed not only at foreigners. For many years, children in Basque areas were punished for speaking their native tongue in public schools; the same was true in the case of Breton, a language spoken by some 800,000 people in Brittany. In recent years there has been a new assertiveness on the part of Bretons, Corsicans, and (to a lesser extent) Alsatians. This assertiveness has many sources: the independence movements of the Third World; the influence of foreign workers; the transnational regionalism and open borders of the European Community; and the examples of culturally determined "regionalization" policies of Belgium, Italy, and other European countries. France has responded to the unique aspirations of her own ethnolinguistic minorities by providing radio broadcasts in Breton and Alsatian, allowing Breton to be taught as a subject in public schools (but not used as a language of instruction), legalizing Celtic proper names, transforming Corsica into a separate region, and promising significant increases in economic development aid. Nonetheless, Corsican, Breton, and Basque separatist movements (or "liberation fronts") have been suppressed. Moreover, the recognition of minority "dialects" —considered as part of the folkloristic treasure of the nation—has not been permitted to interfere with the predominant position of the French

24. Laurence Wylie, *Village in the Vaucluse* (New York: Harper & Row, 1964), p. 208.
25. Ernst Robert Curtius, *The Civilization of France* (New York: Vintage, 1962), p. 28.

language, which has been viewed as the primary tool in an educational system that, from the Third Republic to this day, has been expected to overcome linguistic provincialism and shape a nationally oriented, largely republican, and secular citizenry.[26]

THE EDUCATIONAL SYSTEM

The educational system, like so many other aspects of French life and culture, may be viewed as traditional or innovative, depending upon the observer's criteria. Since the nineteenth century, the school system in France has been public, theoretically uniform, and centralized, with the national Ministry of Education determining the educational policy and curricula at all levels, and supervising virtually all examinations. The primary schools in particular, in which attendance has been compulsory, have served as relatively efficacious agencies of republican, secular, and nationally oriented political socialization, and have prepared most pupils to find a productive place in the economy at the age of fourteen or fifteen years. The French school system was highly stratified, with the children of working class or peasant families rarely going beyond the primary school; and the bourgeois children advancing to the *lycée* in early adolescence, and thence to the university. In fact, the educational content of the *lycée*, which stressed classicism, historicism, rationalism, and formalism rather than technical or "modern" subjects, was little related to the labor market and was essentially designed for the leisure class or for those who already belonged to educated or otherwise privileged families.

In a sense, this hierarchization has extended to the structure of the French educational system. Although in theory most French *lycées* and universities are equal, certain Parisian *lycées* have been much more highly regarded than the less pretentious secondary schools in the provinces. In higher education, a distinction has been made between the ordinary universities and the specialized *grandes écoles*, such as the *Ecole Polytechnique* and the *Ecole Normale Supérieure*. These latter—most of them established in the nineteenth century—which have provided France with her intellectual and political leadership, have catered

26. See Louis-Jean Calvet, "Le colonialisme linguistique en France," *Temps Modernes*, August–September 1973, pp. 72–89. Cf. Michel Phlipponneau, *Debout Bretagne!* (Saint-Brieuc: Presses universitaires de Bretagne, 1970), pp. 153–56; Paul Serant, *La France des minorités* (Paris: Laffont, 1965); Christian Colombani, "Sans Breton, pas de Bretagne," *Le Monde*, 5 December 1975; and Flora Lewis, "West Europe's Minorities Are Getting Their Way," *New York Times*, 23 November 1975 (sect. 4).

essentially to the upper-middle and the upper classes.[27] Moreover, the clear status distinctions among the university faculty ranks (the *professeur titulaire*, the *chargé de cours*, and the *assistant*) and between these and the student, have traditionally been rather precise and rigid, and have been a microcosm of the hierarchism of society at large.

Nevertheless, in the area of educational reforms France has been more innovative and dynamic than most other Western European countries, particularly since the advent of the Fifth Republic. In 1959, it was decided to raise the school-leaving age to sixteen by 1967 (a decision fully implemented only in 1971), and soon there was widespread agreement that secondary schooling was the right of all Frenchmen. In 1963, the government established the observation period (*cycle d'observation*), which was destined to evolve into a uniform middle school for all categories of students of the eleven–fifteen age group. After the age of fifteen, students were to be guided into one of three "streams": the *lycée* (for traditional, humanistic studies), the *collège* (for more modern or scientific studies), or the technical school (*centre d'enseignement technique*)—with only the first two culminating in the *baccalauréat*, the diploma required for admission to a university. As a consequence of these reforms, an ever-increasing number of students have been acquiring some kind of academic secondary education. In 1970, nearly 70 percent of the 210,000 students who took the *baccalauréat* examinations passed them.

The pressures for university entrance created by this fact have caused serious problems for the system of higher education, which in 1974 encompassed some 800,000 students, the largest number of any Western European country. The overcrowding of lecture halls, the inadequacy of physical facilities and libraries, the impersonal relationship between the professor and the students, and above all the persistence of a university curriculum that, despite its overall excellence, has borne a constantly diminishing relationship to the labor market—all these problems demanded solution.

In the 1960s, the government began to establish additional universities, often with American-style campuses, and introduced more "technical" subjects. But these reforms were inadequate and came too late, and the clamor for a thorough overhauling of the French system of higher education figured heavily in the rebellion of May 1968. After this event, Edgar Faure, as minister of education, initiated several significant reforms, including the granting of some autonomy to universi-

---

27. In 1971, the 138 *grandes écoles* enrolled 50,000 out of the total university population of 700,000.

ties in determining curricula; the creation of new technological colleges; the establishment of American-type academic departments (UERs);[28] and a system of "participatory democracy" under which a university's governing personnel would in part be elected by professors, staff, and students. Faure's successor, Olivier Guichard, continued these reforms, particularly in regard to greater decentralization of academic decision making, the establishment of interdisciplinary curricula, and the founding of new university centers in the Paris region in order to relieve the congestion of the old Sorbonne. Moreover, in the past decade, more Frenchmen have recognized that an enlarged place in the curriculum ought to be accorded to such modern subjects as economics, mathematical statistics, sociology, business management, and computer technology. The reforms introduced in 1974 by Education Minister René Haby soon after Giscard d'Estaing assumed the Presidency are continuing this emphasis on a technologically oriented curriculum, which is to be accorded a greater place than hitherto also in the secondary schools.

Some of the reforms have had unforeseen consequences. Thus, the regrouping of related fields into single departments has sometimes been undertaken on the basis of ideological rather than substantive affinities; and the provisions for participatory democracy have apparently not caught on with many students, only about 40 percent of whom regularly take part in elections of administrative personnel. In contrast, the legalization of political organizations for students has tended to distract them from their studies and provided them with frameworks for violent confrontation and physical disturbance.

The academic establishment has welcomed certain aspects of educational reform because they are in consonance with its egalitarian principles. These reforms have included the virtual universalization of the public nursery school (école maternelle); the mixing of the sexes in elementary schools in the Paris region; and the program of basic education (alphabétisation) for illiterate foreigners, which was inaugurated in the early 1970s. But the academic elite has been concerned about the possibility that too great an expansion of educational enrollment might depress standards. The gradual phasing out of Latin as a required subject in secondary schools (which was steadfastly opposed by Pompidou, a former lycée professor of literature) and similar measures of curricular modernization are thought of as destroying the unique character of French education and as contributing to a lowering of literary levels. In recent years there have been complaints that many students taking

28. UER—unité d'enseignement et de recherche (instruction and research unit).

the *baccalauréat* examinations are inadequately prepared in French grammar, style, and verbal sophistication. Many professors have objected to the tenor and content of "modern" curricula because these do not conform to their idea of what one needs to learn to become a cultured person, and because they see their own elite status threatened by a cheapening of the commodity they produce. To paraphrase a French commentator, French intellectuals are often dominated by a preoccupation with the past, a hostility to science, and an aristocratic view of culture—which coexists with egalitarian political convictions—because such a view constitutes a means of feeling superior to the masses.[29]

Such an attitude was brought into sharp focus early in 1976, when the government initiated a proposal to transform the university curriculum in such a way as to channel a large number of students from humanistic to more practical subjects. This transformation is to be accomplished with the participation of the business and industrial sectors. Many professors have opposed the reform on the ground that it destroys the function of the universities as "places where culture is dispensed to those worthy to receive it."[30] Among the students, the reform proposals have sparked unrest because they, too, view "culture" as an autonomous sphere and oppose the use of universities as cooptative devices for the business establishment.

It will be some time before many of the educational reforms now existing on paper are fully implemented. Despite the good intentions of politicians, the rate of expansion of university admissions has been reduced, not only because of subtle resistance by part of the traditional educational establishment, but also because of insufficient funds and the scarcity of positions for university graduates—a phenomenon observed in other industrialized countries also. In 1968, only 12 percent of the students at all universities in France were from workers' families, about one-half the proportion of such students in Britain or the United States, but higher than in West Germany, Switzerland, or the Netherlands. (Since that time, the percentage has not risen significantly in France.) In order to make access to higher education easier for a broad cross section of the population, the government had begun, in the Fourth Republic, to grant scholarship aid (*bourses*) to students, especially from low-income families. But the stipends have often been considered insufficient. Moreover, for France as for most other advanced Western

29. Jean-François Revel, "Les intéllectuels," *L'Express*, special issue, Spring 1970, pp. 100–101.
30. Alfred Kastler, "La réforme de l'université," *Le Monde*, 23 April 1976. See also Jacques Charpentreau, "Le snobisme de la culture," *Revue politique et parlementaire* 78 (March–April 1976): 70–79.

societies, there has remained the question whether hasty or piecemeal measures would provide cultural benefits on equal terms to the lower classes, or motivate them to demand such benefits, for the simple reason that workers and peasants have more pressing priorities. According to a poll conducted in 1969, 58 percent of Frenchmen do not read books, 87 percent do not go to the theater, and 78 percent have never been to a concert.[31] Libraries are ubiquitous in France, but—as elsewhere in Western Europe—they have not been easily accessible to the working class or the peasantry. The French cultural treasure is indeed great, but the masses have been even more effectively alienated from it than from the growing economic treasure.

THE CENTER AND THE PROVINCES

The maldistribution of the economic and cultural output of France is related to the persistent conflict between centralizing tendencies and provincialism. Since the consolidation of national power in Paris under the Bourbon kings of the seventeenth and eighteenth centuries and under Napoleon in the first decade of the nineteenth century, the provinces have declined. Yet the country is so large—by European standards —and its population, physical characteristics, and regional traditions are so diverse, that provincialism and local orientations remain significant, despite the growth of such unifying devices as radio, television, and the automobile. There are regional climatic, culinary, and linguistic differences, and there are differences with respect to the degree of economic and cultural development. Thus the Paris region is relatively "de-Christianized" while Brittany is deeply Catholic; the Northeast near the Belgian border is highly industrialized while the Massif Central is mainly rural; Alsace and Lorraine are dynamic from the point of view of economic growth, while the mountainous South is economically stagnant.

Such regional differences have accounted for ideological diversities throughout France, and for the fact that the city or district (the *arrondissement*) remains to this day the principal political base of parliamentary politicians. But the predominance of Paris is such that all provinces constitute part of a neglected backyard and a cultural and economic desert.[32] In West Germany and Italy, several different and

---

31. *Le Monde*, 19 June 1970. For more recent, and more optimistic, data, see Ambassade de France, Service de Presse et d'Information, *France*, January 1975, pp. 4–5.
32. John Ardagh, *The New France* (London: Penguin, 1970), pp. 176 ff, 263 f.

competing cities serve as cultural, financial, industrial, or political centers. In France there is only one significant city: Paris has the largest number of industries and controls the financial, cultural and political life of the country. With a few exceptions (such as Marseilles, which has an opera house), music, theater, and dance do not exist meaningfully outside the capital.

The continuing dominance of Paris explains why ambitious politicians, intellectuals, and businessmen, even though they may pride themselves on their rural roots, endeavor to maintain a "presence" (i.e., an apartment or office) in the capital; and why many provincial university professors try to obtain supplementary lecture assignments in the Paris area. In order to breathe some economic and cultural life into the provinces—and incidentally to halt the excessive urban sprawl around Paris—the government has undertaken several measures. Thus it began during the Fourth Republic to locate a few nationalized industries in provincial towns and (under the four-year economic plans) to provide tax exemptions and subsidies to private firms willing to build industrial plants in the hinterlands. In the 1960s under André Malraux, the minister of culture, centers for the arts (*maisons de culture*) were established in a number of cities in order to make available musical, theatrical, and artistic offerings to the provincial population. But neither the economic nor the cultural decentralization attempts have been very successful. Where provincial cities and regions have attained some importance, this has been due to accident or to special factors: Lorraine is significant because of its metallurgical industries, which could develop there because of localized iron deposits; Marseilles, because of its location, is an important harbor; Bordeaux has benefited from the fact that its mayor, Jacques Chaban-Delmas, was the French premier until the summer of 1972; and Grenoble has achieved some dynamic growth and importance because of local initiative as well as because the national government saw fit, for reasons of prestige, to spend a great deal of money in that city as the site of the 1968 Winter Olympics.

The provinces and towns of France have been hampered in their attempts at development largely because they have lacked significant powers of taxation. In recent years, the national government has allocated a greater proportion of locally collected revenues to the localities themselves, but not in sufficient amounts. There is increasing discussion of "regionalization," that is, of the devolution of more meaningful administrative powers to the regions, but it will be some time before Paris will be ready substantially to share with the provinces its political and fiscal preeminence.

THE POSITION OF WOMEN

Nowhere is the ambiguous relationship between modernism and traditionalism illustrated better than by the role of women in France. As a Latin and predominantly Roman Catholic country, France has tended to assign to women the customary family and household roles. The Napoleonic code of 1804, under which women were legally incompetent, remained in force until 1938. Since that time, the legal and political disabilities of women have gradually been removed. In 1945, women obtained the right to vote; in 1965, married women were granted the right to open bank accounts without their husbands' express permission and to dispose of property in their own name; and subsequently, to be legal heirs. For all practical purposes, there is now legal equality of men and women.

Women have made even greater progress economically. Approximately a third of the French labor force consists of women, and the pay differential between the sexes in France, which several years ago was 9 percent, has been much lower than in Germany and Italy. Between 1954 and 1962, the number of women in the professions (in particular the teaching profession) rose by 66 percent—double the rate for men. In 1971, women accounted for nearly half of university students, 20 percent of professors, 18 percent of lawyers (about a third of all lawyers in Paris), and 9 percent of physicians.[33] The entry of women into the labor market has been facilitated by the availability (especially in the Paris region) of free nursery schools for children from the age of three.

The political role of women is more difficult to assess. Traditionalism is strong enough so that women remain somewhat less than perfectly "politicized." According to one survey,[34] 37 percent of the women do not read the political news items in their newspapers, as against 20 percent of all readers. Though women account for more than half the population, they make up about two-thirds of the electoral nonparticipants. And many women who do vote are believed either to be heavily influenced by their husbands in their party preferences or to be ideologically more conservative than the latter. Most observers of French politics agree that Gaullist and other moderate, conservative, or Catholic parties have attracted a proportionately larger number of women than men—al-

33. Ibid., pp. 358–59; Carroll, *The French*, p. 117; and Ambassade de France, Service de Presse et d'Information, *Bulletin*, April 1972.
34. P. E. Converse and G. Dupeux, "Politicization of the Electorate in France and the United States," *Public Opinion Quarterly* 26, no. 1 (1962): 1–23.

though precise statistics about this are lacking. In contrast, women running for political office have tended to choose Communist or Socialist labels rather than conservative ones. The only three women cabinet members during the Third Republic served (as junior ministers) in the Popular Front Government of Léon Blum in 1936—one Communist, one Socialist, and one Radical Socialist.[35] Since 1946 only seven women have held cabinet positions, five of them since the accession of Valéry Giscard d'Estaing to the Presidency.

One indication of the changing societal position of women has to do with birth control. The Gaullist party disapproved of contraception and abortion because of the leadership's social conservatism and its desire to encourage the growth of the population. (At a women's convention that took place in November 1970, in Versailles, M. Debré, the defense minister at that time, told the 325 participants to *increase* the birthrate.) Consequently, legal abortions were until recently extremely rare in France; but—largely owing to the housing shortage—the idea of family planning has become more acceptable, and since 1969 contraceptive devices for women can be purchased legally. Since the accession of Giscard, the policy of liberalization in regard to women's rights has been considerably advanced. Abortions can now be obtained legally, and further progress has been made in the direction of securing equal pay for women. As a token of his commitment to women's rights, Giscard created a new Ministry for the Condition of Women.

Since 1964, a wife's adultery is *legally* considered as being no more serious than a man's. But despite this change, old attitudes, deeply ingrained in Latin culture, die hard. The Gabrielle Russier case in 1970, in which a mature female *lycée* professor had a liaison with a teen-aged male student—she was socially ostracized, imprisoned, and driven to suicide, a fate that would have been unthinkable for a male colleague—showed that public opinion and the public authorities accorded women far fewer sexual freedoms than they did to men.

35. Bernard Chenot, *Etre ministre* (Paris: Plon, 1967), p. 28.

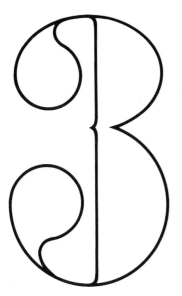

Patterns and
Perspectives of
Political Culture

According to widely accepted criteria of modernity, France is as modern a country as the United States, Britain, or West Germany.[1] Yet, we are told, "the encounters between modernizing tendencies [in France] and the traditional powers seem to have been too massive and too uncompromising to permit the emergence of a shared culture of political accommodation,"[2] a situation that has translated itself into recurrent legitimacy crises and revolutions in France. The language sometimes used by American political scientists and historians, who discuss France in terms of her inability to adapt to change without cataclysms and her reluctance to "marry" the twentieth century,[3] has been conditioned by the self-critical and revolutionary rhetoric that is found in French intellectual discourse. Such rhetoric makes many an institutional pattern that is less than perfect appear like a "blockage," and many a political

---

1. A modern political system is one in which traditional authority has been replaced by "a single national authority," decision-making patterns have become rationalized, political functions have become differentiated, political life in general has become secularized, elite recruitment is by merit rather than ascription, and in which meaningful institutions of (popular) political participation have developed. Samuel Huntington, "Political Modernization," World Politics 18 (April 1966): 378–414. According to Jean Blondel, France was the first modernizing society, having achieved centralization in the seventeenth century. See Blondel, The Government of France (New York: Crowell, 1973), pp. 42 f.
2. Gabriel Almond and Sidney Verba, The Civic Culture (Boston: Little, Brown, 1965), p. 7.
3. Cf. Philip Williams and Martin Harrison, Politics and Society in de Gaulle's Republic (New York: Doubleday Anchor, 1973), pp. 3 ff.

happening appear like a revolution.[4] But American scholars, when look-
ing at France, have also been influenced by the ethnocentric model of
the Anglo-American system, in which constitutions are hallowed by
antiquity and regimes are democratic and stable. France's deviation
from that model is often attributed to defects in her political culture (or
national character) that are detrimental to the maintenance of a stable
democracy. While French intellectuals, speaking in Marxist terms, tend
to explain the gap between the real and the ideal polity in terms of
class and other "contradictions,"[5] American political scientists, using
"value-free" functionalist vocabulary, tend to explain the shortcomings
of the French political system in terms of "dysfunctional" variables.
Thus French political culture is said to be characterized by rigid ideologism, fragmentation, lack of a participant ethos, social mistrust, evaluative (critical) attitudes, lack of subsystem autonomy, and the absence
of civic-mindedness (incivisme); while the American political culture is
noted for its pragmatism, integration, pro-system orientation, a participant ethos, social trust, affective attitudes, high subsystem (e.g.,
group or local government) autonomy, and a significant degree of civic-
mindedness.

The problems with such a catalogue are that the culture traits listed
therein do not always correlate with political behavior; the above-
mentioned negative traits may not be unique to France and—what is
more important—are often canceled out by positive traits that can also
be found in France. Moreover, certain culture traits (if they exist in
France) may be at least as "eufunctional" as they are "dysfunctional,"
that is, may be much more conducive to system maintenance and social
stability than would appear superficially to an American observer.[6] A
few examples will illustrate this point.

Lack of civic-mindedness in France is said to be illustrated by widespread tax evasion, draft-dodging, contempt for law, and that most
notorious of symptoms of alienation: alcoholism. But occasional violations of the laws, or the circumvention or "rectification" of laws by
means of personal arrangements or even bribery, are not demonstrably
more pronounced in France than in the United States, and considerably
less so than in Italy. The French believe (intellectually) in the principle
of government of laws, and tend to be law-abiding if they are con-

4. See Michel Crozier, *The Stalled Society* (New York: Viking, 1973); and Raymond
   Aron, *The Opium of the Intellectuals* (New York: Norton, 1962), pp. 94–95.
5. Aron, *Opium of Intellectuals*, p. 91.
6. See John Frears, "Conflict in France: the Decline and Fall of a Stereotype,"
   Political Studies 20 (March 1972): 31–41. The article debunks Almond's notion of
   France as a conflict-ridden and low-consensus society, and criticizes the "end of
   ideology" approach as well.

vinced that the laws are just and fair. Draft-dodging was bound to be a problem in a country engaged in wars for a longer period than any other democratic regime in the twentieth century—from the outbreak of the Second World War in 1939 to the settlement of the Algerian war in the early 1960s. But draft-dodging has probably been no more significant in France than it was in the United States during the Vietnam war.[7] Moreover, the French are also known for their patriotism and for the readiness with which many of them sacrificed their lives during World Wars I and II and during the German Occupation.

Tax evasion in France is definitely related to an "evaluative" political culture, and to the extent that such evasion exists, it is at least in part indicative of a "low support level" among the population. But tax fraud or tax "negotiations" are probably inevitable in an incompletely industrialized society and serve as a means of accommodating individuals who might otherwise turn against the system in their attempts to secure a minimal livelihood from family enterprises. Tax fraud has therefore certain "eufunctional" aspects; by protecting the small man against the vicissitudes of too rapid economic modernization, it keeps his antisystem proclivities in check and limits the growth of movements of popular fascism, such as Poujadism (see chapter 5). Moreover, in France tax advantages for the wealthy are not so obviously sanctioned by law as they are in the United States and are partly balanced by the extensive system of "negative income taxes"—family subsidies, university scholarships, and social security payments.

The alcoholism that one encounters in France may similarly be attributed to widespread alienation. But excessive wine drinking—apart from its association with conviviality and "Latin" patterns of social intercourse—is also related to the fact that viticulture is a very important element of the French agricultural economy and that wine is as available in France as milk or Coca-Cola or tea in other countries.

The educational elitism described above impedes upward mobility, fortifies inequality, and (theoretically) alienates those social sectors whose chances of educational advancement are blocked, while the "unrealistic" and humanistic content of education also contributes to frustration, as university graduates find that their education is not suited to the market. But educational exclusivity has also been a way to maintain standards and to provide continuity in the cultural tradition, while the multitrack system has contributed to social stability. Moreover, France has done more than any other Western European country to democratize

7. Early in 1973 there were widespread protest demonstrations in France against the abolition of draft deferments for university students.

university admissions, has established many technical schools, and has instituted a system of training civil servants that is far more modern and practical than the training in other Western European countries.

It has been remarked that "in the United States, which has gone further than any other Western society in institutionalizing the ethic of achievement, acute social tensions occur at the lower levels of the reward hierarchy. These are manifested in the exceptionally high incidence of various social phenomena, including homicide, mental illness, drug addiction, alcoholism, juvenile delinquency, petty larceny, and organized crime."[8] Since with respect to most of these phenomena France appears to be better off than the United States, we may assume that France has succeeded better than the United States (with its more "civic" culture) in minimizing the antisocial behavioral tendencies of the disprivileged— both by emphasizing forms of social orientation and organization that we tend to regard as "premodern," parochial, or fragmentative, such as the stress on family or class membership, and by permitting occassional anomic activity and (often harmless) flights of ideological rhetoric.[9]

Both the Frenchman's attitude of distrust of the political system and his preoccupation with his family are attributed not only to his perceptions of the system's failure to do enough for him, but also to what has been called a "fear of face-to-face relations."[10] This fear is said to be manifested in the Frenchman's inability to make friends easily, or his reluctance to invite friends to his home. But failure of the Frenchman to entertain at his home—apart from pointing up certain aspects of Mediterranean "café" culture that have no provable political consequences—may be attributed also to poor housing conditions or to a highly developed sense of privacy. Nevertheless, social relations in France, although they are more formal than in the United States, may often be more lasting; they are in any case counterbalanced by the deep organic ties of family. Moreover, the formality of social intercourse in France is complemented by affective ties to local notables and by a pervasive trust in charismatic leaders. The continuing importance of organic ties may be detrimental to (economic and political) modernization, but such ties are at least conducive to the maintenance of a spirit

8. Frank Parkin, *Class Inequality and Political Order* (New York: Praeger, 1971), p. 68.
9. Antisocial behavior patterns seem to be increasing in direct proportion to the speed with which France is becoming "Americanized." On the recent rise in incidence of juvenile delinquency, betting scandals, kidnappings, and other "modern" forms of antisocial behavior in France, see "La criminalité," *La Nef*, July–September 1975.
10. Cf. Henry W. Ehrmann, *Politics in France* (2nd ed.; Boston: Little, Brown, 1971), pp. 151 ff.; and Crozier, *Stalled Society*, pp. 65–70, 93–99, 112–19.

of community. The Frenchman takes great pride in his city; he is frequently reminded that France is an old country and that each of her cities uniquely reflects the nation's cultural patrimony. Characteristic of this attitude was the project, inaugurated in the mid-1960s by André Malraux, to restore the medieval appearance of the Louvre by excavating the moat around it. Municipal pride is transideological, and to some degree compensates for the Frenchman's critical attitudes regarding the national regime.

Similarly, the predominance of elderly leaders in industry and politics—only gradually being modified by an "accent on youth," especially since the inauguration of President Giscard d'Estaing—has been symptomatic of a preindustrial society and has impeded economic dynamism. But in a country where in 1974 a fifth of the population was over sixty years of age, the gerontocratic cultural orientation has had a positive effect on social stability and has inspired a relatively advanced social policy for the aged. In 1971, information centers for the aged were set up in each department to inform them of their rights, which include generous pension payments, housing allowances, and rebates on public transport. Such an orientation contrasts sharply with that of the United States, where an exaggerated emphasis on "modern" role-determined relationships has tended to produce a bias against the aged that has been reflected in inadequate pension payments.

True, the French are far less inclined to be philanthropic than Americans. But this failing may be more a function of output expectations than of an anti-civic orientation. The United States, with its long tradition of governmental noninvolvement in many social problems, has offered generous tax writeoffs for charity; France, owing to *dirigiste* traditions and legislative concern for welfare, income, and general culture, has had less need for the philanthropic spirit.

The inadequacy of the political system as a whole, and of the socialization process in particular, is nonetheless demonstrated by widespread disaffection with the regime. This disaffection is said to be clearly shown by the prevalence of an ideological approach to politics, by revolutionary rhetoric, by electoral abstentionism, and by frequent outbursts of political violence. There is no doubt that French politics is informed by a high degree of ideological thinking, by "absolute-value rationalities," and by "apocalyptic" visions.[11] Such thinking, which has

11. Gabriel Almond and James S. Coleman, eds., *The Politics of Developing Nations* (Princeton: Princeton University Press, 1960), p. 37. See also Charles Morazé, *The French and the Republic* (Ithaca, N.Y.: Cornell University Press, 1958), pp. 20 ff., which discusses the "passion for theory" prevalent among Frenchmen.

been conditioned by history and by the stress of the educational curriculum upon rationalistic, Cartesian, and systematic approaches to social phenomena, has influenced the Frenchman's interest in philosophical nuances among competing political formulas.[12] Such approaches are said to be particularly remarkable in the case of "Radicals, Socialist and Catholic intellectuals, and Communists,"[13] each of which groups has its own views on the imperfections of the existing regime and the need for revolution.

Are these divisions significant in terms of practical political behavior? The French have encountered numerous revolutions, or at least have participated in numerous attempts to replace inadequate regimes by experiments informed by millennial strivings. But none of the revolutions has ever succeeded completely, and the French have learned not to expect too much from them. ("*Plus ça change, plus c'est la même chose.*") Therefore, "apocalyptic" visions are often pursued as if they had a life of their own—a situation that has been reflected in the behavior of both political parties and ordinary French citizens.

It may happen that individuals adhering to competing political parties, labeled according to conflicting ideologies, such as "Catholics, Communists, [and] Socialists . . . find it impossible to come to common working agreements . . . even when it is in the compelling national interest to do so,"[14] or that "a Communist might spend his whole life in what might be thought of as an ideological enclave in the French political system."[15] But the opposite may be equally true. Political parties and individuals in France, no matter how seriously they swear by a political philosophy, tend to engage in pragmatic compromises just as frequently as do parties and individuals in the United States and Britain. Several years ago, Waldeck Rochet, then leader of the French Communist party, responded to the question, "What is a revolutionary?" by saying, "He does not babble about an armed insurrection; on the contrary, he works for a union of the Left, and the winning of a majority."[16] The transideological collaboration of the Communists, the Socialists, and the Catholics during the period of "tripartism" immedi-

12. "Cartesian" refers to the intellectual tradition inspired by René Descartes through his best-known work, *Discours de la méthode* (1637). According to the popular conception of this method, particulars are deduced from general principles (based on reason) in an orderly, logical, and clear fashion. Cf. Ernst Robert Curtius, *Civilization of France* (New York: Vintage, 1962), pp. 93–96.
13. Almond and Coleman, *Politics of Developing Nations*, p. 37.
14. Gabriel Almond and G. B. Powell, Jr., *Comparative Politics: A Developmental Approach* (Boston: Little, Brown, 1966), p. 62.
15. Ibid., p. 266.
16. *L'Express*, 23–29 October 1967, p. 4.

ately after World War II, and even the (sometimes surreptitious) co-operation of Communists and Gaullists (about which more will be said in chapter 5), are paralleled also by the behavior of the most representative trade unions. Although ideologically fragmented, and although often proclaiming their desire to transform the regime—by revolution if necessary—these unions meanwhile engage (not always successfully) in autonomous bargaining, collaborate for practical reformist goals, and participate in decision-making or consultative agencies.

The perception of the functional autonomy of ideological rhetoric from specific programmatic preferences affects the average Frenchman as well. This is illustrated by the fact that while the majority of Frenchmen adheres to an anticlerical party, an even greater majority opposes the end of subsidies to Catholic schools (see table 3). There is also a

Table 3
Attitudes Regarding Government Support of Private Schools
(in percent)

	All	Commu-nists	Socialists	Center	Gaullists
Increase subsidies	29	24	20	39	40
Maintain subsidies at existing levels	39	27	41	46	39
Reduce subsidies	14	34	23	7	5
No reply	18	15	16	8	16

SOURCE: *Sondages* poll, 1968, cited in Jack Hayward, *The One and Indivisible French Republic* (New York: Norton, 1973), p. 196.

distinction between "verbal political behavior" and "electoral behavior,"[17] which more often than not translates itself into a tendency on the part of the typical Frenchman to incline to the Right on election day. The same Frenchman who loves the idea of revolution also has a penchant for order in his personal life; the citizen who exhibits verbal antimilitarism admires the warriors of the past.[18] The petit-bourgeois harbors a traditional (and intellectually acceptable) contempt for the regime; but

17. Gérard Adam et al., *L'Ouvrier français en 1970*, Fondation Nationale des Sciences Politiques, Travaux et recherches de science politique, no. 13 (Paris: Colin, 1970), p. 75.
18. François Nourissier, *The French* (New York: Knopf, 1968), pp. 117–22.

at the same time, he hopes that his son will be able to enter a career in the service of that regime, whether as a teacher or as a government functionary. The underprivileged worker (especially if he fancies himself a "socialist") may vote for the Communist party (PCF), but such a vote does not necessarily imply that the worker is "alienated" or that his political socialization has been faulty or negative. Many workers who vote for the PCF do so, not because they view that party as being committed to the destruction of the system, but in order to express generalized discontent for not receiving the benefits to which they think they are entitled. Many others vote for that party in the foreknowledge that it will not capture power but merely function as an agency of opposition. Moreover, while it may be an exaggeration to say that "the revolutionary impulse of the [French] working class has been so diminished as to be extinguished,"[19] it is true that workers *have* benefited from a growing measure of general economic prosperity,[20] owing to the policies of the existing bourgeois regime, and they now have more to lose than their chains.

Even if the voters' perception of the incumbent deputy today is not too different from what it was reputed to be during the Fourth Republic —as a person who is guilty of "a flight from responsibility"[21] and of enriching himself at the expense of the public—they may still vote for an incumbent politician because he is a known quantity, and therefore safe. Safe voting, until 1974, often meant voting for a Gaullist candidate, not because of the voters' preference for the Gaullist party as such, but for a de Gaulle or a Pompidou as against a leftist President (or a preference of "order" over "chaos" or uncertainty). During the parliamentary election campaign of March 1967, one candidate, a secretary of state, told his constituents: "If you give me a triumphal . . . majority on the second ballot, the success will make me eligible for [full] ministerial rank, so that I shall be in a position to be useful to this region and to each and every one of you."[22] One may suppose that, if the President of the Republic were a Socialist, electors who have conservative political

19. Norman Birnbaum, *The Crisis of Industrial Society* (New York: Oxford University Press, 1970), p. 34. For a traditional exposition of the cultural alienation of the worker, see Jean Minces, *Un ouvrier français* (Paris: Seuil, 1969), esp. pp. 53f. and 81 f.

20. Cf. Albert Détraz, "Consommation ouvrière et attitude politique," in *Les nouveaux comportements politiques de la classe ouvrière*, ed. Léo Hamon (Paris: PUF, 1962), pp. 248–51.

21. Nathan Leites, *On the Game of Politics in France* (Stanford: Stanford University Press, 1959), pp. 43–49.

22. Pierre Avril, *Politics in France* (Baltimore: Penguin, 1969), p. 77n.

affinities all year round would incline, for similar reasons, to vote for a Socialist rather than a conservative candidate.

Herbert Luethy, in 1957, spoke about "the lack of consequences of political controversy."[23] The widespread feeling that political parties in France—as compared to those of the United States—are even more inadequate today than they were in the Fourth Republic as meaningful vehicles of political expression seems to be supported by the results of a poll conducted in 1958 that indicated that only 25 percent of Frenchmen, as against 76 percent of Americans, could identify their father's political party.[24] It is easier in the United States to identify parties, since there are far fewer than in France. Moreover, in France party labels often change dramatically; people change party allegiance; and adherence to a political party is often less important than an affective relationship to a local notable or a charismatic national figure. Finally, the political party may be eclipsed as an agent of socialization by the educational system, the welfare state system (i.e., the system of outputs), and the (often ideologically oriented) secondary association.

The relative indifference to, and even ignorance of, political parties seem to be particularly significant among French children and adolescents, because the socialization of children to political party identification occurs much later than in the United States—if at all.[25] This indifference among the young does not appear to be compensated for by an affective orientation to a national suprapartisan authority figure, as is often the case with adults—a phenomenon that has been explained by the tendency of French children to rebel against overprotective parents and to transfer their rebelliousness to political institutions and authority figures.[26] This negativism also extends to economic institutions. According to a poll conducted in June 1972, only 15 percent of eighteen-year-olds favored the maintenance of the existing economic system, as compared with 57 percent of adults.[27]

It should, however, be noted that rebelliousness is selective. A large number of students—even from families of comfortable circum-

23. Herbert Luethy, *France Against Herself* (New York: Meridian, 1957), p. 39.
24. P. E. Converse and G. Dupeux, "Politicization of Electorate in France and the United States," *Public Opinion Quarterly* 26, no. 1 (1962): 11.
25. Ibid. See also Frank A. Pinner, "Parental Overprotection and Political Distrust," *Annals of the American Academy of Political and Social Science*, no. 361 (September 1965): 58–70.
26. See Fred I. Greenstein and Sidney G. Tarrow, "The Study of French Political Socialization: Toward the Revocation of Paradox," *World Politics*, October 1969, pp. 107–10.
27. Yves Agnès, "Les jeunes et la politique," *Le Monde*, 17 February 1973.

stances—are leftist in general orientation primarily *because* their parents are;[28] but this leftism does not necessarily imply support of the Communist party because the PCF is either viewed as being too worker-oriented and therefore hostile to students[29] or, conversely, because it is regarded as too "conservative." The vast majority of students (87 percent according to a poll of June 1972) are interested in politics;[30] while this interest extends less to slogans and more to practical socioeconomic questions, it does not necessarily translate itself into electoral participation.

The sometimes significant degree of electoral abstentionism (among the youth as well as the adults) may be related to a growing disillusionment with political parties (see chapter 5), to a trend to "depolitization," or (as in local elections) to a realization of the relative lack of powers of certain elected bodies;[31] but it is not a perfectly convincing indicator of an "evaluative" political culture. Electoral abstentionism is no greater in France than in the United States, and may even be less. Moreover, there is the "reserve mechanism" of anomic articulation.

Anomic behavior should not automatically be equated with revolution or construed as a manifestation of an unreconstructed and persistent alienation of the masses. Spontaneous events may in fact provide useful outlets or social catharses that obviate or impede real system changes or revolutions. This is true even of the May Events of 1968— the general strikes that involved millions of Frenchmen and appeared to challenge the very foundation of the French political, social, and economic system. Many of the participants were anarchists or revolutionary syndicalists; these—and numerous subsequent commentators—naturally invested the Events with momentous ideological meaning and saw them as reflecting both social anomie and a demand for modernization.[32] To

28. Yves Agnès, "L'attitude des jeunes: une nouvelle classe?" *Le Monde,* 18–19 February 1973.
29. Richard Johnson, *The French Communist Party Versus the Students* (New Haven: Yale University Press, 1972), esp. chaps. 6–7.
30. Agnès, "Les jeunes et la politique."
31. See Jean Meynaud and Alain Lancelot, *La participation des Français à la politique* (Paris: PUF, 1965), p. 125. Note that in the municipal elections of March 1971, the abstention rate was 24.9% in the first ballot and 26.4% in the second ballot; and that abstentions in first-ballot cantonal elections from 1958 to 1976 have ranged from 32.6% to 46.0%. *Le Monde,* 9 March 1976. Concerning the extent of electoral abstentionism in France as compared to that in the United States, see William R. Schonfeld and Marie-France Toinet, "Les abstentionnistes: ont-ils toujours tort?" *Revue française de science politique* (hereafter cited as *RFSP*) 25 (August 1975): 645–76.
32. Cf. Bernard Brown, *The French Revolt* (New York: McCaleb-Seiler, 1970), pp. 9–10, 20.

the extent that they were sparked by students, however, the Events must be ascribed not so much to an alienated political culture as such as to the fact that France had a much larger number of students in universities than other Western European countries, and that university structures and curricula remained more archaic than other institutions in France. At the same time, the students' rebellion was an overreaction to the boredom engendered by the technicist and nonideological nature of the political discourse taking place within the streamlined institutions of the Gaullist system, and hence constituted a revolt *against* modernization. On a more mundane level, the students who occupied the buildings of the Faculty of Letters at Nanterre, then a supplementary suburban campus of the University of Paris, wished to make examinations easier; agitated for better dormitory amenities; and expressed doubts whether a diploma from an "inferior" campus would guarantee them appropriate jobs. (Curiously, a public-opinion poll conducted in 1969, less than ten months after the May Events, revealed that nearly 90 percent of French youth between the ages of sixteen and twenty-nine were relatively satisfied with their situation and that most were happy with their scholastic or professional activities.)[33] Many active participants in the Events were intellectuals, who may have jumped on an ideological bandwagon, but did not necessarily hope that these Events would lead to the kind of thorough restructuring of society that might entail a loss of privileges for themselves.

One noted political commentator does argue that France has never fully recovered from the May Events, in the sense that the social and political momentum they created has not been reversed.[34] Among these changes were the gradual breaking of the spell of de Gaulle, the increased demands for "participatory democracy," and the progressive rise of the level of economic expectations on the part of the masses. At the

33. Joint opinion poll of IFOP and *L'Express*, cited in *L'Express*, 17 February 1969, pp. 120–24. For a discussion of the (often contradictory) reasons for rebellion among *lycée* students, see Gérard Vincent, *Les lycéens*, Fondation Nationale des Sciences Politiques, Cahier no. 179 (Paris: Colin, 1971), chap. 7, esp. pp. 311–15.
34. Jacques Fauvet, "A Slow Recovery," *Le Monde Weekly*, 12 May 1973. Of the numerous works on the 1968 rebellion, the following may be mentioned: Patrick Seale and Maureen McConville, *Red Flag, Black Flag* (New York: Ballantine, 1968); Daniel Singer, *Prelude to Revolution: France in May, 1968* (New York: Hill & Wang, 1970); Alain Touraine, *The May Movement* (New York: Random House, 1971); Bernard E. Brown, *Protest in Paris: Anatomy of a Revolt* (Morristown, N.J.: General Learning Press, 1974). For an interesting (though somewhat premature) discussion of the literature on the subject, see Philippe Bénéton and Jean Touchard, "Les interprétations de la crise de mai-juin 1968," *RFSP* 10 (June 1970): 503–44.

same time, it should be kept in mind that many university reforms remained confined to paper innovations; that such novel manifestations of social solidarity as the collaboration between workers and students hardly outlasted the Events; that the rise in consumer demands is not by itself revolutionary; that the radicalization of certain social sectors (for example, the quasi-Catholic trade union, the CFDT) also coincided, on the one hand, with an impressive victory of Gaullist candidates in the parliamentary election of 1968 and, on the other, with the beginning of the "domestication" of the Communist party; and that the disengagement of the French from Gaullist charisma itself indicated a gradual return to institutional normalcy.[35]

Institutional normalcy in the Fifth Republic connotes a system in which the national government clearly dominates over subnational governments, and in which the executive dominates the legislature. The overcentralization of decision making and administration in the unitary regime of France is sometimes considered to be "dysfunctional" from the point of view of subsystem autonomy, because it prevents the development, or contributes to the decay, of "democratic infrastructures"[36] (in contrast to the United States, where federalism is conducive to the maintenance of such an infrastructure). But centralization was deliberately instituted (during the *ancien régime* and Napoleon's First Empire) precisely in order to overcome the historic French provincialism —which is also dysfunctional and antimodern since it fosters parochialism and fragmentation! In recent years, the French have developed certain types of subnational functional units, such as economic and university regions, which aim at practical "deconcentration" (see chapter 9). Local government may still be much weaker than it is in the United States (and local PTAs may be nonexistent), but, in contrast, there are in France "participatory" infrastructures that are unknown in the United States, such as modernization commissions, agricultural regional councils, social security boards, and mechanisms for industrial "co-management."

The current predominance of the President is a much more serious problem, not only because it constitutes a departure from Third and Fourth Republic traditions, but also because most of the existing "countervailing" institutions—such as Parliament, opposition parties, interest groups, and the press—are weak. Although all these countervailing agencies sometimes influence governmental policies, put the executive on guard, and occasionally even effect changes in governmental per-

---

35. See Flora Lewis, "French Still Ponder '68 Revolt," *New York Times*, 27 May 1973.
36. Almond and Verba, *Civic Culture*, p. 7.

sonnel, they are too institutionalized and too constrained to threaten the existing pattern of power relationships.

If the executive predominance in the Fifth Republic has contributed to the elevation of bureaucratic rule, it has also reduced the significance— and destructiveness—of ideological fragmentation as manifested by political party competition in Parliament. In a country in which "politics and administration function in watertight compartments,"[37] bureaucrats can now act without worrying excessively about the clamor of politicians. But while bureaucratic decision making is a hallmark of modernity— and therefore the Fifth Republic is distinctly more modern than its predecessor—that kind of decision making is not particularly democratic, since the civil servants, not being subject to elections, are not directly responsible to the public, a fact that tends to create a certain distance between the masses and the apparatus of decision making. Increased technicism does not mean lack of controversy, nor does it altogether exclude nontechnical and external democratic input. But it does imply the kind of controversy in which the participatory role of the general public is necessarily restricted, despite the institutions of "participatory democracy" that have been mentioned.

Both the widespread perception of the limitations of mass participation in the political system, and the institutional complexity of that system that makes it difficult to understand, have contributed to an evaluative political culture, that is, to the critical attitudes of the French regarding their regime. Pride in the governmental system is found in a far smaller percentage of the French (29 percent) than of Americans (85 percent) or Englishmen (46 percent).[38] However, the percentage is still greater than in Germany (7 percent)—a country that has been moving toward "Anglo-American" (participant and affective) political culture patterns. Moreover, the acceptance by Frenchmen of their political system may not be so negative after all, or may be becoming more positive. In a poll conducted in December 1971, 10 percent of the French respondents thought that the institutions of the Fifth Republic were exactly what was needed; 47 percent felt that they were basically acceptable and needed only minor changes; 23 percent felt that they were acceptable with major changes; and only 5 percent that they were unacceptable.[39] Another poll at about the same time found that 65 percent expressed a high degree of confidence in the President, 65 percent in the mayor, 39 percent in the national parliamentary deputies, 47 percent in

37. Luethy, *France Against Herself*, p. 18.
38. John S. Ambler, "Social and Political Trust in France" (Paper delivered at American Political Science Association, Washington, D.C., 1972), table, p. 12.
39. Ibid., p. 3.

the conduct of affairs by the municipal government (which indicates, perhaps, that parochial orientations are receding), and 66 percent in the meaningfulness of elections in general.[40]

We have already pointed out that there need be no clear correlation between critical attitudes toward the government and voting for opposition parties; a Frenchman may be critical of the government or the regime simply because such an attitude is expected of him, instilled in him, and accords with his perception of himself as an adult intellectual or citizen. Similarly, there may be no clear causal relationships among evaluative attitudes, low support levels, and meaningful policy outputs ("system capacity").

According to a poll conducted in 1971, the pride of Frenchmen in their country's position in international affairs (14 percent) is greater than that of Americans (5 percent), Englishmen (11 percent) or Germans (5 percent); and there is a far larger proportion of Frenchmen (22 percent) than of Americans (4 percent) or Englishmen (13 percent) who are proud of their country's achievements in the arts and sciences— perceptions that hardly seem justified by objective criteria.[41] Conversely, fewer Frenchmen (7 percent) than Britons (10 percent) are proud of their respective economic systems; yet it can be argued that—in terms of accomplishments (e.g., growth rates)—the French economic system is "better" or more dynamic than the British one. Fewer Frenchmen (4 percent) than Americans (13 percent) are proud of their respective social legislation,[42] yet in many respects French social legislation is much further advanced than American. It could be that the Frenchman tends to be more critical of government performance than the Englishman or American, because the Frenchman has accepted the "positive state" much less reluctantly; hence his level of expectations is higher. This attitude is in itself a manifestation of an "instrumental" rather than "symbolic" view of the political system, that is, of modern rather than traditional political culture.

Despite the social fragmentation, critical attitudes, and lack of political consensus found in French society, and despite the "legitimacy crises" that have frequently occurred because of these attitudes, there has also been a great deal of consensus about certain values among Frenchmen. In the face of the impermanence in specific French constitutional arrangements—there having been more than ten different types of regimes since 1789—there has been a persistence in the administra-

40. Ibid., p. 2.
41. International criteria such as military power; cultural-scientific criteria such as the number of Nobel prize winners.
42. Ambler, "Social and Political Trust," p. 12.

tive, legal, and educational structures because such structures have accorded with the Frenchman's values and expectations. It is interesting to note that in the United States, in which there has been a remarkable continuity and consensus with respect to political institutions, the "state" is still a loose concept,[43] while the state has a venerable history in France, and the *idea* of the state has a well-established claim on people's attentions. Moreover, there is a widespread agreement that ultimately the form of that state must be republican. Although the republics that succeeded each other have varied in terms of institutional arrangements, there has been a continuity of political personnel, illustrated by the fact that many politicians have served in more than one regime. Adolphe Thiers, for example, was a prominent politician in the Second Empire, and became the first President of the Third Republic; Léon Blum was a premier in both the Third and the Fourth republics; and Edgar Faure, Antoine Pinay, Maurice Schumann, and René Pleven (to name but a few) were prominent leaders in the Fourth as well as the Fifth republics. In view of such extended tenure, it is not surprising that institutional adaptation in France has not been so discontinuous as it is sometimes thought to be; that (as will be pointed out in chapter 4) many of the adjustments of institutional patterns that we associate with the Fifth Republic were in fact undertaken at the end of the Fourth Republic; that there has been, in short, a continuing commitment to democracy.

43. Cf. Alain Clément, "A System Under Fire," *Le Monde Weekly*, 12 May 1973.

The Fifth Republic Constitution

THE DECLINE AND FALL OF THE FOURTH REPUBLIC

The Fourth Republic was inaugurated in 1946 under rather inauspicious circumstances. In the spring of that year, one attempt to fashion an instrument of government had foundered when the electorate rejected a draft constitution providing for all-powerful unicameral legislature. The Constitution that was put into effect in the fall was approved, but with less than overwhelming enthusiasm. Only 60 percent of the electorate participated in the referendum, and of these only two-thirds voted "yes." Many felt that the Third Republic ought to be continued; others —among them General de Gaulle—thought that the Constitution was foredoomed to failure because of its imperfections; and still others— notably the Communists—*hoped* that it would fail and pave the way for a regime more palatable to them.

There were indeed many structural weaknesses in the Fourth Republic Constitution. The Assembly was altogether too strong, while the role of the Council of the Republic, a pale copy of the Third Republic Senate, was ill-defined and ambiguous. Superficially, the dual executive was reminiscent of the Third Republic: the President, elected by Parliament, was a mere figurehead; and the prime minister, the "efficient" part of the executive, was chosen by, and responsible to, the legislature. The prime minister theoretically possessed the dissolution power, but he exercised this power only once, largely because it was looked upon as an antiparliamentary device.

The Assembly remained sensitive about its constitutionally defined legislative supremacy, but in the absence of coherent and stable majorities that chamber could not fully play its role. Because of its inability or unwillingness to make unpleasant decisions, it delegated legislative or decree powers to cabinets (in violation of the Constitution), only to oust them once decisions had been made. Cabinet instability, moreover, could be attributed to the ambitions of numerous politicians who considered themselves of ministerial caliber (*ministrables*) and were eager for cabinet posts.

Any postmortem of the Fourth Republic is of course incomplete if one disregards the accomplishments of that regime (see chapter 1). Nonetheless, one must say that the imperfections of the Fourth Republic Constitution might well have been transcended by political practice had it not been for the colonial question, the frustration of the military, and the scarcity of strong leaders capable of dealing with these issues.

The military, in particular, brought up with the historical memories of a glorious national army, had in their lifetimes experienced mainly defeats: the fall of France in 1940, the defeat at Dien-Bhien-Phu in Indochina in 1954, the Suez misadventure of 1956, and the continuing inability to pacify the rebellious elements in North Africa. Just as the German officers had blamed the "politicians" for the defeat of Germany in 1918, so the French generals had tried to assign the blame for the lack of victories to the politicians and the "system" that had brought them forward.

The final years and months of the Fourth Republic had seen rapid changes in cabinets: Prime Ministers Mollet, Gaillard, and Pflimlin were each unable to deal with the Algerian problem and, as it turned out, to save the regime. The French Parliament had made a few last-ditch attempts to eliminate certain constitutional difficulties: in 1954 the Constitution had been amended to make the investiture of prime ministers easier—and thus to make deadlocks less likely—by requiring a relative (or simple) rather than an absolute majority. In March 1958, in order to reduce the scope of irresponsible behavior on the part of the deputies, a reform was instituted that forbade back-benchers to introduce bills resulting in an increase of expenditure. Moreover, the Assembly sharply limited its own power to oust a cabinet by a vote of nonconfidence. Specifically, it was provided that if the prime minister made a bill a matter of confidence, the text of the bill was automatically considered adopted unless the Assembly actually produced a no-confidence vote; that a vote of no-confidence could be introduced only if there was a government program before Parliament; and that the President could dissolve the legislature if, after having sat for a minimum of eighteen months, it censured a prime minister who had been in office less than two years. But these reforms came too late; moreover, General de Gaulle, who had "saved" the honor of France in the past, waited in his country home at Colombey-les-deux-Eglises for the opportunity to act as the savior of his nation once more.

In April 1958, the resident military in Algeria, under the leadership of paratroop General Massu, established—in a manner intended to be reminiscent of 1793—a "Committee of Public Safety." Its demand for the return of Charles de Gaulle to power was supported and echoed by the General's political supporters on the mainland of France, including Michel Debré, Jacques Chaban-Delmas, Jules Michelet, and Jacques Soustelle (and later, by General Raoul Salan, the commandant of Algiers). In May, the President of the Republic, René Coty, sent a letter to de Gaulle exploring the possibility of the General's return; de Gaulle held a press conference on May 15 in which he announced his "availability" and shortly thereafter began to take steps to form a government. The *coup de grâce* of the Fourth Republic was finally delivered by President Coty when he (somewhat belatedly) informed the Parliament that he had asked the General to form a government, and that he would resign if the formation of such a government were prevented.[1]

THE SOURCES AND NATURE OF THE NEW CONSTITUTION

On June 1, 1958, de Gaulle was formally invested as prime minister by the Assembly and empowered by the latter to undertake a revision of the Constitution. The Fifth Republic Constitution, which was written in record time, is an eclectic document that incorporates monarchist, plebiscitarian, and traditional republican features (see table 4), as well as specifically Gaullist innovations.[2]

In modern French political history there have been two conflicting constitutional theories: the Rousseauan theory of complete popular sovereignty, as enunciated in the *Social Contract*,[3] and the doctrine of a "mixed government." According to Rousseau's theory, a truly democratic constitution is based on the principle that all political sovereignty rests inalienably with the people, who can delegate decision-making power only imperfectly—if at all—to a legislature. The second consti-

1. For a succinct and useful account of the end of the Fourth Republic, see Nicholas Wahl, *The Fifth Republic: France's New Political System* (New York: Random House, 1959), pp. 18–24.
2. Regarding the haste and confusion amid which the Constitution was drafted, see Nicholas Wahl, "The French Constitution of 1958: The Initial Draft and Its Origins," *American Political Science Review* 53 (June 1959): 358–82.
3. Bk. 3, sect. 4 (1762).

Table 4
Fifth Republic Features and Their Precedents

Feature of Fifth Republic Constitution	Precedent or Model
Popular election of President (amendment: 1962; first election: 1965)	Constitution of 1848 (2nd Republic)
Seven-year term of President	Third Republic
Power to appoint premier without prior parliamentary consultation	Second Republic
Presidential dissolution power	Third Republic (until 1879)
Presidential lawmaking (by decree)	Second Republic
Social and Economic Council	Third and Fourth republics
Referenda or plebiscites for constitutional amendments	1802 (Napoleon Bonaparte made consul for life) 1852 (Napoleon III vested with imperial powers)
Limit of Parliament's budget-making powers	End of Fourth Republic
President as "co-initiator" of legislation	Second and Third republics
President as negotiator of treaties	Second and Third republics
Plebiscitarian appeal to the people	Constitution of 1852 (Napoleon III)
Constitution adopted by referendum	Year I (1792) Year III (1795) Year VIII (1799) Fourth Republic (1946)
Incompatibility of cabinet office with parliamentary mandate	Constitution of 1791 (constitutional monarchy)

tutional principle envisaged a proper mixture of executive, legislative, and judicial institutions, all of which derive equally from the people and are therefore "coordinate" (but not so separate from each other as Montesquieu had envisaged them in his *Spirit of the Laws*).[4] The Rous-

4. Bk. 11, sect. 6 (1748).

seauan doctrine was reflected in the "Jacobin" constitution of 1792, which gave unlimited power to a Constituent Assembly as the best possible articulator of the "general will," and in the Fourth Republic's grant of legislative supremacy to the Assembly. The doctrine of a mixed government was embodied generally in monarchist regimes, e.g., the Constitutions of 1791, 1814, and 1830: in these the principle of popular sovereignty was reaffirmed, but was institutionally reflected only in an elected lower house. That chamber, rather than being the sole decision maker, had to act in "concert" with a nonelective king and a chamber of the nobility.[5] To some extent, the idea of the mixed government was embodied in the spare constitutional articles of the Third Republic, which granted legislative power to the Assembly but gave the executive the power to appoint ministers and to dissolve Parliament.

The Fifth Republic Constitution, on the face of it, adheres neither to the Jacobin principle nor to that of a "mixed" system. The very order of the constitutional provisions—Sovereignty, the President, the Government, Parliament—implies an enhanced position of the executive, and the provisions detailing the power of the legislature are such as to render that branch neither supreme nor even coordinate.

The President's power to preside over the cabinet, to appoint the prime minister, and to dissolve the legislature are basically Third Republic features, though after the "May 16" episode, these powers had atrophied. The provision for the independent (and later direct) election of the President is reminiscent of the Second Republic, while both the monarchical Constitution of 1791 and the Second Empire Constitution had provided for the incompatibility of cabinet office and parliamentary mandate. The extraparliamentary election of the President, his power to introduce legislation via his ministers, and his power to appoint the premier (and, in effect, the cabinet) without prior parliamentary consultation, were based on provisions found in the Constitution of the Second Republic (1848); the plebiscitarian appeal by the President was based on the Constitution of 1852. The President's power to negotiate treaties and to dissolve Parliament, the reconstitution of the Senate and its relatively equal position vis-à-vis the Assembly, and the omission of a clearly stipulated set of provisions regarding civil liberties—all these features are reminiscent of the Third Republic's Constitutional Laws of 1875. The Fourth Republic, too, is heavily reflected in the provisions of the Fifth, notably with respect to the following: the seven-year term of the President, his power to send messages to Parliament and to ask

5. M. J. C. Vile, *Constitutionalism and the Separation of Powers* (New York: Oxford University Press, 1967), pp. 202–3.

Parliament to reconsider bills it has passed, the election of senators by an electoral college of local politicians, as well as provisions concerning martial law and the establishment of a Social and Economic Council, and of course, an Assembly chosen by universal suffrage.

The specifically "Gaullist" aspects of the Constitution are not easy to determine, because the sources of Gaullism are diverse and its nature is intertwined with Bonapartism. In his Bayeux speech of January 1946, de Gaulle, while publicly opposing the first draft of a constitution for the Fourth Republic, had proposed a system of separation of powers; an indirectly elected Senate in which, in conformity with corporatist tradition, socioeconomic and professional sectors would be represented; and a chief executive who would, in the manner once suggested by George Washington, be "above parties,"[6] and who would, moreover, select his prime minister and preside over the cabinet. Some of the Gaullist notions of government had been, in the course of the Fourth Republic, espoused by Michel Debré and René Capitant, who suggested the shortening of the sessions of a Parliament that would operate only within the framework of enumerated powers, as well as the notion of "incompatibility" finally embodied in Article 23.

The central feature of the Fifth Republic Constitution, a strong, quasi-monarchical executive, is considered the most Gaullist innovation, because the General, in his memoirs and public utterances, had consistently advocated it. It should, however, be remembered that de Gaulle merely embraced a constitutional preference that was a recurrent theme in France. The restoration of a genuine monarchy long ago became unthinkable in France, but the glorification of kings and the association of national greatness with monarchical regimes are still emphasized in the schools of republican France. Moreover, most of the French regimes after 1789, including republics, have been adorned (or encumbered) with certain monarchist elements. The Constitution of the Year III (1795) empowered the executive to appoint and dismiss ministers; the Charter of 1814 gave the king extensive legislative powers; the laws of 1830 reaffirmed the royal veto power; the Constitution of the Second Republic (1848) provided for a relatively weak President, but one who was still entitled to convoke the Assembly for special sessions, introduce bills, and negotiate treaties; the Constitution of 1852 (put into effect after the *coup d'état* by Napoleon III) granted most legislative and other powers to the executive; and the Constitutional Law of 1875 (the Third Republic) gave legislative initiative both to the President and to the chambers, and granted the President the power to appoint ministers.

6. Léo Hamon, *De Gaulle dans la République* (Paris: Plon, 1958), p. 70.

In the course of the Third Republic, the Parliament had asserted its supremacy at the expense of the President, whose legislative, appointive, and dissolution powers had gradually atrophied. Parliamentary supremacy and presidential weakness had become republican constitutional norms, which were embodied in the Fourth Republic Constitution of 1946. But throughout the Third and Fourth republics, the "myth" of an authoritarian president had persisted, and had been propagated by various movements and individuals who (like General Boulanger in the 1880s) had viewed Parliament as ill-suited to express the general will. In the Third Republic—particularly in the years 1917–19—attempts had been made to strengthen the office of the President by the *Association nationale pour l'organisation de la démocratie*, by the *Syndicat des français*, and by other groups that advanced various proposals reflecting a growing hostility to deputies for their alleged selfishness and lack of competence.[7] Many Frenchmen then favored an American type of regime. Alexandre Millerand, when he was President in 1923, wanted a stronger executive, to replace what he called the "parliamentary dictatorship."[8] He preferred the election of the President by a large electoral college (instead of by popular vote or by Parliament) as well as the resuscitation of presidential dissolution power.

Immediately after World War II the overreaction to Marshal Pétain's authoritarianism was so widespread that very few Frenchmen seriously thought a strong executive feasible in a republican regime, or would accept the idea of either the people or an electoral college replacing Parliament as the instrument for selecting the executive. Between 1941 and 1943 even Michel Debré, who was later to become the orthodox Gaullist par excellence, had written essays and letters (published in 1945) in which he expressed opposition to a popularly elected President and opposed a presidential regime altogether, because he feared that France would be governed by a general on the basis of pronunciamentos![9]

Nonetheless, at various times throughout the postwar period, especially during the last few years of the Fourth Republic, notions of presidentialism were advocated not only by de Gaulle himself, but also by Socialists, Christian Democrats, and others.[10] The President came to be viewed as an ideal person to hold the overseas territories and France together—perhaps following the example of Britain, where the queen

7. Hughes Tay, *Le régime présidentiel et la France* (Paris: Librairie Générale de Droit et de Jurisprudence [hereafter cited as LGDJ], 1967), pp. 69ff.
8. Ibid., p. 88.
9. Jacquier-Bruère (pseud.), *Refaire la France* (Paris: Plon, 1945), p. 120.
10. Tay, *Régime présidentiel*, pp. 185–94.

was the focal point of cohesion for the Commonwealth. After 1956, many elements of the intellectual Left and Right favored the direct election of the President (i.e., the American presidential model);[11] alternatively, others proposed the direct election of the prime minister (i.e., the de facto British model)[12]—but that was not held out as a serious possibility for France because of her chronic multiparty tendencies and relative lack of party discipline. As we have seen, some reforms had been instituted between 1954 and 1958 to strengthen the executive vis-à-vis Parliament, but these reforms had not been effective or credible because they had not been endorsed by the people.

The plebiscitarian features of the Fifth Republic Constitution, introduced by the Gaullists in order to weaken parliamentary and other intermediaries and to strengthen the President, were not Gaullist innovations but, rather, recurrent and widely used instruments in modern French political history. One aspect of plebiscitarianism, the popular approval of the Constitution, has a particularly hallowed place in French constitutional history: the Constitutions of 1792, 1795, 1799, and 1946 had all been submitted to the people. The same is true of the invalidation of republican rule and its replacement by authoritarian and Bonapartist regimes: the naming of Napoleon I as consul for life in 1802; the establishment of the Bonapartist hereditary line in 1804; the investiture of Napoleon III as Emperor in 1852—all these had been approved by plebiscite.[13] Even where earlier French precedents do not clearly exist, certain Fifth Republic features are not entirely novel in that they probably leaned upon foreign examples. Thus the authors of Article 16 (Emergency Powers) must have based themselves partly upon Article 48 of the Weimar Constitution; and the use of referenda for ordinary legislation may have been based upon the examples of the Weimar Republic, Switzerland, and contemporary Italy.

The Fifth Republic does, however, represent a sharp break with the Fourth Republic, because the Constitution tilts power decisively on the side of the executive, because it mirrors the political doctrines and institutional preferences of one man, and because the circumstances surrounding its establishment are in many ways different from those that had preceded and conditioned earlier attempts at reconstituting republican regimes after authoritarian experiences. The First Republic was the consequence of a rebellion against the monarchs of the *ancien régime*; the Second Republic followed the Revolution of 1848 and the deposition of the July Monarchy; the Third Republic was a reaction to

11. See Club Moulin, *L'Etat et le citoyen* (Paris: Seuil, 1961).
12. E.g., Marc Paillet, *La Gauche année zéro* (Paris: Gallimard, 1964), pp. 235 ff.
13. Hervé Duval et al., *Référendum et plébiscite* (Paris: Colin, 1970), pp. 15–16.

the military failures of Louis Napoleon as well as to the bloody suppression of the Paris Commune; and the Fourth Republic was both a
reaction to the Vichy regime and an attempt to restore the democratic
status quo ante bellum. The Fifth Republic, in contrast, was not a reaction to the authoritarianism of an earlier regime. It did not therefore
represent a step forward in republican terms: for if republicanism is
equated with the elevation of Parliament at the expense of a powerful
executive, then the Fifth Republic must be considered institutionally
retrogressive. But neither did it represent an unusual step backward.
Much of the basic nature of the Fifth Republic Constitution—in particular its executive-administrative character—can be explained by the
fact that the Fifth Republic was historically opportune, i.e., it fitted into
a cyclical pattern of French constitutional development. According to
Dorothy Pickles, modern French political history has been divided into
three-part cycles, each beginning with a moderate monarchy, followed
by a liberalized ("republican") regime, and ending in a conservative
reaction (see table 5). But whereas the conservative reactions to the

Table 5
Political Cycles and Regimes

Moderate Monarchy	Liberalization	Conservative Reaction
Constitutional monarchy of 1791	Republic of 1792	Dictatorial government of 1795
Restoration of 1815	July Monarchy, 1830	Second Empire
Early Third Republic, 1870–79	Third Republic since President Jules Grévy	Vichy regime
	Fourth Republic	Fifth Republic

SOURCE: Based on Dorothy Pickles, *Fifth French Republic* (3rd ed.; New York: Praeger, 1965), pp. 3–5.

Republic of 1792, the July Monarchy, and the Third Republic since the
1880s had been institutionally reflected in empires or dictatorships, the
response to the parliamentary excesses of the Fourth Republic was a
regime in which many republican institutions were retained.

Nonetheless, the Fifth Republic Constitution contains more innovations than its immediate predecessor. There is, first of all, the notion of

presidential *arbitrage*: the President's responsibility for both observing and interpreting the Constitution. Second, there is a limit on the length of parliamentary sessions, a reduction of the number and the power of legislative committees, and the streamlining of the budgetary process in such a way as to leave it essentially an executive matter. Third, there is a specific mention of political parties, including a stipulation (found in the West German and Italian constitutions as well) that political parties "must respect the principles of national sovereignty and democracy."[14] Fourth, there is a sharing of legislative power among the executive, the legislature, and the people, and for that reason a differentiation among organic laws, ordinary laws, regulations, and decrees. Fifth, there is the double responsibility of the premier to the President as well as to Parliament, both of which may, in theory, dismiss him. And finally, there is Article 16 (discussed more fully in chapter 7), which gives the President vast discretionary power to act in case the constitutionally established institutions do not function normally. It might even be argued that the Fifth Republic is unique because, unlike other Republics, it was inaugurated in a slightly unconstitutional manner.

The government itself (a provisional government) was given constituent powers immediately after de Gaulle was invested as prime minister by the Fourth Republic Parliament, despite Article 90 of the Fourth Republic Constitution (which was still in effect) that provided that constitutional amendments could be initiated only in Parliament. Hence one prominent anti-Gaullist has argued that the installation of the Fifth Republic was a *coup d'état* that had only a thin veneer of legality.[15] Indeed, the law of June 3, 1958, which empowered the government to draw up a new constitution, could be considered almost as "unconstitutional"—and the result as "illegal"—as the law of July 10, 1940, by which the National Assembly of the Third Republic had ceded all power (including the power to set aside the constitution) "to the Government of the Republic, under the authority and signature of Marshal Pétain."[16] This does not mean that the Gaullist regime should be compared to the Vichy regime, because the Fifth Republic Constitution, unlike Pétain's "French State," was endorsed in a popular referendum and therefore legitimated. Indeed, if one attaches a quantitative element to the criterion of popular endorsement, one may even argue

14. The Fourth Republic Constitution (Art. 2) had merely referred to "political associations," whose aim is the "preservation of the natural . . . rights of man," specifically, "liberty, property, security, and resistance to oppression."
15. Pierre Mendès-France, "De Gaulle's Betrayal of de Gaulle," *Le Monde Weekly*, 18 November 1970.
16. Michel-Henri Fabre, *Principes républicains de droit constitutionnel* (2nd ed.; Paris: LGDJ, 1970), pp. 339 f.

that the Fifth Republic Constitution (which was approved by 80 percent of the electorate) was more "legitimate" than its immediate predecessor (which had been endorsed by only about 40 percent of the registered voters). It remains true that in France, popular sovereignty is the source of a republican constitution, just as it is in Britain, where parliamentary enactments or cabinet actions that have the consequence of "amending" the constitution are based on general or "mandate" elections.

However, the new Constitution was also legitimated by its internal character, that is, by virtue of the fact that it stipulated certain traditional republican principles. First, the principle of universal suffrage continues to apply, as before, for the election of the Assembly. Second, the government, although selected in the first place by the President, continues to be subject to criticism and revocation by the Parliament. Third, there is an independent judiciary. The inclusion of these features was demanded by the multipartite Consultative Committee, the Council of State, and other agencies and individuals whose advice was sought in the constitution-drafting stage. Without these provisions, the Fifth Republic Constitution would very likely have been rejected in the popular referendum.

CONSTITUTIONAL INTERPRETATION
AND ADAPTATION

There is no reason to believe that democratic political patterns cannot in the future be further developed by amendment, interpretation, and practice. Not all the formal constitutional amendments to date have tended toward democratization in the customary parliamentary direction, possibly because the French now, as in earlier regimes, have not been able to make up their minds between plebiscitarian and representative democracy. While the amendment of November 1962, which provided for the popular election of the President, was a shift in the plebiscitarian direction, the failure of the constitutional amendment of April 1969, which attempted to reform the Senate out of existence, demonstrates that institutions traditionally associated with republican regimes (or with "parliamentary supremacy") cannot be abolished so easily.

But constitutional practice has tended to reinforce habit patterns that are reminiscent of earlier regimes. The Fifth Republic has had to operate at least in part within the parameters of traditional republican expectations because—apart from de Gaulle himself—a large number of Fifth Republic cabinet members had been prominent politicians in the Fourth Republic, and many more deputies, especially in the early years of the Fifth Republic, were "holdovers" from the Fourth Republic's National Assembly. It was natural for such politicians to operate according to their traditional styles, and to help perpetuate old practices. Among these have been the (occasional) practice of investiture, the custom of proxy voting in Parliament, the phenomenon of party discipline (in some parties), and the simultaneous service of deputies as regional or local councilors or mayors.

There have, however, been certain actions that fall in the twilight zone between constitutional and unconstitutional behavior. Did de Gaulle act constitutionally when, in October 1962, he dissolved Parliament after the latter had adopted a no-confidence motion against Premier Pompidou? According to Article 50, the premier, when censured, must submit the resignation of his cabinet (therefore ceasing to be premier). According to Article 8, the President names the premier; and according to Article 11, the President can dissolve the Assembly, but before doing so must consult the speakers of the two chambers and the premier. The question is whether an ousted premier is still premier, or whether there is any premier left to "consult"! Even if one admits that these provisions are sufficiently vague as to lend themselves to presidential interpretation for political purposes—in this case the political purpose of taking revenge upon, and thereby cowing, the Assembly—could one not say that the spirit of the Constitution was violated?

The Gaullist interpretation of presidential power in such a way as to undercut the premier's independent position even more than envisaged by the constitutional wording (as in the fact of the President, rather than the premier, choosing the cabinet) is of course an expansion of presidential power; but one must remember that in the Fourth Republic, a regime characterized by parliamentary supremacy, the prohibition against "delegated legislation" (Article 13 of Fourth Republic Constitution) was disregarded when Parliament in fact granted decree powers to cabinets (see table 6, page 62).

Having noted the violations of, or digressions from, the text of the Fifth Republic Constitution, one should not automatically assume that France does not have a constitutional regime. In Britain, too, adaptations of the constitution have become necessary in order for democratic government to function, such as the "complementing" of the principle of parliamentary supremacy by the practice of cabinet government. In France, the de facto situation has often differed from the de jure situation, and constitutional provisions have been sidetracked or adapted not only in the Fifth Republic, but in the Third and Fourth republics as well;

Table 6
Constitutional Principles and Constitutional Adaptation

	Principle	Practice
Third Republic	Presidential dissolution and appointive powers	Parliamentary arrogation of these powers
	President to serve seven years	Premature abdication of several Presidents forced by Parliament
Fourth Republic	Prohibition against delegated legislation	Decree powers in fact given to the cabinet
	Investiture of prime minister	"Double investiture" of premier and cabinet
Fifth Republic	Appointment of cabinet by premier	Appointment in practice by the President
	Incompatibility of cabinet office with parliamentary mandate (Article 23)	Cabinet members permitted to seek parliamentary mandate
	Prohibition against undemocratic parties (Article 4)	Certain "undemocratic" parties (e.g., the PCF) permitted to exist
	No precise enumeration of civil rights	Continuation of traditional liberties (e.g., freedom of speech)
	Separation of church and state (Article 2)	Governmental support of parochial schools; public salary of clerics in Alsace; church holidays are legal holidays
	Equality of all before the law (Article 2)	Extensive legal disabilities of women, only recently being abolished
	Vote of censure by Parliament leading to resignation of cabinet	Vote of censure by Parliament leading to its dissolution
	Prohibition against binding instructions upon members of Parliament (Article 27)	Enforcement of party discipline in several parliamentary parties

this adaptation has not necessarily been antidemocratic or "dysfunctional" for the system. In the Third Republic, the constitutional provisions regarding strong presidential powers had to be ignored, and certain executive powers had to be permitted to atrophy, in order to facilitate democratic political development. In the Fourth Republic, provisions against delegated legislation had to be violated in order to allow decisions to be made by *someone* (usually the prime minister). In the Fifth Republic, not all failures to adhere strictly to constitutional provisions, and not all extraconstitutional practices, have merely enhanced presidential power. Thus the interpretation of Article 23 so as to permit cabinet members to seek formal election to parliamentary seats (which they do not occupy) provides a grass-roots legitimation of ministers. The constitutional reference (Article 2) to France as a secular state has not interfered with legislation (e.g., the *Loi Debré*) providing for governmental support of parochial schools—nor should it, given the historic and present importance of Catholicism in France. In interpreting the constitutional requirement (Article 4) that political parties adhere to a democratic order, France could have followed the German example by declaring the Communist party to be illegal. But such a "strict construction" might well tear apart the body politic, given the importance and the considerable electoral following of the French Communist party, and make a mockery of the principle of majority rule.

Most of the adaptations of Western constitutions have been legitimated by their popular acceptance and democratic intent. This is true of the Fifth Republic Constitution as well; even its interpretation tending to favor presidential power to the detriment of parliamentary power is democratic because the President himself is (since 1965 at any rate) a creature of popular sovereignty and a product of majority rule.

Some adaptations may be considered undemocratic if one does not like them, and all of them may be considered "unconstitutional" if the criterion of constitutionality is a strict interpretation of the letter of specific provisions. But who is to decide? Since there is no judicial review in the American (or West German) sense, practices and statutes that conflict slightly with the Constitution are considered nonetheless valid if constitutional violations (such as the procedural violation by de Gaulle in 1962 in connection with a referendum to change the Constitution) are "vindicated" by popular sovereignty (see page 191); other adaptations are legitimated by the fact that they are anchored in French traditions. Certain constitutional evasions are legitimate not only because they are confirmed by popular sovereignty, but even "legal" in the sense that they are based on statutes that antedate, and coexist with, a particular constitution. This is similar to the situation in West Ger-

many, where statutes providing for punishment of "seditious" statements, or giving the police extensive power to make preventive arrests,
continued for many years to coexist with provisions in the Basic Law
regarding freedom of speech and procedural due-process protections.
Thus while the Fifth Republic Constitution provides (by implication)
for freedom of speech and assembly, there are (still valid) statute laws
permitting the government to punish speech that is seditious or lèse-
majesté; while the Constitution provides for equality, there were, until
recently, laws putting women in a legally inferior position.

Neither the "rules of the game" nor notions of legitimacy in France
—and, indeed, in several other European countries with twentieth-century constitutions—can be based exclusively (or even predominantly)
on the text of a particular document. French constitutions have been
revised frequently, even before the legal norms contained therein were
fully absorbed in the Frenchman's political consciousness. In the face of
this constitutional impermanence it has been natural for intellectuals,
lawyers, and citizens to base many of their notions of legality on the old
statute laws, and their ideas of legitimacy on popular sovereignty. It
is in this light that constitutional practice (or adaptation) must be viewed.

The Fifth Republic Constitution has, like others, its share of uncer-
tainties and internal contradictions, of which the following may be cited
as examples. Article 23 provides for the incompatibility of a parliamentary mandate with incumbency in other governmental office, but
Article 25 permits Parliament to provide legislation on the eligibility of
members of Parliament that may moderate this incompatibility. Article
16 provides for purely presidential action in emergency situations, but
Article 36 provides for the declaration of martial law by the cabinet,
and the prorogation of that law by Parliament. Article 21 provides that
the premier is in charge of national defense, but Article 15 makes the
President commander of the armed forces. Article 20 says that the
government "determines the policy of the nation," but Article 5 says
that the President is the "guarantor of national independence [and] the
integrity of its territory."[17]

Under de Gaulle and his successors, these contradictions have been
resolved by a kind of "preferred position" doctrine under which—when
the situation was in doubt—presidential power would prevail. But this
has been the case only because such an interpretation has appeared
legitimate and has been supported by the French people. It must be

17. For a more detailed treatment of textual ambiguities, see Stanley Hoffmann, "The
    French Constitution of 1958: The Final Text and Its Prospects," American Politi-
    cal Science Review 53 (June 1959): 332–57.

realized that the exercise of presidential power in France is not determined solely by what the Constitution permits, or by what it does not forbid. The English queen has many awesome political powers, but British political culture and habit do not tolerate their exercise. In France, similarly, the exercise of presidential powers is possible only to the extent that it is sanctioned by historical precedent and popular acceptance.

The subversion or nonobservance of certain provisions of the French Constitution by General de Gaulle may be considered legitimate insofar as Frenchmen themselves accepted the fact that he was its main institution, and insofar as this institutionalization of de Gaulle was confirmed by popular vote. But legitimation of one-man rule by direct democracy tends to undermine several institutions built into democratic constitutions, such as parliaments, political parties, and interest groups, and therefore traditional constitutional government itself. Moreover, the danger of the personalization of a constitution, even though based on popular sovereignty, is that a charismatic President must constantly buttress and renew his "legitimacy" by providing periodic circuses to maintain the people's interest in, and support of, his rule.

It is questionable whether this kind of legitimation can carry over completely to de Gaulle's successors. The French Constitution (Article 3) provides that "national sovereignty belongs to the people who exercise it through their representatives and by means of the referendum." When de Gaulle was President, the people permitted him to rely largely on the referendum and the presidential election as expressions of the popular will. But when Pompidou announced (in December 1972) that any new government that might be constituted after the parliamentary election of March 1973 would base itself on the policies of the President alone rather than "this or that electoral combination," he was widely criticized for misinterpreting the Constitution.[18] Apparently Pompidou, who lacked de Gaulle's personality and institutional qualities, was expected to be bound more closely than his predecessor to the letter of constitutional provisions.

That is not to say that constitutional adaptation depends solely on a particular hero-figure, because many other types of legitimation exist for constitutional evasion or development. In the Third Republic, constitutional development was in the direction of proscribing governmental (i.e., executive) power, because the state was viewed as an enemy of

18. See, for example, Jean-Denis Bredin, "Inquiétude et désarroi," *Le Monde,* 20 December 1972.

liberty,[19] and the President represented the state better than any other institution. In the Fifth Republic, parliamentary power has been reduced because Parliament—owing to its mismanagement during the Fourth Republic—was viewed as an enemy of the state, the nation, or the "general will." Constitutional development, then, is also legitimate if it conforms to the spirit of the time and is accepted (or at least not opposed) by public opinion.

Every constitution is said to be based on a particularly dominant principle and to be instituted for an overriding political purpose. Thus the basic principle of the American Constitution is separation of powers; of the British Constitution, the idea of a gradual development of freedoms, and the progressive adjustment of relations between certain dominant institutions (e.g., queen, Parliament, and cabinet); of the Fourth Republic Constitution, the idea of parliamentary supremacy; and of the Fifth Republic Constitution, the idea of the "solitude" of the executive.[20] The Olympian position of the President, as well as other features of the Fifth Republic Constitution, in addition to being based on specific Gaullist ideas, French and other precedents, and "republican" requirements, are also reflective of the need for mechanical readjustments of institutional relations that were viewed as "dysfunctional" for the preceding regime, which, in the phrase of Dorothy Pickles, makes the present constitution "a plan for winning the last war."[21] But the Fifth Republic is not unique in that sense. Just as the makers of the Fifth Republic Constitution were haunted by the specter of an immobilized but theoretically omnipotent legislature, so the writers of the Bonn Constitution, in instituting the "positive vote of no-confidence," had been haunted by the cabinet instability of the Weimar Republic.

In some respects, the rationale behind the making of a new constitution in France in 1958 was similar to that which applied to constitution making in the Fourth Republic, in postwar Italy, and in postwar West Germany. In these three regimes, the constitutions were of a negative character in that they contained articles embodying an overreaction to a bad past, i.e., the dictatorial governments of Hitler, Mussolini, and Marshal Pétain. That is why all three constitutions contained clear definitions of human rights, and certain programmatic features (e.g., social and economic rights), and most of them also had a very restricted

19. William G. Andrews, *Constitutions and Constitutionalism* (New York: Van Nostrand, 1968), p. 67.
20. Roger-Gérard Schwartzenberg, "Le président français," *Le Monde*, 30 January 1973.
21. Dorothy Pickles, *The Fifth French Republic* (3rd ed.; New York: Praeger, 1965), p. 12.

place, or none at all, for plebiscitarian decision making—since under Hitler this had been very much abused. In contrast, the Fifth Republic Constitution was an overreaction primarily to experiences of ineffective government.[22]

The Fifth Republic Constitution is unusual in the twentieth century, in that, like the American, British, and Third Republic Constitutions, it is essentially mechanistic; unlike the Italian, Bonn, and Fourth Republic Constitutions, it contains virtually no "programmatic" features and no Bill of Rights. While the Fourth Republic Constitution spelled out (in its Preamble) the right to work, to organize trade unions, to strike, to collective bargaining, to family protection, to health and old-age provisions and unemployment benefits, to free and secular education, to worker co-management of business, and so on, the Fifth Republic Constitution shies away from such clear specifications.[23] However, Article 2 contains a reference to the fact that France is a "secular, democratic and social" republic, and guarantees "the equality of all citizens before the law." Furthermore, there is in the Preamble a statement of "acceptance" of the Declaration of the Rights of Man of 1789 and of the civil rights and privileges mentioned in the Fourth Republic Constitition. The Preamble has no clear binding force; however, there is a plethora of customary rights and freedoms existing alongside the Constitution, which have been periodically extended by means of legislation, especially under the Presidency of Giscard d'Estaing.

22. Carl Friedrich, *Constitutional Government and Democracy* (4th ed.; Boston: Ginn, 1968), p. 151.
23. For a more general discussion of the differences between mechanistic and programmatic constitutions, see Karl Loewenstein, *Political Power and the Governmental Process* (2nd ed.; Chicago: University of Chicago Press, 1965), pp. 136–43.

Political Parties
and Elections

The political party system in France—at once the lifeblood of various republican regimes and the cause of their instability—is renowned for its complexity and diversity. Multipartism is not unique to France: the "political families" that have provided the ideological underpinnings of parties—conservatism, liberalism, Catholicism, radicalism, socialism, and communism—are found elsewhere in Western Europe. But several characteristics peculiar to French parties make it difficult to compare them to American or British parties. In France, the party is not merely a mechanism of elite recruitment, a focus of political responsibility, or an instrument of government. For the past hundred years, parties have been established or splintered over certain questions that had been solved gradually—or depoliticized—in Britain and the United States: the place of religion in politics, the question of the legitimacy of the regime, and the relationship of the executive to the legislative power. Each political party has tried to represent a set of principles in which these issues were more or less balanced; such a position often made it difficult for political parties to compromise and to adapt to a changed social or economic situation. It has been said that in France "there are two fundamental principles: that of the Right and that of the Left; three main tendencies, if one adds the Center; six 'political families'; ten parties, small or large, each opposed by multiple currents; fourteen parliamentary groups, highly undisciplined; and forty million opinions."[1] This was the situation that obtained toward the end of the Fourth Republic and was in some measure responsible for the discrediting of the parliamentary regime,

1. Jacques Fauvet, *La France déchirée* (Paris: Fayard, 1957), p. 22.

in which the parties were given free rein but were incapable of governing stably. To be sure, there has been a simplification of the party spectrum; in the mid-1930s, there were nineteen recognized parties in the Assembly, whereas in the early 1970s there were only six: the Gaullists, Giscard's Republicans, the Center, the Radicals, the Socialists, and the Communists. Yet each of the six represents a political force that has shown a remarkable persistence in French political life.

GAULLISM

The Gaullist organization at first pretended not to be a political party at all, but rather a national movement and an alternative to parties. For as long as possible, it shunned a clear-cut ideology and organizational structure and based itself on the charisma and mystique of one man—General Charles de Gaulle. It has been the only political force in a century to capture an absolute majority of parliamentary seats, and has been the first organized party of the Right supported by the masses.

The original Gaullists, the leaders of "Free France" in London, were a disparate group. They included Maurice Schumann, a devout Catholic who was later to become a leader of the Christian Democratic party (the MRP); René Pleven, subsequently leader of the UDSR, the mildly socialist party of the Resistance; and René Cassin, a prominent jurist who later became president of the Council of State. These men, and others, were united in accepting the idea that de Gaulle embodied the national and republican spirit of France.

To many Frenchmen, the Fourth Republic was unsatisfactory. General de Gaulle's oratory, in which he attacked the weakness of France, and attributed that weakness to a feeble executive and a Parliament that was immobilized by too many parties, led to the formation of the Rally of the French People (*Rassemblement du peuple français*—RPF). The RPF soon participated successfully in municipal elections: in October 1947, it received more than a third of the votes and gained control of many large cities. The main tenets of the RPF—the reassertion of France's role in the world, and the desire for a stable and effective government—were popular with the majority of the French. At a press conference in 1952, de Gaulle had declared that "every Frenchman is, was, or will be Gaullist." The eclectic nature and appeal of Gaullism at once becomes clear when one considers the success with which the RPF enticed French political leaders who, while still committed to distinct non-Gaullist parties, yet found enough in Gaullism to suit them. Among these were Edmond Michelet, a Christian Democrat; Jacques Soustelle, a Socialist; and Jacques Chaban-Delmas, a Radical Socialist.

But when the RPF became too successful, i.e., when it captured about 20 percent of the seats in Parliament after the election in 1951, it began to lose its effectiveness as a Gaullist opposition instrument. Many RPF deputies were coopted into the system when they supported government coalitions and especially when they joined the right-of-center cabinet of Antoine Pinay, thereby becoming part of the hated Fourth Republic. These Gaullists came to be known as the Social Republicans, and de Gaulle dissociated himself from them in 1953.[2]

The election of 1956 indicated a decline in the Gaullist party's fortunes: it won only 12.4 percent of the popular vote and its representation in the Assembly was reduced from 120 to 22. The reasons for this decline are complex: the French economy was making appreciable advances, and the Fourth Republic functioned in a relatively acceptable fashion; the Poujadists (see page 77) drew away potential supporters from Gaullism; in addition, the growing conservatism of the MRP drained off much Catholic and conservative support from the Gaullists.

But this setback was temporary. Gaullism as a political force was revived in 1958, when de Gaulle was recalled to power and needed a new tool for organizing parliamentary elections. The Union for the New Republic (*Union pour la nouvelle République*—UNR) was established in October 1958 as an amalgam of Gaullist groupings that either had continued to hold aloft the banner of Gaullism in the last years of the Fourth Republic or had sprung up spontaneously. These included individuals who looked upon de Gaulle as the guarantor of continued French rule in Algeria; and others again—of the traditional Right—who saw in de Gaulle an embodiment of heroic leadership.

Nevertheless, the Gaullist party is a "modern" party of the Right because Gaullism has embraced technocracy and the business ethos. Moreover, Gaullism has tried to be a "catchall" party by exploiting ideologies found in both right-wing and left-wing political formations. Thus the Gaullists have shared their antiparliamentary attitudes with the Communist party (PCF); their positive view of the church with the MRP; and their imperialism with some Radicals and many Socialists. Indeed, plebiscitarianism itself—the penchant for referenda and other mechanisms of direct democracy—is also a left-wing preference. Clericalism can be associated with economic progressivism, and nationalism cuts across a number of social classes and ideologies.

Despite de Gaulle's attack on the notion of the class struggle, his relative indifference to socioeconomic domestic issues, and his denigra-

2. On the cooptation of the RPF and the hibernation of Gaullism, see Roy Pierce, "De Gaulle and the RPF—A Post-Mortem," *Journal of Politics* 16, no. 1 (February 1954): 96–118.

tion of internationalism, many voters of the Left deserted to Gaullism. In 1958, the SFIO leadership supported de Gaulle because the Gaullist constitution had retained a number of traditional republican institutions; many Socialists viewed Gaullism as the only alternative to civil war and as a bulwark against communism. Some Socialists supported de Gaulle for what they perceived to be his uncompromising stance on Algeria, just as others subsequently supported him for precisely the opposite policy, i.e., the decolonization of Africa.

In the beginning of the Fifth Republic there had been some hope that Gaullism would turn leftward on economic issues. Attempts were made to establish separate political entities for that segment of the working class which might rally around de Gaulle. The most important of these was the Democratic Union of Labor (*Union démocratique de travail*—UDT) led by René Capitant, a university professor who liked the plebiscitarian aspects of Gaullism, and hoped that de Gaulle would "impose" great domestic reforms upon the country. In 1962 the UDT formally associated with the UNR, and in 1967 the two groups combined for electoral purposes, becoming the Democratic Union for the Republic (*Union démocratique pour la Ve République*—UDR). But in view of de Gaulle's increasingly conservative domestic policies, his relative neglect of the working class, and his quasi-permanent coalition with the business-oriented Independent Republicans, left-wing Gaullism had become an illusionary orientation. The only *raison d'être* of the UDT remained the support of the leadership of de Gaulle. Until 1965 de Gaulle had not encouraged the transformation of the UNR into a disciplined, organized party, possibly because he did not wish to see any institutional substitutes for himself as the center of Gaullism.

After de Gaulle left the political scene, Gaullism briefly appeared to have become more pro-European, more progressive, more disciplined, and more pragmatic. Spokesmen of the Gaullist "Left," such as Louis Vallon, argued that Pompidou betrayed Gaullism by his lack of enthusiasm for de Gaulle's notion of the "association" of capital and labor via such schemes as *intéressement*, i.e., the buying of industrial stock by workers.[3] Others, e.g., André Malraux, argued that Gaullism was inconceivable and "idiotic" without de Gaulle.[4] Still others promoted a "dynastic" Gaullism; in 1972, two rival associations were established to back the presidential candidacy of Admiral Philippe de Gaulle, the General's son. The Pompidou entourage contained a few old-line Gaul-

3. Cf. Louis Vallon, *L'anti-de Gaulle* (Paris: Seuil, 1969).
4. *Le Monde*, 27 July 1972. On the background, ideology and appeal of Gaullism, see the excellent discussion by Jean Charlot, *The Gaullist Phenomenon* (New York: Praeger, 1971).

lists who considered themselves the interpreters of "genuine" Gaullism. In addition, some two or three dozen clubs saw to it that Gaullist ideology did not disappear.

Pompidou was certainly a Gaullist in a broad sense; by and large he shared de Gaulle's foreign policy, his view of the office of the President, his penchant for referenda, and his general social and economic orientations. But Pompidou was also a realistic politician who knew that, while under de Gaulle the power of the party had rested on the mystique of one man, under his successor it had to rest on an expanded electoral base. This realism could be seen in the diverse nature of the personalities and tendencies that dominated Pompidou's cabinets: the etatism and ultranationalism of Michel Debré and Pierre Messmer; the Catholic sentimentalism of Maurice Schumann; the "liberal" façade of Chaban-Delmas; the technicism of Olivier Guichard; the opportunism of Edgar Faure; the economic conservatism of Giscard d'Estaing; the small-town orientation of Jacques Duhamel—the latter two, leaders, respectively, of the Independent Republicans and the PDM. These diverse tendencies were less important than the fact that there was a Gaullist machine, which by the mid-1960s had become fairly structured and disciplined and had shown itself capable of seeking and maintaining power—at least until 1974—regardless of the uncertain nature of the doctrines espoused by party leaders. No doubt the strength of Gaullism was due also to the disorganization of its rivals.

Despite the UDR's majority status in Parliament, Pompidou proved far less successful than his predecessor in holding the various strands of Gaullism together. He could neither exploit the Resistance nostalgia nor retain the support of the working class. Moreover, the majority status of the party contributed to a lessening of its unity, and the growth of internal strife inspired the resignation of a number of prominent Gaullists from the UDR.[5] In the early 1970s, a group of deputies united in the association *Présence et action du gaullisme*, in order to safeguard the traditional conservatism of Gaullism. Conversely, in mid-1971, an attempt was made to unite various "left" Gaullist groups into the *Comité d'action pour le rassemblement*. The conservative Gaullists retained the upper hand; there was a growing lack of cordiality between

5. In 1970, several members of the Gaullist "Left" resigned because of disillusionment with the conservatism of Pompidou; in 1971, ex-cabinet minister Fouchet resigned because he felt that without the General, Gaullism had become senseless; and in 1972 M. Jeanneney, another former minister, switched to the opposition Centrists in protest against Pompidou's statement that if in the election of March 1973 the UDR should lose its parliamentary majority, he might ignore that outcome in his cabinet appointments. *Le Monde*, 2 July 1970, 2 October 1971, and 11 November 1972; and *New York Times*, 13 February 1971.

the UDR executive and Premier Chaban-Delmas, who was considered too moderate. UDR dissatisfaction with the premier was put in abeyance immediately following Chaban's victory in the parliamentary by-election in Bordeaux in September 1970, but revived soon thereafter—culminating finally in his ouster from the cabinet.

The public image of the UDR declined because of the involvement of some Gaullist deputies in real estate and other scandals, and the absolute loyalty to Gaullism of the parties associated with the majority became increasingly questionable. Candidates of the UDR and the Independent Republicans, who had often collaborated previously, competed with each other in the senatorial by-elections in certain districts in 1970. In 1969, there had been 360 deputies (274 Gaullists, 61 Independent Republicans, and 25 Centrists) solidly behind Pompidou, but that majority began to crumble in 1972, with some 40 deputies voicing protests against the economic policy of the UDR and against the continuation of one-man rule.[6] As for the Center, those deputies who officially supported Gaullism and who were united in the Assembly under the label of *Centre de la démocratie et du progrès* (CDP) wished to remain "true to themselves" even while adhering to the majority.[7] Early in 1970, the leaders of the pro-Gaullist CDP met with leaders of opposition Center factions and together constituted a group of about 75 parliamentarians, the *Union parlementaire du Centre.*

For the parliamentary election of 1973, the UDR, aware of its growing weakness, decided to join the Independent Republicans and the CDP in an electoral alliance that provided that candidates belonging to the various components of the majority coalition run under the common label of the Union of Republicans for Progress (*Union des républicains pour le progrès*—URP) on the first ballot. But in many districts, candidates of the three formations continued to run against each other under their distinct labels. The elections indicated the extent of the decline of the UDR: it received only 34.5 percent of the first-ballot votes as compared to 43.7 percent in the election of 1968—the consequence of a loss of 1.3 million votes; and after the second ballot the UDR's parliamentary representation declined from 273 to 185. The UDR retained its parliamentary plurality only because many Independent Republicans and Centrists (Reformers) had switched to the UDR as a more palatable alternative to the leftist coalition. This plurality, too, lost much of its meaning with the election of Giscard as President in 1974. Already before that event the UDR had been weakened by defections, by a lack

6. Cathérine Nay, "La majorité en miettes," *L'Express*, 13–19 November 1972, pp. 12–13.
7. *L'Année politique 1970*, p. 28.

of decisive leadership, and, during Pompidou's fatal illness, by a fight for the succession. At the end of the campaign, during which the moderate Chaban-Delmas had been pitted against the more orthodox Messmer, the Gaullists were forced to support Giscard d'Estaing, the candidate of the Independent Republicans, on the second ballot.

At the beginning of Giscard's Presidency it looked as if the Gaullist party would become a mere component of his right-of-center presidential majority rather than—as Chirac hoped—its foremost pillar. According to one view, the party had become a group of "aging notables and young careerists"[8] attempting to stay as close to national power as possible, and its membership, which in 1973 had been 150,000 to 200,000, had declined dramatically. But in 1976 Chirac assumed the leadership of the party, which, under a new label, experienced a revival. It demonstrated that it could exist (at least as far as one could foresee) without a national hero to lead it and that its appeal as a "populist" movement cut across class lines. Before the parliamentary elections of 1978, it had managed to strengthen its local machines, and claimed a membership of 600,000.

THE PRO-GAULLIST RIGHT

The traditional French Right—the Catholic, non-Bonapartist conservatives representing the established classes—began as an antirepublican force. But as soon as the Third Republic was firmly established, the "Right" divided itself into two major groups. One segment continued to be adamantly against the Republic, and organized itself into extraparliamentary clubs or movements—e.g., the *Action française*, the *Croix de Feu*, and the *Cagoulards*—the heirs of which still survive. The other group adapted itself to republicanism, particularly after an encyclical issued by Pope Leo XIII in 1891 had suggested that republicanism need not be incompatible with Christian values. This group may still have believed that the best of all possible forms of government was monarchy, but the hope for its restoration had become unrealistic; in any case, it was more important to fight the demands of a growing working class and thus to preserve the social and economic privileges of the bourgeoisie.

Two of the pro-republican right-wing movements, the *Alliance démocratique* and the even more conservative *Fédération républicaine*, eventually combined in the Chamber of Deputies to form the National Center of Independents and Peasants (*Centre national des indépendants*

8. Bertrand Fessard de Foucault, "Enfin, la vérité," *Le Monde*, 17 December 1974.

et paysans—CNIP). During its heyday in 1936 that party won 42.5 percent of the vote, but its popular support dwindled in 1945 to 14 percent. In the Fourth Republic, traditional conservatism never recovered its former importance because conservatives had failed to solve pressing social problems and were considered to have been too eager to compromise with the Vichy regime. Furthermore, the supporters of the traditional Right were fragmented: in 1945, many Catholics voted for the MRP; in 1951, a number of old "Bonapartists" and antirepublicans voted for the RPF; and in 1956, economically frustrated petit-bourgeois opponents of the Republic voted for the Poujadists. The UNR and UDR retrieved a large proportion of these elements in 1958 and thereafter, but a traditional Conservative party managed to survive. In the early days of the Fifth Republic, certain members of the CNIP—Giscard among them—diverged from the rest of the party's deputies in approving both the new Gaullist system in 1958 and its Algerian policy, and later in favoring the government's position on the Evian Accords (granting independence to Algeria) and the referendum concerning the direct election of the President of the Republic. Early in 1962, this small faction of deviants organized a "study group." Although it remained a force in the Senate and in municipal elections, the CNIP ceased to be important in the Assembly; after the parliamentary election of 1962, that party's representation was reduced from 121 to 29 deputies.[9] Of these, seven joined Lecanuet's Democratic Center, four attached themselves to the Radical Socialist party, and eighteen reunited with Giscard's original supporters in a new parliamentary faction, the Rally of Independent Republicans (*Rassemblement des républicains indépendants*—RI).

The RI, like its mother party and rival, was conservative. It had no mass following, no national congress (until 1971), and no challenges by local politicians to the national leadership, into which Giscard "emerged" almost from the inception of the party.[10] The RI was like the UDR in that the national organization encouraged the establishment of local clubs; and it was like the Radical Socialist party in its lack of both discipline and ideological uniformity.

Although the RI supported the UDR on most issues, its relation to the Gaullists remained ambiguous. Giscard's early support of de Gaulle had earned him an appointment, in 1959, as secretary of state in the Finance Ministry and, three years later, as full minister of finance. In

9. Malcolm Anderson, *Conservative Politics in France* (London: Allen & Unwin, 1974), pp. 254–55.
10. Ibid., pp. 261ff.; and Jean-Claude Colliard, "Les Républicains Indépendants: Doctrine et programme," *Revue politique et parlementaire*, March 1972, pp. 32–43.

1966 he was replaced in that position by Michel Debré (in part because de Gaulle wished to abandon the "economic stabilization" policy with which Giscard's name had been associated), and refused a proffered demotion to another cabinet post. In the same year Giscard transformed the RI into a full-fledged party, primarily in order to give himself a new political platform.[11] In 1967, he attacked de Gaulle's "lonely exercise of power" and criticized individual aspects of de Gaulle's policies, although Giscard was neither anti-Gaullist nor able to produce alternative programs.[12] The fence-sitting of the RI was probably unavoidable in a party that accommodated itself to the "law-and-order" Gaullism of Marcellin (minister of the interior) and Giscard's disagreement with Gaullism on economic policy. But this flexibility paid political dividends: the parliamentary representation of the RI increased from 35 in 1962 to 42 in 1967. Giscard's fortuitous absence from the cabinet in 1968 enabled him to escape much of the blame for the May Events, with the result that in the ensuing parliamentary election the RI increased its Assembly representation to 61. This representation did not suffice to give the RI the balance of power in Parliament, since the UDR alone held an absolute majority of 292 out of 485 seats. In 1969, Giscard, while supporting regional reforms, publicly opposed de Gaulle's referendum on the reform of the Senate (though the majority of RI deputies favored it).[13] After the defeat of the referendum and de Gaulle's departure, Giscard supported Pompidou in the presidential election that followed. The new President reappointed Giscard as finance minister in the government of Chaban-Delmas, whose 39 members included seven Independent Republicans.

The enhanced fortunes of the RI illustrate the success of that party as a vehicle for Giscard's political advancement. While Giscard served Pompidou faithfully, the RI kept its options open. For the RI, Gaullism was not ideological but "institutional"; the party consistently supported the Fifth Republic, but it did not have any clear views about where France ought to be going, or any coherent notions about social progress.[14] The party—which reflected a hodgepodge of liberalism, moderate

11. Anderson, *Conservative Politics*, p. 263.
12. Giscard's qualified Gaullism is perhaps best illustrated by the story about a television appearance during the parliamentary election campaign of 1967, during which he "took a piece of paper and in front of the viewers wrote in two columns the negative and positive sides of Gaullism in power." Charlot, *Gaullist Phenomenon*, p. 52.
13. Colliard, "Les Républicains Indépendants," pp. 38–40; and cf. same author, "Le rôle et l'équation personnelle de Valéry Giscard d'Estaing," *Revue politique et parlementaire*, March 1972, pp. 44–48.
14. Charlot, *Gaullist Phenomenon*, p. 98.

Catholicism, republicanism, and tactical Gaullism—has been essentially centrist in that it has desired to avoid extremes, to depoliticize problems as much as possible, and to look at them from a technical perspective. Hostility to the PCF and the Left in general may have been more pronounced in the RI than in the UDR, and it is questionable whether the RI would have accommodated itself as easily to the foreign policy of the USSR as did the UDR. In domestic policy the RI has been more liberal than the UDR; it has been a supporter of traditional civil rights, and opposed the Gaullist policy of using the public media of information as a government propaganda machine. It has preferred a laisser-faire approach to economics, although it has issued certain statements, as the occasion demanded, in favor of economic redistribution and social justice. The adaptability of the RI led it, in 1971, to propose the establishment of a "large centrist federation" that would include the PDM and the Radicals.[15] Such an attempt was premature; until 1974 the RI remained a minority party.

The social base of the RI, a well-organized elite party, was rather small, as was its implantation in local political offices. In 1971, only 17,000 of the 463,000 local and regional councilors were members of the party. Nevertheless the RI remained a significant party, not only because of its dynamic leader, who was a member of almost every cabinet since 1958, but also because it could be counted on to be safely Gaullist on crucial issues. With the election of Giscard d'Estaing as President in 1974, the Independent Republican party has moved into a privileged position; it has become the crucial element of the presidential majority and the main connecting link between traditional Gaullism and the Center.

THE NON-GAULLIST RIGHT

Two additional parties of the Right in the Fourth Republic were the *Parti républicain de la liberté* (PRL), and the Poujadist party. The PRL, which was anticollectivist and slightly pro-monarchist, had little mass following. The party had thirty deputies until 1951; toward the end of the Fourth Republic it disappeared when some of its politicians and many of its supporters joined the CNIP and the others, the Gaullists.

A much more important phenomenon was the Poujadist movement. Originally not a party at all, its core organization was an interest group, the Union for the Defense of Shopkeepers and Artisans (*Union pour la défense des commerçants et des artisans*—UDCA), which was estab-

15. Anderson, *Conservative Politics*, p. 267.

lished in 1953 by Pierre Poujade. As its name implies, the UDCA tried to defend the small shopkeeper and other members of the traditional French economy, whose livelihood was being progressively threatened by the consequences of industrialization, the consolidation of enterprises, and the economic planners' emphasis on productivity and the mass market. The UDCA fought against what it considered an unfair tax system, and it favored a governmental policy of continued subsidies to the small enterprises and family firms that were especially numerous in the provinces. Since it was a movement fighting the rich, it was supported in some localities by the PCF in the early 1950s. But Poujadism was always a reactionary movement; it was antiparliamentary, imperialistic, and xenophobic—and during the premiership of Mendès-France in 1954 it became openly anti-Semitic. Poujadism could, in fact, be considered a variant of fascist populism. Poujade's father had been a member of the ultrareactionary *Action française*, and he himself had been associated with a fascist group in the 1930s.[16] In 1956, the UDCA sired a political party, the French Union and Fraternity (*Union et fraternité française*—UFF). In the parliamentary election of 1956, the UFF obtained 12 percent of the popular vote, and briefly functioned as a parliamentary party under the leadership of Tixier-Vignancour (who ran as an extreme-right candidate during the presidential election of 1965, receiving a little over 5 percent of the popular vote). In 1958, Poujadism collapsed as an effective political force. Convinced that de Gaulle would destroy the hated Fourth Republic and that he would keep Algeria French, most Poujadist deputies supported his return to power, and most of the Poujadist adherents were absorbed into the UNR (in the same way that in West Germany the neo-Nazis were largely absorbed by the CDU). The UDCA, which still exists, no longer has a viable party of its own; in the parliamentary election of June 1968, Poujade asked his followers to vote for Gaullist candidates.[17]

THE POLITICAL CENTER

There has been, at least since the last two decades of the Third Republic, a "political family" in France that has tried to steer a middle

16. See Stanley Hoffmann, *Le mouvement Poujade* (Paris: Colin, 1956); and Philip Williams, *Crisis and Compromise* (Garden City, N.Y.: Doubleday, 1966), pp. 174 f.
17. René Chiroux, in *L'extrême droite sous la Ve République* (Paris: LGDJ, 1974), distinguishes among the following three phases of the non-Gaullist Right: (1) in 1958, the struggle to keep Algeria French; (2) after 1962, absolute opposition to de Gaulle and his regime; and (3) after the May 1968 Events, rallying to the regime and waging war on communism.

course between the antiparliamentary conservatives and the Jacobin revolutionaries, between the ideology of the upper bourgeoisie and that of the industrial working classes, and between the backward elements of the provinces and the class-conscious leftists of the large cities. It has tried above all to commit itself to republicanism and to social reform, without upsetting too abruptly the structures of society and without alienating the conservative elements of the electorate. In the Third Republic, the most representative element of this political family was the Radical Socialist Party, which had allied itself with the Left for electoral purposes and with the Right in parliamentary politics. It was the true Center party, because of the ease with which Radicals could participate in right- or left-oriented cabinets (see page 83).

In the beginning of the Fourth Republic, a new force, the Popular Republican Movement (*Mouvement républicain populaire*—MRP) arose, which soon competed with the Radical party in occupying the center position in the French party spectrum. The MRP, like the Radicals, was pro-republican and anti-Communist, but unlike the Radicals, it was interested in combining republicanism and social reform with a Catholic outlook. Moreover, whereas many Radicals, though they retained their local political machines, had forfeited much of their mass appeal because of their readiness to compromise with Pétainism, the MRP, by contrast, arose out of the Resistance and was the party considered most loyal to de Gaulle's wartime efforts to secure the continuity of republicanism. The roots of the MRP go back to the Third Republic, specifically, to the *Parti démocratique populaire* (established in 1924) and to a number of Catholic youth organizations with somewhat leftist inclinations. In the Third Republic, the progressive-Catholic combination was not yet fully credible, with the result that the *Parti populaire* obtained barely 2 percent of the popular vote in the election of 1936. But at the end of World War II in France—as elsewhere in Western Europe— left-wing and republican Catholicism had become quite respectable; "Christian democracy" in France was widely supported by local priests who were fearful that unless political Catholicism acquired a progressive outlook, the masses might be alienated from the church and enticed to support socialist parties.

The rise of the MRP to political prominence was phenomenal. In August 1945 the MRP had 100,000 members, a force that was parlayed to 5 million votes in that year's parliamentary election; and by 1946, it had become the largest parliamentary party (with 28 percent of the total vote). The MRP's appeal cut across class and geographical lines; what united the working-class voters (about 20 percent of the party's supporters) with those from the peasantry, the petite bourgeoisie, and the upper middle classes was a common rejection of the class struggle, a spirit of community, and above all, a commitment to Christian values. The party militants were rather leftist, a circumstance that facilitated the participation of the MRP in the tripartite coalition, from 1944 to 1947, with the anticlerical Socialists and Communists. This alliance was an uneasy one, in view of the fact that the MRP competed with the Communists for the title of the largest mass party, and capitalized on its anticommunism. After the tripartite coalition ended, the MRP continued to be the most important political fulcrum of the Fourth Republic; it participated in every government coalition until 1954—supplying five prime ministers—and supported every government until the fall of the Republic, with the single exception of the Mendès-France cabinet of 1954–55.

This central position had a corruptive effect on the MRP, and its ideology became subject to change and confusion. While many deputies supported social reform legislation, the party, following the lead of its electorate, gradually became more conservative in the early 1950s. (In a 1953 opinion poll a majority of MRP voters expressed their opposition to further nationalization of industries.)[18] In foreign policy, the MRP favored reconciliation with Germany, European integration, and the steadfast support of the Atlantic Alliance; but while most of the militants of the party were antiimperialist, some of its leaders—e.g., Georges Bidault and Maurice Schumann—supported an imperialist policy in North Africa. With the rise of the RPF in 1947 and the implantation of that party in Parliament in 1952, a large number of MRP voters switched to Gaullism, and most of its leaders cooperated with the Gaullist party; indeed in 1951 many MRP deputies owed their election to Parliament to the tacit support of the Gaullists. The party began to decline as rapidly as it had arisen: of its 200,000 members in 1946, it retained only 40,000 in 1957; its voter support, which had been 5.6 million in June 1946, was reduced to 2.5 million in 1951 and 1.8 million in 1958, while its parliamentary representation dwindled from 169 in 1946 to 84 in 1958.

In the Fifth Republic the MRP continued its existence in a weakened fashion; while the growing conservatism of the MRP caused many of its working-class voters to switch to the SFIO, its bourgeois Catholic elements turned increasingly to the new Gaullist party, the UNR. Those who had not joined the Gaullists were a mere fragment in the Assembly, with 36 deputies after the parliamentary election of 1962. This group could not by itself constitute a "third force" between the Gaullists and

18. Pierre Fougeyrollas, *La conscience politique dans la France contemporaine* (Paris: Denoel, 1963), p. 93.

the Communists. In the same year the few remaining MRP deputies associated, together with some unaffiliated "moderates" and non-Gaullist "independents," in a new parliamentary grouping known as the Democratic Center (CD), but even that enlarged centrist group had only 59 parliamentary seats. Its leader, Jean Lecanuet, ran for the Presidency in 1965; however, he was unsuccessful in mobilizing mass support. The hope of some Centrists that the party could join in an alliance that was both anti-Gaullist and anti-Communist—and that would also include the Socialists and the Radicals—was frustrated by the establishment of the Federation of the Democratic and Socialist Left (FGDS), and by the electoral alignment of that Federation with the PCF, under the leadership of Mitterrand (see page 88).

After the election of 1967, the MRP ceased to exist as a political party. The 42 members of the CD who remained in Parliament had meanwhile been reorganized into the Party for Progress and Modern Democracy (*Progrès et démocratie moderne*—PDM), which had been formally established in 1966. This parliamentary party, which harbored some old local notables of the MRP, some conservative Radicals, and some former members of the Party of Independents and Peasants of the Fourth Republic, obtained only slightly more than 10 percent of the popular vote in the parliamentary election of 1968, and was reduced to 30 deputies, barely enough to be recognized as a separate faction.

The effectiveness of the PDM was limited because it divided into two major groups. The group led by Lecanuet continued to dream of making common cause with the Radicals and even the Socialists in opposing Gaullism. The last attempts of Lecanuet's faction at meaningful anti-Gaullism were its (successful) opposition to the referendum of April 1969, which resulted in the resignation of President de Gaulle; and the (unsuccessful) candidacy of one of its leaders, Alain Poher, president of the Senate, to succeed de Gaulle.

The other component of the PDM, led by Jacques Duhamel and Joseph Fontanet, was inclined to support the Gaullists. Several members of that group had owed their election to Parliament in 1968 to the support of the UDR (some of whose candidates abstained in the second ballot in favor of Centrists); others were converted to the support of the Gaullists in 1969, when Pompidou, de Gaulle's successor, appeared to embrace a more pro-European policy. In the same year, thirty pro-government Centrist deputies formally associated with the parliamentary majority and renamed their group the Center of Democracy and Progress (*Centre pour la démocratie et le progrès*—CDP).

During the last three years of Pompidou's Presidency the pro-Gaullist and the anti-Gaullist Centrists each conjured up a formula for reuniting the two factions and for making the Center into a viable alternative to Gaullism and socialism.[19] In 1972, Lecanuet's faction joined with the moderate Radical Socialists to establish the Reform Movement (*Mouvement réformateur*); in 1974 this group was enlarged with the inclusion of the pro-Gaullist CDP and, with Giscard's election to the Presidency, became a component of the new majority.

Since the spring of 1974, the various centrist parties have been engaged in several attempts to overcome their fragmentation, to maintain their individuality as a "reformist" element within Giscard's majority, and to emphasize their distinction from Gaullism. At the end of 1974, the CD proposed the construction of close links with the RI; a few months later, a new group, the "Federation of Reformers," came into being. This electoral combination, which formalized a parliamentary alliance that had been previously established, included the Reformers' party (see page 85), the CDP, and a number of politicians with their unique clubs or "tendencies."[20] These efforts at alliance building progressed steadily[21] and culminated, in May 1976, in the fusion of the CD and CDP into the *Centre des démocrates sociaux* (CDS). Eighteen months later, this new party joined the Radical Socialists and Republicans in the *Union pour la démocratie française* (UDF), a "Giscardian" electoral combination.[22]

THE RADICAL SOCIALISTS

The oldest and perhaps most typical of French political groupings is the Radical Socialist party. Formally established in 1901, its roots go back to the beginning of the Third Republic. From the first, Radical Socialism embodied a generalized desire for a moderate republic, containing a strong, preferably unicameral Parliament in which the rising urban bourgeoisie would be heavily represented. "Classical" radical doctrine had been built on a number of ideological preferences and specific demands, such as anticlericalism and democratic elections. The establishment of the Radical Socialist party itself was accompanied by a move to the left, since the party's espousal of such goals as the democratization of society by means of universal suffrage, the nationalization of certain sectors of the economy (e.g., the railroads), and the

19. Colette Ysmal, "Adhérents et dirigeants du Centre démocrate," *RFSP* 22 (February 1972): 77–88.
20. These tendencies have appeared under a variety of labels, e.g., *Mouvement progrès et liberté, Mouvement de la gauche réformatrice, Centre républicain*, etc.
21. "Le regroupement des courants centristes est toujours à l'ordre du jour," *Le Monde*, 19 June 1974. Cf. *Le Monde*, 19 November and 19 December 1974.
22. See pp. 294 ff.

institution of a progressive tax system left the more moderate republicans behind.

Originally based in Paris, and Jacobin in principle, the party hoped for an alliance with industrial workers. After the rise of the Socialist party, such an alliance, however, proved difficult to achieve. Moreover, toward the end of the Third Republic, the party's support base had shifted to the provincial artisans and shopkeepers who were interested in the protection of property rights and feared the socioeconomic experimentation that was being demanded by a growing proletariat. Most of the leaders of the Radical Socialist party were local notables (often mayors) who maintained their power bases by adjusting their ideologies to an amorphous and largely conservative electorate. By the 1920s, the Radical Socialist party's leftist rhetoric had acquired a hollow ring. As a party that had been instrumental in the fight against the church, it continued to preach laicism even after "disestablishment"—carried out in 1905—had transformed state-church relations into a minor issue.

In its quest for self-preservation, the Radical Socialist party frequently changed its position in the light of changed circumstances. For example, at the turn of the century the party favored the abolition of the Senate, but later reversed itself after that chamber had become a stronghold of Radical Socialism. In 1940, many Radical Socialist deputies, despite their allegiance to a party that had traditionally favored parliamentary republicanism, voted for the investiture of Marshal Pétain and even served in his regime.

Throughout the Third and Fourth republics, the Radical Socialist party's center position made it a useful ally to the left and moderate factions; therefore it is not surprising that of the twenty-four cabinets between 1944 and 1958, ten were led by Radicals, and most of the other cabinets included them.[23] A notable exception was the party's refusal to join the coalition of the Communists, Socialists, and Christian Democrats immediately after the Liberation because the Radical Socialists could not bring themselves to embrace the collectivism of these coalition partners.

A precise placement of the Radical Socialist party on an ideological continuum is difficult. During the Fourth Republic, the party itself was divided into at least five distinct groupings: (1) the "left-Radicals," led by politicians close to organized labor, some of whom eventually joined other leftist parties; (2) the "neo-Radicals," who were close to big business; (3) the "Mendèsists," who wished to rejuvenate the party,

23. Francis de Tarr, The French Radical Party (London: Oxford University Press, 1961), pp. 249–50.

strengthen its organization, and incline it toward a modern economic progressivism; (4) the "Gaullist Radicals," who were enamored of de Gaulle and eventually joined his party; and (5) the pragmatic "administrative Radicals"—such as Premier Henri Queuille—who were interested mainly in the manipulation of political power.[24] The Radical Socialists remained a party of individualists held together by dominant personalities such as Edouard Herriot, leader of the party from 1945 to 1957, or Pierre Mendès-France, prime minister in 1954.

Whereas during the Third Republic the Radical Socialist party had controlled about 25 percent of the seats in the Chamber of Deputies, the party won only 11.5 percent of the seats in the 1946 elections. In 1949, the percentage climbed slightly to 13.7 percent, and in 1956 the party controlled 15.8 percent of the Assembly seats.

By the end of the Fourth Republic, the Radical Socialists had lost popular support. Even before then, they had compromised their basic commitment to laicism when, in 1951, many of them voted for the *Loi Barangé*, which granted public financial support for parochial schools. The party had also lost adherents because it was so strongly identified with a discredited regime. As the agricultural sector declined, the growing urban electorate that demanded genuinely "radical" economic reforms deserted to the Socialists and Communists; the more conservative artisans and shopkeepers organized separately in the Poujadist movement; others again, for a variety of reasons, converted to Gaullism.

After Mendès-France resigned from the party in 1957, it lacked a central figure to galvanize support; in the parliamentary elections of 1958 and 1962, it suffered severe defeats, in each case winning less than 10 percent of the first-ballot popular votes. Subsequently, the Radical Socialist party was too weak to operate electorally alone, and had to align itself with other progressive formations. The party was beset by the same ambiguities as in the Third and Fourth republics: it could not easily strike a balance between its "progressive" past, which made it consider itself a formation of the Left, and its petit-bourgeois electoral base. The one caused the party to make electoral alliances with the Socialists, and the other inclined it to vote in Parliament with the more conservative factions on social and economic issues.

Since the late 1960s there has been a movement to revive the party. In February 1970, Jean-Jacques Servan-Schreiber was elected leader of the Radical Socialists. He won an upset victory in the parliamentary by-election in Nancy later that year. Meanwhile he had published a manifesto, *Ciel et Terre* ("Heaven and Earth"), which stressed the

24. Ibid., pp. ix–xiii and passim.

modernization of the economy, competition, the expansion and democratization of educational opportunity, the reform of the tax system (including a sharp increase in the inheritance tax), and greater regional administrative autonomy that would breathe new life into the provinces.[25] While this program was hardly revolutionary, it made use of progressive vocabulary perhaps in order to cut into the ideological vacuum between the Gaullists and the Communists. It tried to preempt the "progressivism" of the non-Communist Left without, however, alienating the more traditional sector of the economy that had supported the Radical Socialist party for generations.

The manifesto was an attempt to put a modern face on party doctrine, and perhaps to enable the Socialists to look with favor upon an electoral alliance with the Radical Socialists. The Radical party's progressivism did not appear convincing enough to the Socialists, because of the connections of its leader with the business and managerial elite in various Western European countries. However, its doctrine appeared too "radical" for a large proportion of the party's own members. Many of the party's Fourth Republic "leftists" had abandoned it earlier, while most of the remaining leadership of the party continued to be more inclined toward economic conservatism than toward collectivism. Nevertheless, in the spring of 1972 Servan-Schreiber tried to make overtures to the Socialists, but the latter, having been enticed into an electoral coalition with the much more potent Communist party, rebuffed him. It was under these circumstances that he joined with Jean Lecanuet's Democratic Center in the Reform Movement.[26] Although still in the Opposition ranks, the Reformers held out the possibility that if, after the parliamentary election of 1973, the UDR fell short of a majority in the Assembly, they would consider collaboration with the Gaullists if the latter made certain (not clearly specified) policy compromises. In 1973, the left wing of the Radical Socialists, led by Maurice Faure, entered an electoral alliance with the Socialists under the label of the Union of the Socialist and Democratic Left (UGSD). A year later, while the UGSD joined the Communists in supporting the presidential candidacy of Mitterrand, the Reformers, together with the Gaullists and their old allies, backed Giscard d'Estaing's candidacy in the runoff ballot. The Radical Socialist party, once a proud and progressive power broker, is still solidly implanted in the provinces; but, with its leaders coopted

---

25. On the Radical Socialists' view of regionalization, see Jean-Jacques Servan-Schreiber, *Le pouvoir régional* (Paris: Grasset, 1971).
26. In October 1974, the Reform Movement became a party in the formal sense under the name of Radical-Socialist and Reformist party (*Parti radical-socialiste et réformateur*).

into Giscard's administration, it is temporarily eclipsed as an independent national political force.

THE SOCIALISTS

The major party of the French non-Communist Left during the Third and Fourth republics was the French Section of the Workers' International (*Section Française de l'Internationale Ouvrière*—SFIO). It was established in 1905 in an attempt to unite four dominant varieties of socialism: utopian, syndicalist, revolutionary, and reformist. Although the SFIO was the most disciplined party in France—until the appearance of the Communist party in 1920—it was in fact a federation of independent regional units. Officially, at least until after the end of World War I, the revolutionary rhetoric of Marxism was dominant; however, the actual behavior of the party was often quite moderate and pragmatic. Although in principle the SFIO was opposed to participation in bourgeois governments, it felt compelled to join coalitions whenever the "Republic" seemed to be in danger—for the party was clearly committed to a traditional parliamentary democracy—or when opportunities of officeholding proved irresistible. Thus the SFIO participated in a broad coalition government upon the outbreak of war in 1914—the "sacred union" in defense of France against the German attackers; and in 1936, the Socialist leader, Léon Blum, headed the antifascist Popular Front government. However, in 1940 the majority of SFIO deputies voted in favor of granting exceptional powers to Marshal Pétain.

The SFIO emerged again in 1944 and was rebuilt by Daniel Mayer, its secretary-general, into the third largest party by the time the Fourth Republic was inaugurated. Mayer attempted to steer the SFIO to a reformist outlook, while participating, from 1944 to 1947, in the tripartite coalition with the MRP and the PCF. In 1946, the SFIO elected as its secretary-general Guy Mollet, who was to hold that position for more than twenty years. Under his leadership, the party continued to adhere to the Marxist line while joining various coalition governments. In 1951, the SFIO entered the ranks of the Opposition in order to safeguard the party's revolutionary mystique. Moreover, any Socialist participation in government would have had to be with either the Left or the Center: if the Left, there was danger that the SFIO would be eclipsed and ultimately absorbed by the PCF. It seemed clear that the SFIO could not effectively compete with the Communists in appealing to the working class, despite the Socialists' retention of an official belief in the class struggle, revolution, social equality, and the nationalization of industries. In the Fourth Republic, hardly more than 5 percent of Socialist deputies belonged to the working class. Moreover, many of the party's adherents came from among the lower-echelon civil servants who were not inclined to make a revolution against a system that employed them. Finally, many leaders of the SFIO were university or *lycée* professors or lawyers, whose empathy with industrial workers might be suspect. Socialist deputies sponsored progressive legislation in the Fourth Republic Parliament, but they were not alone: Catholic and Communist deputies did likewise. The SFIO could not commit itself unreservedly to an alliance with the Center, i.e., the MRP or the Radicals, because the MRP, although it began with a rather left-wing attitude on economic policy, was still clericalist, and the Radicals were stigmatized by the economic outlook of the property owners. That the SFIO's behavior was not always impeded by its own ideological restrictions became clear in 1956–57, when the SFIO's leader, Mollet, headed a government and compromised the party's pacifism by advocating military solutions to the problems of Algeria and the Suez Canal.

In 1958, when the Fourth Republic appeared definitely to be in danger, most of the leaders of the party endorsed the investiture of General de Gaulle as prime minister and later pronounced themselves in favor of the Fifth Republic Constitution, which violated so many institutional notions dear to the Socialists; and Mollet himself joined the first cabinet of the new republic. Other leaders, who were disillusioned by what they regarded as Mollet's abandonment of the Socialist commitment to a truly republican system, bolted the party and, together with some Radicals, established the PSA (*Parti socialiste autonome*).

In the early 1960s, even the pragmatic Socialists were disillusioned by aspects of de Gaulle's new regime, notably the impotence of the Assembly, the unnecessary invocation of Article 16, and de Gaulle's conservative social and economic policy, all of which led the party again to go over to the Opposition. The party membership had meanwhile declined dramatically, having been reduced to fewer than 100,000. The SFIO tried to broaden its base of support by modernizing its ideology and by establishing alliances with other leftist political organizations. Such attempts demonstrated a deep split within the party between what came to be called "Defferrism" and "Molletism." Gaston Defferre, mayor of Marseilles and leader of an important regional federation of the SFIO, wanted to move the party toward *travaillisme*, i.e., the evolutionary, reformist democratic socialism characteristic of the British Labour party. He wished to accommodate to the more "liberal" socioeconomic position of the Radical Socialist party as well as to the clericalism of the MRP by including both parties in a new coalition of the Left, while leaving out the Communists. In 1963, Defferre promoted his candidacy for the presidential election of 1965, and as a vehicle for this candidacy he proposed a Socialist-Democratic federation, in which the SFIO would be structurally merged with other non-Communist Left formations and progressive Centrist elements. Nothing came of such a merger, because the split between the laicist and clericalist forces appeared irreconcilable.

Guy Mollet distrusted the PCF as much as Defferre did, but he was not willing to give up the old revolutionary doctrine. At a Socialist Congress in July 1946, Mollet himself had pushed through a resolution condemning "all attempts at revisionism, especially those . . . [whose] aim is to obscure . . . the class struggle."[27] He still supported the idea that the SFIO had "no enemies to the Left." He was also not willing to weaken the SFIO's apparatus in which many Socialists had spent much of their adult lives. Meanwhile, the more dynamic young Frenchmen who had not compromised with Gaullism and who were interested in socialism saw their political future in the PCF.

In 1965, Defferre's candidacy collapsed largely for want of clear support by the SFIO's leadership.[28] In a public-opinion poll conducted a year earlier it had already become apparent that Defferre would not be a viable candidate: de Gaulle received 42 percent, and Defferre only 13 percent (and an undesignated Communist candidate 10 percent).[29] In order to broaden its base of support among anti-Gaullist elements, the SFIO—with the approval of the PCF, PSU (see page 93), and Radicals —selected François Mitterrand, leader of the CIR (see page 92), as the presidential candidate of a united Left, and at the same time established a new electoral alliance: the Federation of the Democratic and Socialist Left (*Fédération de la gauche démocratique et socialiste*—FGDS).

The FGDS—which included the SFIO, the Radicals, and the CIR but neither the MRP nor the Communists—hardly got off the ground because ideological disagreements were never completely ironed out, because the SFIO did not wish to give up its separate identity, and because the other parties felt that they were being "used" by the SFIO. In 1966, the FGDS, in order to show a constructive attitude and a

27. Quoted in G. Willard, *Socialisme et communisme français* (Paris: Colin, 1967), p. 143.
28. Mollet was unenthusiastic about Defferre's candidacy not only because he feared that it would undermine his own authority within the SFIO, but also because that candidacy had been promoted by a business association (*Jeunes patrons*) and other questionable interests. Cf. Georges Suffert, *De Defferre à Mitterrand* (Paris: Seuil, 1966), p. 27; and René Remond, "L'élection présidentielle et la candidature Defferre," *RFSP* 14 (June 1964): 526.
29. *L'Année politique 1964*, pp. 62–64.

readiness to govern, formed a "shadow cabinet." It would have been desirable to include Mendès-France, who had once been a strong prime minister, in this shadow cabinet. But Mendès-France had never joined the FGDS; moreover, disagreements between Radical Socialists and Socialists persisted on economic and social policy issues.[30]

The FGDS was beset with even weightier problems: in order to be an effective political force, it had to encompass the entire spectrum of political opinion between Gaullism and communism, and beyond that, to establish a means of electoral cooperation with the Communist party. In the 1967 and 1968 elections, an alliance between the FGDS and the PCF was agreed to—which was in effect a confirmation of the informal electoral accord between the PCF, the SFIO and the Radicals that had already existed during the parliamentary election of 1962. Though this alliance frequently broke down on constituency levels, it was effective enough to secure the election of 121 non-Communist Left candidates in 1967 (compared to 109 in 1962 and 87 in 1958) and 73 Communist candidates (41 in 1962 and 10 in 1958). In the 1968 election the alliance was, however, ineffective in view of the public backlash to the May Events, as a consequence of which the representation of the non-Communist Left was reduced to 44 and that of the PCF to 34.

Before the presidential election of 1969 the alliance of the Left had broken down. The SFIO reached the nadir of its political position when its candidate, Defferre, received only 5.1 percent of the first-ballot votes (as compared to Communist Jacques Duclos, who won 21.5 percent), and the party was forced to support Alain Poher, a Centrist, on the second ballot. After the election, the SFIO ceased to exist formally. It was reborn as the *Parti socialiste* (PS), an amalgamation of the old SFIO and a few leftist clubs. Mollet was succeeded as secretary-general by Alain Savary, and the new party adopted a more pragmatic outlook when it absorbed the (less "revolutionary") CIR in June 1971 (see page 92).

The revitalized Socialist party has shown a remarkable adaptability and dynamism. The choice in 1971 of Mitterrand as secretary-general of the PS was a fortunate one; in 1965 he had been a strong enough presidential candidate to force de Gaulle into a runoff election, and he had worked hard since then at constructing an electoral alliance with the Communists. With the help of this alliance, the Socialists succeeded in 1973 in doubling their parliamentary representation to over 100, and in 1974 very nearly captured the Presidency. There has been a rejuvenation

---

30. For a highly personal account of the evolution of the FGDS by a member of its executive committee, see Claude Estier, *Journal d'un fédéré* (Paris: Fayard, 1970).

of the party's leadership and candidates, a reinforcement of its alliance with the Radical party's left-wing and other social-democratic elements, and an increase of its membership (from fewer than 70,000 in 1969 to more than 150,000 in 1975). This membership now includes the most diverse elements: old notables, leftist intellectuals, practical reformers, and even Catholic utopians. In 1973, workers made up 37 percent of the Socialist electorate—an indication of the party's renewed credibility as a progressive force.

The Socialist party still retains a tactical dependence on the Communist party, with which it had agreed on a "Common Program" in 1972. This program, a 150-page document, advocated guaranteed minimum wages coupled with an escalator clause, and a forty-hour work week; the extension of social benefits; the strengthening of union rights; the gradual elimination of parochial schools; the rescission of Article 16; the reduction of the President's term to five years; and a return to the proportional system of elections. What meaning can be attached to the Common Program is open to question. The concern expressed in the Program for a return to parliamentarism may be unrealistic and hollow: both parties of the left coalition greeted Giscard's assertion of presidential supremacy in August 1976 with relative indifference. Similarly, the references to decentralization cannot be taken too seriously, given the Left's tradition of preference for centralized government. Finally, the proposals regarding the nationalization of industries may remain largely a slogan, given the increasing concern (shared by the Socialists) with productivity, the cost to the public treasury that "expropriation" of the private sector entails, and the continuing disagreement within the Left alliance—and the Left electorate—regarding the speed and scope of nationalization.[31]

The Socialist party's relationship with the PCF remains an uneasy one, not only because the Common Program failed to resolve certain disagreements between the two parties—notably on aspects of economic and foreign policy—but also because the Socialists have eclipsed the PCF in terms of both parliamentary representation and electoral support. According to a public-opinion poll conducted at the end of 1974, 34 percent of the populace would vote for a Socialist candidate, compared

31. See *Programme commun de gouvernement du parti communiste et du parti socialiste* (Paris: Editions Sociales, 1972). A poll commissioned by Giscard early in 1976 revealed that while half the electorate would vote for the Left coalition, 70% of Frenchmen disapproved of the Common Program. *Le Nouvel Observateur*, 30 August 1976, pp. 22–23. On the evolution of attitudes (and membership) within the Socialist party, see Jean-François Bizot et al., *Au parti des socialistes* (Paris: Grasset, 1975); and Paul Barrois, "Le parti socialiste aujourd'hui: diversité et unité," *Etudes*, February 1975, pp. 165–76.

to 18 percent for a Communist one. The ascendancy of the Socialists over the Communists was demonstrated in the cantonal elections of March 1976, in which the former got 27 percent of the total vote (and control of twelve regional councils) and the latter, 22 percent (and two regional councils).

THE NON-COMMUNIST LEFT SPLINTER PARTIES

Democratic socialism, because it tries to combine a commitment to Marxist historical interpretation with a firm belief in traditional democratic values, lends itself to a variety of interpretations. It is therefore not surprising France has had several minor socialist political parties. These parties have sometimes competed with the major Socialist party (and with one another) and prevented it from duplicating the success of its counterparts in other Western European countries.

In the Fourth Republic, one of the most interesting splinter parties was the UDSR (*Union démocratique et socialiste de la Résistance*), which was established in 1946. The party began as a federation of several Resistance movements, and it owed its existence and representation in Parliament less to any clear-cut ideology than to the fact that its leaders and deputies were local notables who possessed independent political machines and shared a certain nostalgia about the Resistance. The UDSR was widely regarded as socialist in orientation. But in the beginning of the Fourth Republic, the UDSR distrusted the SFIO leadership and resented that party's collaboration with the PCF. Moreover, the UDSR was a party of individualists with disparate ideologies, of which socialism was only one. Although deputies of the UDSR supported cabinets in which anticlerical Radicals were represented, the party also voted for the *Loi Barangé* in 1951. Although many of its leaders were closer to socialism than radicalism in economic policy, the UDSR entered into a parliamentary alliance with the Radical Socialists, forming the Rally of the Republican Left (*Rassemblement de gauche républicaine*—RGR). By the late 1940s, many of the pro-Gaullists had departed from the UDSR, an occurrence that clarified somewhat the political orientation of the party and allowed it to become more "socialist." But this ideological evolution did not matter too much: the party supported both the Right and the Left, whichever suited the political ambitions of its leaders. After the 1951 election, the UDSR, with nine deputies, managed to maintain its status as a parliamentary party only because some deputies from Africa joined it to give it the required minimum of fourteen seats.

At the beginning of the Fifth Republic, the UDSR was decimated when René Pleven and others who backed Gaullism abandoned the party, leaving Mitterrand (who opposed de Gaulle) as its leader. The UDSR's few deputies in the early 1960s could no longer function as a separate parliamentary party (since it fell short of the new minimum of 30 seats) and were joined to the Radicals. By the mid-1960s, the UDSR became a component of the CIR.

The *Convention des institutions républicaines* (CIR) was established in 1964 as an association of a score of political clubs of varying "progressive" tendencies. It included groupings that were at one time close to the Mendès-France, or leftist, wing of the Radicals; others that were close to the PSU; still others that were ideologically linked to the SFIO but not necessarily enthusiastic about its leadership; and—although most of the CIR's components were anticlerical—some Catholic groups. What united these disparate elements was anti-Gaullism. The CIR transformed itself into a political party after 1965, when it ran candidates for Parliament under its own label. In 1967, the CIR elected seventeen deputies (six of whom were former members of UDSR). In 1965, the main purpose of the CIR seemed to be the promotion of Mitterrand's candidacy for the Presidency; thereafter it saw itself as a principal force for advancing the unity of the non-Communist Left. Above all, the CIR remained what the UDSR had been before it: the political instrument of Mitterrand. He was its leader, and when the CIR joined the FGDS, he headed that enlarged federation, too. With the collapse of the Federation in 1968, Mitterrand briefly lacked a meaningful political organization (he still headed the CIR, but served in Parliament as an unaffiliated deputy). In 1971, the CIR merged into the *Parti socialiste*, which is now, of course, headed by Mitterrand.

Another group of the non-Communist Left is the *Parti socialiste unifié* (PSU). It consists of an even greater variety of elements than the CIR, although its general outlook is far more extreme-leftist. It was formally established as a party in 1960, functioning as an expanded forum for the *Parti socialiste autonome*, which was its nucleus. The PSU has participated in most elections in the Fifth Republic, but its electoral support has been relatively feeble. In the parliamentary election of 1962, the party received less than 2.5 percent of the popular vote; in subsequent parliamentary and presidential elections the popular vote has never risen above 4 percent. In 1974, the party failed to nominate its own candidate for the first ballot, and in the second supported the presidential candidacy of Mitterrand.

There are several reasons for the weakness of the PSU. Although the party has emphasized "purity of doctrine," it remains ideologically eclectic. It has always been anti-Gaullist, and it has favored both the abandonment of Fifth Republic presidentialism and certain "structural reforms" of society and the economy (notably workers' control of industry), but it has no monopoly with respect to such attitudes. Tactically it was clearly desirable for the PSU to affiliate with like-minded political groups. But although many members of PSU favored its joining the FGDS, the majority opposed it, because the SFIO and the Radicals did not accept one of the preconditions of the PSU—the admission of the PCF into the federation—and because the PSU did not wish to abandon its structural independence. The party has appealed more to academicians and students than do other socialist parties, and has not addressed itself to those who are supposed to be the real beneficiaries of the PSU's socialist policies: the working class. (In 1971, the party claimed only 15,000 members, of whom less than 16 percent were workers.)[32] In the election of 1973, the PSU received only 3.2 percent of the total vote, failing to get a single deputy elected. At the end of 1974, a minority faction of the party (including its leader, Michel Rocard) decided to accept the Common Program—having been attracted particularly to its anticapitalist references. Soon thereafter, when the Socialists (PS) appeared to have endorsed the PSU's positions regarding nationalization, democratic planning and worker self-management (*autogestion*), Rocard and his group joined the PS. Most of the remainder of the PSU drifted into the newly formed *Ligue communiste révolutionnaire* and other extreme-leftist organizations.[33]

THE COMMUNISTS

The Communist party of France (*Parti communiste français*—PCF) is the second largest Communist party in Western Europe (after Italy), and the most disciplined outside the Eastern bloc. It was established in 1920 at the Congress of Tours held by the SFIO, when about three-quarters of the delegates decided to join the Third International that had been set up by the Russians after the Bolshevik Revolution.

Since its founding, the development of the PCF has, to some extent, paralleled that of the SFIO, and the PCF has shared many of the SFIO's characteristics, notably its steadfast adherence to Marxism, its appeal to the working class, and its espousal of such domestic policies as minimum wages, the nationalization of crucial industries, the democratization of education, the reform of the tax structure, and the expansion of the

32. Jacques Capdevielle and Roland Cayrol, "Les groupes d'entreprise du PSU," *RFSP* 22 (February 1972): 89–107. For an extensive treatment of the party, see Michel Rocard, *Le parti socialiste unifié et l'avenir socialiste* (Paris: Seuil, 1969).
33. See *Le Monde*, 24–25 November and 17 December 1974.

welfare state. The PCF has had a fairly reliable electoral appeal, obtaining in the Fourth Republic more votes than any other single party. Its share of the total vote has ranged from a high of 28.6 percent (in November 1946) to a low of 18.9 percent (in 1958). It has been a significant party in the industrial north of France, in certain rural regions of the Midi and Massif Central, and in the working-class suburbs, the "Red Belt," of Paris. Although only about 60 percent of its members and less than 50 percent of its voters have been working class (with about 9 percent being intellectuals); although only one in every four workers has consistently supported the party; and although, in short, the working class is not entirely Communist nor is the PCF entirely working class—the PCF has nonetheless been the workers' party par excellence. According to a noted scholar of the PCF, the party has capitalized on the fact that the French working class feels a strong sense of alienation that has not been significantly diminished by improvements in the workers' living standards.[34]

In general, the PCF has been in the Opposition, except where tactics, or the dictates of Moscow, have imposed a different form of political behavior on the party. Beginning in 1934, because of the rise of fascism in France and elsewhere in Europe, the party advocated collaboration with other left-wing parties; and in 1936, the PCF joined an electoral coalition with the SFIO and the Radical Socialists, and supported the Socialist-led Popular Front government—though refrained from joining it. As a result of the Nazi-Soviet Pact of 1939 and the PCF's defense of Stalin, many of the party's members became disillusioned. Dissolved by Pétain, the PCF continued in a clandestine fashion, and, following the German invasion of the Soviet Union in 1941, the party began to fight seriously against fascism and compiled such an impressive Resistance record that it emerged from World War II with an enhanced image. The party entered the government for the first and only time in French political history when it participated in the postwar tripartite coalition.

During the Fourth Republic, the stand of the PCF was often not so much a reflection of domestic demands as of the foreign policy positions of the Soviet Union. Thus in 1947, the PCF opposed the Marshall Plan; in 1948, it denounced Tito and his experiment with "national communism" in Yugoslavia; in 1949, it opposed NATO, using the CGT, its trade-union "transmission belt," to organize general strikes; in 1952–54, it fought against the European Defense Community and its corollary, the rearmament of Germany; and in 1956, it justified the Soviet sup-

---

34. Annie Kriegel, *Les Communistes* (Paris: Seuil, 1968), p. 15.

pression of anti-Stalinist communism in Hungary. Such support of the USSR made the PCF appear as the most "Stalinist" of all Western European Communist parties and occasioned periodic rebellions among the leadership and membership, rebellions that were frequently resolved by purges. The most widely publicized purge took place in 1970, when Roger Garaudy, a prominent Marxist theoretician, was ousted from the party for having advocated a more "humanistic" approach to Marxism. Some years ago the PCF began to manifest a modest degree of independence of Moscow. In the late 1960s it criticized the trial and conviction of Daniel and Sinyavski, two dissident writers in the Soviet Union; in 1968, it expressed (somewhat halfhearted) disapproval of the Soviet invasion of Czechoslovakia; and in the summer of 1972 it deplored as a "negative action" the purges of "unreliable elements" in that country.[35] Still, the PCF continued to be informed by considerable ideological rigidity, which made collaboration with other leftist parties —notably the SFIO—difficult.

But the PCF, like other parties, has not always behaved as its ideology would seem to dictate. Although in the past the PCF preached the principle of violent revolution, and although it was the only anti-Gaullist party that opposed *en bloc* the establishment of the Fifth Republic, it passed up several chances to promote a revolution against the regime. During the May Events of 1968, the PCF discouraged a widening of "spontaneous" rebellion and favored a "law and order" approach. In the presidential election of 1969, after its own candidate, Jacques Duclos, was eliminated in the first ballot—he had come in third—the PCF decided to "sit out" the second ballot, preferring not to exercise a choice between the "cholera and the plague," that is, between the Gaullists led by Pompidou and the Centrists led by Poher, although the latter was clearly anti-Gaullist. This abstention, too, may have had a tactical explanation: odious as the continuation of Gaullist domestic policies would be to the French Communist party, Pompidou would at least continue to promote a foreign policy favored by the USSR.

Although its leaders talked about a "reform of structures," the PCF fought (often with the tacit support of Gaullist governments) against leftist movements that spoke even more convincingly of such reform. It was commonly held that the PCF expected to see the bourgeois regime discredit itself by domestic policy failures, so that a Communist regime would inevitably follow. (Despite such an attitude, the PCF has consistently lent support to reformist endeavors.) Second, the PCF does not want to be outflanked by political movements to its left, which it

35. *Le Monde Weekly,* 12 August 1972.

brands as "irresponsible," because the PCF wishes above all to retain its monopoly as *the* most revolutionary party. Third—and paradoxically —the PCF may have become part of the establishment. Although all the general secretaries and a large number of deputies of the PCF have originated from the working class, many Communist city councilors and mayors have come from the bourgeoisie, and these have behaved no differently from their colleagues belonging to other parties. Finally, there are intellectuals in the PCF who are Marxist in an academic or even aesthetic sense but do not expect the party to achieve power.

The PCF still adheres to some Marxist-Leninist slogans, and obviously cannot accept a bourgeois—or even Social-Democratic—view of the purpose of politics. At the same time, its increasing domestication has been reflected in its regular participation in electoral politics, the frequent articulation of its desire to achieve power by peaceful means, and its acceptance of such bourgeois values as party pluralism, civil liberties, and even nationalism. The conversion of the PCF (and of its leader, Georges Marchais) to parliamentary methods—a process that began in the late 1960s and is still continuing—may be largely a tactic used in order to persuade the non-Communist Left parties to make electoral alliances with it. In any case, it is widely believed that a majority of Frenchmen now would accept the participation of Communist ministers in a coalition government.[36]

The improved public image of the PCF has been, in part, a logical consequence of that party's success. The electoral alliance between the PCF and the Socialists was effective enough in the parliamentary election of 1973 to reduce the Gaullist majority in the Assembly to a mere plurality; and in the 1974 presidential election to bring the united Left within a hair's breadth of the Presidency. But postelectoral relations have not always been harmonious. The PCF has accused the PS of ignoring the Common Program and of attempting to use the Communists to gain electoral victory while intending to exclude them from any future share

36. According to a poll conducted in January 1976, only 33% of respondents believed that the PCF wanted to make a revolution if the time was opportune; while 44% were favorably inclined to Communist participation in government (as compared to 31% in 1964). Cited by Raymond Barrillon, "Une nouvelle visage," *Le Monde*, 3 February 1976. Such attitudes are in sharp contrast to the views held in official U.S. circles. According to one fanciful scenario, the appointment of Communist ministers in the wake of a victory of the Left would lead to a massive flight of capital, the collapse of the franc, a denial of American credits, and a general strike engineered by Communist-dominated trade unions. See James Goldsborough, "Big Win by France's Commies [sic] Drops Franc and Other Shoe," *New York Times*, 8 April 1976.

in government. The PCF has resented the fact that in parliamentary and cantonal elections, the Socialists have frequently backed out of the bipartisan electoral agreement (see page 111) and have therefore had greater electoral successes than the PCF. Moreover, the Communists were annoyed when, in October 1974, the PS invited the PSU and CFDT, but not the PCF—which is by far the largest socialist formation[37]—to a "national conference on socialism."

The Socialists, in turn, have distrusted the PCF, alleging that it lacked commitment to democratic methods and that it used the alliance merely to gain respectability for communism.[38] In order to neutralize such distrust, the PCF, following the example of the Italian Communist party, went to great length, at its twenty-second Congress (in February 1976) to forswear violence, to announce its abandonment of the principle of the "dictatorship of the proletariat," to reaffirm its belief in democratic processes, to assure its adherence to the Western Alliance, and to declare its independence of Moscow. As Georges Marchais put it, the new, advanced democratic society built by the party would "fly the French flag."[39] It is a matter of controversy whether this is a sincere conversion, and whether the PCF, once having attained power, would revert to its original principles, especially in view of the fact that the PCF has retained its tightly centralized structure and internal discipline (in contrast to the PS with its loose federal structure and ideological diversity). While this controversy continues, there is little hope of a permanent merger of the Left, and the PCF will remain "a party unlike other parties."

37. Precise figures are elusive. For 1976, the PCF cited a membership of 600,000, organized into 10,000 cells (*Le Monde*, 10 February 1976). According to Flora Lewis ("French Reds Drive to Plug Party," *New York Times*, 24 March 1976), there were 500,000 members in 23,000 cells (8,000 industrial, the rest local or rural). The lowest figure, provided by the government, is 100,000 members in 8,000 cells (a fourth of them industrial). French Embassy, Press and Information Division, *France*, March 1976, pp. 4–5.
38. "Gaining respectability" is not without political risk for the PCF; too much moderation might make it difficult for many voters to distinguish between Socialists and Communists and deprive the latter of support by those who have in the past been attracted by the PCF's reputation for anomic activism. See *Le Monde*, 24 October 1974.
39. Cf. *Le Monde*, 21 January, and 7, 8, and 9 February 1976. On the PCF's "de-Stalinization" and emergence from political isolation, see André Laurens and Thierry Pfister, *Les nouveaux communistes* (Paris: Stock, 1973), esp. pp. 61–82 and 181–236; and the generally sympathetic analysis by a Jesuit, Louis de Vaucelles, "Le XXe Congrès du parti communiste français," *Etudes*, April 1976, pp. 535–51.

POLITICAL FRINGE GROUPS, CLUBS, AND MOVEMENTS

On the periphery of the party system in France there exist political "grouplets" (*groupuscules*), protest movements, and clubs. Among these are numerous New Left (*gauchiste*) organizations, which tend to be anarchist, Trotskyite, or Maoist and which oppose the traditional Marxism espoused by the PCF. They operate mainly among marginal sectors of society—the slum dwellers, the immigrant workers, and the *Lumpenproletariat*—as well as in the university student community. They appeal also to ex-farmers and others who have recently come to the cities and are in process of proletarization. Most of these groups are ephemeral and relatively unknown, although a few have achieved a certain amount of fame or notoriety.[40] Perhaps the most active was the *Gauche prolétarienne*, a Maoist organization that believed in the spontaneity of the masses and their capacity to overthrow the system. Its leader, Alain Geismar (formerly secretary-general of a radical-left teachers' association), became a hero of the Opposition in 1970 when he was arrested and when the group's journal, *La Cause du Peuple*, was declared subversive.

The New Left began to decline in influence not long after the May 1968 Events, partly because of backlash, and partly because of the internal fragmentation of its components. New Left groups cannot usually become political parties because their appeal, and hence their aggregative potential, is limited; nor do they wish to do so, lest they be accused of compromising with the political establishment. Nonetheless, these groups enliven the political scene by publishing numerous journals, engaging in clandestine (or "subversive") activities, and occasionally organizing demonstrations and violent confrontations.

Clubs are part of an old tradition in France, which goes back to the Revolutions of 1789, 1848, and 1870. However, clubs were relatively weak in the Fourth Republic, probably because the rigid-list proportional representation system then in operation encouraged a sufficient number of political parties. The club phenomenon reasserted itself during the Fifth Republic, when in the face of the new electoral law producing aggregative parties, the (temporary) mass support of de Gaulle, and the weakness of the Parliament, parties proved inadequate as vehicles for the promotion of specific ideologies or goals. Thus clubs arose for such purposes as criticizing the "permissive society" resulting from socio-

40. On gauchiste organizations, see "Panorama de l'extrême Gauche révolutionnaire," *Le Monde*, 3 April 1970. See also issue on "Les gauchistes," *La Nef*, July–September 1972.

economic modernization, fighting Gaullism, combating fascism, promoting laicism, suggesting reform ideas, and providing forums of discussion or instruments of political education.[41]

A large number of political clubs are Gaullist in orientation. These have to be distinguished according to whether they support Gaullist orthodoxy or whether they wish to broaden Gaullism by infusing into the party some concern for the masses. Among the left-wing Gaullist groups are the *Jeunes progressistes*, the *Union travailliste*, and the *Mouvement pour le socialisme par la participation* (a group that supports worker participation in management). There is also the *Comité d'études pour un nouveau contrat social*, a pro-Gaullist group (led by Edgar Faure) ideologically close to the Center. There is the *Alliance républicaine indépendante*, ideologically close to the Independent Republican party. There is the *Mouvement progrès et liberté* (led by Jacques Soustelle), a Centrist movement with Catholic and nationalist overtones.

Since 1958, the non-Gaullist extreme Right has confined itself largely to political clubs and other extraparliamentary associations. Many of these have been ad hoc, such as the Secret Army Organization (OAS), which in the early 1960s fought in vain to prevent the granting of independence to Algeria. Recently there has been a revival of the *Action française* (now called the *Nouvelle action française*). Under its auspices a new party, the *Ordre nouveau*, was founded in May 1970. This group, which is frankly fascist (and partly royalist), has made an effort to appeal to the working class and has participated in recent municipal elections. In the 1974 presidential election it fielded a candidate who received less than 44,000 votes. In November 1974, another right-wing party was founded, the New Forces (*Parti des forces nouvelles*). It has been attempting to appeal to extremely conservative Gaullists and ultranationalists, and has announced its readiness to fight against both Marxism and liberalism. However, there are relatively few extreme right-wing organizations, because most hard-line conservatives— who feel far less "alienated" than their counterparts on the Left—can find appropriate places in a hospitable Gaullist party.[42]

Although many political clubs have been close to political parties or ancillary to them, what has differentiated clubs from parties is the fact that most clubs do not seek political power; they do not usually promote candidates to political office, and they have weak organizations

---

41. Frank L. Wilson, "The Club Phenomenon in France," *Comparative Politics* 3 (July 1971): 517–28. For a historical treatment, see Jean-André Faucher, *Les Clubs politiques en France* (Paris: Didier, 1965).
42. For a recent discussion, see Bernard Brigouleix, "L'extrême droite," *Le Monde*, 12, 13, and 14 June 1976.

and a fluctuating membership. Two political clubs have had exceptional influence, however: the CIR, which became a political party (see page 92), and the Club Jean Moulin. Established in 1958, the Club Moulin has included Mendèsists, left-wing Catholics, and "nonpolitical" civil servants who were impatient with the ideological dichotomies found within the party system. Republican and moderately leftist in general orientation, the Club Moulin has concentrated on research, education, and the advocacy of pragmatic institutional reforms. The Club Moulin briefly (and somewhat halfheartedly) participated in the promotion of Defferre's candidacy for the Presidency in 1963. In recent years, the Club's influence has declined.

THE FUNCTIONAL RELEVANCE OF POLITICAL PARTIES

The preceding discussion has given the reader some idea of the diversity of French political forces and ideologies. While such a discussion is meaningful from a historical point of view, the question remains as to how the ideological distinctions relate to the political process and political behavior. Many scholars have pointed out that the multiplicity of parties has in the past rendered difficult the construction of stable governments, since the governments all had to rest on tenuous coalitions. In theory, the insistence of each party on its uniqueness has been an expression of the aspect of French political culture known as "absolute value rationality,"[43] which has impeded the aggregative process. Yet it would be a mistake to conclude that interparty philosophical differences always prevented the achievement of common outlooks and policies. In the Fourth Republic there was a vast area of agreement among most parties about certain essentials, such as the maintenance of the political system, the establishment of minimal welfare state policies, and the necessity for economic planning. Moreover, among members of Parliament, there has been, from the Third to the present Republic, the same kind of *esprit de corps* that is found in other democratic legislatures. Robert de Jouvenel may have exaggerated when he asserted that "there is less difference between two deputies, one of whom is a revolutionary and the other is not, than between two revolutionaries, one of whom is a deputy and the other is not";[44] nevertheless, it is true that often enough

43. Cf. Gabriel Almond and G. B. Powell, *Comparative Politics: A Developmental Approach* (Boston: Little, Brown, 1966), pp. 108–9, 263–66.
44. Robert de Jouvenel, *La République des camarades* (8th ed.; Paris: Grasset, 1914), p. 17.

members of political parties have not behaved in a manner conforming to the party's ideology when they entered alliances, or when they voted on issues. There has always been a certain amount of opportunism (called "pragmatism" when found in Anglo-American systems) among party leaders—particularly deputies—which has accounted for the widespread notion among Frenchmen, from Rousseau's time to the present, that parliamentary parties are mainly power seeking and selfish, are collectively enemies of the people, and are guilty of betraying by coalition deals the ideologies to which they are ostensibly committed.

Such a view can be substantiated by reference to a number of political practices. First of all, there have been "unnatural" preelectoral and parliamentary alliances involving political parties representing mutually hostile ideologies. Alliances have been determined by accidents of geography and personality, the institution of the single-member district system of elections, and perhaps the fear of being left behind by political developments and of having to forgo a share of power. In 1944 and 1945, clericals and anticlericals collaborated in the tripartite coalition in Parliament; the PRL, originally an antirepublican party, made an electoral pact in some departments with the Radical Socialists—archdefenders of the Republic—prior to the parliamentary election of November 1946; in 1958, the SFIO supported the return of de Gaulle and the Gaullist constitution, despite the SFIO's frequently articulated reservations about both the man and the regime. In 1968 and 1969, the Communists tacitly supported the maintenance of the Gaullist regime despite their continuing criticisms of the reactionary nature of Gaullism; for the past decade, the PCF has seemed to favor gradual political change by parliamentary processes despite its traditional commitment to revolution. The MRP had been committed to the welfare state and had been a major partner in a leftist coalition immediately after World War II; but by the end of the 1950s, the conservatism of the party's adherents had asserted itself in sufficient measure for them to flock to the Gaullist banner. The successors of the MRP, the Centrists, remained in the Opposition until 1969, when half the members of the party, under the label of PDM, went over to the majority. The other half, led by Lecanuet, remained oppositionists while there was still hope that the Gaullist majority would disintegrate.[45] The indecisiveness of both factions of the Center was manifested in 1971 when the pro-majority and the pro-Opposition Centrists joined together in a parliamentary association! In

45. "Le Centre démocrate attend toujours l'éclatement de la majorité," *Le Monde*, 24 January 1970.

1972, the Radicals became interested in making an electoral alliance with the non-Communist Left while still trying to retain the support of petit-bourgeois and business elements, and even keeping open the possibility of joining a Gaullist majority in 1973.

Second, France has been notorious for the political wanderings of deputies from one parliamentary party to another—a practice made possible by the semicircular physical arrangement of the chambers, in which a deputy's slight move to the right or left is not nearly so dramatic an action as "crossing the aisle" in the British House of Commons. Thus Debré and Edgar Faure moved from the Radical to the Gaullist party without much difficulty; Pierre Mendès-France from the Radical to a left-socialist party (the PSA); and Mitterrand in the past thirty years to four or five political organizations.[46]

Third, the "core ideas" of many historic parties have become somewhat irrelevant. The anticlerical stand of the Radical Socialists is now less meaningful because the growing urbanization of France has brought about a significant weakening of clericalism, and the class-struggle notions of the PCF have become less compelling today because of the growing *embourgeoisement* of the working class. Republicanism (of one sort or another) is so well entrenched that the Radical Socialist party has lost its former quasi monopoly in propounding it. In economics, the split between parties advocating liberalism and those advocating interventionism is a false dichotomy today; most political parties—from the Giscardians and Gaullists on the Right to the Socialists and Communists on the Left—have long ago been converted to some measure of *dirigisme* (the intervention of the state in economic affairs). The argument that divides the parties is not whether there should be economic planning, but what kind of incomes policy there should be, and what social content or what degree of sectoral participation a particular economic plan should entail. Colonialism or anticolonialism ceased to be relevant issues in the early 1960s after France had completed her decolonization process. To be sure, political parties still remain divided over such foreign policy questions as participation in NATO, the nuclear striking force, and the Arab-Israeli conflict; but (except for European economic integration, which all parties save the PCF and a small wing of the UDR favor) these are not matters that exercise the vast majority of Frenchmen.

Anyone trying to understand the meaning and purpose of the parties is, moreover, confounded by contradictory assessments available for

46. Mitterrand was a leader of the UDSR, the CIR, the FGDS, and the Socialist party (PS)—all of them different vehicles for an essentially consistent ideological position.

each one. Thus one writer insists that the UDR and its predecessors have had a clear and coherent doctrine,[47] while another has emphasized the ideological eclecticism of the party.[48] One Socialist took pains to criticize the SFIO for its organizational sclerosis and ideological irrelevance,[49] while another saw its successor, the *Parti socialiste*, as a modern force of reform.[50] One writer (an ex-Communist) has viewed the PCF as a totalitarian party whose concern for the working class is often secondary to its overall strategy,[51] while another sees the party as a domesticated humanistic force of democracy and as the only significant instrument of socioeconomic justice.[52]

These clashing perceptions have contributed to the Frenchman's growing impatience with political parties and help to explain his electoral fickleness.[53] An individual may still vote for a particular party because its interpretation of social phenomena may be intellectually appealing, although he knows that this interpretation need have no clear relationship to specific programs or policy expectations. In a poll conducted in 1952, doctrine was the most important reason for the choice of parties of all but voters for Gaullism (where leadership was the most important reason);[54] platforms, however, were of only secondary importance to supporters of all the major parties. In a 1954 public-opinion

47. Bernard LeCalloc'h, *La Révolution silencieuse: Du gaullisme au pouvoir* (Paris: Didier, 1971).
48. Charlot, *Gaullist Phenomenon*. A SOFRES poll conducted in 1974 revealed that half of the UDR's *electorate* considered that party to be to the right, while most of its *membership* considered it to be to the left of Giscard and the Independent Republicans. Cited in *Le Monde*, 24 October 1974.
49. André Philip, *Les Socialistes* (Paris: Seuil, 1967).
50. Alain Savary, *Pour le nouveau parti socialiste* (Paris: Seuil, 1970).
51. André Barjonet, *La révolution trahie de 1968* (Paris: Didier, 1968). Cf. Frédéric Bon et al., eds., *Le communisme en France et en Italie*, Fondation Nationale des Sciences Politiques, Cahier no. 175 (Paris: Colin, 1969), pp. 255–303.
52. Bertrand Fessard de Foucault, "La sincérité communiste," *Le Monde*, 27 September 1972. Cf. the round-table discussion on "L'enigme communiste," *L'Esprit*, vol. 43, February 1975.
53. Nearly half of the electorate switched parties between the elections of 1956 and 1958, and about a third (excepting the Communists) switched between 1958 and 1962. See Georges Dupeux, "Le comportement des électeurs français de 1958 à 1962," in *Le référendum d'octobre et les élections de novembre 1962*, ed. François Goguel et al. (Paris: Colin, 1965), pp. 181–82. The fickleness of the non-Communist voters may also be due to their awareness of the social gap between them and the party leaders (members of a transpartisan "political class"). E.g., the founders of the MRP were urban intellectuals, but the party's appeal was to the peasantry (Gordon Wright, "Catholics and Peasantry in France," *Political Science Quarterly* 68 [December 1953]: 540); most SFIO leaders were intellectuals, but the party's aim was to appeal to workers.
54. Fougeyrollas, *La conscience politique*, p. 54.

poll, as large a proportion of voters for the SFIO (that is, 36 percent) were opposed to the nationalization of industries as favored it (37 percent); but in a poll conducted in 1958, 67 percent of Socialist voters indicated opposition to the capitalist system![55]

Class differences, attitudinal divisions, and "output expectations" have never been clearly represented within the party spectrum. It may be true that the Communist or Socialist parties have represented the working class, that the Center parties have mirrored Catholic and/or small-town attitudes, or that the Radical Socialist party has represented the petite bourgeoisie; at the same time, all the major parties have attempted to expand their electoral bases. Thus in the election of 1974, Mitterrand appealed to "progressive" Gaullists against a common foe: the business-oriented Independent Republicans; in 1975, the PCF increased its efforts in farming communities,[56] and in 1976 that party called upon Catholics to join a "union for socialism" in preparation for the parliamentary election of 1978.

The position of particular parties on individual issues has not always been clear-cut or consistent (see table 7), and the political ideologies and behavior patterns of individual party leaders have often been at variance with the positions professed by the party as a whole. The Gaullists' relatively unimportant left wing has occasionally favored a more collectivist approach to economics. The Radical Socialist party has remained divided on economic issues, with one wing favoring the dynamic business sector and the other, protection for the small businessman. That party was in the past opposed to the Fifth Republic, but its dominant personality, Servan-Schreiber, has not been averse to the idea of a strong Presidency, should he ever capture that office. From 1966 to 1969, the Centrists remained in the Opposition because they were critical of the excessive power of the President and the weakness of Parliament; but their leader, Jean Lecanuet, himself had run in the presidential election of 1965 as a candidate projecting a "Kennedyesque" image of the dynamic executive.

Popular political party alignments cannot, therefore, be explained simply in terms of the leaders' ideological consistency. The French have often voted for a politician because he is a local notable, or because he may have connections in Paris that his constituents expect him to exploit in their behalf. The voters have no absolute assurance that a deputy of their choice, even if he remains in that party after the election, will adhere to the principles the party stands for. An inquiry conducted in 1970 revealed that (in case of conflicts with their constituents) more

55. *Sondages*, no. 1 (1954); nos. 1 and 2 (1958).
56. Alain Giraudo, "Le démarchage et le prêche," *Le Monde*, 27 December 1975.

Table 7
Overlapping Cleavages in Attitudes of Parties, Fifth Republic

	UNR	UDT	RI	PDM (CDP)	Reformers / Center / Democratic Center	Radicals	Socialists	PCF
Gaullism Favors maintenance of existing political system	+	+	+	+	?	?	—	—
Clericalism Favors maintenance or increase of level of public support for Catholic schools (or does not oppose it)	+	+	+	+	+	—	—	—
Collectivism Favors greater collectivism, interventionism, redistribution of income, welfare statism	—	+	—	?	?	?	+	+
Foreign Policy Generally pro-U.S. or pro-NATO	—	—	?	+	+	+	?	—
Actively pro-European integration	—	—	+	+	+	+	?	—
Favors independent French nuclear force	+	+	?	—	—	—	—	—

+ Yes
— No
? Divided or uncertain

[a]In 1977 the PCF suddenly reversed its position by advocating an independent French nuclear capacity. See chapter 13.

SOURCE: "Les programmes électoraux des principaux partis," *Le Monde*, 27 and 28 February, 1 March 1973; and "Les positions des principaux candidats sur les grands problèmes du moment," *Le Monde*, 4 May 1974.

deputies are in fact guided in their parliamentary behavior by their conscience than by their political party (see table 8).

Table 8
Determinants of the Political Behavior of Deputies

	Total	Commu- nists	Social- ists	Radi- cals	Cen- trists	Gaull- ists	Independent Republicans
Conscience	74	48	50	70	84	78	79
Party	8	37	33	—	—	4	2
Local electorate	7	—	3	—	3	7	15
No response	11	15	14	30	13	11	4
	100%	100%	100%	100%	100%	100%	100%

SOURCE: Roland Cayrol et al., "Les députés français et le système politique," *RFSP* 25 (February 1975): 84.

The feeling that parliamentary election results have little impact on the content of policy has led to the depolitization of a large number of Frenchmen. In a poll conducted in 1962, 54 percent said that their interests could be best promoted by interest groups; 10 percent, by parliamentarians; and only 8 percent, by political parties.[57] In the Fifth Republic, decision making has tended to be not parliamentary but rather presidential or technocratic, and neither type of decision making has involved political parties as the chief vehicle of popular representation. The popular input into presidential decision making has been a septennial exercise in plebiscitarianism, a popularity contest between two individuals during the second ballot, supplemented by periodic referenda on specific issues. Many Frenchmen showed by their massive support of de Gaulle from 1958 to 1968 that they were beginning to put more stock in the aggregative efficacy of a charismatic leader whose outlook—at least in the beginning of the Fifth Republic—transcended that of the traditional political parties. Between 1958 and 1973 the Gaullist movement became, of course, a viable political party; but the fact that it was a

57. Philip Williams and Martin Harrison, *Politics and Society in de Gaulle's Republic* (London: Longmans, 1971), p. 21 n.

catchall party dominating political life in general, and the Assembly in particular, contributed greatly to the simplification of the political spectrum (see table 9, pages 108–9), the confusion of the Opposition, and the "regression of ideological politics."[58]

PARTIES, VOTERS' CHOICES, AND THE ELECTORAL SYSTEM

During de Gaulle's incumbency, many Frenchmen tended to vote with specific reference to his personality, his achievements, or his failures rather than for the UNR (or UDR) as such, particularly in presidential elections where the party label of the Opposition candidate was less significant than the fact that he was an alternative to de Gaulle. In the presidential election of 1965, many North African repatriates who had voted for extreme conservative candidate Tixier-Vignancour on the first ballot switched in the second to "Popular Front" candidate Mitterrand mainly because of their hatred of de Gaulle.[59] Ideology was obviously of little importance there. The popularity of de Gaulle—as measured in public-opinion polls—was consistently higher than the votes received by individual Gaullist candidates or the Gaullist party as a whole on the first ballot of parliamentary elections (see table 10).

The devaluation of the political party as an instrument of popular choice has also had an adverse effect on the party's importance as a significant training ground for the "grass roots" participation of the masses, who have turned to street demonstrations and general strikes as a means of political articulation. Similarly, the continuing interest of young Frenchmen in politics has not implied an active involvement in political parties. According to a recent report, membership in youth groups of *all* parties in 1973 was less than 100,000, or one out of every 150 young people aged 15 to 29.[60]

Most political parties have continued to provide some formal opportunities for the involvement of political activists; and there is still competition for the more than 450,000 municipal or communal council seats. But local elections frequently involve party labels that are only vaguely—if at all—related to national parties. Mere local party participation, moreover, is often meaningless—except for the election of senators—because of the powerlessness of local authorities, and because only a relative handful of politicians in the councils of small towns are able to use their office as a springboard for national political ambitions. National

---

58. Fougeyrollas, *La conscience politique*, pp. 253–68.
59. Williams and Harrison, *Politics and Society*, p. 75.
60. Colette Ysmal, "L'attitude des jeunes," *Le Monde*, 20 February 1973.

Table 9

The Consolidation of Political Parties

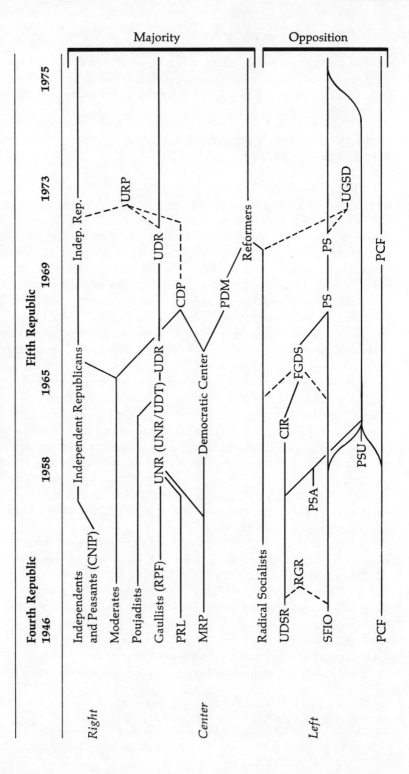

CDP—Center for Democracy and Progress: pro-Gaullist centrist party established in 1969
CIR—Convention of Republican Institutions: center-left formation of various political clubs
CNIP—National Center of Independents and Peasants: an amalgam of various economic conservatives, supporters of business, and/ or agricultural elements

FGDS—Federation of the Democratic and Socialist Left: an electoral alliance, between 1965 and 1968, of Radicals, CIR, and SFIO
MRP—Popular Republican Movement: Christian-Democratic party
PCF—French Communist Party
PDM—Progress and Modern Democracy: anti-Gaullist centrists; component of Reformers party
PRL—Republican Party of Liberty: conservative, generally antirepublican party
PS—Socialist party: successor to SFIO (since 1969)
PSA—Autonomous Socialist party: splinter party, 1958–59, composed of anti-Gaullist Socialists and Radicals
PSU—Unified Socialist party: established in 1960 by Marxist dissidents from SFIO, PSA, and PCF
RGR—Rally of the Republican Left: coalition, in mid-1950s, of Radical Socialists and UDSR
RPF—Rally of the French People: first Gaullist party, established in 1947
SFIO—French Section of Workers' International: name of Socialist party until 1969
UDR—Democratic Union for the Republic: Gaullist party (1968)
UDSR—Democratic and Socialist Union of the Resistance: a non-Communist progressive party
UDT—Democratic Union of Labor: left-wing component of Gaullism.
UGSD—Union of the Socialist and Democratic Left: electoral alliance of PS and left-wing Radical Socialists (1973)
UNR—Union for the New Republic: Gaullist party (1958)
URP—Union of Republicans for Progress: Gaullist electoral alliance (since 1972), composed of UDR, RI, and CDP

NOTE: Unbroken lines indicate evolution of party. Broken lines indicate alliance. Brackets indicate Majority/Opposition alignment since 1974.

109

Table 10
Gaullism and de Gaulle: Comparative Popularity

	Gaullist Party Popular Vote in Parliamentary Elections (1st ballot) % of total	Popularity of de Gaulle % in favor
1958	17.5	68.0
1962	36.0	60.0
1967	38.0	63.0
1968	48.0	55.0

SOURCE: *Sondages* no. 1 (1966); and IFOP poll, cited in Charlot, *Gaullist Phenomenon*, p. 49.

party conventions are indeed forums of representation for local party activists, but delegates at such conventions often pass resolutions concerning ideologies rather than platforms. Even when certain "action programs" came into vogue (as in the case of the SFIO in the early 1960s and of the Radicals in 1970), these programs were not seriously thought to be binding on politicians. Moreover, it has been very difficult for conventions to alter significantly the elite structures of most political parties, which have been led either by self-perpetuating gerontocracies (e.g., in the PCF and the old SFIO), or by fortuitous combinations of notables from important localities (e.g., in the case of the Center and the Radicals).

A politician's claim to continued local leadership, and to continued candidacy for parliamentary office, has rested on his past electoral successes, which in turn have to some extent depended upon his choice of party. But the electoral success of a party has often had less to do with the strength of the party's social base and the credibility of its philosophical appeal than with the advantages or disadvantages accruing to a party from the electoral system. Under the "pure" proportional representation system that prevailed in France at the onset of the Fourth Republic, each party had theoretically equal chances. Thus the anti-system PCF, the Catholic MRP, and the laic and republican SFIO each had approximately 20–25 percent of the parliamentary seats from 1945 to 1951, the number of mandates rather faithfully reflecting the proportion of the popular vote received by each party. For the parliamentary elections of 1951 and 1956, new electoral laws provided that if any party, or combination of parties, obtained an absolute majority of the total vote in a multimember constituency, that party could appropriate all the seats allocated to the constituency and divide them among various components of the electoral alliance on the basis of prearranged formulas. This measure was intended to provide advantages to the pro-system parties near the Center—the SFIO, the Radicals, and the MRP—among whom electoral alliances were easily possible, and to reduce the representation of those antisystem parties—the PCF and the RPF—that could not easily combine (s'apparenter) with "neighboring" parties. Thus, while in the election of 1951, the popular vote of the PCF was nearly twice as large as that of the MRP, the parliamentary representation of the PCF was only slightly larger than that of the MRP.

In 1958, France returned to the electoral system that had prevailed throughout most of the Third Republic: the single-member district system of elections with two ballots. Under that system, which is in force today, a candidate is elected on the first ballot if he has received an absolute majority of the votes; if no one has received such a majority, there is a runoff election a week later in which a candidate has merely to obtain a plurality of the votes. Since 1976, regulations provide that any candidate receiving at least 12.5 percent of the total first-ballot votes of a constituency may stay in the race for the second ballot; but realism has demanded the withdrawal (désistement) of all relatively weak candidates. Such withdrawals are, in principle, based on prior agreements between parties on a national level. Thus, since the early 1970s, agreements between the PS and the PCF provided that whichever of the two parties got the larger first-ballot vote could expect the other to withdraw in its favor. In fact, each constituency party has made its own decision; and on many occasions the Socialist candidate—whether for reasons of personal ambition or ideological distrust—has preferred either to remain in the race, thus enhancing the electoral chances of a conservative candidate, or to throw his support to a Radical (or Reformer).

In any case, the preelectoral aggregation process that has traditionally characterized Anglo-American politics has also been at work in France, with the result that the party preferences of Frenchmen are revealed even less precisely than before by the parliamentary representation of various political parties. The PCF's popular vote was relatively stable from 1951 to 1973, ranging from about 4 million to about 5.5 million, its registered membership remaining stable, too, at about 400,000; but its parliamentary representation fell from a high of 183 in 1946 to a low of 10 in 1958. Had the proportional representation system of the Fourth Republic been operative in the November 1958 election, the PCF would have received 88 seats instead of 10; the SFIO, 72 seats instead of 40; and the UNR, 82 seats instead of 189.[61] There is no question that the electoral system of the Fifth Republic has been heavily weighted in favor of the Gaullists (see table 11).

Table 11
Gaullists and Communists in the Fifth Republic:
Popular Votes and Parliamentary Representation

Assembly Elections	Gaullists		Communists	
	Percentage of Popular Vote in First Ballot	Percentage of Assembly Seats	Percentage of Popular Vote in First Ballot	Percentage of Assembly Seats
1958	18	40	19	2
1962	32	49	22	8.8
1967	37.8	50	22.5	15
1968	43.7	58.3	20	7
1973	23.9	37.7	19	14.9

The reduction of the parliamentary representation of some political parties and the simplification of the party system as a whole cannot be attributed entirely to the electoral system, since most of the "Fourth Republic" or anti-Gaullist parties lost popular votes. By 1967, much of the loss of the MRP and the CNIP was due to defection to Gaullism, with the "rump" of each party going over to the so-called Center. The Gaullists were political beneficiaries because the Opposition could not effectively aggregate its ideological differences despite such temporary electoral coalitions as the FGDS; because the Gaullists, successfully capitalizing on the nationalism that runs through all French parties, made significant inroads into the traditional electorate of these parties; and because the Gaullist party had become *the* system party par excellence, and benefited from the coattail effects of General de Gaulle.

61. Cf. J. M. Cotteret et al., *Lois électorales et inégalités de représentation en France 1936–1960* (Paris: Colin, 1960), p. 372.

The Gaullist preponderance in the Assembly can be weighed against the dominance of anti-Gaullist parties in the Senate. Since the Third Republic, there has been an institutionalized political inequality in the latter chamber, its composition never adequately reflecting the distribution of popular votes. The participants in the electoral college that chooses the senators are local politicians and the majority of them—given the large number of communes in France—come from rural areas. This non-Gaullist control of the Senate is not so important as it may seem, in view of the lack of meaningful legislative power of the upper chamber. But it can be argued as well that even if the Assembly were to reflect adequately the popular votes received by the various political parties, it might make little difference with respect to political decision making. This argument might explain why Giscard has been sympathetic to the demand—frequently made by the Left—for a return to the proportional-representation system of parliamentary elections.

Given the widespread conviction that a particular party lineup in Parliament need have no decisive effect on the content of legislation or on the composition of the cabinet, it is possible to view the political party—irrespective of the type of electoral system that prevails—largely as a vehicle for mobilizing voters for or against a presidential candidate or a certain position in a referendum. In the sense that the French voter must choose between a yes or no vote in a popular consultation, or between a Gaullist (or "post-Gaullist") President and his opponent (or between "order and stability" versus "anarchy and totalitarian communism"), the choice is no longer among traditional political parties, but between polar opposites.

BIPOLARISM OR MULTIPOLARISM?

This dichotomy between supporters and opponents in a referendum, or between ins and outs, has led certain scholars to argue that France is moving toward the two-party norm of the Anglo-American democracies.[62] On the one hand, there are the Gaullists and their conservative and centrist allies, with a solid majority in the Assembly, and with the magnet of officeholding that can attract other wavering parties; on the other hand, there is the Left Opposition. Moreover, the virtual disappearance of antirepublicanism on the Right and (assuming the domestication of the PCF to be genuine and lasting) the programmatic unification of the Left have contributed to a new kind of institutional consensus politics and to a reduction in the number of viable parties. The stress on

62. See Maurice Duverger, "The Non-Official Opposition," Le Monde Weekly, 28 October 1970

bipolarity is a theme particularly attractive to those who are eager to find a parallel between socioeconomic and electoral "Americanization." However, the positing of such bipolarism is premature, not only because it sometimes rests on the questionable assumption that "it is essential to stability" or the equally questionable (and tautological) proposition that "it is the only alternative to a return to some form of pre-Gaullist fragmentation,"[63] but also because it presupposes a structural merger between the PS and PCF on the one hand, and the UDR, the Giscardians, and their allies, on the other. Since all these parties retain their independence, one scholar has described the evolution of the French party system in terms of the quadripolar norm of Scandinavian democracies: as a quadrille in which "senior partners" on each side (the Giscardians and Socialists) are joined by "junior partners" (the Gaullists and Communists, respectively).[64] This quadrille does not, however, fit into the four-party model once propounded for the American system—i.e., two congressional and two presidential parties—because in France the bipolar legislative party alignment is not matched by a parallel bipolar executive party system.[65] Moreover, a clear distinction between junior and senior partners cannot be made, because parties, like their leaders, have survival instincts, and because each of the partners possesses particular attributes not possessed by the other—attributes that are necessary for electoral success. On the Left, the Socialists' acceptability to many centrist voters—and the Socialists' recent electoral successes—must be matched against the solid and apparently irreducible electoral base of the Communists (ca. 20 percent of the votes in the past fifteen years). On the Right, the ideological flexibility and presidential incumbency of the Independent Republicans must be juxtaposed to the parliamentary plurality of the Gaullists and their control of local political machines.

It has been said that the Center parties as such were "the great

63. Bruce Campbell, "On the Prospects of Polarization in French Electoral Competition" (Paper presented at the Western Political Science Association, Denver, Colorado, April 1974), p. 3. On the (questionable) causal relationship between bipolarism and stability, see Giovanni Sartori, "European Political Parties: the Case of Polarized Pluralism," in Political Parties and Political Development, ed. J. La Palombara and M. Weiner (Princeton: Princeton University Press, 1966), pp. 137–76.
64. M. Duverger, "Le quadrille bipolaire," Le Monde, 27 January 1976. Duverger took us one step further: he predicted that in the parliamentary elections of 1978 the Socialists would capture about 30% of the total vote, and will thus be in the same position as the Scandinavian Labor parties. See "Le 'décollage' du parti socialiste," Le Monde, 13 March 1976.
65. James MacGregor Burns, The Deadlock of Democracy: Four-Party Politics in America (Englewood Cliffs, N.J.: Prentice-Hall, 1963), esp. pp. 257–64.

casualty of the Fifth Republic."[66] The Center parties have certainly suffered from the aggregative effects of the Fifth Republic electoral system, especially insofar as presidential elections are concerned (see table 12). The Centrists are temporarily disorganized, but it would be rash to write them off permanently. In the cantonal elections of March 1976 (second ballot), the candidates of miscellaneous pro-majority centrist parties received 21 percent of the vote—as much as the combined vote for the Gaullists (11.9 percent) and the Independent Republicans (9.1 percent), and more than the PCF (17.3 percent).[67] And after the election, centrist formations still held the presidencies of half the general councils.[68] In the Senate, the presence of the Center is even more apparent: the combined Center factions located between the UDR and the PS account for 160 out of 283 seats (or 100, if the RI is subtracted). Presidential bipolarism is imperfectly reflected even in the Assembly, where the multiparty system continues to exist; where the combined representation of all the parties situated between the UDR and the PS amounts to more than a fourth of the total; and where the various Center formations have not given up their organizational identities but are constantly engaged in efforts at reconstituting themselves into a united "third family" distinguishable from both Gaullism and the non-Communist Left. This centrist force has been able to play off the UDR and occasionally the Left against Giscard, and in so doing to secure appropriate political payoffs, in terms of cabinet positions for itself. The very existence of the Center—and its intermittent interest in building an alliance with the non-Communist Left—has enabled the PS to enhance its position within the Left alliance, because a Center-Left arrangement is still viewed by some Socialists (the "Defferrists") as an attractive alternative to a Socialist-Communist one. Just as the alliance between the PS and the Radical-Socialists enabled the non-Communist Left to poll 20 percent of first-ballot votes in 1967 and 1968, a PS-Center combination would have produced 32 percent of the first-ballot vote in 1973. If such an alliance were to be constructed in future elections, and the PCF and UDR were each to run separately, France would be transformed into a three-party system.

A tripolar system would certainly be consonant with the profound centrism of most Frenchmen, which has been more permanent than their episodic Gaullism (which lasted exactly a decade) and more sig-

66. Jean Blondel, "The Rise of a New-Style President," in France at the Polls: The Presidential Election of 1974, ed. Howard Penniman (Washington, D.C.: American Enterprise Institute, 1975), p. 49.
67. Le Monde, 17 March 1976.
68. Le Monde, 20 March 1976.

Table 12
Parliamentary and Presidential Elections, 1958–74
(in percent of votes cast)

| | Commu-nists | Social-ists | Center | | | Moderates Inde-pendents | Gaull-ists |
			Radi-cals	MRP	Demo-cratic Center		
		Left		Center		Right	
Parliamentary Elections							
1958							
first ballot	18.9	15.5	11.5	11.6		19.9	17.6
second ballot	20.7	13.7	7.7	7.5		23.6	26.4
1962							
first ballot	21.7	12.6	7.5	8.9	9.6[a]	4.4[b]	31.9
second ballot	21.3	15.2	7.0	5.3	7.8	1.6	40.5
1967							
first ballot	22.5	18.8[c]			17.9[d]	37.8[e]	
second ballot	21.4	24.1			10.8	42.6	
1968							
first ballot	20.0	16.5[e]			10.3[f]	43.7[e]	
second ballot	20.1	21.3			7.8	46.4	
1973							
first ballot	21.5	21.2[g]			13.1[h]	36.4[e]	
second ballot	20.6	25.1			6.1	46.2	

nificant in behavioral terms than their intellectual leftism (*sinistrisme*).[69] If the Center parties were satellites of the UDR under Pompidou, the UDR has, under Giscard, itself been reduced to a kind of satellite status. On the first ballot of the presidential election of 1974, Giscard, who was supported by the Centrists, Radicals, and even some Socialists, received 32.6 percent of the total vote, while the Gaullists received only 15.1 percent. During the election campaign, both major presidential candidates had avoided highly polarizing positions, and most Frenchmen viewed neither a victory of Giscard d'Estaing nor a victory of Mitterrand

69. This centrism was once emphasized by M. Duverger in *La démocratie sans le peuple* (Paris: Seuil, 1967), esp. pp. 218–34. Cf. Jack Hayward and Vincent Wright, "Presidential Supremacy and the French General Election of 1973," *Parliamentary Affairs* 26 (Summer 1973): 274–306, for a discussion of the tripolar system that emerged in the spring of 1973.

Table 12
Parliamentary and Presidential Elections, 1958–74
(in percent of votes cast)

	Commu-nists	Social-ists	Radi-cals	MRP	Demo-cratic Center	Moderates Inde-pendents	Gaull-ists
		Left		Center		Right	
Presidential Elections							
1965							
first ballot		32.2[i]			15.8[j]		43.7[k]
second ballot		45.5					54.5
1969							
first ballot	21.5[i]	5.1[m]			23.4[n]		43.9[o]
second ballot		42.4					57.6
1974							
first ballot		43.2[i]				32.6[p]	15.1[q]
second ballot		49.2				50.8	

[a] anti-Gaullist centrists
[b] Independent Republicans (RI)
[c] FGDS
[d] Democratic Center
[e] UDR and allies
[f] PDM
[g] UGSD
[h] Reformers
[i] Mitterrand
[j] Lecanuet
[k] de Gaulle
[l] Duclos
[m] Defferre
[n] Poher
[o] Pompidou
[p] Giscard d'Estaing
[q] Chaban-Delmas

SOURCE: Partially based on Hayward, *One and Indivisible Republic*, p. 66.

NOTE: Tixier-Vignancour, a candidate of the extreme Right who received 5.3% in the first-ballot presidential election of 1965, has been omitted from the table. All other first-ballot candidates, who received less than 5% of the total vote, have also been omitted. The vertical lines denote the divisions between Opposition parties (to left of line) and governmental coalitions (to right of line).

as an evil. The "centrist" behavior of many Gaullist supporters of Giscard and the "social democratic" pronouncements of many Communist supporters of Mitterrand made the runoff election appear rather similar to an American presidential contest. But a true "Americanization" of the French party system can be expected only with the softening of the Gaullist orthodox faith (which has not yet disappeared despite the progressive disintegration of the UDR) and the permanent conversion of the Communist party to a democratic alternation of parties in power.

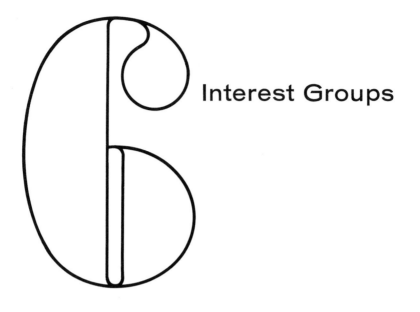

Interest Groups

It is only natural that in a country such as France, with her social and economic complexities, interest groups should have a significant place. At present a myriad of secondary associations ranges from trade unions and business organizations with large memberships to small, ideologically exclusive groups of students. From the Third Republic onward, interest groups have played an important part in socialization, policy formulation, and even the support of republican institutions. Groups have been involved politically via the linkage of their leadership to the formal decision-making organs, their alliance with political parties, and their direct colonization of Parliament and the civil service. The impact of interest groups has been uneven and has depended upon the group's membership, financial situation, internal cohesion, and image.

TRADE UNIONS

Among the most important interest groups are the trade unions, from the point of view of age, well-established linkages to political parties, mass membership, and the mobilization of support for or against government policies. The oldest trade-union roof organization, the General Confederation of Labor (*Confédération générale du travail*— CGT), was established in 1895. As a catchall union of syndicalist-Marxist and revolutionary inspiration, it was as much concerned with general political goals—e.g., the restructuring of the political system as a whole—as with bread-and-butter issues. After World War I, workers inspired by Catholic principles split away from the CGT to form their own union, the French Confederation of Christian Workers (*Confédération française des travailleurs chrétiens*—CFTC). In 1947, many workers who disliked the increasing dependence of the CGT on the Communist party, the CGT's preoccupation with politically inspired general strikes that had little to do with the concrete and immediate economic concerns of the workers, and its questionable loyalty to the Republic, established (with some American encouragement) a new union, the Workers' Force (*Force Ouvrière*—FO). The CGT, with membership figures variously estimated from 800,000 to more than 1,500,000, remains the largest trade union. Although not all its members are Communist, the fact that most of its leadership is also prominent in the PCF hierarchy and that many of its activists are reliable supporters of the PCF, has often made the CGT appear like an obedient and effective "transmission belt" for the party.[1] The FO has about 350,000 to 500,000 members; during the Fourth Republic it was a significant union because it was ideologically linked to the SFIO. Like the latter party (and unlike the CGT), the FO firmly supported the regime and was convinced that benefits could be gained for workers through orderly collective bargaining and through lobbying. The FO approximates the Anglo-American type of union in its avoidance of ideological approaches to labor-management relations and in its staunch anti-communism.[2]

The CFTC was closely allied to the MRP. This alliance, coupled with the CFTC's rejection of the class struggle and the deeply held conviction that "man does not live by bread alone," enabled that union to recruit many traditionalist members of the working class. But the CFTC lacked dynamism and was in danger of losing much of its membership to the CGT, which never tired of pointing out that clericalism could not be credibly combined with the promotion of workers' interests. In response to this claim, the bulk of the CFTC's membership and leadership "deconfessionalized" the union in 1964 and renamed it the French Democratic Confederation of Labor (*Confédération française démocratique de travail*—CFDT). The bylaws of the CFDT do not mention Christianity at all, but merely refer to man's "spiritual needs." The persistence of a vestigial Catholicism in the CFDT is indicated by that union's strong implantation in the consultative committees for parochial education; in

1. See André Barjonet, *La CGT* (Paris: Seuil, 1968), pp. 124–29. According to this source, the CGT is not a complete transmission belt, yet relationships are so close that the CGT often neglects concrete economic policies in favor of general anti-system politics.
2. For a history of French trade unionism, and the FO's "nonideological" position, see Georges Vidalenc, *La classe ouvrière et le syndicalisme en France de 1789 à 1965* (Paris: Confédération Force Ouvrière, 1969), esp. pp. 441–502.

the December 1975 committee elections, the CFDT received 39 percent of the votes.[3] (A rump of the old CFTC officially remains in existence, but, with a membership of about 80,000, it is of little significance.) The CFDT, whose membership is between 400,000 and 800,000, has become the second largest trade-union federation.[4] In the late 1960s, the CFDT's leadership became more revolutionary, more Socialist, and more amenable to ideas about the class struggle, an evolution that made it possible for the union to entice members away from the CGT.[5]

The existence of several ideologically fragmented trade unions has provided a certain amount of competition, which has often forced a union to adopt radical rhetoric in order to appeal to potential members and to trump its rivals. Ideological conflicts have not been the only factors in the fragmentation of the employees' groups. In France, as elsewhere in Western Europe, the white-collar segment has organized separately in order to maintain its status distinction. The CGC (*Confédération générale des cadres*) is such a white-collar union, and it counts among its 200,000 members not only clerks, but also supervisory office personnel. Not all white-collar employees are in the CGC; many are in fact found within the three major trade-union federations. The latter, in order to keep the white-collar elements within their ranks, have insisted that salary differentials between white- and blue-collar workers ought to be retained; this is true even of the CGT, which has tried to combine its egalitarian ideology with opposition to a policy of complete leveling of wages.

The prospect of unity among the different trade unions is uncertain. The ideological division among them, which in the past was buttressed by their relationship to patron parties, is weakening now, because of the simultaneous decline of political parties and of Parliament. Moreover, the fragmentation of trade unions sometimes exists on a level that is functionally autonomous. All major trade unions share a commitment to higher wages and fringe benefits for workers; to socialism (democratic

3. *Le Monde,* 29 January 1976.
4. One source has cited the following membership figures for 1967: CGT, 1,500,000; CFDT, 600,000; FO, 400,000. Jacques Capdevielle and René Mouriaux, *Les Syndicats Ouvriers en France* (Paris: Colin, 1970), p. 74. Membership figures for French interest groups (and political parties) are notoriously unreliable. The figures issued by an organization tend to be inflated, and those issued for its rivals are usually understated. Thus (according to *L'Année politique 1974,* p. 158), the FO claimed 850,000 members at the end of 1973—an obvious exaggeration. There is, however, considerable agreement that in recent years the CFDT's membership has surpassed that of the FO.
5. See Edmond Maire and Jacques Juilliard, *La CFDT d'aujourd'hui* (Paris: Seuil, 1975).

or other); to *co-gestion* (co-management by workers at factory levels)—
though the CFDT is most enthusiastic and the CGT most reserved about
such an approach; to the nationalization of industries; and to democratic economic planning. Interunion rivalries are sometimes occasioned
by differences in approach to general politics, with the CGT and CFDT
favoring direct political involvement and the search for parliamentary
and other allies, and the FO proclaiming its "independence" of political
forces. But there is a growing feeling among the rank and file that purely
ideological preoccupations detract from the pursuit of pragmatic goals.
In a poll conducted in October 1969, 54 percent of the respondents
felt that trade unions should not mix in general politics.[6] That is perhaps
why doctrinal differences present at the trade unions' central headquarters have not prevented a degree of interunion collaboration, as in
joint demonstrations, intersyndical bargaining committees (in the nationalized industries or the bureaucracy), and strikes.[7] Thus in September 1969, the three major industrial unions arrived at a common view
about the size of the minimum wage, and in July 1970, these three unions
negotiated, jointly and successfully, with the CNPF for the monthly
payment of wages (*mensualisation*) to metalworkers.[8]

Nevertheless, "autonomous bargaining" in the Anglo-American
sense is weak in France. The ideological splits in the labor movement
have weakened the trade unions' position in bargaining with a relatively
unified employer. For factories in which workers' membership is split
among several unions, the National Labor Relations Board (*Commission
supérieure des conventions collectives*), which includes trade-union and
business representatives, may, in theory, certify one union as the bargaining agent for all workers; in practice, however, the workers are
represented at the bargaining table by several unions.[9] Monolithic trade-
union organization, like that of Sweden or Austria (where about 80 per-

6. Paul Silvestre and Paul Wagret, *Le syndicalisme contemporain* (Paris: Colin,
   1970), p. 19. In consonance with this theme, Georges Séguy, the secretary-general
   of the CGT, declared at his union's congress in 1969 that "the era of politically-
   based factions [within the unions] is past," and that the CGT would not be a
   camp of "ideological fratricide." *Le Monde*, 15 January 1970.
7. See "L'action syndicale," *Après-demain*, no. 125–26 (June–September 1970): esp.
   40–44.
8. Industrial workers have favored *mensualisation* not only because that is the
   method of payment for white-collar employees, and therefore a prestige issue,
   but also because it brings with it better protection against dismissal and better
   social security benefits. (In 1973, about 75% of the industrial workers in the
   private sector were paid on a monthly basis.)
9. John Sheahan, *An Introduction to the French Economy* (Columbus, Ohio: Merrill,
   1973), pp. 43–45.

cent of the workers are unionized), is difficult to achieve in France because there is no union shop in that country. Until recently, union recruiting activities on the factory level were forbidden; if a worker wished to join a union, he had to register at a local branch office. Unlike in Britain, there is in France no automatic payroll checkoff system; dues have had to be collected—with dismal success—by the local union officials. The result has been that only 25–30 percent of the workers are unionized, and that the union coffers have been relatively empty. Since 1971 collective bargaining at the plant level has been legalized, but the union locals are still so weak that they tend to rely on national union-management agreements (*accords-cadres*). And since these agreements often involve the government as a third party, the latter becomes in effect a co-negotiator whose goodwill is crucial.

There is a vicious circle regarding the relationship between the trade unions and the government. The government is sometimes inclined to discriminate against the unions because it feels that the political system may be threatened by the latter's historic syndicalist ideology; and the unions cannot easily replace their belief in the politics of confrontation by a commitment to the politics of accommodation, i.e., acquire a businesslike bargaining outlook, as long as they are convinced that bargaining opportunities as well as fruitful access to government are restricted.[10]

There is also a vicious circle regarding the power of unions. On the one hand, the lack of inclusiveness of unions has made them ineffective in collective bargaining, and the lack of strike funds has prevented them from engaging in lengthy and credible strikes. On the other hand, unions find it difficult to recruit new members, and often to retain old ones, because of their weaknesses. Therefore, French unions have never placed much faith in "autonomous bargaining" and have instead concentrated on political goals and syndicalist action.

BUSINESS ASSOCIATIONS

The business sector is, in many ways, in a better position than labor, because the former has more money and greater unity. These advantages apply in particular to big business, which since 1946 has been organized in the National Council of French Employers (*Conseil na-*

---

10. On unions and collective bargaining, see Gérard Adam, *La négotiation collective en France* (Paris: Editions ouvrières, 1971).

tional du patronat français—CNPF).[11] During the Second World War, the business community (then still represented by the *Confédération générale de la production française*) discredited itself politically by its collaboration with the Vichy regime. The weak Resistance record of industrialists, and their virtual absence from de Gaulle's London entourage, prevented a *rapprochement* between organized business and a postwar government dominated by left-wing political parties.[12] The poor image of business was in some measure reflected in the nationalization of many industries and in the enactment of numerous laws in favor of the workers.

To the extent that economic decision making was parliamentary, organized business was less well placed than the trade unions or the agricultural associations, because it was only feebly implanted in the Assembly.[13] Nevertheless, throughout most of the Fourth Republic, the CNPF proved, for a number of reasons, to be an effective interest group. The government's commitment to capitalist planning transformed the business community into a crucial partner in economic policy making (see chapter 11); the disunity of organized labor frequently permitted business to ignore collective contracts; and the *pantouflage* relationship to the higher echelons of the civil service gave business favorable access to the authorities. This relationship made it possible for a business leader to slip (*pantoufler*) into the bureaucracy, and, conversely, for bureaucrats who had proved their goodwill toward the business community to exchange their jobs for lucrative positions in that community. By and large, the leadership of the CNPF is still dominated by a long-tenured, conservative gerontocracy, which has had less than satisfactory contacts with individual business firms. In recent years, the CNPF has tried to work toward an improvement of its image and a "rejuvenation" of its leadership by setting up new rules providing that the maximum age of the organization's president and vice-president be seventy years.[14] Under the prodding of the Young Employers (*Jeunes patrons*), a group of dynamic businessmen until recently vaguely affiliated to the CNPF,

11. The CNPF—a "roof organization" of about 400 constituent associations—also harbors smaller enterprises among its 900,000 industrial, commercial, and banking components, but big business is clearly dominant.
12. Henry W. Ehrmann, *Organized Business in France* (Princeton: Princeton University Press, 1957), pp. 58–100, 103.
13. In 1945, only 20 (out of 522) deputies were representatives of business; about 40 in 1951 and 1956, and 54 (out of 465) in 1958. Figures cited in Jean Meynaud, *Nouvelles études sur les groupes de pression en France* (Paris: Colin, 1962), p. 186.
14. Jacques Ehrsam, "Renouveler le patronat," *Le Monde*, 7 February 1970.

the latter has acquired a more competitive business outlook and has learned to exert considerable leadership in the French economic planning process.[15] Small business is separately organized in the General Confederation of Small and Medium-Sized Enterprises (*Confédération générale des petites et moyennes entreprises*—CGPME), an association that, while formally remaining a constituent part of the CNPF,[16] has tried vainly to maintain traditional family businesses in the face of international competition and the modernization of industry.

In the Third Republic, the small-business sector was well enough protected, even coddled, by virtue of its links to the Radical and other centrist parties based in the provinces. But that sector began to feel threatened when, in the early years of the Fourth Republic, France committed herself to a policy of economic modernization by adopting voluntaristic planning. The Union of Shopkeepers (UDCA), established in 1953, attracted a membership of more than 350,000 and, as a political party (the UFF), attained considerable electoral success in 1956 (see page 78). The most articulate contemporary spokesman of small business is the CID-UNATI (see page 17), whose main strength is in the provinces. Because of what it considers the big-business bias of the government, and because it possesses neither an effective patron party in Parliament nor meaningful access to executive and other decision-making institutions, the CID-UNATI has become quite radicalized and has increasingly preferred anomic and violent forms of political articulation—which in 1970 led to the imprisonment of its leader, Gérard Nicoud. The "martyrdom" of Nicoud may have accounted for the fact that between 1970 and 1971 the membership of CID-UNATI grew eightfold—from 23,000 to 189,000.[17] Nonetheless, there is little question that small business cannot now effectively articulate its interests, given the pressure of the Common Market for the consolidation of enterprises.

15. The extent of "modernization" of business, and of the CNPF, remains a matter of controversy. The myth prevailing in the 1930s about the "200 families" running the French economy is gradually being replaced by a counter-myth about the distinction between stock ownership (which is still largely confined to the upper strata) and control by management (i.e., polytechnicians who facilitate access to the economic bureaucracy). See André Vène, "Qui sont les nouveaux patrons?" *Revue politique et parlementaire* 74 (October 1972): 29–42.
16. The picture of organized business is somewhat confused by the fact that the Christian Employers (*Centre du patronat chrétien*) and a group of directors of big business (*Association des cadres dirigeants de l'industrie*), although generally sympathetic to CNPF, are both unaffiliated with it.
17. *Le Monde*, 7 March 1972.

AGRICULTURE

The weakness of small business is paralleled in the agricultural sector, which has had some difficulty in preserving its position. Although until the advent of the Fourth Republic agriculture was a dominant economic force, and several political parties in Parliament were spokesmen of farmers' interests, today agriculture must rely largely on its own organizational strength. But agriculture, like labor, suffers from fragmentation and internal competition. The largest farmers' association is the National Federation of Farmers' Unions (*Fédération nationale des syndicats des exploitants agricoles*—FNSEA), which is a roof organization of a score of specialized farmers' groups. Although it has 700,000 members, it includes only about a third of the two million farmers in France, a poor showing compared to the 90 percent of British farmers included in the National Farmers Union. The FNSEA embraces primarily independent farmers and is generally thought to be conservative in political outlook, although one of its constituent groups, the Young Farmers (*Centre national des jeunes agriculteurs*—CNJA), themselves led by the Christian Agricultural Youth (*Jeunesse agricole chrétienne*—JAC), tried briefly to infuse "progressive" (and Catholic) attitudes into the FNSEA. In late 1969 and early 1970, some leaders of the Young Farmers resigned from membership in certain regional associations of the FNSEA, charging that the parent organization did not represent farmers as much as it did the farming industries, that is, the processors of farm produce.

Fragmentation of agriculture along ideological lines was fairly widespread before the war, when the *Sociéte nationale d'encouragement à l'agriculture* was close to the Radicals, and the *Confédération générale de l'agriculture* was close to the SFIO.[18] Today there are still agricultural associations that are ideologically oriented. Thus, the FNSEA tends to be Catholic and right-of-center (most of its leaders were politically close to the MRP and are now close to the Centrists); the *Confédération nationale de la mutualité de la coopération et du crédit* is close to the Radical Socialists; and MODEF (*Mouvement de coordination et de défense des exploitants agricoles familiales*) is sponsored by the Communists to represent the very poorest farmers. The ideological identification of agricultural associations has been declining, however, and fragmentation is increasingly based on agronomic specialization: single-

---

18. François Goguel and Alfred Grosser, *La Politique en France* (Paris: Colin, 1964), p. 137.

crop producers, such as beetgrowers or winegrowers, and economic groups, such as credit or cooperative marketing associations.[19] The various agricultural organizations are united—if that is the word—only under "corporatist" auspices, in the sense that they all elect representatives to the agricultural chambers. These chambers, which exist on regional and national levels, are officially sanctioned "bodies of public law" that the government calls upon for expert advice and for the occasional performance of public-administrative tasks, such as the implementation of farm price and credit policies.[20]

THE ACCESS AND INPUT OF INTEREST GROUPS

The preceding summary of the major interest groups, though far from complete, indicates that organizational frameworks exist for the important economic sectors in France. But the extent of organization does not by itself indicate a group's position and power in French political life. In terms of her pluralistic reality, and in conformity with the freedom of association found in all democratic regimes, France has certainly been receptive to a vigorous interest-group politics. However, in modern French political history there has always been a school of thought inspired in particular by Rousseauan theories, which held any political role of interest groups, secondary associations, and even political parties to be unnecessary interpositions between the public and the government, and therefore destructive of the "general will." In consonance with this doctrine, the *Loi Le Chapelier* in 1791 declared all intermediary bodies (*corps intermédiaires*) illegal, and secondary associations were not permitted until 1884, when that law was rescinded. Since that time interest groups have indeed flourished, and they have made their political influence felt in a variety of ways.

In the Third and Fourth republics, various economic or ideological groups were strongly linked to political parties, exerted considerable influence on them, or were at least ideologically close to them. In the Third Republic, the Freemasons considered the Radical party as their spokesman; in the Fourth Republic, the MRP was seen as reflecting the views of the Catholic church, and the veterans' organizations supported the RPF because it represented their interests well. A clear party linkage

19. See Yves Tavernier, *Le Syndicalisme paysan* (Paris: Colin, 1969), for the history of, and interrelationships among, the agricultural associations. On the multitude of farmers' groups, see also Yves Tavernier et al., *L'univers politique des paysans dans la France contemporaine* (Paris: Colin, 1972), pp. 367–557.
20. On elections to the agricultural chambers, and on the various public services provided by these bodies, see "Les nuances du corporatisme agraire," *Le Monde*, 18 February 1976.

enabled interest groups to colonize the Parliament directly by having group leaders elected deputies. Thus by the end of the Third Republic, the Senate had begun to establish its reputation as the "Chamber of Agriculture," and in the Fourth Republic, many trade-union officials were elected to the National Assembly under Communist or Socialist party labels. Interest-group input was facilitated by the numerous specialized legislative standing committees in the Fourth Republic, with the trade unionists establishing "squatter's rights" in the Committee on Labor, and the representatives of the farmers' associations in the Committee on Agriculture. This input was supplemented by the special access of certain interest groups to "their" particular ministry, and by the acceptance of ministerial portfolios by a leader of a client group: for example, in the Fourth Republic, the minister of agriculture was usually a person linked to an agricultural association. In addition, interest-group representatives were often recruited (albeit on a temporary basis) to a minister's own official team. The pervasive presence of interest groups—whether real or imagined—made governmental institutions, from Parliament to the bureaucracy, appear like a complex of fiefdoms. To the extent that this situation obfuscated the distinction between the public and the private domains, it helped to bring the Fourth Republic into disrepute.

Since 1958 the power of interest groups has declined considerably. In part this has been due to the etatist philosophy of de Gaulle, who had as little use for interest groups as he had for political parties, having considered both as particularistic and therefore out of harmony with the public interest. Since the concept of *concertation*—inadequately translated as "harmonization"—was a favorite with de Gaulle and his followers, it has been argued that de Gaulle's views regarding groups were protofascist. Like the Nazis, who wanted to eliminate the independent existence of groups by "coordinating" or merging them into the official authority structure, de Gaulle wanted to bring about an evisceration of trade unions by making them part of a "capital-labor association" and by depoliticizing them.[21] In fairness, however, it should be noted that *concertation* has also been a catchword of non-Gaullist planners and post-Gaullist politicians, and that it had been viewed as a device for technocratic decision making even during the Fourth Republic.

In the Fifth Republic, interest groups and political parties could of course not be eliminated from the French scene, but the institutional

21. Alexander Werth, *De Gaulle: A Political Biography* (Baltimore: Penguin, 1967), pp. 197, 203–6.

framework could be so arranged as to minimize their political influence. Parliament has not been a fruitful access point for interest groups; until 1973 the traditional "patron parties" of prominent interest groups (notably labor and agriculture) were relatively insignificant in the Assembly. The electoral system based on proportional representation, which in the Fourth Republic had permitted a party to articulate the views of specific interests and social sectors or classes more clearly, has now been replaced by the single-member district system, which forces a party to be more aggregative and hence to become a less reliable reflector of the demands of a particular interest group. The Communist party can still be said to represent the workers' point of view—if such a representation does not conflict with the party's general strategy at a particular time; the Socialist party still reflects the views of such "promotional" groups as the League of Human Rights (*Ligue des droits de l'homme*); and the anticlerical attitudes of educational associations are still embodied in official Radical-Socialist philosophy.

Such ideological affinities may sometimes be more useful to a political party than they are to an interest group. Moreover, if a group's ideological orientation is excessive, a rival association adhering to different principles may be established, with the result that a specific objective interest can no longer be effectively articulated. This has been the case in particular with student associations. Most of these associations—including SNESup, UNEF, and UEC—have been leftist, but have been divided along Trotskyist, Maoist, and "orthodox" Communist lines.[22]

Conversely, too much transideological collaboration among interest groups may conflict with the broader political aims of an "associated" party. In the past decade, all the student associations have favored increases in student subsidies, including the UEC, the Communist-sponsored union. The PCF several times "purged" the UEC because the latter had become more interested in intergenerational rather than interclass conflict; and, on a more pragmatic plane, the PCF felt that its support of the students' demands would not be appreciated by the working class, since the money for subsidies would have to be paid out of the taxes of the workers.[23] During the Fourth Republic, the SFIO, especially when it was in power, constrained the Socialist FO to re-

22. SNESup—*Syndicat national d'enseignement supérieur*, a leftist association of university teachers; UNEF—*Union nationale des étudiants de France*, a Trotskyist organization; UEC—*Union nationale des étudiants communistes de France*, allied to the PCF.
23. Richard Johnson, *The French Communist Party Versus the Students* (New Haven: Yale University Press, 1972), pp. 45 f, 53 ff.

sponsible behavior, as did the PCF with respect to the Communist CGT in 1968.[24]

There may be cases where linkage with party politicians is of benefit to an interest group. In the parliamentary election of 1968, several high officials of agricultural associations (including a former president of a regional chamber of agriculture) ran for Assembly seats as Gaullists, and a few officials ran under the labels of the PDM and FGDS.[25] But one must guard against exaggerating the benefits accruing to organized agriculture as a result of this kind of "colonization." The voice of a representative of agriculture in the Gaullist party may be drowned out by that of the nonagricultural interests; in the Opposition parties, agricultural representatives may have as inadequate a hearing as the party as a whole. Moreover, Parliament itself is now so rationalized that traditional lobbying, or even colonization, would pay questionable dividends to an interest group. While in the Fourth Republic about 30 percent of all bills introduced in the Assembly were private members' bills—many of which had originated with particular interest groups—such bills now account for less than 15 percent of the total. Since the legislative committees in the Fifth Republic Assembly are largely unspecialized, they can no longer be viewed as preserves of particular groups. The influence of interest groups upon the executive—exercised via Parliament—is equally limited, because the President need have no regard for the interests represented in Parliament when he constructs his cabinets.

The preceding discussion explains why farmers' associations, veterans' groups, and even trade unions often proclaim their independence of political parties and seek extraparliamentary access points. Thus the CFDT and the JAC, while ideologically still related to Christian democracy, both stressed their desire not to be considered the exclusive preserve of the MRP (when that party still existed).[26] The desire for autonomy has been reflected, especially since 1969, in efforts by the CFDT, UNEF, and even the CGT to avoid ideological slogans and to emphasize wages and other concrete demands. This independent stance does not, of course, mean that there is no longer any collaboration between a political party and an interest group. Occasionally, the various trade unions have joined in protest demonstrations with socialist political factions, and have cooperated with them in attempts to form an

24. Alain Bockel, *La participation des syndicats ouvriers aux fonctions économiques et sociales de l'Etat* (Paris: LGDJ, 1965), p. 222.
25. *Le Monde*, 30 June 1968.
26. Goguel and Grosser, *Politique en France*, p. 137.

enlarged "movement" on the Left. But the kind of endorsement given by the leadership of an interest group to a political party now increasingly depends on the party's specific positions. Moreover, such endorsement is not reliably translated into support of that party by the group's rank and file. Although the CGT apparatus gave nearly automatic backing to the PCF during the parliamentary election of 1973, over 40 percent of CGT members voted for other parties; and although the leadership of the CFDT generally endorsed various leftist and left-of-center candidates, more than a quarter of that union's membership voted for candidates of the government coalition—and nearly two-thirds of the members of that Catholic-inspired union voted for anti-clerical parties (see table 13). During the presidential election of 1974

Table 13
Trade Union Membership and First-Ballot Votes
In the 1973 Parliamentary Elections
(in percent)

Trade Union	PSU	Communist Party	Socialist Party	Reformers	Gaullist Coalition	Extreme Right
CGT	1	58	29	3	6	3
CFDT	11	21	30	6	27	5
FO	3	20	43	5	23	6
Unorganized	4	23	20	14	36	3

SOURCE: SOFRES poll, cited in Jean-Daniel Reynaud, "Trade Unions and Political Parties in France: Some Recent Trends," *Industrial and Labor Relations Review* 28 (January 1975): 222.

the CFDT, having clearly embraced socialism, endorsed the candidacy of Mitterrand; while the CNPF remained undecided between Chaban-Delmas and Giscard until after the first ballot—but certain business firms were reported to have made financial contributions to all three candidates![27]

The relationship between interest groups and political parties has

27. Jacqueline Grapin, "Le patronat joue son propre tierce," *Le Monde*, 27 April 1974.

been so complex as sometimes to obscure the functional distinction between the two. Strikes, demonstrations, and other tactics of group
action often involve the encouragement and participation of political
parties;[28] conversely, trade unions (notably the CGT and CFDT) participate in the formulation of party ideologies and the construction of
leftist electoral coalitions.[29] There is, however, a growing tendency for
interest groups to function separately from political parties when it
comes to concrete issues. They increasingly seek to present their points
of view by means of audiences with the President and the premier, or
by means of written communications to various members of the cabinet
and the civil service.

FUNCTIONAL REPRESENTATION AND
CONSULTATIVE ADMINISTRATION

Access of interest groups to the formal decision makers has been
highly institutionalized in France. Social and economic interests are
represented in the Social and Economic Council (originally established
at the end of the Third Republic as the Economic Council), which is
often consulted by the government in the preparation of bills involving
domestic issues. This agency of functional representation includes
among its more than 200 members delegates of trade unions, agricultural associations, business organizations, and professional groups,
as well as unaffiliated experts and civil servants.[30] The Council is supplemented by numerous advisory bodies that have proliferated around
ministries and by the regional "modernization commissions" that help
to shape the French four-year economic plan.[31] In the early 1970s there
were well over 4,000 such bodies, with more than 100 found in each
ministry (in addition to a myriad of consultative bodies attached to
departmental prefectures). The institutionalized consultative process

28. A recent example: in December 1975, the CGT, CFDT, and FEN issued a declara-
    tion jointly with the PCF and PS, and organized a common mass demonstration
    in protest against the "antisocial and repressive" policies of the government.
    Le Monde, 17 December 1975. Cf. *L'Année politique 1974*, p. 173. The evolution
    of the CFDT's ideology—e.g., its commitment, in 1976, to "anti-imperialism,
    anti-sexism, anti-racism, and anti-etatism"—has tended at once to reduce
    divergences between the CFDT and the CGT and to facilitate the adhesion of
    industrial workers in *both* unions to the Socialist party. René Mouriaux, "Le 37e
    Congrès de la CFDT," *Etudes*, July 1976, pp. 119–23.
29. Between 1972 and 1975, the CFDT acted as an "honest broker" in efforts to
    unify the PS, PSU, and PCF.
30. Meynaud, *Nouvelles études*, p. 272. This is a comprehensive work that mentions
    several hundred nationally organized interest groups.
31. See Stephen S. Cohen, *Modern Capitalist Planning: The French Model* (Cam-
    bridge, Mass.: Harvard University Press, 1969), pp. 220 ff.

has already inspired a substantial literature, which conveys the impression that policy making at the national level is a genuine partnership between the government and the private interests, and an extension of the "social partnership" said to characterize relations between labor and business. But there is inconclusive information about how often these advisory councils meet and how important is the impact of interest-group representatives on the civil servants who tend to dominate the councils. Civil servants frequently ignore the advice furnished by interest-group representatives because the government has already made up its mind about a policy, because the demands made by a particular group do not fit into the councils' frames of reference, or because the civil servants are not impressed with the qualifications of interest-group spokesmen.

In France, qualification is a very important criterion for interest-group consultation. French bureaucrats, with their highly developed notion of the public interest, consider excessive involvement of interest groups in the decision-making process as endangering both democracy and the "objective" resolution of a problem.[32] Since the civil servants' principal aim is to obtain information, and not necessarily to listen to advice, they tend to make a distinction between pressure groups, which they view as harmful, and professional associations, which have expertise and are equipped to interpret the bureaucracy's activities to the outside.[33] Such a distinction had been greatly exaggerated during the Vichy regime when, in a manner characteristic of fascist systems, the government refused to acknowledge "private" groups and dealt only with chambers and other bodies of public law that were coopted for public purposes. Today, the existence of privately organized groups is officially recognized as a sine qua non of a free society; however, the government has at the same time retained a hierarchy of "approved" organizations, with which it prefers to deal. The government prefers to consult professional orders (ordres professionnels) where possible, rather than pure interest groups (syndicats).[34] These "orders" have many tasks: the maintenance of intraprofessional standards and discipline, the control of access to the profession, the supervision of training, and finally, "consultative administration." The meaning of that term is not entirely clear. At best it refers to significant participation in rule

32. Ezra Suleiman, *Politics, Power and Bureaucracy in France* (Princeton: Princeton University Press, 1974), pp. 316–51.
33. Henry W. Ehrmann, "French Bureaucracy and Organized Interests," *Administrative Science Quarterly* 5 (1961): 534–55; and Ehrmann, "Les groupes d'intérêt et la bureaucratie dans les démocraties occidentales," *RFSP* 11 (April 1961): 541–68.
34. Bernard Chenot, *Organisation économique de l'état* (Paris: Dalloz, 1965), pp. 257 ff.

making: for example, the agreements by "national professional commit-tees on horses and mules" regarding prices, marketing, and production standards, which the Ministry of Agriculture may use as a basis for its regulations.[35] At worst, consultative administration implies a dangerous corporatization of economic interests which threatens to extend the government's control over associations and undermines the articulation of economic demands.

Corporatization may sometimes forcibly engineer interassociational cohesion; however, some interests cannot be easily corporatized because they are too large, too diverse, or too "syndicalist" in orientation. In the name of industrial democracy, the government must give such interests formal access also, but the access can be controlled. The fragmentation of, and competition among, interest groups strengthens the government's power to determine which association should be considered the "true" spokesman for a particular socioeconomic sector. Interest-group repre-sentation in bodies in which access to the decision-making authorities is highly institutionalized depends upon legitimation by the government, and this legitimation is frequently accorded on a selective basis. In some cases, the question of whether this or that association shall represent a particular interest is decided by the criterion of professionalism—and where professionalism is inadequate, by such criteria of representative-ness as an association's inclusiveness, degree of internal democracy, or even the extent to which a group is in tune with governmental policy. Thus, the Ministry of Social Affairs bargains on the matter of doctors' fees with the Federation of Medical Associations (Confédération des syndicats médicaux—CSM), rather than with another medical associa-tion, because of the CSM's professionalism. (Although the Ordre des médecins is even more professional in outlook, it is less cooperative.)[36] Similarly, the Ministry of Education bargains with the Fédération d'Edu-cation Nationale, an association of school teachers, because the FEN (which has a membership of about 500,000) is all-inclusive and not oriented toward a particular ideology (except laicism).[37] Conversely, the Ministry of Education has recognized one rather than another parents'

35. Ibid., p. 244. See also Jean-Louis Bonnefoy, ed., Aperçu sur l'administration consultative (Paris: Documentation française, 1964), Notes et études documen-taires, no. 3133.

36. Cf. Jean Meynaud, Les groupes de pression (Paris: PUF, 1962), p. 16. The Ordre des médecins suffers from the stigma of having been created during the Vichy regime and hence of being a vestige of fascist corporativism. This fact—and the Ordre's attempt to scuttle the implementation of legislation on birth control—has led the government to suggest internal reforms, and the Socialists to en-courage the establishment of a rival medical group.

37. James M. Clark, Teachers and Politics in France (Syracuse: Syracuse University Press, 1967), pp. 30 and passim.

association because it is secularly rather than confessionally oriented, and therefore more "qualified" than a rival association.[38]

Frequently, when the government has a choice, it selects as spokesmen of organized labor representatives of more tractable and less syndicalist trade unions. Since the establishment of the Fifth Republic, the number of union representatives in the Social and Economic Council has been approximately equal for the FO and CGT, although the latter has had three times as many members as the former. Both labor and agricultural associations have periodically complained about being underrepresented in the Social and Economic Council, particularly in relation to business and the civil servants. The growing "governmentalization" of the SEC is indicated by the fact that while in 1946, 8 percent of the SEC's members were individuals nominated by the government, the proportion had risen to 30 percent in the Fifth Republic.[39] In the modernization commissions dealing with the Economic Plan, trade unions are underrepresented because the Plan as a whole tends to adhere to a business rather than a union outlook and concentrates on productivity rather than wages or social policy.

Even where interest-group representation is more equitable, the input of interest groups can be minimized by the governmental practice of ignoring recommendations that do not fit into a preconceived policy framework. Thus in the late 1950s, the advice rendered by the *Conseil supérieur de l'éducation* was ignored because it differed from the ideas of the minister of education; and in the early 1960s, the government ignored the recommendations made by the multipartite committee of inquiry (the *Commission Toutée*) regarding an "incomes policy" in the public sector. The *Comité supérieur de l'emploi*, in which trade unions can theoretically make recommendations regarding manpower retraining, meets only once a year. The National Labor Relations Board, which advises the government on minimum wages and other labor-contract issues, meets more often. However, the unions claim that the government representatives on that body usually confront organized labor with a fait accompli.

Interest groups that are underrepresented or whose demands are ignored can do little but articulate their frustrations, or else boycott the advisory councils, a policy occasionally adopted by trade unions and agricultural associations (see chapter 11). If, conversely, group representatives prove amenable to a governmental policy even when it goes

38. *Le Monde*, 9 August 1972.
39. Jack Hayward, *Private Interests and Public Policy: The Experience of the French Social and Economic Council* (New York: Barnes & Noble, 1966), pp. 23–24.

against the interests of the group, the representatives are viewed by their organization as having become corrupted by the governmental aura. In that event they lose their connection with the rank and file and can no longer effectively commit their group to a policy favored by the government.

The gap between the membership and the representatives of an interest group is considerably minimized whenever the group has the power to select its own spokesmen to bodies concerned with social and economic matters, as in the case of agricultural chambers, factory councils, boards of nationalized industries, social security boards, or labor courts. Such representation is in most cases determined by elections, for which electoral lists are set up by ideologically competing associations. In the 1970 elections to the agricultural chambers, the Communist-oriented MODEF won 33 percent of the seats in those *départements* where it competed with the FNSEA, and demanded recognition as a legitimate spokesman for the farmers. Several months earlier, Jacques Duhamel, the minister of agriculture, had refused to recognize the group, asserting that "its representative character . . . in a professional sense had not been demonstrated." Eventually MODEF secured this legitimation, but not without charging that the public authorities had misreported the election results by attributing only 16.49 percent of the vote to that organization.[40]

In the competition to name trade-union representatives, the CGT has received by far the largest number of votes, the CFDT the second largest, and the FO the smallest.[41] But such a predominance may not be particularly meaningful, because the scope of decision making in advisory bodies is limited. In the factory councils, which were set up to provide opportunities for co-management, decisions tend to be limited to such mundane subjects as work shifts, lunchrooms, and factory lighting, collectively referred to as *oeuvres sociales*. Theoretically, interest-group representation in nationalized industries is much more relevant for economic decision making, because the working conditions and wages established for that sector have a "ripple effect" on the private sector. The administrative councils of most public or mixed enterprises are tripartite in composition, with the workers, the consumers and the administration represented equally. The workers' spokesmen are indeed chosen by the unions themselves, while the consumers are represented not only by consumers' and family associations but

---

40. *Le Monde*, 7–8 June 1970.
41. Cf. Gérard Adam, "La représentativité des organisations syndicales," *RFSP* 18 (April 1968): 278–307.

also by delegates of local assemblies and even members of Parliament. Frequently the so-called consumers' representatives vote on the side of the administration. Furthermore, the workers' interests may be slighted by the constant meddling of the minister of finance, who is concerned with ensuring "budgetary equilibrium" in the nationalized industries.[42]

Similar limitations appear to apply to the *conseils de prud'homme*, the special functional tribunals (modeled to some extent after the "labor courts" in West Germany) that decide disputes arising in connection with labor legislation. These tribunals include representatives of trade unions, employers' associations, and similar interested associations who participate in rendering verdicts (which are arrived at by simple majority). It is, however, not clear whether this participation is meaningful for interest groups, except in the most perfunctory sense, because each group, taken by itself, has only minority representation; because the scope of decision is narrowed by existing codes of labor law; because the presiding judge, who is not a spokesman of any interest group, has considerable prestige and can often sway the "lay assessors"; and finally, because decisions rendered by the tribunals can be appealed to, and reversed by, ordinary courts.

Hence it is not surprising that workers' participation in the elections to the *conseils de prud'homme* is seldom higher than 25 percent.[43] Participation in the elections of trade-union representatives to the social security boards (*caisses*), which administer health-insurance programs and family subsidies, is somewhat higher, but the elections do not generate great interest. This has been true especially since 1967, when the representation ratio favorable to trade unionists was abolished and parity of representation was granted to the employers—in effect giving the latter control over the boards. (Curiously, the trade unions did not mount loud protests against the change.)[44] If trade-union input was in the past taken seriously within these boards, it may have been due to the fact that a particular union had privileged access to a party in Parliament that could help alter in the unions' favor the legislation under which the boards operated. But until 1973, the unions most strongly represented on the boards, the CGT and the CFDT, had no such assistance because "their" respective parties were insignificantly represented in the Assembly.

---

42. Bockel, *Participation des syndicats ouvriers*, pp. 237–38.
43. William H. McPherson and Frederick Meyers, *The French Labor Courts: Judgment by Peers* (Urbana, Ill.: University of Illinois Press, 1966), pp. 62–63.
44. Peter Coffey, *The Social Economy of France* (London: Macmillan, 1973), pp. 25–26.

PROSPECTS AND LIMITS OF GROUP POLITICS

An interest group becomes less dependent upon the intercession of a political party (or a local notable) if it is powerful enough to react to governmental economic policies by striking, interfering in the work of the tax collector, or influencing election outcomes. The exercise of such power becomes more credible when a group acquires a sizable membership; but by such growth the group transforms itself from an articulative into a largely aggregative instrument. The constituent associations of the FNSEA, and even more of the Chamber of Agriculture, represent such a multiplicity of clashing agricultural perspectives—farm laborers, large landowners, marketing cooperatives, vintners, and dairymen—that *the* agricultural interest can no longer be clearly expressed. Similarly, the competition for size has caused trade unions to include in their ranks blue-collar, white-collar, and professional members, and even foreign workers. This admixture of members tends to blunt the cutting edge of a union's most radical elements. In order to project dynamism *and* retain its internal unity, an interest group may concern itself with general political issues—e.g., UNEF's fight against the war in Algeria, and the CGT's stand against NATO in the late 1940s and against promoting a revolution in 1968. But any interest group that underemphasizes concrete economic issues in favor of general political ones (especially if the position taken is in opposition to government policy) runs the risk of not being taken seriously as an issue spokesman or bargaining partner by the government.

It can be asserted that an interest group today has greater legitimation and more secure access to the public authorities if its basic aims are roughly in accordance with—or encapsulated in—the policy orientations of the executive, as in the case of big business, big agriculture, and perhaps clerical groups. Since the beginning of the Fifth Republic, finance ministers have been close to business as an economic sector, though they were not specifically the "patrons" of the CNPF. Furthermore, the teams of officials serving other ministries have included a number of men temporarily coopted from business, many of whom, like the career bureaucrats, have been graduates of the National School of Administration. This relationship has led to the abandonment by business of its old view of the government as the enemy and has made the CNPF publicly receptive to social goals embraced by the government, such as improved factory conditions, job security, and worker participation in certain aspects of management.[45]

45. On the "patronat de gauche," see Pierre Drouin, "Un timide 'aggiornamento,'" *Le Monde*, 11 July 1968; and Jacqueline Grapin, "Le patronat après les élections," *Le Monde*, 21 March 1973.

Conversely, some interest groups—despite the fact that these, too, are partly institutionalized—have been unsuccessful in their "lobbying" efforts, to the extent that their goals do not correspond with those of the governmental decision makers. There has been the failure of the veterans' organizations to get pensions restored, probably because of the government's businesslike (and therefore negative) attitude to the non-productive sector; the failure of agricultural associations to obtain meaningful economic support for family farmers, because of a new emphasis on agricultural competitiveness; the failure of the alcohol lobby to secure tax exemptions, because of the government's concern about alcoholism;[46] the failure of the anticlerical associations to prevent passage of the *Loi Debré* (in 1959) by which the government can make educational "contracts" with parochial schools, because of the Gaullists' interest in retaining the loyalty of the Catholic sector;[47] and the failure of the trade unions to secure wage increases sufficiently commensurate with the rise in the cost of living and—until 1968—to obtain the right to organize in the factories. It is possible to interpret the extension of factory democracy since 1975 as a victory of organized labor, and especially of the CFDT. But such new measures are due less to effective "lobbying" in the conventional American sense than to the government's desire to depoliticize the conflict between management and labor and thus partially to escape the onus for failing to pursue a sufficiently redistributive economic policy.

The access of trade unions is restricted to the extent to which their orientation is seen to be syndicalist and therefore antistatist. Similarly, the bureaucracy has not been very accommodating to the organizations representing small businessmen because of their hostility to government efforts at economic modernization. This remains true despite the fact that there exists a Ministry for Small Business, which was created by President Pompidou in the early 1970s largely for electoral reasons.

The government's policy of retraining redundant agricultural labor-ers in the mid-1960s was attributed to the presence of agricultural associations in planning and other advisory councils;[48] and the granting of low-interest loans for agricultural modernization and the improve-ment of social security coverage for farmers in the early 1970s were

46. Cf. Bernard E. Brown, "Pressure Politics in the Fifth Republic," *Journal of Politics*, August 1963, cited in *Comparative Politics: Notes and Readings*, ed. Macridis and Brown (Homewood, Ill.; Dorsey, 1964), p. 162.
47. See the comprehensive account in Joseph Franceschi, *Les groupes de pression dans la défense de l'enseignement public* (Paris: Librairies techniques, 1964).
48. Jacques-Noel Chatanay, "Participation des agriculteurs à l'élaboration du Ve Plan," *Revue de l'Action populaire*, no. 193 (December 1965): 1185–95.

interpreted as a victory of M. Debatisse, the president of the FNSEA.[49] In large measure, the successes of the "farm lobby" have been due less to institutionalized access of the FNSEA than to the fact that most officials of that organization have been mayors or members of municipal councils, and some have been deputies.[50] The linkage between FNSEA and certain Centrist politicians could not completely compensate for the undercurrent of that organization's hostility toward de Gaulle, because the Centrists remained in the opposition until the General's resignation. The FNSEA's weakness was reflected in the fact that the increased fiscal outlays for agriculture, particularly in 1965–66, were earmarked more for the consolidation of landholdings than for social investments, and benefited principally the big farmers.[51] Even after de Gaulle's departure, governmental measures have generally been insufficient to counteract the rural exodus or resolve the question of the lagging incomes of farmers because of the government's determination to promote a policy of "structural modernization" of agriculture.

The problem of neglected interests is particularly acute in the case of groups that pursue a goal that runs counter to the national culture—e.g., the Breton or Basque cultural and autonomist groups. Their access is hampered by lack of a patron party in Parliament as well as by the monolithic notions of French culture that pervade the intellectual and political elite.

In France (as elsewhere in Western Europe) interest groups may be weak also because of their "abnormal" origins. It is frequently asserted that in liberal democracies interest groups arise when a collection of individuals recognizes a common, "objective" economic interest that must be protected against adverse governmental policy. Some interest groups have indeed arisen in this voluntaristic, "Anglo-American" way; while others—e.g., MODEF, UEC, and the Union des femmes françaises —were created by the PCF as ancillary organizations.[52] Some, like the National Federation of Social Security Organizations (FNOSS), have arisen in consequence of novel administrative arrangements which have produced new categories of quasi-public professionals;[53] and others

49. Le Monde, 1–2 October 1972.
50. Tavernier, Syndicalisme paysan, p. 74.
51. See Philippe Tallois, "Les politiques agricoles de la Ve République," Revue politique et parlementaire, October 1969, pp. 29–36.
52. Meynaud, Groupes de pression, p. 46.
53. FNOSS—Fédération nationale des organisations de sécurité sociale, a roof organization embracing several associations of specialists administering governmentally established programs of health insurance, children's subsidies, retirement benefits, etc.

again—e.g., the French Confederation of Labor (CFT)—have been created by (or with the encouragement of) the government. Fifth Republic governments, which have not been close to organized labor, have realized that in multipartite bodies there must be *some* representation of the workers.[54] It was hoped that the CFT would provide a workingman's input that was pro-system and otherwise convenient for the conservative political establishment.[55]

If an interest group adjusts its general ideology and moderates its demands, it is rewarded by legitimation and by a privileged position within the consultative structures of the public authorities, but the result is an even further reduction of its power to bargain autonomously. Such a reduction might not be too great a price to pay if functional or quasi-institutionalized representation provided meaningful political participation for interest groups. Unfortunately, many forms of access accorded to the groups have been neither meaningful nor equitable (see table 14). Given these weaknesses, interest groups that refuse to be coopted or "corporatized" become even more powerless, since, with the relative deparliamentarization of decision making, there are few alternative access routes.

In federal countries such as the United States, West Germany, and Switzerland, and even in unitary Britain (with its tradition of significant decision making at county levels), inadequate access to national authority structures can frequently be compensated for by interest-group activities at provincial or local levels. In France, with her centralistic tradition, locally oriented group activities are often of doubtful value. In many localities there are *syndicats d'initiative*, organizations of hotelkeepers and other entrepreneurs that, like American chambers of commerce, suggest ways of improving the local business climate and of enticing tourists. In recent years, volunteer civic associations (*groupes d'animation municipale*) have been established in a large number of cities. Composed of interest-group representatives and unaffiliated citizens, these associations have tried to infuse dynamism into the city councils; but their success has been limited owing to the cities' great financial dependence upon the national government (see chapter 9).

In view of all the obstacles to effective interest-group politics, it is not surprising that (according to a poll conducted in 1963), 49 percent of Frenchmen felt that they could not rely on any interest group to

54. See Bockel, *Participation des syndicats ouvriers*, pp. 19, 427.
55. The CFT (*Confédération française de travail*), which until recently was considered Gaullist in orientation, has tended to organize immigrant workers and "scabs," particularly in the private automobile industry.

Table 14
Interest Groups and Decision-Making Institutions

Form of Access	Political Institution	Weaknesses
Audiences with interest-group spokesmen	President, Premier	Unreliable, episodic, selective
Multipartite negotiations or agreements	Cabinet	Agreements may be ignored or fail to be fully implemented
Advisory councils	Bureaucracy	Advice is often ignored
Occasional colonization via party linkages	Parliament	Specific weaknesses of legislative committees, which are no longer a preserve of groups; general weakness of Parliament
Ideological connections	Political parties	Parties are becoming more aggregative
	Social and Economic Council	Growing preponderance of government representatives; role is consultative only
Direct representation	Economic planning commissions	Frame of reference is restricted; unequal representation
	Social security boards	Reduction of scope of decision making
	Specialized tribunals (*Conseils de prud'homme*)	Minority representation of interest groups

promote their aims.[56] The result of frustrated interest-group access is a growth of spontaneous or extrainstitutional political action exemplified by general strikes, street demonstrations, and violence. The frequent wildcat strikes of the workers, the blocking by farmers of the doors of the Ministry of Agriculture in 1962, the dumping of such valuable prod-

56. *Sondages*, no. 2 (1963).

uce as truffles by farmers disgruntled with the agricultural price structure, the Breton farmers' brandishing of pitchforks to "welcome" tax
collectors, the violence against tax collectors committed by provincial
shopkeepers in 1970, and the May Events of 1968—all these are manifestations of the frustration of interest articulation by normal means.[57]

Occasionally, such extrainstitutional agitation may soften up the
authorities and accomplish goals desired by interest groups that could
not be accomplished by "ordinary" access. Thus the general strike of
two million workers in 1936 resulted in the Matignon Accord of that
year in which the government, the unions, and management leaders
agreed to workers' demands for comprehensive collective contracts; and
the general strike of 1968 resulted in the Grenelle Accord, which provided for significant wage increases. Similarly, the imposition of a 12
percent import tax on cheap Italian wines in 1975 was a victory for the
French winegrower. In this case, the government moved not in response
to successful lobbying by the vintners' associations, but in order to
terminate the violence associated with the vintners' "direct action." The
government may also react by hardening its attitudes. The "Anti-
Breakers' Law" passed in 1970 subjects the organizers and activists of
mass demonstrations in certain cases to criminal penalties, thus restricting even extrainstitutional interest articulation.

The foregoing presentation of the institutional difficulties standing
in the way of interest-group politics conforms to some extent to the
"administrative action" model, in which society is "stalemated" and in
which whatever policy is produced emerges from "intrasystemic" (i.e.,
intragovernmental) inputs, occasionally supplemented by crisis-resolving
mass violence.[58] This model applies to some extent to all industrial
democracies; conversely, it is not always applicable to France. Many
French policies in the Fourth and Fifth republics have been the results
of incremental and pluralist approaches, involving compromises among
legislators, parties, interest groups, civil servants, and the executive. The
value-added tax policy of the early 1960s took into account the pressures
of small and medium-sized business; the university reforms of 1968
involved the ideas of Education Minister Edgar Faure as well as those
of the teachers' and students' unions,[59] and some of the agricultural

57. See Henry W. Ehrmann, *Politics in France* (2nd ed.; Boston: Little, Brown, 1971),
    pp. 192–94.
58. See Martin Heisler, "Patterns of European Politics: The 'European Polity' Model,"
    in *Politics in Europe*, ed. Heisler (New York: McKay, 1974), pp. 38 ff.
59. See Jacques Fomerand, "Policy Formulation and Change in Gaullist France: the
    1968 Orientation Act of Higher Education," *Comparative Politics* 8 (October
    1975): 59–89.

policies of the 1960s and 1970s were compromises between the government and the farmers' associations.

Since the accession of Giscard d'Estaing to the Presidency, the image of interest groups has improved, and no efforts have been contemplated to restrict their establishment or activities.[60] The *encadrement* (i.e., institutionalized encapsulation) of interest groups in advisory and planning councils, which had been contrived in preceding regimes, has been retained. But this *encadrement* now appears to have far less restrictive consequences for interest groups than in previous years, because Giscard's brand of liberalism (or neo-liberalism) presupposes economic policy making on the basis of genuine dialogues between the government and the groups. In contrast to de Gaulle's disdain for intermediaries and Pompidou's business bias, Giscard's pattern is to encourage interest groups to fashion their own agreements[61] and to supplement these by frequent consultation with the heads of trade unions and agricultural associations.[62] Such dialogues help to arrest tendencies to uprisings on the part of workers and farmers who have been caught in the vise of inflation, dislocation, and unemployment.

60. A notable exception is the army. Attempts made in 1975—with the alleged encouragement of the CFDT and left-wing parties—by the 330,000 soldiers (mostly draftees) to unionize have been strenuously opposed by the government.
61. Examples are the *accord-cadre* signed by the CNPF and various unions in October 1974, regarding the continued payment of wages to dismissed workers, and a similar accord on the improvement of working conditions signed in March 1975. Both agreements were subsequently "ratified" by parliamentary legislation.
62. *Le Monde*, 18 March 1975.

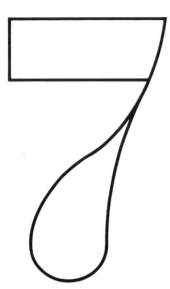

Instruments and Patterns of Decision Making: The Executive

Western democratic regimes usually conform to one of two models. The first is a parliamentary system in which there is an executive composed of two "units": a monarch or a figurehead President, and a prime minister and his cabinet, the latter two selected by, and ultimately responsible to, a Parliament. The alternative is a presidential system in which a President who is popularly elected functions as both the chief of state and the head of government and is independent of the legislative branch of the government, and in which both branches cooperate and balance each other.

In terms of both tradition and the political institutions mentioned in its Constitution, the Fifth Republic is a hybrid system, embodying features of standard continental parliamentary democracies and of various types of presidentialism. Parliament, however, occupies a secondary place in the system, and was put there for the sake of French custom as well as in order to appease certain non-Gaullist members of the Constitutional Consultative Committee. These members, knowing de Gaulle's ideas as expressed in the famous Bayeux speech of June 16, 1946, feared that he might set up a dictatorial regime.

On June 1, 1958, the Assembly invested de Gaulle as prime minister (by a vote of 329 to 224) after he had assured the deputies that, at the age of sixty-seven, he would hardly be likely to launch a career as a dictator. Nevertheless, there was some question in the minds of the deputies as to whether they could absolutely depend upon such assurance. Hence the Parliament, in authorizing de Gaulle to draft a new constitution, passed a law that obliged him to retain in it the separation of the President's from the premier's office, as well as provisions making the premier and the cabinet responsible before Parliament. Yet the Fifth Republic Constitution was tailor-made for de Gaulle, with the clear assumption that he would be its first President, and it is the Presidency that is the cornerstone of the political edifice of the Fifth Republic. The President is mentioned first in the Constitution and the legislature second, a reversal of the order of the Fourth Republic's Constitution.

THE POSITION OF THE PRESIDENT

The President in France is extremely powerful and virtually independent of other branches of government. His term of office is seven years, as it had been in the two previous republics. Whereas in the Fourth Republic a President was limited to two terms, there is today no such limitation. In previous republics, the President was elected by Parliament, was subject to its controls and pressures, and did not possess an independent popular mandate. In the Fifth Republic, the President was until 1962 chosen by an electoral college composed—much in the manner of the electoral college for the French Senate—of members of Parliament and municipal councils; thereafter, his election has been by direct, popular vote. The President appoints the prime minister, presides over the cabinet, initiates referenda, and dissolves the National Assembly.

A number of labels have been used to describe the special character of the Fifth Republic, such as principate, elective monarchy, and plebiscitarian monocracy. The system is similar to that which prevails today in Austria, Finland, Ireland, and Iceland, in that the President is popularly elected. But in these countries the President is in fact much weaker than their respective constitutions would suggest, because his role is circumscribed by his being subject to ouster by Parliament (as in Iceland), by the strong legislative powers that Parliament possesses (as in Finland), or by the role of strong, disciplined parties (as in Austria). The French President, in contrast, suffers from none of these limitations. He is like the President in Weimar Germany in that he is granted special emergency powers as well as the right of dissolution, and in that, theoretically, he is one part of the "bicephalous" executive; that is, he shares power with a prime minister. But he is like the American President in that he "reigns as well as rules." He is like an elective monarch: he possesses, in theory and in practice, all the powers that the English queen now possesses only in theory.

But he can also be compared to an Orleanist monarch—albeit an elective one—rather than to a British monarch, because, like Louis Philippe after the revolution of July 1830, he has an important political influence that tends to be nationalistic, conservative, and (at least until 1974) Catholic. In order for him to assert power effectively, the king had insisted on having a cabinet that enjoyed his confidence rather than that of an elected assembly. Like Louis Philippe, de Gaulle did accord a place to an elected assembly—but he wanted to see it counterbalanced by the traditional (conservative) pillars of society—i.e., the provincial elite that in the early Gaullist regime was expected to be reflected in the Senate, as it had been during the July Monarchy.[1]

The President is the head of state—in fact, "the highest authority of the state"; the guarantor of national independence; the individual chiefly responsible for seeing that the Constitution is observed; the person who ensures the "functioning of governmental authorities"; the "arbiter" over political and institutional conflicts; the principal appointive officer; diplomatic negotiator; and the commander-in-chief of the armed forces. He is also the "guide of France"; he is "in charge of the destiny of France and the Republic"; and he is "the inspirer and orienter of national actions."[2] He conveys general principles of policy to the people and Parliament by means of presidential messages; he has the right of pardon and reprieve; and his signature is necessary in order for acts of Parliament to be valid. He is, in addition, like a monarch in that he is aloof and above political battles—in theory he does not demean himself by overt identification with political parties—and in that he represents the continuity of the state.

The presidential "mediation" role was intended to apply primarily to the areas of defense and foreign affairs. The Third Republic Constitution (Article 8, Law of July 16, 1875) specifically granted the President the initiative in foreign affairs, e.g., in the negotiation of treaties, and early Third Republic presidents had a voice in choosing the foreign minister. Presidential power to make foreign policy atrophied, especially after World War I, when President Poincaré left Premier Clémenceau free to negotiate the Versailles Treaty. The Fourth Republic Constitution merely said that the President was to be "informed" about international negotiations, and that he signed treaties. In the Fifth Republic, the President negotiates *and* signs treaties (Article 52).[3] Since (under Article 15) the President is commander-in-chief of the armed forces, he has

1. Maurice Duverger, *Institutions politiques et droit constitutionnel* (11th ed.; Paris: PUF, 1970), p. 731.
2. Radio address by General de Gaulle, 20 September 1962.
3. See François Goguel and Alfred Grosser, *La Politique en France* (Paris: Colin, 1964), p. 206.

always taken defense *policy* as his own domain. For a number of reasons, most Frenchmen accepted de Gaulle's predominance in the two areas of defense and foreign affairs. In the first place, the precedent of continuity in foreign policy had already been set in the Fourth Republic, when, in the face of constant reshuffling of cabinets and premiers, there was remarkable stability in the Foreign Ministry: while there were seventeen premiers (in twenty-three governments), there were only eight foreign ministers. Second, de Gaulle came to power largely because the premiers under the Fourth Republic's institutional arrangements had been unable to solve the Algerian problem. If one of the principal reasons for calling upon de Gaulle was to solve that problem, he had to be given a relatively free hand. Third, implicit in de Gaulle's political philosophy was the reassertion of the international role of France, a position that would necessitate a strong executive.

Although the Presidency is associated with other institutions, in fact, all those for which there are specific headings in the Constitution, these institutions are relatively impotent to check the presidential office, and tend to be under the President's control. The Constitution provides that the President chooses the prime minister, and then ratifies or confirms the premier's selection of his cabinet colleagues. A rigid interpretation of the Constitution would have it that, once the cabinet is constituted, the President cannot dismiss it, but Parliament can. However, parliamentary dismissal of the cabinet is difficult and fraught with political risks to the deputies, because the Assembly itself is subject to dissolution by the President. Certain bills, constitutional amendments, referenda, and the invocation of emergency powers involve the consultation of the Constitutional Council, but three of its nine members, including its presiding officer, are appointed by the President. One of the few national institutions that would seem to be independent of the President is the Social and Economic Council; that body, however, has only consultative powers.

THE PREMIER

Many of the powers the premier possessed in the Fourth Republic are now, either in theory or in practice, possessed by the President. In the Fourth Republic, the President "presided" over cabinet meetings during ceremonial occasions, but the premier was the real chairman of the cabinet. In the Fifth Republic, the premier is merely the "head of the government," while the President is the actual decision maker. He leaves to the premier the role of being a link between the Presidency and the Parliament, particularly on matters in which the President is not interested. Thus the premier's position is almost analogous to that of the provincial prefect in France, who provides a linkage between the national government and the municipal mayor and council. The President, rather than the premier, makes all decisions in the "reserved domain," which includes, besides foreign policy and defense, constitutional concerns and whatever else may attain great importance in an ad hoc sense, such as sensitive social or economic problems. When these latter cease to be headline issues, they devolve upon the ministers.[4] Significant policy decisions made by the President have included Algerian independence in 1962, the withdrawal of France from the integrated command of NATO in 1966, the embargo on military supplies to certain Mideast countries in 1967, the blocking of British entry into the Common Market in 1963 and 1966, the initiation of constitutional amendments in 1962 and 1969, the devaluations of the franc in 1969 and in 1971, and the reduction of petroleum imports in 1974.

The long list of presidential powers and decisions would appear to be so exhaustive that the notion of the "dual executive" is a myth, at least in terms of a sharing of powers. True, the Constitution allows some independence to the premier once he has been appointed because, according to a strict interpretation, only the Assembly, and not the President, can get rid of the premier. Moreover, according to the Constitution, the premier has a respectable number of powers and responsibilities. He is expected to manage government bills and see them safely through Parliament; but his task is facilitated by the short sessions of Parliament, the government's (i.e., the President's) control over the agenda, and the presidential threat of dissolution. The premier prepares budget bills; he defends government policy in Parliament and answers parliamentary questions. And he—as well as the other ministers—supervises the work of the ministries and departments and the civil servants who staff them; he also issues regulations for the ministries. But these regulations can be vetoed by the President. Furthermore, the premier's control over the ministries is somewhat limited by the fact that the President may take direct charge of the work of some ministries, and may ignore the cabinet.

Some presidential decisions have not required cabinet input or participation at all, such as decisions on the dissolution of the Assembly, and the invocation of Article 16 (see page 167). Although in these two cases the consultation of the premier is mandatory, such consultation probably has little meaning beyond the requirement that the premier be

4. Michel-Henri Fabre, *Principes républicains de droit constitutionnel* (2nd ed.; Paris: LGDJ, 1970), p. 371.

informed of the President's intentions: if the premier should object, the President could react in the same way that President Lincoln was said to have reacted when his seven-member cabinet unanimously voted against a policy he had embraced: "seven nays, one aye; the ayes have it."

At a press conference in January 1964, de Gaulle said that "it cannot be accepted that a diarchy exist at the top."[5] He considered that he was free to listen to or to ignore his premier, and, in fact, to replace him. It has been asserted that this attitude about presidential monopoly, which prevailed from 1958 to 1963, was subsequently modified by the development of a more genuine "co-pilotage" between President and premier, in the sense that de Gaulle withdrew from clearly articulated leadership in domestic affairs and gave his premier a freer hand in this area.[6] It has also been argued that the role of the premier under de Gaulle's immediate successor had increased because Pompidou lacked de Gaulle's charisma, did not have to face the same domestic and foreign policy problems (e.g., the May Events or Algeria), and, having been "victimized" by his powerlessness when he was premier, would not, in turn, as President become the victimizer. But Pompidou as President fully shared his predecessor's attitude to the premier. At a press conference on March 16, 1972, Pompidou outlined in the following way what he required of his premier: (1) he must have ideas which correspond as closely as possible to those of the President; (2) he must completely accept the institutions of the Fifth Republic, meaning the preeminence of the chief of state in matters of general policy direction and in the most important decisions; (3) "he must be capable of carrying out his own duties—a heavy load . . . since it means not only directing daily policy, but also . . . being responsible for government policy before the Assembly and the Parliament; and, finally, carrying out relations with the Majority.'"[7] President Giscard d'Estaing appears to have endorsed unreservedly the ideas of his predecessors. In a televised interview in June 1976, he insisted that he alone determined basic policies, and viewed his premier as a "loyal and active" spokesman for them.[8]

From the lack of independence of the premier's office it might be inferred that premiers of the Fifth Republic have been nonentities chosen with the same kind of care for their lack of political ambition or

5. *Major Addresses, Statements and Press Conferences of General Charles de Gaulle,*
   1958–1964 (New York: French Embassy, 1964), p. 248.
6. Fabre, *Principes républicains*, p. 347.
7. Ambassade de France, Service de Presse et d'Information, *Bulletin 72/65*, p. 13.
8. *New York Times*, 17 June 1976.

sagacity that was used for the selection of Third Republic Presidents. But all premiers thus far have been highly educated and prestigious individuals, with wide governmental experience either in elective office or the civil service. They have been selected because of their qualifications, their political backgrounds, and their precise suitability to the presidential temper.

The original party allegiances of the premiers has been diverse: Michel Debré and Jacques Chaban-Delmas were Radical Socialists in the early years of the Fourth Republic; Georges Pompidou and Pierre Messmer had been briefly affiliated with the Socialist party; while the backgrounds of Maurice Couve de Murville, Jacques Chirac, and Raymond Barre could be considered genuinely "nonpolitical." Debré, before he became premier, had been a senator, a civil servant, a writer, and an important ideologist of Gaullism, and one of the chief architects of the new Constitution. Pompidou had been by turns a professor of literature at a Parisian *lycée*, a member of de Gaulle's "kitchen cabinet" in 1945, a civil servant, and a director of the Rothschild banking house. Couve de Murville had been a respected professional civil servant and had served as de Gaulle's foreign minister for several years. Chaban-Delmas had been a hero of the Resistance, mayor of Bordeaux (a position he still holds), and speaker of the Assembly. Messmer had been a civil servant, cabinet member, and colonial "troubleshooter." Chirac had held a number of important civil service positions and, after 1968, a variety of cabinet posts. Barre, a professional economist, had been minister of foreign trade.

All the premiers until August 1976 had been loyal Gaullists; all had been prominent in either the Resistance or the Free French movement (except for Pompidou, who sat out World War II and the Occupation in Paris, and Chirac, who was too young) or else had had close personal relations with de Gaulle; and all but one had experience in the government bureaucracy. Four premiers have had parliamentary experience—Debré, Chaban-Delmas, Messmer, and Chirac—and three—Pompidou, Couve de Murville, and Barre—have not, although in 1968 Couve tried unsuccessfully to run for a seat in Parliament in a Paris constituency. Moreover, all have stood for a theme considered politically desirable by the incumbent President. Debré, the orthodox Gaullist, helped to launch the new regime he had done so much to shape; Pompidou represented a technocratic outlook and a business orientation; Couve de Murville, clearly an interim premier, represented nonpartisanship; Chaban, in view of his Radical-Socialist background, was chosen to appeal to the Center forces with his quest for a "new society"; Messmer, a conservative Gaullist, was installed largely for the purpose of retrieving the support of orthodox adherents of Gaullism; and Chirac was chosen because he combined a background of Gaullism and technocracy and had the wisdom to prefer Giscard d'Estaing over Chaban-Delmas in the first ballot of the presidential election of 1974. Barre was chosen ostensibly because of his technocratic orientation and lack of political ambition. Despite their obvious qualifications, however, the premiers have all taken a back seat to the Presidency and have had a somewhat groveling relationship to the President. In the case of a number of premiers, political genuflection was probably calculated behavior; it might be assumed that they were prepared to play second fiddle in the hope of someday succeeding to the Presidency (as Pompidou had done).[9]

In view of the relative devaluation of the premiership it has been suggested that the office be abolished altogether—and that the powers of the President be reduced. The Club Moulin some years ago proposed that the premier be replaced by a vice president (or assistant to the President) much like the American prototype. But there are at least three reasons why no French President—if he is a Gaullist or shares the Gaullist view of the Presidency—would accept such a reform. The vice president would run together with the President, be his political shadow and possible successor, share the plebiscitarian mandate with the President, and politically compete with him, a situation as unacceptable to the present chief of state as it was to de Gaulle and Pompidou (see page 293). It would be a violation of the French republican tradition, which has always had a dual executive; and it would look like an obvious imitation of the United States.

THE CABINET

In terms of size, if not power, the typical Fifth Republic cabinet resembles those of earlier French regimes. It has ranged from twenty-four members under the provisional premiership of General de Gaulle in July 1958 to forty-three under Premier Chirac in January 1976. The nature and distribution of ministerial portfolios have reflected the problems and pressures of the day. In the Fourth Republic, ministerial posts were established for Veterans' Affairs, Colonies, and even Algerian Affairs. Under de Gaulle's Presidency, ministries for Cultural

9. Cf. Pierre Viansson-Ponté, *Lettre ouverte aux hommes politiques* (Paris: Albin Michel, 1976), pp. 69–87, 120–26. The author is particularly harsh in his judgments of Debré, who frequently changed his policy positions, and Chirac, who is depicted as an "apolitical" person who might easily have become a Socialist instead of a "Gaullist," had circumstances been different.

Affairs, Scientific Research, Information, and International Cooperation were created. De Gaulle's first Fifth Republic cabinet also included a Minister for Overseas France, in order to provide a spokesman for the former French colonies in Africa that were components of the "French Community" (until the early 1960s, when most of them opted for complete independence). President Pompidou established a Ministry for Craftsmen and Small Businessmen, and President Giscard d'Estaing added a Ministry for the Quality of Life. France does not have a "patron" ministry for Bretons or Basques that would be analogous to the British ministries for Scottish or Welsh affairs; nor is she likely to have such a ministry, given her refusal to recognize these ethnic groups as deserving special government attention.

Although occasionally a person may be coopted from the world of business or banking, a cabinet like that of President Eisenhower, which consisted of "nine millionaires and a plumber," would be unthinkable in France. Whereas in the United States, an intellectual as cabinet member is a rarity, the typical French cabinet since the Third Republic has included a high proportion of university and *lycée* professors and freelance intellectuals. In Fifth Republic cabinets there has been a significant proportion of graduates of the elite schools. For example, ten of the fifteen full ministers in the Chirac government were graduates of the *grandes écoles*.[10]

As in previous republics, each cabinet minister has the specific functions of supervising the civil servants in his particular ministry (which may include several departments or agencies), of developing policy in his domain, of helping to draft bills and steer them through Parliament, of providing expertise to the cabinet, and of defending government policy touching upon his jurisdiction. The cabinet reflects a complex hierarchy of titles and positions, indicating both the importance of a portfolio and the political position of the minister. At the top are the full ministers—among them the ministers of Finance, Defense, Foreign Affairs, Justice, Interior, and Education. (Occasionally the title "Minister of State" may be granted to a full minister in order to indicate his special relationship to the President—as in the case of André Malraux under de Gaulle and Jean Lecanuet, Michel Poniatowski and (since August 1976) Olivier Guichard under Giscard. Below the ministers are the secretaries of state ("junior ministers"), of whom there are two categories: those who are autonomous (i.e., have their own departments), and those who are attached to the premier's office or to that of

10. Three graduated from ENA (Premier Chirac, Interior Minister Poniatowski, and Finance Minister Fourcade), and four from the *Institut d'Etudes Politiques*.

a full minister.[11] For example, in the Chirac government constituted in May 1974, the secretary of state for Posts and Telecommunications was autonomous; the secretary of state for the Condition of Women was attached to the premier's office; and the secretary of state for Preschool Education, to the minister of education. Occasionally, a junior minister may acquire great importance, as in the case of Mme. Alice Saunier-Seité, appointed in January 1976 as secretary of state for Universities: she has borne the chief onus for the most recent university reforms.

The principle of collective cabinet responsibility has been retained, that is, the notion that individual cabinet members must publicly agree with the general cabinet position on all issues. This principle was often violated in the Fourth Republic because cabinets were coalitions of great ideological eclecticism, and political parties frequently insisted that their representatives in the cabinet stand by the party's position on specific issues against the inclinations of members of other parties in the cabinet. Moreover, ambitious ministers were sometimes interested in deliberately creating cabinet disunity, so that a cabinet would collapse, and they would, they hoped, be able to move up when it was reconstituted—move, for example, from the Ministry of Finance or Labor to the premiership. If, after a reshuffle, ministers did not get a cabinet post at all, they did not lose everything, since they retained their parliamentary seats. In the Fifth Republic, an ousted cabinet minister, even though he may have been recruited from Parliament, has no formal right to return to it. The ideological diversity that had given rise to cabinet disunity can be easily avoided today, since cabinet making does not depend any longer, at least in principle, upon party alignments in Parliament.

What power does the cabinet have? In the Fourth Republic, the cabinet was as powerful as the premier; however, the premier's position was insecure because Parliament was so jealous of its prerogatives that it was hesitant about granting meaningful decision-making powers to him—and tended to oust premiers who asserted themselves too much. In the Fifth Republic, premiers and cabinet members are relatively powerless because the President is jealous of *his* prerogatives; hence the constitutional provision (Article 20) giving the "government" policy-making power is less a serious prescription for "co-pilotage" than it is "a vestige of the parliamentary phase of French politics."[12] Since premiers and cabinets do not depend so much upon the support

11. The "pecking order" established by protocol (and not based on relative political power) has remained virtually the same as in the Fourth Republic: President of the Republic, premier, president of the Senate, speaker of the Assembly, and finally, the rest of the cabinet.
12. Pierre Avril, *Le régime politique de la Ve République*, (Paris: LGDJ, 1967), p. 43.

of Parliament as upon that of the President, the role of the cabinet is more often than not that of a sounding board for presidential ideas. This is especially true of foreign affairs, which, particularly in the early 1960s, were hardly ever the object of discussion in the cabinet. While de Gaulle was President and Couve de Murville foreign minister, the other ministers would simply listen to an exposé by the latter that reflected the former's ideas. Furthermore, the cabinet and premier today share whatever power they have with other bodies, such as the staff of the presidential office, or with "gray eminences" or personal friends of the President who are part of a "kitchen cabinet."

That is why the frequency of cabinet meetings is in itself no indication of the extent to which the President consults his ministers when he makes a decision. The custom prevailing in the Third and Fourth republics of having frequent meetings of an "inner cabinet" of a half-dozen ministers was abandoned under the Presidency of de Gaulle, and there were a significant number of meetings of the full cabinet (including secretaries of state). But it was soon apparent that cabinet meetings involving nearly thirty ministers were inefficient, and such meetings were therefore convened mainly for ceremonial purposes. In order to streamline discussions, de Gaulle and his successors have tended to follow the British example in excluding junior ministers from cabinet meetings, save for individuals of that rank who are invited when problems in their specific domains are being discussed. Furthermore, the custom arose of establishing interministerial committees (*conseils* or *comités restreints*), in which the President, but not the entire cabinet, would participate. Some of these committees, such as the Committee on National Defense or the Committee on Foreign Affairs, took on a permanent character, while others remained ad hoc. Between 1958 and 1965 there were more meetings of interministerial committees than of the cabinet.[13] At a press conference on September 9, 1965, de Gaulle, in trying to prove that he did not act merely on the basis of counsel with himself, said that in his first term of office (1958–65) he had 302 meetings with the cabinet and 420 meetings with interministerial committees; he received the premier in his office 605 times, the president of the Assembly 78 times, and individual ministers 2,000 times. In addition, he had about 1,500 meetings with experts, civil servants, or officials of associations.[14] These consultative practices, which gave de Gaulle a great deal of free-

13. Duverger, *Institutions Politiques*, p. 687. For a more detailed treatment of the composition and functions of ministries, see Jean-Dominique and Pascale Antoni, *Les ministres de la Cinquième République* (Paris: PUF, 1976).
14. Jean Lacouture, ed., *Citations du Président de Gaulle* (Paris: Seuil, 1968), pp. 39–40.

dom to determine the overall concepts of a policy, made the cabinet appear as little more than a defender of executive policy before Parliament and an agency for the preparation of details, the drafting of bills and speeches, and other general "staff" work.[15]

Under Pompidou there was a slight upgrading of the cabinet, which met more frequently than under his predecessor. This upgrading was probably due to two circumstances: (1) the relative absence of international conflicts involving France turned the President's attention more to domestic problems, in which *arbitrage* functions were less important than economic and other technical expertise (which are often found in the cabinet); and (2) the cabinets contained certain old Gaullists or pro-Gaullists whose stature was too great for Pompidou to ignore them— notably Michel Debré, the first premier under de Gaulle, and Valéry Giscard d'Estaing, minister of finance and leader of the Independent Republicans. But even under Pompidou's Presidency there was no reliable evidence indicating that consultation with the cabinet as a basis of presidential decisions occupied a more preeminent place in relation to other consultative mechanisms than it did under de Gaulle.

Under President Giscard d'Estaing, the fifteen full cabinet ministers (sixteen as of January 1976) have been meeting weekly, ostensibly in order to discuss policy, with the secretaries of state being called upon to participate only occasionally. In addition, Giscard is in almost daily contact with his premier and consults frequently on an informal basis with selected cabinet members, in particular with Michel Poniatowski, the minister of the interior (who has become, in effect, a "co-premier"). Giscard's consultative activities have not been confined to cabinet members. He relies heavily on the advice of several dozen bureaucrats in executive departments and planning offices, as well as the personnel of his own Office of the Presidency, which has grown to about 300 men and women.

In view of the foregoing, it is difficult to know which decisions arrived at by the cabinet have owed their inspiration to the President or to his ministers. All Presidents have occasionally stretched the definition of the presidential "reserved domain" and made decisions about (or "interfered" in) relatively minor matters that might well have been left to the discretion of ministers. In the case of de Gaulle, these decisions have included the vetoing of an appointment to the *Académie Française*; the refusal, in 1965, to lower the retirement age of workers; opposition to the reforms of the *baccalauréat* examination in 1966; the decision in 1968 to raise the minimum wage by 3 percent; and frequent

15. Pierre Avril, *Politics in France* (Baltimore: Penguin, 1969), p. 114.

intervention in budget making.[16] In the case of Pompidou, presidential intrusions involved, among others, the limitation of the height of buildings in the Paris area, and the decision, at the end of 1972, to lower the value-added tax on meat and other foodstuffs. In the case of Giscard, an acknowledged expert in economics, presidential decisions have involved prices, wages, the floating of the franc, and many other economic matters. Moreover, he has gone beyond the practice of his predecessors in scrutinizing the texts of ministerial communiqués and in personally editing the language of bills prepared by civil servants (thus bringing the bureaucracy more under direct presidential control).[17]

Presidents have slighted the cabinet in other ways as well. De Gaulle undertook periodic *tours de France* in order to "consult" the people.[18] Pompidou followed that practice, making a trip to the provinces every summer during his five-year tenure as President. Moreover, both de Gaulle and Pompidou used the referendum, which allowed them to bypass the cabinet and obtain legitimation of a purely presidential decision. Although Article 11 of the Constitution specifies that a referendum must be "proposed" by the government before it is submitted to the people, de Gaulle in September 1962 *announced* to the cabinet that *he* would propose to it a referendum on the direct election of the President.[19] Similarly, it was Pompidou, rather than the cabinet, who initiated the April 1972 referendum on the question of Britain's membership in the Common Market.[20] Under Giscard, consultation with the people has so far not involved referenda. Instead, it has taken the form of "walking tours" through Paris, frequent meetings with spokesmen of national economic organizations, and highly publicized encounters with ordinary citizens.

THE CONSTRUCTION AND RESHUFFLING OF CABINETS

The Constitution stipulates the necessity for ministerial countersignature to a presidential action, a provision that seems to harness

16. Fabre, *Principes républicains*, p. 373n.
17. Bertrand Fessard de Foucault, "Le grand conducteur," *Le Monde*, 28–29 July 1974.
18. *L'Express*, 7–13 August 1972, p. 17. Between 1959 and 1969, de Gaulle had managed to pay a visit to every department in metropolitan France.
19. See Peter Zürn, *Die Republikanische Monarchie* (Munich: Back, 1965), p. 109.
20. In addition to the referendum of September 1958, on the Fifth Republic Constitution, there have been five popular consultations: January 1961, on self-determination for Algeria; April 1962, on the Evian Agreement granting independence to Algeria; October 1962, on changing the method of electing a President; April 1969, on amending the Constitution so as to reform the Senate —a referendum culminating in de Gaulle's resignation; and, finally, the referendum of April 1972.

individual ministers more specifically to a decision-making role. But a minister owes his position to the President in the first place. Although ministers are in theory picked by the premier—after the latter has himself been selected by the President—most ministers are in fact chosen by the President. The rumor that every cabinet member, from the premier on down, deposits on the President's desk an undated letter of resignation is difficult to confirm. What is clear is that all three Fifth Republic Presidents have asserted for themselves complete discretion in regard to the retention and dismissal of cabinet members. At a press conference in 1964, de Gaulle made a reference to "the President who . . . names . . . members of the government, who has the possibility of changing [the cabinet] either because he views its tasks as accomplished, or . . . because he no longer approves of [it]."[21] Pompidou clearly agreed with de Gaulle's interpretation of presidential discretion. Pompidou's position was articulated by his premier, Messmer, when he announced on television that the President would, after the spring 1973 elections, form a government on the basis of policies he wished to pursue and not on the basis of a particular parliamentary party lineup.[22]

In 1962, de Gaulle personally selected Maurice Schumann as minister of information; in 1966, de Gaulle insisted that Debré, Giscard, and Faure participate in the third cabinet of Pompidou; and in 1968, the Couve de Murville cabinet was said to have been "totally constructed" by de Gaulle.[23] It has been asserted that Messmer himself did not choose his cabinet colleagues, that they were chosen by a "kitchen cabinet" confidant of Pompidou, and that Messmer made his personal choice only in the case of a few secretaries of state.[24]

The foregoing should not be taken to mean that Presidents have been completely willful in the construction of cabinets. Despite the independence of the President, all the chiefs of state of the Fifth Republic have been concerned with the political composition of the Assembly, the electorate at large, or both. The first Fifth Republic cabinet, which was installed in January 1959, reflected an attempt to strike a balance between a few old Gaullists, who had to be rewarded for their political loyalties, and leaders of non-Gaullist parties whose support of the Fifth Republic during its initial phase was considered important. However, as if to illustrate de Gaulle's contempt for party politicians, more than a third of the cabinet members were nonparty technicians

21. *Le Président de la Ve République*, Documents et Etudes, Droit Constitutionnel et Institutions Politiques, no. 6 (Paris: Documentation Française, 1970), p. 27. Cf. *Major Addresses*, pp. 246–49.
22. *Guardian Weekly*, 13 January 1973.
23. Fabre, *Principes républicains*, p. 367n.
24. *L'Express*, 17–23 July 1972, p. 12.

or civil servants, a proportion that was retained until the end of 1962. The depolitization of the cabinet during those years was reflected in the composition of the *cabinets des ministres* (the ministers' own official teams) as well; while in the Fourth Republic they had been composed largely of the ministers' party associates or personal friends, there has been a tendency in the Fifth Republic to coopt civil servants to staff these offices.

Between the parliamentary election of 1962 and that of 1967, the number of civil servants in the cabinet was progressively reduced while the number of Gaullists was steadily increased, roughly in proportion to the growth of the Gaullist majority in the Assembly.[25] After the parliamentary election of 1968, the cabinet assumed an even more Gaullist coloration, clearly corresponding to the overwhelming majority of the UDR in the new Assembly. The repolitization of the cabinet was balanced by the choice of a nonparty technician (Couve de Murville) as premier.

Under Pompidou, the repolitization of the cabinet was virtually complete; more than three-fourths of his cabinet ministers were Gaullists, and nonpartisan technocrats were entirely excluded until the parliamentary election of 1973. Although Pompidou shared de Gaulle's notions about the independence of the President, and owed his election to a new presidential majority, he was in fact less independent vis-à-vis the Gaullist party establishment. No deputies had been elected on the coattails of President Pompidou; moreover, although he openly asserted his leadership over the UDR, his Gaullist credentials were being challenged, and he was forced to silence these challenges with political payoffs. Moreover, the Independent Republicans also had to be rewarded with cabinet positions, as had that wing of the Centrists (the CDP) that had supported him during the presidential election of 1969.

After the parliamentary election of 1973 and the collapse of the Gaullist majority in the Assembly, the President's sensitivity to Parliament increased slightly. Although the idea of presidential continuity was conveyed in the retention of a genuine Gaullist as premier, most of the other important holdovers in the cabinet were nonorthodox Gaullists, Independent Republicans, and Centrists.

With the election of Giscard, the cabinet was entirely recast in a manner reflecting at once the composition of the Assembly, the new President's penchant for technicians,[26] and his rather centrist presiden-

25. From 1967 to 1968 the proportion of Gaullists in the cabinet increased despite their loss of majority status.
26. The 43 members of Chirac's cabinet, as reconstituted in January 1976, included 31 with professional civil service backgrounds.

tial majority (see table 15). Specifically, one-quarter of the cabinet seats was assigned to nonparty people, and UDR representation was reduced to a third of the total. Nonetheless, the presidential dependence on Parliament should not be exaggerated. Even if the President, in constructing a cabinet at some future time, should be totally oblivious of party alignments in the Assembly, it is not likely to take great risks in opposing him, because censure motions are difficult to pass, and because the President maintains the power of dissolution.

Since presidential discretion applies equally to cabinet appointments and dismissals, and since there have been only three Presidents in the Fifth Republic, there has been much greater cabinet stability than in the Third and Fourth republics. But this stability has not been absolute. The Fifth Republic (between 1959 and 1976) has had only seven prime ministers and sixteen "governments," but there has been a significant turnover of ministers—and a corresponding lateral movement of the ministers' higher civil-service staffs. From January 1959 to April 1969, there were ten ministers of Education, ten of Information, eight of Scientific Research, six of Industry, and five each for Justice, Interior, Health and Agriculture.[27] In contrast, there has been relatively great stability in crucial ministries, such as Foreign Affairs (with Couve de Murville holding the portfolio for six years), Defense (Messmer for seven years), and Finance (Giscard for nine years). From January 1959 to January 1976, there have been altogether thirty-five cabinet reshuffles, but not all of them have involved the appointment of new faces.[28] By virtue of their stature or political connections, a number of individuals have been extremely ministrable and have held several different portfolios, e.g., Maurice Schumann (Social Affairs and Foreign Affairs), Jacques Duhamel (Agriculture and Culture), Michel Debré (premier, finance minister, and defense minister), Edgar Faure (Social Affairs and Education), Maurice Couve de Murville (Foreign Affairs and premier), and Jacques Chirac (Interior, Agriculture, and premier).

While in the Fourth Republic cabinet reshuffles were usually the result of shifting parliamentary party alignments and disagreements among coalition partners, reshuffles throughout the Fifth Republic have

27. Based on Daniel Amson, "Les secrétaires d'état sous la Ve République," *Revue du droit public et de science politique* 88 (May–June 1972): 661–76. On the lateral movement of prime ministers' civil service staffs, under three Presidents, from and to the Council of State, the Court of Accounts, the prefectoral corps, and private business, see Bertrand Badie and Pierre Birnbaum, "L'autonomie des institutions politico-administratives: le rôle des cabinets des présidents de la République et des premiers ministres sous la Cinquième République," *RFSP* 26 (April 1976): 286–322.
28. *Le Monde Hebdomadaire*, 7–13 January 1971; and *Le Monde*, 14 January 1976.

Table 15
Political Composition of Fifth Republic Cabinets

	4th Republic de Gaulle July 1958	5th Republic Debré Jan. 1959	De Gaulle Presidency					
			April 1962	Pompidou Dec. 1962	Jan. 1966	April 1967	May 1968	Couve July 1968
UNR(UDR)	3	6	9	15	15	21	19	26
RI				3	3	3	3	4
Independents	3	5	3					
MRP	3	3	5					
PDM(CDP)								
Radicals	2	1	1	1				
Socialists	3							
Miscellaneous	1	2			3[a]			
Nonparty	9	10	11	7	7	5	7	1
Total cabinet, including premier	24	27	29	26	28	29	29	31

| | Pompidou Presidency | | | | | | Giscard Presidency | | |
| | Chaban | | | Messmer | | | Chirac | | Barre |
	June 1969	May 1972	July 1972	May 1973	Jan. 1974	June 1974	Jan. 1975	Jan. 1976	Aug. 1976
UNR(UDR)	29	31	22	24	19	12	12	13	9
RI	7	7	5	7	5	8	8	9	10
Independents									
MRP									
PDM(CDP)	3	3	3	3	2	2	2	2	2[c]
Radicals						6[b]	5[b]	5[b]	5
Socialists									
Miscellaneous				1	1				
Nonparty				3	2	8	11	14	10[d]
Total cabinet, including premier	39	41	30	38	29	36	38	43	36

[a] Included one Democratic Centrist and two left-wing Gaullists.
[b] Reformers (Moderate Radicals and Centrists formerly in the Opposition).
[c] Known under the new label of Centre des démocrates sociaux (CDS).
[d] Collectively designated as "presidential majority."
SOURCE: Based on *L'Année politique*; Office of Information, French Embassy, *Bulletins*; and *Le Monde*, 8 July 1972, 11 June 1974, 14 January 1976, and 30 August 1976.

taken place mostly because of disagreements between ministers and the President—the cause of virtually all the seventeen resignations of ministers between May 1959 and May 1972. Thus in 1959, Socialist and Radical ministers left the cabinet because of disenchantment with de Gaulle's domestic policies; in January 1960, Antoine Pinay quit the Finance Ministry because he disagreed with Premier Debré and President de Gaulle; in February of the same year, Jacques Soustelle quit over the government's Algerian policy; in May 1962, five ministers—all former members of, or close to, the MRP—resigned in disagreement with de Gaulle's "anti-European" policies; in April 1967, Edgard Pisani resigned as minister of housing because he took exception to de Gaulle's invocation of Article 38 (the parliamentary grant of decree powers to the executive) to solve pressing economic problems; and in April 1969, René Capitant quit as minister of justice after the resignation of de Gaulle because he was convinced that no successor on the horizon could maintain a genuinely "Gaullist" policy.[29] In July 1974, Jean-Jacques Servan-Schreiber was asked to resign from the cabinet shortly after his appointment as minister for administrative reform because of his public disagreement with President Giscard over continued nuclear testing.

Sometimes the President may oust the premier or a cabinet minister because of the need for a scapegoat upon whom blame can be fixed for a policy failure. Thus President de Gaulle replaced several ministers of education as a consequence of public criticism concerning university reforms; and he replaced Premier Pompidou by Couve de Murville after the May Events of 1968. In January 1975, President Giscard d'Estaing replaced Pierre Lelong as minister of posts because he had mishandled a postal strike in the preceding fall (and had insulted postal workers by depicting mail sorting as "idiots' work"); and in the spring of 1975, Jean Soufflet was replaced as minister of defense because of unrest in the army over low pay and unsatisfactory living conditions.[30] Cabinet reshuffles may also occur if the President decides to give the government a new orientation or image—as when Pompidou appointed Chaban-Delmas as premier in 1969 in order to veer the Gaullists toward the Center, and conversely, when he appointed Messmer in 1972 in order to return them to the Right; or he may reshuffle the cabinet in order

29. "Le Remaniement du gouvernement," *Le Monde*, 16 May 1972.
30. In a subsequent reshuffle (January 1976), Pierre Abelin was replaced as minister for cooperation partly due to his being blamed for mishandling the Claustre Affair—his failure to secure the release of a French anthropologist held captive in a former French colony in Africa.

to make room for a politician whose party has moved from opposition to majority support—as when the PDM in 1969 decided to support the Gaullists and its leader, Jacques Duhamel, was rewarded with a cabinet post.

The elevated position of the premier as chief of the "government" is of small consolation to him, because he is in as great a condition of dependence as the rest of the cabinet upon the President's goodwill. One might even argue that in the cabinet-making enterprise he is worse off than his colleagues. In the Fifth Republic, whenever there has been a cabinet reshuffle (which does not always involve a change of premiers), most ordinary ministers have not been ousted from the cabinet, but have been given another portfolio. A notable exception to this pattern was the cabinet constituted by President Giscard d'Estaing after his election. Only eight of the thirty-six members of the first Chirac government were holdovers from the Messmer government. However, when the premier himself is dismissed, it is usually for a political reason, which renders it difficult to retain him in any position in the succeeding cabinet. In fact no Fifth Republic ex-premier has been named a minister under such circumstances. (Michel Debré *was* recalled to the cabinet four years after his ouster as premier, and until 1973 served successively as minister of finance, foreign affairs, and defense—but his recall to the cabinet was necessary in order to placate the orthodox Gaullists.) In the unlikely event that the premier should refuse to resign if the President no longer had any use for him, it is conceivable that the President— if he had a parliamentary majority supporting him—could "persuade" the Assembly to oust the premier on a vote of no-confidence; and even if the President lacked parliamentary support, he could accomplish the same purpose by the threat of dissolution.

THE EXECUTIVE AND PARLIAMENT

The fact that four of the seven premiers have been recruited from Parliament, that *all* members of the cabinets of Chaban-Delmas and Messmer had parliamentary "origins,"[31] and that most premiers have found it desirable to go before Parliament to be "invested" by the deputies, may make it seem as if the Fifth Republic has been evolving from pure presidentialism to a British-style parliamentary democracy.[32] But investiture by Parliament is neither legally required under the

31. *Le Monde*, 8 July 1972.
32. Cf. Georges Vedel, "Un régime pas si présidentiel," *Le Monde*, 14 July 1972.

present Constitution nor is it essential.[33] Sometimes, in fact, the cabinet is "presented" quite a few days or even weeks after its formal appointment, and after it has already been functioning.

Michel Debré went before Parliament in 1959, together with his program, as did Chaban-Delmas in 1969 and Chirac in 1974; Pompidou, in contrast, did not even bother to secure a post-factum "confirmation" of the cabinet (constituted in May 1968), and neither did Messmer seek that confirmation after his appointment in July 1972.[34] Why the first three, and not the latter two? Obviously, the decision as to whether the premier "needs" to be invested is purely a presidential one, although it may be influenced by a premier-designate's prior relations with Parliament. Debré, Chaban, and Chirac, as former members of Parliament, still had some respect for that institution; Pompidou, who had no parliamentary experience, and Messmer, who only a short time before had been elected to a parliamentary seat, viewed their careers to be entirely dependent upon the President of the Republic. But the public esteem that Chaban had frequently pretended to hold for Parliament did not prevent his being replaced by Messmer, that is, to be in precisely the same state of dependence upon the President as the other premiers.

As indicated above, Presidents *may* pay some attention to Parliament; but the confidence of that institution, while it may sometimes be desirable, is only "a subsidiary condition" for the retention of a premier.[35] As Pompidou said, "the President of the Republic takes the composition of the Assembly into consideration . . . [but] he is not its slave."[36] While in the Fourth Republic, a President had to accept the resignation of a premier when the latter lost the confidence of Parliament, the President of the Fifth Republic may retain the premier despite the latter's loss of parliamentary confidence—as de Gaulle did when he retained Pompidou as premier in October 1962—in order to demonstrate his indifference to, or even contempt for, parliamentary feelings. Conversely, the President may dismiss the premier because the latter enjoys *too much* confidence in Parliament. Pompidou's dismissal of Chaban-Delmas in

---

33. In Britain, a formal investiture of the cabinet is not necessary; still there is an implied investiture, because any new cabinet set up after a general election "presents itself," as it were, together with the government's program—the Queen's Address—which is always voted on. If the Queen's Address is received with critical amendments, this, in essence, indicates lack of confidence in the government, or parliamentary failure to "invest" it.
34. Based on *Le Monde*, 29 September 1972, and updated.
35. Jean Petot, "La Ve République et la continuité du pouvoir sous de Gaulle et Pompidou," *Revue du droit public et de science politique* 90 (November–December 1974): 1655–56.
36. Press Conference, 28 September 1972, reported by Raymond Barrillon, "Preeminence Underlined," *Le Monde Weekly*, 30 September 1972.

July 1972 was in part prompted by the latter's receipt of a massive vote of confidence (368 to 96) in the Assembly. The low turnout of the electorate—only 60 percent voting, including 7 percent casting blank ballots—in the April 1972 referendum on Britain's entry into the Common Market had been interpreted as an indication of Pompidou's waning popularity. Chaban's dismissal may therefore have been prompted by Pompidou's jealousy of his premier's own strong showing. Chaban's popularity, as measured by public-opinion polls, was consistently higher than that of Pompidou as premier; and, more important, it was also higher during the last three years of Pompidou's Presidency.[37] In the words of Pompidou, the retention of Chaban would have created a situation in which "the Premier . . . ends up becoming too powerful and reducing the President of the Republic to a symbolic role . . . or else to . . . a kind of director of the cabinet."[38]

"Political jealousy" was not the only reason for the dismissal of Chaban. Negative feelings toward the premier had been developing because of the exposure early in 1972 of his failure to pay taxes, and because of his inability to implement his "new society" program, which had promised more telephones, more money to students, more roads, more employment opportunities, and more housing. As the campaign for the forthcoming parliamentary election was approaching, Pompidou needed to restore the image of the Gaullist party, and to do so he had to purge a government in which there had been instances of corruption and scandal. Moreover, the President wished to remind the country that in addition to a parliamentary majority, there was also a presidential one, and he wished to make the former dependent upon the latter.

This strategy is also apparent in the case of President Giscard d'Estaing, whose appointment of a substantial number of Independent Republicans and Reformers to the Chirac government reflected a new presidential majority. While his choice of a Gaullist as premier and his inclusion of a few additional Gaullists in the cabinet attested to the continued plurality of the UDR in the Assembly, Giscard demonstrated his desire to transform the UDR itself into a presidential machine by encouraging his premier to assume the leadership of that party. The Gaullist parliamentarians are in turn adjusting to the new presidential majority. Although the UDR in the beginning promised only "qualified" support for Giscard, the party (with some reluctance) soon closed ranks behind the President because he continued to pursue certain policies acceptable to it and because of the inevitable drift of that party to a Giscardian centrism.

37. *Sondages*, nos. 1 and 2 (1974): 24–25.
38. *Le Monde*, 23 September 1972.

The invocation of a presidential majority in the chief executive's relation to Parliament should not be thought of as a Gaullist or conservative monopoly. If Mitterrand had been elected President in 1974, he probably would have had no more regard for the Assembly than had Gaullist Presidents. In a television debate with Giscard, which took place early in May 1974, Mitterrand clearly indicated his belief in the dominance of the presidential majority over the parliamentary one: if elected, he said, he would appoint a Socialist government, and if the (non-Socialist) Assembly should oust it, he would use his power of dissolution.

It is interesting to speculate about what might happen if the President belonged to one party (a conservative one) and the Assembly were controlled by another (a left-wing party or combination of parties). If the President had participated in the parliamentary election campaign culminating in the victory of the Left, he would have to interpret the outcome as a personal defeat: he "would find himself publicly disavowed by [the most recent expression of] universal suffrage."[39]

Early in 1978, in the face of predictions by public-opinion pollsters that the Left was likely to win the forthcoming parliamentary election, Frenchmen discussed a number of scenarios that might follow such an event. The President might try to fashion a minority government composed of Gaullists and Centrists, but such a government would be faced with almost certain dismissal by the Assembly. He might appoint a cabinet of technicians, but such a cabinet would meet a similar fate. He might dissolve Parliament; dissolution can be undertaken only once a year, however, and would be fraught with risk, because popular resentment over such a step might result in even greater electoral victories for the anti-presidential political parties. Having thus been rebuffed, the President might resign—as Marshal MacMahon had done in 1879—with the danger that his successors would revert to the figurehead role chiefs of state had occupied during the Third and Fourth republics.

In fact, Giscard, unwilling to provoke a constitutional crisis, had already hinted that in case of victory of the Left, he would adjust to the realities of the situation and appoint Mitterrand (or perhaps another Socialist) as premier.[40] He would probably also have seen to the construction of a cabinet that included Radical Socialists and Centrists.

39. Roger-Gérard Schwartzenberg, "Deux scénarios," Le Monde, 6 May 1976.
40. In the campaign speech delivered on 27 January, Giscard, while reminding his listeners that "the President's mandate is longer than that of deputies," emphasized that the electors would decide "who would govern France next spring." "Les élections législatives de mars 1978," Le Monde, Dossiers et Documents, p. 66.

Such a move would of course be predicated on the assumption that the Socialists would abandon their alliance with the Communists. But what if the Socialists insisted on the continuation of their alliance and the inclusion of Communists in the cabinet, and encouraged the parliamentary majority to behave in a manner construed by the President as "irresponsible"? It is virtually certain that de Gaulle and Pompidou would have fought Parliament by invoking their own popular mandate.[41] It is not entirely certain what Giscard would have done, had he not been "saved" by the outcome of the 1978 elections. Most French observers believe that Giscard, as a non-Gaullist known for his commitment to good relations with Parliament, would have behaved like a British monarch rather than resort to the presidential emergency powers found in the constitutional arsenal of the Fifth Republic.

ARTICLE 16

One of the most awesome instruments possessed by the President is Article 16 of the Constitution. It provides that "when the institutions of the Republic, the independence of the nation and the integrity of its territory . . . are threatened in a grave and immediate manner, and when the regular functioning of the constitutional governmental authorities is interrupted, the President shall take the measures commanded by these circumstances." The constitutions of several parliamentary democracies have contained such emergency provisions, which have been aimed not at destroying constitutional government but at preserving it: amputating a limb in order to preserve the body politic. Article 16 provides that whenever the President invokes emergency powers, he must inform the nation in a message; and the steps he undertakes "must be inspired by the desire to ensure to the constitutional governmental authorities, in the shortest possible time, the means of fulfilling their assigned functions." It is provided further that the Constitutional Council shall be consulted with regard to any measures; and that Parliament shall meet during the emergency period. Article 16 was thus far invoked only once, during the abortive generals' putsch in Algeria. That putsch began on April 23, 1961, and was effectively put down a few days later; yet Article 16 remained in effect until September 30, that is, more than five months.

Article 16 leaves a number of questions that are difficult to answer. Is Article 16 necessary at all, in view of the existence of Article 36—

---

41. Press Conference of 9 January 1973, Ambassade de France, Service de Presse et d'Information, *Bulletin,* 73/12/H.

which deals with martial law? That article provides that martial law shall be decreed by the cabinet, but can be extended beyond twelve days only by Parliament. It is therefore not an instrument of the President, and it may have seemed too restrictive to de Gaulle. Article 16, however, may be too "open-ended," because it is not clear whether any meaningful checks exist against its abuse or excessively prolonged invocation. If Parliament is in ordinary session, it cannot be dismissed during the exercise of Article 16; if it is not, it must be called into special session. But what is Parliament entitled to do while sitting? When de Gaulle first announced the invocation of Article 16, he told Parliament that, in its special session, it had legislative and surveillance powers; but at the same time, in a communication to the premier (Debré) he said the opposite, namely, that Parliament could *not* legislate. It is difficult in any case for Parliament, in special session or otherwise, to legislate against the wishes of the President, since the government would continue to control the agenda. Furthermore, what are the protections—if any—against an unwarranted interpretation of "danger" to the Republic? What measures are allowed, or forbidden, to the President? Can he suspend civil liberties? The Weimar Constitution's emergency powers clause (Article 48) authorized the President to suspend only *some* of the rights guaranteed by the Constitution, and these were specifically named. But there is no specific Bill of Rights in the Fifth Constitution; ergo, can the President suspend all the rights that exist by statute law or custom? The provision that the measures taken by the President must be inspired by a desire to return to a "normal" state of affairs is not very helpful. What if there is a will to return to normal constitutional government, but no way (as the President sees it)? And what is considered a "regular functioning of constitutional institutions"?

De Gaulle's actions during his Presidency raised some doubts about the extent to which he was interested in "guaranteeing" the Constitution. He violated Article 11 a number of times, when he bypassed Parliament before submitting a bill to a referendum—the most notorious case being the referendum of 1962 regarding the direct election of the President; Article 29, by refusing to accede to the demand of the Assembly for a special session in March 1960; Article 38, by unnecessarily asking for special decree powers in May 1967; and Article 50, by refusing to dismiss Pompidou as premier in 1962, after the latter had been ousted by a vote of censure in the Assembly. And while de Gaulle adhered to the letter of Articles 23 and 16, he so interpreted them as to violate their spirit or intent. Although traditionally emergency powers have been designed for use during civil disorders, insurrections or wars, both Presidents de Gaulle and Pompidou hinted on a number of occasions that Article 16 might be used for largely political purposes, especially in order to overcome a hostile parliamentary majority.[42]

Most of the Communists, Socialists, and other anti-Gaullists—and even the members of the nonpartisan Club Moulin—who may have come to adjust to other features of a powerful Presidency, have favored the elimination of Article 16, because they are reminded of how a similar provision in the Weimar Constitution was abused by an anti-republican President and contributed to the downfall of democratic government in Germany. Moreover, they had no illusions about de Gaulle's habit of manipulating the Constitution so as to weaken any institution or policy aimed at minimizing the role of the executive.

In the last analysis, the decision to invoke Article 16 depends on the degree of public support a President has. With public opinion on his side, he would be less hesitant to dissolve a Parliament that might obstruct his efforts at dealing with emergencies without invoking Article 16. The dissolution power would therefore seem to make Article 16 superfluous. Hence it is doubtful whether its elimination would be sufficient to reduce the powers of the President, which, after all, depend also upon a weak Parliament and weak opposition parties. Moreover, the President is powerful because a strong executive—whether king, emperor, or charismatic leader—is in consonance with a certain strain in French political tradition.

THE PRESIDENCY AND CHARISMA

We have already noted the periodic irruption of charismatic rule in French political history. It is useful to recall that Bonapartism has always appealed to a wide ideological spectrum, and that Napoleon I, Napoleon III, Boulanger, and de Gaulle were supported both by the Right and by the Left (though not necessarily at the same time) because these "heroes" were expected to rectify the disorders and injustices perpetrated by parliamentary bodies.[43] To be sure, the Right and the Left have been Bonapartist for different reasons: the Right because they hoped that a charismatic authority figure would help to maintain the existing social and economic order and temper a Parliament in which the underprivileged and demanding classes were represented; and the Left because they expected such a figure to counterbalance a Parliament which was viewed in the opposite way—as the preserve of the privileged

42. Maurice Duverger, "L'Article 16," *Le Monde*, 19 November 1966.
43. Cf. Jacques Fauvet, *The Cockpit of France* (London: Harvill House, 1960), pp. 80–81.

classes—and also, perhaps, because the "psychic income" of vicarious glory and national greatness radiating from a hero executive was a substitute for economic wealth.

Moreover, as Crozier tells us, "the conception of authority that continues to prevail in France is universal and absolute, and retains something of the political tradition of absolute monarchy with its mixture of rationality and entertainment."[44] Stanley Hoffmann has remarked that most Frenchmen have been socialized to the acceptance of an authority figure which is abstract, impersonal, and removed from the people, yet at the same time embodies personal charisma.[45]

The factors cited above are insufficient for explaining why a people such as the French, who have a reputation for rationalism and political skepticism, and a preference for institutional orderliness, accepted for more than a decade General de Gaulle's suprainstitutional assertions of omnipotence, his claim that he had "embodied national legitimacy for twenty years," and his statement—reminiscent of Louis XIV—"that the indivisible authority of the State is confided entirely to the President . . . that there is no [authority]—ministerial, civil, military or judicial— except that which is conferred and maintained by him; and that it is up to him to share with others that supreme power. . . ."[46]

Personalization of power is, of course, not confined to France. In the United States the presidential election has, in this age of television, become a political popularity contest, and the President's collaborators in Congress often owe their election to the presidential coattails; moreover, the way in which the vast powers of the Presidency are exercised and expanded depends upon the individual incumbent's unique view of presidential "stewardship."[47] In Britain, the leader of a party is elected or reelected—nowadays in a largely plebiscitarian fashion—as prime minister because of his views regarding the direction of public policy, the size and nature of the cabinet, the timeliness of his dissolution of the House of Commons and, above all, the leadership image he projects to his countrymen. However, in these two Anglo-American democracies "countervailing" powers are found that may be significant: in the United States, Congress can effectively block presidential legislative programs, and even in Britain it is possible for backbenchers to

44. Michel Crozier, Le Phénomène Bureaucratique (Paris: Seuil, 1963), p. 288.
45. Stanley Hoffmann, "Heroic Leadership: The Case of Modern France," in Political Leadership in Industrialized Societies, ed. L. Edinger (New York: Wiley, 1967), pp. 108–54.
46. Press Conference of 31 January 1964, cited in Lacouture, Citations du Président de Gaulle, p. 39.
47. Cf. Clinton Rossiter, The American Presidency (New York: New American Library, 1956), pp. 18–19, 111–12.

rebel against the leadership. In France, by contrast, countervailing institutions are weak.

Still, the personalization of power under de Gaulle should not be compared to that of Hitler or Stalin, or that of absolute monarchs of an earlier age. In the first place, the presidential office in France is non-hereditary and it is fallible. Like Hitler and Stalin, de Gaulle wished to be judged by history;[48] but unlike these two, he was also judged by public-opinion polls, a free press, and unfettered plebiscites whose outcome was not always predictable, and which ultimately caused him peacefully to abandon the Presidency. De Gaulle, like imperious rulers in nondemocratic regimes, virtually monopolized the media of mass communications, and used the press conference neither to enlighten his people nor to seek advice but to appeal for national unity, promote excitement, and demand public support for his policies.[49] But that support was not a foregone conclusion. He had to submit to elections— no matter how infrequent; and he was limited—no matter how imperfectly—by a constitutional framework that provides for some traditional supplementary or balancing institutions such as Parliament. Even if the legislative powers of Parliament have been weakened, it still has the power to propose, to criticize, and to complain publicly. Parliament, to be sure, does not appoint Presidents or governments. But parliamentary (and municipal) election results, much like the parliamentary by-election in Great Britain, serve as political weather vanes and occasionally inflect presidential policies.

In France, as in other democratic countries, the extent to which personal power can be exercised depends upon the support of the political parties and, ultimately, the people. Some of the personalization of power—and the charismatic image of an executive—in France, the United States, Britain, and West Germany is no doubt due to the *vedettisation de la politique* (i.e., the orientation of politics around a celebrity)[50] by the mass media, which capitalize on the average citizen's need for excitement, for an emotional focus, and for a flesh-and-blood symbol of national aspirations. De Gaulle filled that need more than any corresponding figure in other Western countries because of his towering personality, his martial figure and background, his Resistance leadership, and his image as the prophet of legitimacy—all of which were enhanced even more by comparison with the premiers of the Fourth Republic,

---

48. Léo Hamon and Albert Mabileau, eds., *La personnalisation du pouvoir* (Paris: PUF, 1964), p. 296.
49. See Jean-Claude Maitrot and Jean-Didier Sicault, *Les conférences de presse du Général de Gaulle* (Paris: PUF, 1969).
50. Hamon and Mabileau, *Personnalisation du pouvoir*, p. 375.

most of whom were relatively colorless political birds of passage. None of de Gaulle's qualities, however, proved in the end sufficient to overcome the "anti-executive itch"—it has been especially characteristic of the French Left—that helped to secure de Gaulle's departure from the political scene in 1969.[51]

Pompidou had all the constitutional weapons of his predecessor, and in his press conferences between July 1969 and January 1973, repeatedly emphasized his desire to affirm presidential authority.[52] But he did not inherit the political crises that had brought about de Gaulle's accession to the Presidency; moreover, although he was widely considered the heir-apparent to a "president-king,"[53] Pompidou showed, by his frequent outbursts of temper, that he possessed neither the royal hauteur nor the "institutional" qualities of de Gaulle. (It was unlikely that Pompidou could credibly perpetuate de Gaulle's Caesarian habit of referring to himself in the third person.) Instead, Pompidou portrayed himself as an ordinary Frenchman. In an appeal to the voters during the presidential election of 1969 he said: "As President of the Republic, I would constantly remind myself that I am only one Frenchman among many, and therefore that I am able to understand them and their problems."[54] Like Alain Poher, his rival for the Presidency, who was even more "ordinary," he donned the *petit chapeau* of the typical Frenchman—an illustration of the maxim that in bipolar electoral contests, rivals tend to become mirror images of each other. In any case, Pompidou's efforts at identification with the populace failed—or perhaps misfired. In his election to the Presidency, the abstention rate was 31 percent on the second ballot, contrasted with abstention rates of less than 16 percent in the case of de Gaulle and less than 13 percent in the case of Giscard. Whatever authority Pompidou possessed was essentially derived from the fact that he wore de Gaulle's mantle, and from his ability to make crucial decisions. Unfortunately, the last two years of his Presidency were characterized by a politics of drift and indecisiveness,[55] which was exemplified when, in April 1972, he abdicated part of the presidential domain by using the referendum on a foreign policy issue—British entry into the Common Market. The public disavowal of

51. Stanley Hoffmann, *Decline or Renewal? France Since the 1930's* (New York: Viking, 1974), p. 103.
52. See Raymond Barrillon, "Le régime à l'épreuve," *Le Monde,* 3 October 1972.
53. Pierre Viansson-Ponté, "Un dimanche tous les sept ans," *Le Monde,* 1 November 1972.
54. Quoted in Robert Rocca, *Pompi-deux* (Paris: Editions de la pensée moderne, 1969), p. 55.
55. See Hans O. Staub, "Gaullistische Gretchenfrage," *Weltwoche* (Zurich), 21 November 1973.

his rule—and the temporary eclipse of the Presidency—were demonstrated the following year by the UDR's loss of its parliamentary majority.

Giscard's authority rests primarily on the image he portrays of a modern-minded and competent technocrat, who has less need than his predecessors for such political prostheses as staged press conferences, full dress uniforms, and parades. But there is no question that he fully believes in a strong Presidency. Giscard said at his first press conference after his election that as "a product of universal suffrage" and "a guardian of the existing constitution" he was clearly committed to a presidential regime, in which the President initiates policies and "propels" them by means of the government he appoints.[56] He promised, however, not to go beyond the bounds of constitutional provisions, to accord a larger role to the Constitutional Council in safeguarding public liberties, and to give a greater role to Parliament and, in particular, the Opposition within it. Yet it would require a degree of optimism to suggest that such developments will, in the foreseeable future, lead to a significant reduction of presidential power.

56. *Le Monde*, 27 July 1974.

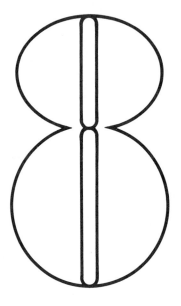

Instruments and Patterns of Decision Making: The Parliament

The conception of republicanism that was traditional in France from the 1870s until 1958 rested on parliamentary supremacy. The Parliament, as the main expression of popular sovereignty, occupied the central role in the French decision-making structure. Parliament was supreme in that it had, at least theoretically, a monopoly on legislative power; it was exclusively responsible for the selection of the President of the Republic; it invested and dismissed prime ministers and cabinets at will; it controlled the budgetary process; it exercised regularly its power of surveillance over the executive by means of questions, interpellations, and votes of censure; and it was the absolute master over such matters as special sessions, internal parliamentary rules, and the dissolution of the Assembly prior to the calling of new elections. Parliamentary legislative monopoly did not permit—in principle—"delegated legislation," i.e., the granting of power to the executive to enact decrees, nor were parliamentary decisions subject to judicial review or nullification.

In many modern societies, the idea (or myth) of the supremacy of Parliament continues to prevail because the legislature is considered to be the agency par excellence of democratic representation and popular sovereignty. But in reality the power of parliaments has declined everywhere. Among the causes of this decline have been the development of the welfare state, the frequency of plebiscitarian elections, the restriction of parliamentary initiative in the interest of efficiency, and the increasingly technical content of policies, about which ideologically oriented deputies and parties are ill informed.

The British Parliament has appeared to be an effective decision maker because it is usually dominated by a disciplined party that has an absolute majority in the House of Commons, a chamber "managed" by the prime minister, who is undisputed leader of the majority party. However, the House of Commons may also be considered an obedient ratifying body for decisions initiated by a strong cabinet. Both in West Germany and in Italy, the Parliament's main role is in effect to confirm decisions made by the party leadership; and even in the United States, where "all legislative powers [granted by the Constitution] are vested in Congress," the President has virtually preempted the area of foreign affairs, leaving the Senate only a feeble and intermittent role in that sphere. Whereas in these countries the theoretical supremacy of Parliament could be tolerated in view of the growing importance of the executive, the French Fourth Republic had a Parliament that was in reality dominant.

PARLIAMENT IN THE FOURTH REPUBLIC

That dominance did not, however, mean that Parliament was a decision maker. The sovereign legislature was unable to use its powers because it lacked effective management; none of the parties in Parliament had an absolute majority, and few of them were disciplined. Coalition cabinets were unstable because of the extreme individualism and ambition of the deputies. Many members of Parliament considered themselves capable of being cabinet ministers, and deputies were easily persuaded to express lack of confidence in an existing cabinet, in the hope that as a result of the next cabinet reshuffle (or "replastering") they would get portfolios.

In order to speed the resignation of a cabinet, the bills initiated by the government were often sabotaged in Parliament. The legislative standing committees (of which there were nineteen in the Fourth Republic Assembly) were particularly adept at butchering a government bill. If the committee, which tended to be the preserve of special interests, did not pigeonhole a government bill, its *rapporteur* (the committee member assigned as the principal "steering" person for the bill) would report a "counter-bill" (*contre-projet*) that embarrassed the government and sometimes led to its resignation. The government, in order to stay in power, got into the habit of refraining from introducing controversial legislation, thus failing to reverse economic stagnation, to introduce meaningful budgets (or any budget at all), or to alleviate the discontent of workers, peasants, and pensioners. The prime minister who epitomized this safe adherence to the status quo was Henri Queuille, a Radical political leader who, when asked to what he attributed his success in remaining in office for thirteen months, replied that when a problem came up he would do nothing but wait until it became irrelevant.

Budgetary and other crucial measures were frequently dealt with by cabinet decree, based on a broad framework law (*loi cadre*) that Parliament enacted in order to grant the executive full powers, and in order to enable deputies to escape responsibility for unpopular legislation. Yet in the Third and Fourth republics it was still meaningful to speak of a parliamentary system; the very existence of a government depended upon parliamentary approval or at least tolerance—for Parliament could prevent the *permanent* dominance of political leaders by cutting short their terms of office. Despite the fact that in the Fourth Republic many prime ministers enacted decree laws even after they had lost the confidence of Parliament (that is, while they were acting as mere chairmen of "caretaker" governments), they did so with the implied permission of Parliament, and in the clear knowledge that they would soon be replaced.[1]

Rightly or wrongly, many Frenchmen came to equate the failures of the Fourth Republic—and not its achievements—with the excessive strength of Parliament. The general public developed a measure of cynicism due to the deputies' frequent manifestations of opportunism, their endless perorations, and their fruitless ideological quarrels. All these tendencies made the deputies appear the enemies of the electorate and reinforced the substratum of antiparliamentary thinking current in France.

In order to salvage their prestige (and save the Republic), deputies during the 1950s had become interested in reform so as to make Parliament more capable of action. For the parliamentary elections of 1951 and 1956, the system of *apparentement* was adopted, which provided that any party list gaining an absolute majority of votes in the multimember district would gain not merely a majority of seats, but *all* seats for that district—in order to encourage various parties to combine and (it was hoped) to have the effect of reducing the number of parties in Parliament. To the same end, in 1957, the minimum number of deputies required for a parliamentary group was raised from fourteen to twenty-eight. In 1954, ordinary parliamentary sessions, which sometimes lasted nine or ten months, were reduced to a maximum of seven months. In 1956, private members were barred from obstructing a governmental

1. Cf. Fernand Bouyssou, "L'introuvable notion d'affaires courantes," *RFSP* 20 (August 1970): 645–80.

budget bill; and in January 1958, a constitutional amendment was proposed that would forbid backbenchers to introduce bills raising expenditures or decreasing revenues. But all these attempts at reform came too late. According to a poll conducted in the last days of the Fourth Republic,[2] a vast majority of Frenchmen still held negative views about Parliament.

PARLIAMENT IN THE FIFTH REPUBLIC

As much as the Gaullists might have preferred to eliminate Parliament altogether, given their preference for plebiscitarian rule, they knew that that institution must be preserved in the Fifth Republic. Parliament was the sine qua non of republicanism, and therefore the Gaullist constitution makers had no choice but to establish *"un régime parlementaire assaini,"* i.e., one in which Parliament would be rationalized and in a position to collaborate efficiently with the executive.[3]

The Fifth Republic Parliament emerged as a mere shadow of its predecessor. The forms are observed: Parliament still has a legislative function, and the government is still responsible to Parliament. In terms of its size, structure, and procedures, the Fifth Republic Parliament does not differ radically from parliaments in earlier regimes. The *Palais Bourbon*, the venue of the Assembly, is a closed and intimate club, in which the traditional *esprit de corps* of politicians, though somewhat weakened since 1958, is still present and still transcends party labels. The deputy spends his working week much in the same way as he might have done during the Fourth Republic—and much as does his American congressional counterpart. A typical week of a deputy is as follows:

Tuesday	A.M.:	Arrival in Paris, after spending night on the train. Reading mail accumulated since Saturday.
	P.M.:	Meeting with parliamentary faction. Assembly session. Cocktail.
Wednesday	A.M.:	Work in legislative committees.
	P.M.:	Assembly session. Preparation of reports.
Thursday	A.M.:	Legislative committees.
	P.M.:	Assembly session. Visits to ministries. Miscellaneous duties. Meeting constituents.
Friday	A.M.:	Legislative committees. Visits to ministries.
	P.M.:	Assembly session. Departure for the constituency.

2. Pierre Fougeyrollas, *La conscience politique dans la France contemporaine* (Paris: Denoel, 1963), chap. 3.
3. Pierre Avril, *Le régime politique de la Ve Republique* (Paris: LGDJ, 1967), p. 13.

Saturday   A.M.:—At home; visits to mayor; seeing important voters.
             Meeting with departmental party federation.
             P.M.:—At home.
Sunday   A.M.:—Public gatherings (inaugurations, ceremonies).
             P.M.:—Attending a soccer match. Banquets.
Monday   A.M.:—At home. Contacts with local administration.
             P.M.:—Study of legislative materials. Departure for Paris.[4]

The present Parliament has retained the bicameralism that has been traditional in French republics. The Assembly's 490 members are elected for a five-year term on the basis of universal suffrage; the 283 senators are elected for nine years by an electoral college composed of deputies and local politicians. As in the Fourth Republic, there is a speaker in each house, elected by its respective membership, who is assisted by a "steering committee" known as the Presidents' Conference. This Conference consists of the leaders of the various parliamentary parties, and is, in a formal sense, responsible for the allocation of committee seats and the allotment of time for debate on most legislative items. The management of the ·Assembly and the Senate is the respective *bureau*, which, as in previous republics, consists of the speaker, six deputy speakers, fourteen secretaries (who take minutes and count votes), and three questors (who are in charge of supplies).

As in most parliaments, specialized legislative committees are charged with examining bills, amending them if necessary, and reporting them out to the floor of the chamber. The Fifth Republic's legislative committee system is a compromise between the systems found in the United States Congress and in the British House of Commons. As in Britain, there are in the Assembly (and in the Senate) only six standing committees, and as in the United States, they are specialized. Their size ranges from 61 members (foreign affairs, economic affairs, defense, and constitutional or administrative matters) to 121 (cultural and social affairs, and productivity). Deputies are assigned to committees on the basis of the proportional representation of recognized parliamentary parties. In the Fifth Republic, a parliamentary party must contain a minimum of thirty deputies—a requirement that has forced relatively isolated deputies to align themselves with larger groups and thereby contributed to the aggregative process within the legislature. As was the case in previous republics, the chairman of a committee has little power.

4. Jean-Claude Lamy and Marc Kunstlé, *Au petit bonheur la chambre* (Paris: Julliard, 1972), pp. 36–38.

He is elected by its members and does not necessarily belong to the largest party.

In the beginning of the Fifth Republic, as in the Fourth, legislative committees met four times a week, from Tuesday to Friday; but since 1969, many committees have met only once a week. Although each bill must be sent to a committee, its decision-making power is now minimal. Committees are no longer permitted to produce a counter-bill that distorts the original legislative intent of the government. The committees are in any case too large and too unwieldy for the development of genuine expertise. In the early years of the Fifth Republic, the UNR insisted that legislative committees should have no authority to subdivide themselves, probably because that party feared that smaller subcommittees might develop into anti-Gaullist power centers. But such subdivision has in fact taken place; "working groups" (*groupes de travail*)—in effect, subcommittees—have been formed frequently, and in recent years they have been more or less officially sanctioned. Neither the subcommittees nor the full committees, however, can function meaningfully other than as components of the legislative conveyor belt, for the committee must report back to the chamber within three months or even sooner, if the government (which under Article 48 of the Constitution has the power to assign priority status to a bill) has attached the label of "urgent" to a measure. Sometimes the legislative committee may provide no input at all. It has happened that the government has so arranged the agenda and so rushed a bill that it has come up for floor debate before the committee has prepared its report on the bill or even had time to discuss it.[5]

At the request of either the government or a parliamentary chamber, a special committee may be named to consider a particular bill. In the past, the government tolerated the establishment by the Assembly of special committees in which the subjects under discussion were not highly partisan (e.g., subsidies for repatriates from North Africa, or birth control). After 1968, the government became more amenable to the creation of special committees dealing with a broader scope of problems, since the absolute majority that the Gaullists enjoyed in the plenum of the Assembly (see table 16) was reflected in the makeup of the special committees.

The setting up of ad hoc parliamentary committees of inquiry into government operations (such as the functioning of the public services or nationalized enterprises) has been authorized since the promulgation

5. Avril, *Le régime politique*, p. 49.

Table 16
The Composition of the National Assembly Since 1956

Parliamentary Election	Total Seats	Gaullists and Allies	Conservatives and Moderates	MRP and Center	Radicals and Allies	Socialists	Communists	Miscellaneous or Unaffiliated
1956	596	22	97	84	94	99	150	50
1958	552	206	129	56	40	47	10	64
1962	482	268[a]	55[e]		43[h]	66	41	9
1967	487	242[b]	41[f]		121[i]		73	10
1968	487	344[c]	34[f]		57[j]		34	18
1973	490	270[d]		34[g]	100[k]		73	13

[a] Including 35 RI.
[b] Including 42 RI.
[c] Including UDR, RI, and CDP.
[d] Including 185 UDR, 55 RI, and 30 CDP.
[e] Democratic Center.
[f] PDM (Progress and Modern Democracy).

[g] Reformers, consisting of Lecanuet's Centrists and (moderate) Radicals led by J.-J. Servan-Schreiber.
[h] Rassemblement démocratique.
[i] FGDS (Federation of the Democratic and Socialist Left), joined by PSU.
[j] Figure was reduced by about a dozen after the breakup of FGDS a few months after the elections.
[k] UGSD (Union of Socialist and Democratic Left) composed of Socialists and left-wing Radicals.

SOURCE: L'Année politique 1956–1973.

of an ordinance in November 1958.[6] But there are major restrictions on the conduct of such inquiries. The investigative committees are, to begin with, limited by a set time period and a narrow frame of reference (in contrast to the Third and Fourth republics, during which there were standing subcommittees of control). Such committees may not be created if the problems they are to deal with are bound to give rise to judicial proceedings—a prohibition intended to obviate interference in the work of the Ministry of Justice. Members of commissions of inquiry are selected not on the basis of proportional representation, but by vote of the majority, which may decide the rules of conduct of the committee and exclude deputies belonging to minority parties likely to be interested in embarrassing the government. The results of the inquiry must be reported to a permanent (standing) committee that (because of its pro-government majority) might reject the report. Finally, the committees can meet only in closed session, with the result that government mismanagement can be exposed mainly by means of leaks (and the parliamentarians' disregard of the pledge of secrecy). Despite such restrictions, the executive—particularly during the incumbency of de Gaulle—discouraged the appointment of committees of inquiry. Between 1958 and 1973 the Assembly proposed the creation of forty-four committees of inquiry or control, but only a few were set up: in 1959, an Assembly committee on the control of the Cinematographers' Union; and in 1971, Senate committees on the radio and television networks (ORTF) and on real estate corporations (as well as an Assembly committee on the latter subject in the same year).

The issue of parliamentary investigative powers became particularly important in 1973 after revelations about governmental wiretapping activities. French parliamentarians were impressed by the Watergate hearings conducted in the American Senate, "which show that it is truly a parliament."[7] The wiretapping issue—referred to in France as "Watergate-on-the-Seine"—had come before both the Senate and the Assembly, and in both chambers, the response of the government to questions on the matter had been unsatisfactory. Calls by left-wing deputies for an Assembly investigating committee were rejected; the Senate succeeded in establishing such a committee, but the government refused to cooperate with it (and the Senate, in turn, took revenge by cutting govern-

6. According to M. Boulloche, a Socialist deputy, "it is impossible [for Parliament] to know the total expenditures of the different sectors of administration." Parliament is, however, apprised of the finances of nationalized industries by an annual report submitted to it directly by the Court of Accounts. Patrick Francès, "Les leçons et promesses de l'année parlementaire," Le Monde, 24 Décember 1975.

7. R. G. Schwartzenberg, "Une enquête exemplaire," Le Monde, 16 June 1973.

mental appropriations for wiretapping).[8] After the election of Giscard d'Estaing to the Presidency, the Senate had a freer hand, and set up committees to investigate ORTF (again), price-fixing by nationalized petroleum companies, and the management of the telephone system.[9]

Formal parliamentary procedure basically follows the pattern established in previous French republics (see figure 1). As in the Fourth Republic, and in Britain, West Germany and Italy, a distinction is made between government bills (*projets de loi*) and private members' bills (*propositions de loi*), with the former accounting for most of the bills introduced in the Assembly. When a bill is introduced, it is sent first to the *bureau*; and the Speaker, who heads that unit, transmits the bill directly to a legislative committee. When the committee has done its work, the *rapporteur* formally reports the bill to the floor for what is technically the initial "reading" of it. The ensuing debate, which provides an opportunity for the introduction of amendments, is followed by a vote. After its passage by the Assembly, the bill is transmitted to the Senate. If that chamber accepts the original version of the bill, it is sent to the government for signature. If the Senate rejects the bill, the subsequent procedure varies. There can be a resort to the shuttle (*navette*)—the sending of a bill back and forth between the two chambers until a common version is achieved; second, the government may request the establishment of a conference committee (*commission mixte paritaire*); third, the government may ask each chamber for a "second reading," i.e., a reconsideration and new vote on the original bill; and fourth, if disagreement persists, the government may ask the Assembly to determine the final version of the bill by simple majority vote.

The foregoing description of procedure, though it hints at a streamlined process, is not a complete indication of the diminished role of the legislature. Although the Constitution clearly spells out the powers of each house of Parliament, the executive can in fact determine the extent to which each of the chambers contributes to the decision process. This is particularly true of the Senate.

THE SENATE

Physically and institutionally, the Senate has not changed much, compared to its predecessors in previous republics. The senators are, as before, elected not by the people directly, but by an electoral college composed of the 490 deputies, more than 3,000 general councilors, and

8. *L'Année politique 1973*, p. 59.
9. R. G. Schwartzenberg, "Parliament as a Public Investigator," *Le Monde Weekly*, 12 April 1975.

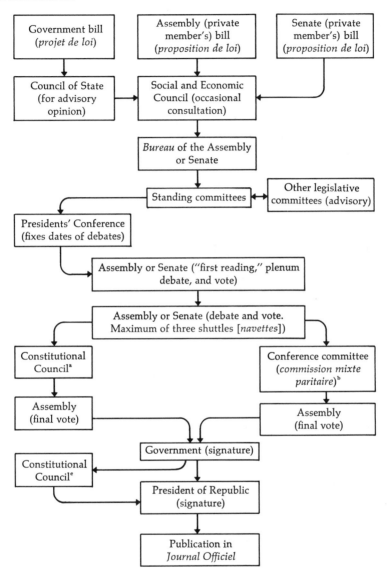

Figure 1. Steps in the Legislative Process

[a] In case of disagreement between the government and either chamber on the constitutionality of a bill.

[b] In case of disagreement between the two chambers.

[c] For organic law.

SOURCE: Based on Jean-Charles Maoût and Raymond Muzellac, *Le Parlement sous la Ve République* (Paris: Colin, 1971), pp. 68–69.

more than 100,000 delegates of city councils. Thus, more than 95 percent of the electors are representatives of localities.

During the Third Republic, the Senate was a very powerful legislative chamber. It was virtually equal to the Assembly in the sense that the Senate could render an absolute veto over an Assembly bill. The Senate, like the Assembly, could produce a vote of censure; and it competed with the Assembly as a body from which many cabinet members were recruited. In the Fourth Republic the Senate was abolished; in its stead there was a "Council of the Republic," which had only a suspensive veto. The founding fathers of the Fifth Republic, among them notably Michel Debré, wished to restore the Senate to the position it had occupied in the Third Republic because they expected that chamber—composed as it was of conservative local politicians— to be a guardian of conservative views as against the more left-wing views traditional in the Assembly, and thus be an institutional supporter of de Gaulle's Presidency. The writers of the Constitution lengthened the senator's term of office from six to nine years, strengthened the powers of the Senate as compared to those of the Council of the Republic, and made the Speaker the acting president in case of a vacancy of the office of President of the Republic.

The Senate has continued to be, as its Third and Fourth Republic predecessors had been, basically an "agricultural chamber"; but it turned out to be anti-Gaullist. The Senate has often had a negative opinion of the Gaullist government because the economic policies of modernization advocated by the latter tended to discriminate against the provincial, agricultural, and more "backward" clientele of the Senate. By the end of the 1960s, the Senate had become an arena of opposition to the executive not only because of the upper chamber's ideological anti-Gaullism, but also because of its awareness that its power to contribute to the legislative process was extremely limited. The weakness of the Senate relative to the Assembly is reflected in the fact that between 1959 and 1974, the Senate held an average of sixty-six sessions a year, as compared with ninety-one sessions for the Assembly.[10] It is also reflected in the fact that of 108 bills passed by Parliament in 1969–70, two originated in the Assembly but none in the Senate, and of 90 bills passed in 1970–71, nineteen originated in the Assembly but only four in the Senate.[11]

However, it cannot be said that the Senate's contribution to the

10. Edouard Bonnefous, "Crise des institutions: restaurer le contrôle parlementaire," *Revue politique et parlementaire* 74 (October 1972): 20.
11. The maximum number of days of Senate sessions was 95 in 1963; the minimum, 48 in 1962. The Assembly maximum was 118 in 1963; the minimum, 67 in 1969. Alain Guichard, "Le parlement à l'heure de la vérité," *Le Monde*, 21 March 1975.

legislative process is negligible. The upper chamber occasionally attempts to modify government bills that encounter little or no resistance in the Assembly. Such Senate modifications occur particularly when government bills deal with subjects about which the Senate is quite sensitive, e.g., regional reforms, the economic protection of the agricultural sector, or the privileges of shopkeepers and artisans. Thus in the late spring of 1972, the Senate amended government bills on regional reforms—in order to give greater fiscal powers to regional councils—and attempted to alter a social security bill in order to raise old-age pension rates for artisans and shopkeepers.[12] The Senate's increased activity is reflected in the steady increase in the number of hours that chamber has met in plenary session: 216 in 1969–70, 239 in 1970–71, 259 in 1971–72, and 305 in the spring and fall sessions of 1975.[13] But senators have complained that most of this increase has had the effect of reducing the time available for the much more valuable committee meetings. They have also argued that the legislative ideas of the Senate are taken seriously by the government only when a failure to do so—especially on agricultural matters—might lead to extrainstitutional protest actions. (The strikes of artichoke growers in 1961, of chicken farmers in 1966, of hog raisers in 1967, and of dairy farmers in 1972 were all in protest against low price ceilings established by the government.)[14] But when the government is adamant about a bill (particularly if there are no threats of anomic action), the Assembly normally overrides Senate objections to it in a "second reading," thus reducing the action of the Senate to a mere suspensive veto.

According to one view, the Senate today represents less a participant in legislative activities or even a chamber of conservatism than a body that, not being subject to dissolution by the President, is an institutionalized opposition and "censor" of the government.[15] The Assembly can be dissolved if the President does not like its composition; if the President does not like the Senate, he can minimize its legislative participation even more than the Constitution has already done. After the election of 1968, there was a diminished need to restrict, ignore, or control the Assembly, by an invocation of Article 16, or of Article 38, or the threat of dissolution—the Assembly then being controlled by an overwhelming Gaullist majority. But the Senate has remained almost as anti-Gaullist (see table 17) as it had been under the leadership of Gaston Monner-

12. *Le Monde,* 9 June 1972 and 13 June 1972.
13. Bonnefous, "Crise des institutions," p. 20; and Francès, "Leçons et promesses."
14. *Le Monde,* 28–29 May 1972.
15. See Jean-Pierre Marichy, *La deuxième chambre dans la vie politique française* (Paris: LGDJ, 1970).

Table 17
The Composition of the Senate Since 1959

	Total Seats	Gaullist and Allies	Inde-pendents	Peasants	MRP	Democratic Left (mainly Radicals)	Socialists	Commu-nists	Unaffiliated
1959	307	41	92		34	64	51	14	11
1961	307	40	93		34	56	51	14	19[e]
1965	274	30	79		38	50	52	14	11
1968	283	29	80		40	50	54	17	13
1973 (October)	283	36[a]	60[b]	16	46[c]	38[d]	48	18	21
1974 (October)	283	33[a]	57[b]	13	48[c]	42[d]	51	20	19

[a] UDR
[b] RI
[c] Center Union
[d] Reformers
[e] Including 9 Democratic Rally for Algeria
SOURCE: L'Année politique 1959–74.

ville, the Radical speaker of that chamber in the first decade of the Fifth Republic. When de Gaulle bypassed the Senate (and the Assembly) in introducing as a referendum a constitutional amendment aimed at providing for the direct election of the President, Monnerville stopped speaking to him. And Alain Poher, the Centrist who succeeded to the Senate speakership in 1968, ran against Pompidou for the Presidency in 1969.

Since de Gaulle could not dissolve the Senate, he attempted to neutralize it by reforming it out of existence. The constitutional reform bill prepared by the government in the fall of 1968 proposed to have only half the members of future Senates elected by the usual method—by regional and local politicians—and the other half in a corporative fashion, i.e., by organized socioeconomic sectors such as trade unions, farmers' associations, and business groups, and to permit the Senate to co-legislate only on clearly enumerated social, economic, and cultural matters. It would be totally excluded from decision making on "general" political matters, as defined by the government. To sweeten the pill, the government associated the dismemberment of the Senate with a popular reform: the grant of greater autonomy to regions. Most people favored such regional reform but opposed the reform of the Senate, as is shown by a poll taken before the referendum of April 1969 (see table 18). The referendum lost; de Gaulle, in consequence, resigned the Presidency. Opposition to the referendum occurred in part because the reform was an affront to those who had always associated republicanism with the existence of a viable Senate, and in part because of objections to the *procedure* chosen for the reform, i.e., the referendum.

Table 18
Political Party Attitudes Toward Referendum of 1969
(in percent)

		PCF	Non-Communist Left	UDR	RI	Center
Regional reform:	favor	26	29	74	71	66
	oppose	63	40	8	14	18
Senate reform:	favor	7	6	47	31	14
	oppose	67	66	15	28	61

SOURCE: Alain Lancelot and Pierre Weil, "L'évolution politique des électeurs français de février à juin 1969," *RFSP* 20 (April 1970): 254.

LIMITS ON PARLIAMENTARY DECISION MAKING

Despite the "victory" of the Senate, General de Gaulle had left in the wake of his departure a Parliament that has been devalued and put under such effective tutelage of the government that the question arises whether France is still to be considered a parliamentary democracy. Parliament no longer participates in the election of the President, or in the selection of the prime minister and his cabinet; it no longer enjoys a monopoly in lawmaking but must share legislative power with the executive and with the people (via the referendum); and it has lost its power of dissolution. Parliamentary officials no longer determine the agenda; instead, there is a priority agenda established by the government, which "informs" the Presidents' Conference about matters to be taken up, and a complementary agenda determined by the speaker of each house and approved by it. (The latter agenda, in the Assembly at least, is influenced strongly by the government majority.) The duration of parliamentary sessions has been reduced to five and a half months a year: two and a half months in the fall (October–December) and three months in the spring session (April–June). No backbencher input or obstruction is permitted when budget bills are considered. Whereas in the Fourth Republic, Parliament's legislative competence was absolute, the Fifth Republic Constitution spells out in detail what falls into the domain of "laws" requiring parliamentary participation. Article 34 specifically mentions civil rights, conscription, criminal law, taxation, education, social security, the nationalization of industries, property rights, employment, and the jurisdiction of local communities. Presumably, all matters not enumerated can be decided by the President and/or the government. Such decisions are decrees or ordinances rather than laws, yet they have the force of a law enacted by Parliament. Virtually the entire area of foreign and defense policy has been preempted by the executive. There may be debates in the legislative committees of Parliament on aspects of foreign policy, but often these debates are in closed session and do not cause the government to modify its decisions. The Assembly does vote to ratify treaties—most often on Common Market matters where parliamentary ratification is stipulated —but it rarely if ever rejects a treaty.

Even areas that are constitutionally within the competence of Parliament can be "invaded" by the executive. Article 38 of the Constitution provides that the government may ask the legislature to delegate to it the power to make ordinances—albeit for a limited period and purpose. By their nature, such legislative grants are not much different from British "statutory instruments" provided by the House of Commons so that the cabinet can issue "orders-in-council," i.e., rule by decree. But unlike Britain, France has resorted to delegated legislation rather frequently and in particularly delicate areas. Thus in 1960, Parliament authorized the government to make ordinances on "social scourges" such as alcoholism and prostitution, and in the same year, to control political disturbances in connection with the government's policy on Algeria. Furthermore, France does not have a parliamentary institution similar to the British Select Committee on Statutory Instruments, which sees to it that ordinance-making power is not abused.

By means of its power to determine the agenda, the government can ensure that its bills have priority over private members' bills. Moreover, it can stipulate in the case of a particular bill what the extent of debate shall be, what sections of the bill shall be open to amendments, and how much time shall be allocated to specific sections of a bill. Finally, the government may request either chamber to vote on a bill— and often on its integral, unamended, text. This procedure, the "blocked vote," as provided by Article 44, Section 3 of the Constitution, effectively eliminates parliamentary input on details. Under de Gaulle and Pompidou, the blocked vote was used frequently. Until the end of 1970, 122 bills were introduced in this fashion in the Assembly, which rejected only 5. In the Senate, 211 blocked-vote bills were introduced, of which 83 were rejected. It is clear that the Senate has been far less cooperative than the Assembly, which, between 1962 and 1973, had a relatively obedient Gaullist majority, save for the 1967–68 interlude. But the Senate's opposition can easily be overcome, because the degree of legislative involvement of the upper chamber depends to a large extent upon the government's discretion. Since most of the blocked votes relate to financial matters, the Senate's relative lack of cooperation with the government is of little consequence. On the annual budget bill, the government is virtually complete master. According to Article 47 of the Constitution, the Assembly is limited to forty days in which to process a finance bill, and the Senate to fifteen days. If within a seventy-day period the two houses of Parliament have not formally approved a budget bill submitted to them by the government, the latter can enact the budget by decree.

The prohibition against private members' bills on appropriations may be extended to virtually any public matter. If, as one politician remarked, a deputy introduced a bill to abolish the death penalty, this bill could be declared inadmissible, inasmuch as guarding a prisoner under life sentence would cost more than executing him.[16] Such an

16. René Pleven, cited in Michel-Henri Fabre, *Principes républicains de droit constitutionnel* (2nd ed.; Paris: LGDJ, 1970), p. 408.

interpretation may be extreme and unrealistic. There is, however, no doubt that the possibility of the government's use of its various trump cards has had a chilling effect on the introduction of bills by private members. In 1957, at the end of the Fourth Republic, 71 of the 198 bills passed by Parliament were private members' bills; in 1959, during the first legislature of the Fifth Republic, only one of the 52 bills was a private member's bill; in the second legislature (1962–67), 55 out of 437; and in the third legislature (1967–68), 40 out of 168.[17] The percentage increase of private members' bills in 1967–68 was due in large measure to the fact that the proportion of Gaullists in the Assembly had been reduced as a consequence of the legislative election of 1967. No doubt the fear on the part of de Gaulle that parliamentary power was on the rise, and his conviction that the balance in favor of the executive should be restored, were instrumental in his decision to dissolve Parliament in 1968 and strive for more solid Gaullist control of the Assembly thereafter.

THE CONSTITUTIONAL COUNCIL

The power of Parliament has been further reduced by the creation of a new institution, the Constitutional Council, which has been assigned certain functions that had once been exercised by the legislature. In the Fourth Republic, Parliament could deal with any nonfinance bill or resolution it wished; today the French Constitution distinguishes among several types of laws or "rules." There are (1) ordinary laws, relating to social, economic, and other matters specifically enumerated in Article 34, which are enacted by Parliament; (2) organic laws, relating to the organization of public powers and their relationship to each other (Article 46), which are also passed by Parliament, but only after the Constitutional Council has certified that they are "constitutional"; (3) constitutional amendments, which the executive proposes, on which the Parliament advises, and which the people may ratify; (4) regulations (règlements complémentaires), which are made by the President or the premier in order to implement parliamentary law; and (5) decrees (règlements autonomes), which are made by the President or premier without any reference to Parliament whatsoever, so long as the Constitutional Council certifies that the matters dealt with by decree have regulatory character. Except for the scope of regulations (4)—which is a matter for the Council of State (see page 216)—the Constitutional Council determines which problems are subsumed under the various

17. Ibid., p. 409. See Jean-Charles Maoût and Raymond Muzellac, *Le Parlement sous la Ve République* (Paris: Colin, 1971), p. 74, for divergent figures.

laws or rules; in short, it determines what is within the purview of government or Parliament. It must be consulted whenever the government decides to invoke Article 16, and whenever there is a question about the constitutionality of any bill (*before* it is enacted) or an international treaty (*before* it is ratified).

Most decisions of the Constitutional Council have tended to favor the government, even to the point of permitting a government decision to violate constitutional procedures. The most famous case was the constitutional amendment of October 28, 1962—providing for the direct election of the President—in which the government had decided to use the popular referendum while bypassing Parliament. The Council, in an advisory opinion, had originally asserted that the procedure chosen by the government had been unconstitutional: it violated Article 89, which stipulated that a referendum could be used only *after* each chamber of Parliament had passed the amendment bill by simple majority. (An alternative method of amendment—which obviates a referendum—requires a vote of three-fifths of the members of both houses sitting jointly.) After its advisory opinion was ignored and the referendum had taken place, the Council—impressed by the popular verdict in favor of the amendment—declared itself unable to judge on the issue (see page 63).

For many years the Constitutional Council was not expected to function as a checks-and-balances device in relation to the executive. Between 1958 and 1975, the Council made 484 "decisions," which included 35 certifications of results of elections and referenda. During the same period, it examined the constitutionality of organic laws only twenty times, of Assembly regulations twenty-two times, of ordinary laws eleven times, and of international treaties only once.[18] The judicial self-restraint of the Council derives from the absence of a tradition of constitutional review (in the American sense) as well as from its method of appointment. Of the nine members of the Council—all appointed for a term of nine years—three are chosen by the President, three by the speaker of the Assembly, and three by the speaker of the Senate. (All Assembly speakers since 1962 have been Gaullists; all Senate speakers have been anti-Gaullists.)

Despite the inevitable Gaullist bias of the Council, legislators succeeded at least once in using that institution to fight the executive. In 1971, the government had introduced a bill that would infringe upon the traditional right of free association (confirmed by statute in 1901)

18. Louis Favoreu and Loic Philip, "La jurisprudence du Conseil constitutionnel," *Revue du droit public et de la science politique* 91 (January–February 1975): 165–200.

by permitting prefects to block the establishment of groups whose aims were viewed as "subversive." The bill was passed by the Assembly but rejected by the Senate; its speaker, Alain Poher, referred the bill to the Constitutional Council, which declared the bill unconstitutional. Although the Council continues to sanction violations of the letter of the Constitution by the executive, there is some prospect of the Council's assuming greater independence. In 1974, one third of its membership was renewed, and now includes Gaston Monnerville, the former Senate speaker known for his zealousness in asserting the role of Parliament.

In the same year, the Constitution was amended to permit the Council to judge a bill's constitutionality (after parliamentary passage but before promulgation) not only on the request of the government or the presiding officers of the two chambers, but also on the petition of sixty deputies or senators. This quasi-judicial review—which is to be used particularly in the case of bills touching upon civil liberties—falls far short of the American practice (which is admired by elements of the Left opposition), but it will doubtlessly impede the "railroading" of questionable bills by the government.[19]

Thus far, when the Assembly has succeeded in opposing or modifying government bills, it has done so with the help not of the Constitutional Council but of external, nonjuridical forces. This was the case in the "Anti-Breakers' Law," introduced by the government in the spring of 1970. The law as finally passed—providing for punishment of participants in an assemblage that results in disorder or damage to property—was less stringent than the original version, as a result of modifications introduced by the Assembly. Behind the modifications of this bill, and of bills passed in the 1960s on agriculture, veterans' benefits, and education, were the pressures exerted from outside of Parliament by trade unions and other interest groups.[20]

Even if a law that significantly reflects the ideas of parliamentarians (and especially senators) is passed, the law may not take effect. The executive may express its contempt for parliamentary lawmaking by failing to implement the legislation. For example, Parliament passed a law on birth control in December 1967, but the law was applied only in 1975. A law on abortion was passed in January 1975 (substantially "confirming" a similar measure passed earlier); but although the more recent law stipulated that implementing regulations must be passed within six months, the minister of health refrained from doing so as long as possible. According to one calculation, nearly a third of all laws

19. See Maurice Duverger, "Un gramme de démocratie," Le Monde, 11 October 1974.
20. Cf. Revue politique et parlementaire, February 1972, p. 74.

passed by Parliament between 1968 and 1973 had not been equipped by the executive with the necessary regulations.[21]

QUESTIONS AND CENSURE MOTIONS

No matter how many facets of legislative initiative have been taken over by the executive in Britain and elsewhere in Western Europe, parliaments in these countries have retained two basic rights: the right to ask questions of the government, and the right to dismiss it. In the Fifth Republic, the Parliament has such rights, too, in conformity with French Republican tradition (and Article 48 of the Constitution). There is a question period once a week; a deputy addresses written queries to a member of the government, and the deputy may supplement them—as is the custom in the House of Commons—with extemporaneous oral questions. Oral questions are divided by the Presidents' Conference into questions with or without debate. In the former, the deputy is given fifteen or twenty minutes time for comment after the minister's response; in the latter, only five minutes.[22]

Written questions are by far the more numerous; there is a stipulation that ministers must reply to them within one month after they have been submitted. This stipulation has often been ignored. According to statistics issued by the Assembly, 6,666 written questions were submitted in 1973. Of the 4,413 responses, 526, that is, 12 percent of the total, were supplied within the required period; 48 percent within two months; 24 percent within three months; and 16 percent after three months.[23] Naturally, the delayed answer is a technique for blunting the immediacy of the problem. A minister may refuse to respond at all; or he may delegate an "incompetent" secretary of state or even a deputy to read a written reply, prepared by the ministry, on which the reader cannot elaborate orally.[24] Question periods in the French Assembly are

21. Schwartzenberg, "Parliament as a Public Investigator." See also *L'Année politique 1972*, p. 50.
22. Eliane Guichard-Ayoub et al., *Etudes sur le parlement de la Ve République* (Paris: PUF, 1965), pp. 100–101.
23. Cited in *Le Monde*, 9–10 February 1975. See also Michel Ameller, *Les questions instrument du contrôle parlementaire* (Paris: LGDJ, 1964), pp. 80–81. According to this study, which covers the period up to 1963, the proportion of questions not answered within the stipulated time periods, which ranged from 17.5% to 23.6%, was not appreciably higher than during the last two years of the Fourth Republic. The proportion of questions answered eventually by the various ministers, however, ranged from 96% to 100% during the first legislative sessions (December 1958 to May 1960).
24. See Philip Williams, *The French Parliament* (New York: Praeger, 1968), pp. 19, 46–51.

scheduled on Friday afternoon (they take place on Tuesdays in the Senate), an inconvenient day because many deputies have adopted the tradition of the long weekend and therefore do not attend at that time. In sum, the question period has not proved to be the effective instrument of controlling or embarrassing the government that it is in Britain.

Since his election to the Presidency, Giscard d'Estaing has encouraged the Assembly to alter its regulations in order to allow the Opposition to question the government on important matters at least once a week, and he has encouraged his ministers to answer questions personally. But nothing may prevent the minister from responding with banalities. In the Fourth Republic inadequate ministerial answers would frequently lead to an enlargement of the scope of "innocent" factual questions, i.e., to a debate on the general policy of the government. The debate might then be followed by an "interpellation"—a vote on the question of confidence in the conduct of the government policy—and might lead to the resignation of the government. Today, with the permission of the leadership of the Assembly, the question period may still be followed by a debate. However, such a debate no longer has meaningful political consequences, since it cannot culminate directly in a vote of no-confidence.

Theoretically, distinct procedures are available to Parliament for ousting a government. Under Article 49, the premier may pledge the responsibility of his government to a general policy, a program, or even the text of a bill. If the Parliament indicates its disapproval, presumably by simple majority, the government must resign. But disapproval can be expressed only by a formal no-confidence procedure, which is cumbersome; a motion of censure must be co-signed by at least 10 percent of the members of the Assembly. The vote on the motion can occur only after a "cooling off" period of forty-eight hours, and the motion must be adopted by an absolute majority of *all* members of the Assembly. A deputy's opportunity to participate in motions of censure is somewhat limited, because any deputy has the right to co-sponsor a censure motion only *once* during each parliamentary session.

Since the establishment of the Fifth Republic, there have been more than two dozen censure motions; however, only one of these was successful, or, to put it more accurately, *would* have been successful if the President of the Republic had adhered to his own Constitution. De Gaulle's unconstitutional procedure in connection with the change in the method of electing the President (see page 191) had provoked a storm of protest in both houses of Parliament; and the Assembly, in October 1962, succeeded in voting no-confidence in the government headed by Georges Pompidou. Instead of dismissing Pompidou, de Gaulle expressed his lack of confidence in Parliament by dissolving the Assembly. After the new parliamentary election in November, the Gaullists had an absolute majority in the Assembly, and Pompidou could therefore be safely retained as premier. The Parliament has so far been unable to oust a single premier; moreover, the failure of Parliament to produce votes of censure has allowed the government to rule by decree, or to make policy by simple declaration. The ineffectiveness of the censure procedure must be largely attributed to the fact that the Opposition has normally lacked the necessary votes. Moreover, even Opposition deputies can sometimes be dissuaded from voting for censure by possibilities of executive cooptation, i.e., by the enticements of participation in future cabinets. In October 1972, the "moderate" Radicals, led by Servan-Schreiber, did not support a censure motion because they anticipated continued Gaullist control of the Assembly after the 1973 parliamentary election, and they wished to keep a bridge open to the UDR in the hope of being asked to join a postelection coalition.[25]

THE INCOMPATIBILITY CLAUSE

The position of government vis-à-vis Parliament has been strengthened by the "incompatibility clause," Article 23 of the Constitution, which provides that no person may hold simultaneously a parliamentary mandate and a cabinet position. The incompatibility clause was a measure introduced not so much to provide for "separation of powers" in the American sense, as it was to reduce the dependence of members of the government upon Parliament. If a deputy had a reasonably good chance of getting a cabinet post once a cabinet were overturned and a reshuffling took place, then he might be sorely tempted to hasten such a reshuffle by doing everything possible to embarrass the government and cause its resignation. If his colleagues did the same to him a few months later, as happened in the Fourth Republic, the deputy would still retain his parliamentary seat.[26] Nowadays, the political future of a deputy who becomes a part of a newly constituted cabinet is much more uncertain. If a cabinet minister offends the legislature, he risks little, in view of the difficulty of passing censure motions; if he loses the President's support and is ousted from the cabinet, he cannot automatically return to the legislative chamber from which he came.

The incompatibility clause has not prevented the government from

25. See Raymond Barrillon, "Hardening of UDR Attitudes," Le Monde Weekly, 24 October 1972.
26. Cf. M. Duverger, "Le nouveau parlement," Le Monde, 29 April 1959.

recruiting many of its members from the Assembly. A deputy who is asked to join the cabinet has a fifteen-day period in which to make up his mind. If he opts for the cabinet, his alternate (*suppléant*) takes over his parliamentary mandate. The system whereby each candidate for an Assembly seat runs with an alternate, whose name also appears on the ballot, precludes the necessity of frequent by-elections. A by-election must, of course, be held if there is a vacancy created by the resignation or death of both the deputy and the alternate. Nothing prevents a deputy from having a prior understanding with the alternate that, in case the deputy wishes to return to Parliament after a stint in the cabinet, the alternate would resign, thus forcing a by-election and (presumably) facilitating the parliamentary reentry of the deputy.

The spirit—if not the letter—of Article 23 has been repeatedly violated. Many members of the cabinet have run for Parliament, in which they have no intention to serve. President de Gaulle himself encouraged his ministers to seek parliamentary seats, perhaps in order to enhance the image of a cabinet consisting of members having support in the country at large. But why did (and do) electors vote for a candidate for Parliament if they know full well that he will resign his seat right after the elections? The electors are aware of the weaknesses of Parliament; they would much rather strengthen their bonds with a person who is closer to power, and who therefore can do much more for his constituency than a mere member of Parliament, and they may even *hope* that the deputy they elected will not take his seat. The proof that the "transfer" from Parliament to the cabinet has become quite a normal procedure in the Fifth Republic is seen in the fact that, between 1958 and 1967, seventy-three cabinet ministers were recruited from among the membership of the National Assembly. While it has clearly become desirable to the President to use the Parliament as a pool of competent members of the executive, the political risk to the deputy which is implied in Article 23 limits both the deputy and the President.

This risk has led to another method—first invoked in October 1972—of circumventing the incompatibility rule: the government's practice of selecting several deputies as "parliamentary delegates (*parlementaires en mission*) who are attached to ministries or who participate in interministerial committees, but retain their parliamentary seats (thus becoming, in effect, "part-time" ministers). In order to resolve the problem of incompatibility, the Chirac government supported a constitutional amendment that would have permitted ministers to resume their parliamentary seats automatically six months after relinquishing their cabinet posts. The amendment failed when, in October 1974, it fell short of the necessary three-fifths vote in a joint session of Parliament.

THE ROLE OF THE DEPUTY

The members of Parliament are themselves aware of the state of impotence to which the Gaullist regime has reduced them. A recent poll of Assembly deputies revealed that only a small proportion of legislators believe the role of Parliament to be very important, or even satisfactory, although, as is to be expected, members of the majority party attach a greater significance to Parliament than do opposition party members (see table 19). In view of this negative institutional

Table 19
Deputies' View of the Role of Parliament

Role of Parliament in % of Responses	PCF	Soc.	Rad.	PDM	UDR	RI
Very important	—	—	—	4	1	—
Satisfactory	—	—	—	15	53	30
Not sufficiently important	100	100	100	78	45	68
No response	—	—	—	3	1	2

SOURCE: Roland Cayrol et al., "L'image de la fonction parlementaire chez les députés français," *RFSP* 21 (December 1971): 1185.

self-image, why do deputies choose their political profession? One scholar has distinguished among four "typologies of motivation": status (social prestige), program (influencing public policy), mission (giving meaning to one's life), and obligation (the fulfillment of a moral duty to society).[27] The "mission-motivation" of French legislators must play a larger role than it does in the case of American legislators, because the payoff is more limited for the former. French deputies do not have the large staffs and salaries of their American congressional counterparts

27. Oliver H. Woshinsky, *The French Deputy* (Lexington, Mass.: Lexington Books, 1973), esp. chap. 1. The author's findings: 38%, mission-motivated; 28%, program; 20%, status; 14%, obligation. The interview responses about the *effect* of deputies on public policy are inconclusive.

and enjoy fewer fringe benefits. True, only about half their salaries (which in January 1976 amounted to about 10,000 francs a month—a sum calculated on the scale for senior civil servants) is taxed. In addition, they receive allowances for secretarial services, housing, and miscellaneous expenses; a reduction in telephone rates; seventy-five free airline trips annually to their constituencies; and unlimited railroad travel for themselves and half fare for their spouses. Moreover, some deputies (especially Gaullists and Communists) receive monthly supplements from their parties (while others—notably Socialists and Independent Republicans—must pay monthly contributions to their parties). Yet many deputies are financially hard-pressed, for they must maintain two residences (and employ two secretaries) and entertain frequently.

Deputies are not so indignant about their limited powers and benefits as they might be, because many of them enjoy compensatory prestige and emoluments as active local politicians—mayors or regional councilors. But this simultaneous officeholding only adds to the deputies' tendencies to absenteeism in the Assembly. The regulations providing for reduction in the per diem pay of deputies for excessive absence have not reversed such tendencies, since these regulations are not consistently implemented. An attempt was made to counteract the Fourth Republic pattern, under which an absent deputy could have his vote cast for him by proxy, by instituting a system of electronic voting. This led to a new practice, that of having colleagues press the buttons for absent deputies. That practice, too, is officially outlawed; but the ban is enforced only in the case of censure motions.[28] It is probable that absenteeism would be even higher than it is were it not for the fact that the Assembly meets in Paris, and many provincials will sojourn in the capital at the slightest excuse.

Absenteeism, cynicism, and frustration of legislators are to be found as well in other democratic countries where the decision-making process has been rationalized. In Britain, for example, a crescendo of complaints has arisen about the "dictatorship" of the cabinet and the reduction of the role of the backbencher;[29] but in that country, backbencher rebellions, though infrequent, are still possible, and ordinary members of Parliament still have the chance to influence the cabinet informally, to force ministers to account for their activities, and to turn public opinion against the executive. Whereas in the early 1960s a

28. Jean-Luc Parodi, Les rapports entre le législatif et l'exécutif sous la Cinquième République, 1958–1962 (Paris: Colin, 1972), p. 28.
29. See A. H. Hanson and Bernard Crick, eds., The Commons in Transition (London: Fontana-Collins, 1970), chap. 12; and Andrew Roth, Can Parliament Decide? (London: McDonald, 1971).

British cabinet member was forced by the House of Commons to justify his questionable personal behavior, a French premier, Chaban-Delmas, when charged in February 1972 (not by Parliament but by a newspaper —the satirical weekly, *Le Canard Enchaîné*) with tax evasion, defended himself not in Parliament, but on the television screen. However, according to one writer, the French Parliament is said still to possess "the less spectacular but more important function" of political education.[30]

The French Parliament occasionally does play an educational role. For example, in June 1970 there was an extensive parliamentary debate on the Sixth Economic Plan. Since a French economic plan is not equivalent to a legislative measure, it does not have to be approved by Parliament; therefore, the activity of the latter may have been designed to promote wide public discussion of economic policy. But there is no evidence that this discussion persuaded the government to alter the main outlines of the plan. Moreover, parliamentary discussion is frequently a sterile exercise because it may not reveal anything new to the public; such discussion may take place in response to information about policy compromises engineered between the government and interest groups, which have "already been presented to, and commented on by, the press."[31] Furthermore, neither public nor parliamentary discussion can compete with the French radio and television networks, which are under the direct control of the premier and have often been monopolized for government—and antiparliamentary—propaganda.

The emasculation of Parliament and, more particularly, of the power of individual deputies was, to be sure, not entirely a Gaullist invention. As we have seen, the immobility of Parliament in the Fourth Republic had called forth, from the mid-1950s onward, measures to streamline the legislative process. These measures were sufficient neither to save the Fourth Republic nor to satisfy the growing number of Frenchmen who criticized, and wished to reduce, the role of Parliament. Among these critics were not only adherents of the (Gaullist and non-Gaullist) Right, but also liberal Anglophiles who envied the tight management of the House of Commons, and certain leftists who (while, as a matter of principle or tactics, wishing to have *no* effective decision-making institution) criticized the failure of Parliament to resolve urgent social and economic problems. Even a number of politicians most strongly identified with traditional parliamentary government occasionally voiced doubts about a strong, uncontrolled legislature. For example,

30. Claude Nicolet, "Régime présidentiel ou régime parlementaire?" *Le Monde,* 22 March 1972
31. Francès, "Leçons et promesses."

Mendès-France, the Radical leader of the Fourth Republic, argued that the Parliament could not function alone, and ought to be aided by a specialized, quasi-corporative chamber.[32] It could even be asserted that those who were skeptical about the dominant role of Parliament reflected the attitudes of a majority of Frenchmen. In the past hundred years, the French tended frequently to vote for Opposition parties that were undemocratic or whose commitment to parliamentary government was questionable; for parties that could not, for lack of discipline, effectively transform Parliament into a instrument of government; or for a charismatic leadership that was, by definition, antiparliamentary; or else have participated in periodic "happenings" that were intended to supplement the decision-making activities of Parliament.

The negative views of Parliament evinced by politicians in the past have, in recent years, been reflected by the general public in a somewhat ambivalent fashion. According to a poll conducted in 1972, 59 percent of Frenchmen thought Parliament should determine basic policies while 27 percent thought the President should.[33] According to an earlier poll (1969), 52 percent of the respondents found Parliament useful, as against only 15 percent who did not.[34] But that positive view of Parliament as an institution has apparently not translated itself into a favorable view of the deputy. According to a poll conducted in 1973, 92.6 percent of the respondents considered deputies to have lower prestige than other professions; 95.1 percent thought that deputies had less freedom of action; and 95.7 percent attached less importance to tasks accomplished by deputies as compared to those accomplished by members of other professions.[35] The Frenchman who votes for a deputy doubts not only the latter's "instrumental" efficacy as a legislator, but also his ability to intervene in behalf of his constituency with the higher civil service.

It has been asserted that "if the relations between the administration and the minister are characterized by a deep mutual distrust, those that exist between the administrator and the deputy bear witness to such an abyss that one may doubt even the existence of any sort of relationship."[36] This gulf between the deputy and the civil servant, which dates to the Third Republic and is based on the existence of two conflicting perspectives, has never been overcome, although it has been

32. Pierre Mendès-France, La République moderne (Paris: Gallimard, 1962), pp. 73–108.
33. SOFRES, May 1972, cited in Bonnefous, "Crise des institutions," p. 16.
34. SOFRES, November 1969.
35. Ezra Suleiman, "L'administrateur et le député en France," RFSP 23 (August 1973): 733.
36. Ibid., p. 731.

somewhat narrowed since 1959—doubtlessly because many deputies, in particular those belonging to Gaullist and allied parties, have shared de Gaulle's affinity for "nonpartisan" professionals as representatives of the state, have shared social and educational backgrounds with the higher civil servants, or have had civil service experience (see table 20).

The negative view of the French deputy is not shared by all political scientists; some would argue that backbenchers today have nearly as much opportunity to participate meaningfully in debate as they had in previous republics, particularly on domestic issues. (Between 1959 and 1967, 21.8 percent of parliamentary debating time was devoted to finances, 13.2 percent to interior (e.g., police and public order) problems, 12.6 percent to agriculture, 12 percent to social affairs, but only 4.9 percent and 3.6 percent respectively to defense and foreign affairs. In the same period, 64.6 percent of the debate time was used by the parliamentary parties, 16.9 percent by legislative committees, and 18.5 percent by the government.)[37] Political scientists also argue that Article 34, which enumerates the areas of parliamentary jurisdiction, has not taken any powers away from Parliament that it had possessed previously. They assert that the decline in the number of laws passed by Parliament had begun in the Fourth Republic, but that as many *important* bills are passed by the Assembly today as had been passed previously.[38] While it is true that deputies are now accorded less time for debate than previously, they *need* less time because the new system has obviated onerous and fruitless debates on government competence. Since parliamentary investiture is no longer required, there is no call for a discussion of the merits of a newly constituted government. Moreover, owing to the consolidation of parliamentary parties and the diminution of ideological concerns, there is less scope for long-winded oratory about matters of principle.

Nevertheless, in contrast to those who say that there is now a much better balance between the executive and the legislature,[39] others, while asserting that the balance has been destroyed, point to the fact that the same fate has befallen other countries, such as the United States, where Congress has been ignored by the President, and Italy, Britain,

37. François Platon, "Le contenu des débats parlementaires sous la Cinquième République," *RFSP* 20 (February 1970): 93–104.
38. The average number of laws voted by Parliament annually was as follows: 1947–54, 255; 1955–57, 175; 1959–68, 85. See François Goguel, "Parliament under the Fifth French Republic: Difficulties of Adapting to a New Role," in *Modern Parliaments: Change or Decline?*, ed. Gerhard Loewenberg (Chicago: Aldine-Atherton, 1971), pp. 81–109.
39. Ibid. Goguel, a political scientist who was once chief secretary of the Senate (and a member of the Constitutional Council since 1971), argues that the decline of the National Assembly is as much its own fault as that of the President.

Table 20
Professional Backgrounds of Deputies, 1969–70
(in percent)

	UDR	RI	PDM	RS[a]	PS	PCF	All Deputies
Higher civil service	14.0	17.0	12.5	20.0	17.0	—	14.0
University professors	2.0	4.0	—	—	—	—	2.0
Secondary school teachers	3.5	2.0	7.0	—	24.0	—	4.5
Primary school teachers	0.5	—	3.0	10.0	20.0	26.0	4.0
Middle-echelon civil servants	1.0	—	—	—	—	—	1.0
Lawyers and related legal professions	10.0	14.5	7.0	10.0	7.0	—	9.5
Military officers	2.0	—	—	—	—	—	1.0
Total "statist" professions	33.0	37.5	29.5	40.0	68.0	26.0	36.0
Workers	1.0	—	—	—	—	37.0	2.0
White collar	0.5	—	3.0	—	3.0	15.0	2.0
Artisans	0.5	2.0	—	—	—	8.0	1.0
Farmers	5.0	14.5	26.0	10.0	3.0	—	7.0
Shopkeepers	6.0	4.0	3.0	10.0	—	—	5.0
Total lower- and lower-middle-class professions	13.0	20.5	32.0	20.0	6.0	60.0	17.0
Managerial class, private sector	10.0	—	10.0	—	—	—	7.0
Physicians and dentists	13.0	14.5	3.0	—	7.0	—	11.0
Veterinarians and pharmacists	5.0	5.0	3.0	30.0	3.0	3.5	5.5
Engineers	4.0	2.0	3.0	—	7.0	3.5	4.0

[a] Radical Socialists

SOURCE: Adapted from Roland Cayrol et al., *Le député français* (Paris: Colin, 1973), p. 40. A number of statistically insignificant professional categories have been omitted, as have the backgrounds of unaffiliated deputies.

and West Germany, where legislative initiative has been lost to the executive and the selection of premiers and cabinets to the political party leadership and the electorate.[40]

The decline of Parliament, and the occasional realization that non-parliamentary substitute agencies of legislative initiative and representation (e.g., the Social and Economic Council and the ministerial advisory bodies) may be quite pragmatic and even democratic, are of small consolation to the deputy who feels that he as an individual and the Assembly as a collective body no longer have wills of their own. In the Fourth Legislature (1968–73), 95 percent of the bills that were passed had been initiated by the government, and most of the rest by private members who belonged to the majority, and whom the government permitted (or encouraged) to present certain bills. Successful private members' bills have dealt with such politically innocuous topics as limitation of imports of household pets, the legal disposition of communes in French Polynesia, the medical coverage of domestics and janitors, etc. Perhaps 1 percent of the legislation had been introduced by an opposition deputy, whose efforts represented "audacity" more than a meaningful legislative contribution.[41] The deputy's role seems increasingly to be that of processing requests from local constituents to the government. The pork-barrel concerns of the deputy have been, to some extent, forced upon him by the single-member district system of elections, under which a deputy tends—in Anglo-American fashion—to be the victor in a local popularity contest. He continues to justify his popularity, and assures his future reelection, by securing the help of the national government in solving local problems. But in order to do this, he must cooperate with the government and not alienate it by being a parliamentary troublemaker—that is, an oppositionist.

Of course, the impotence of Parliament in France in the first decade of the Fifth Republic depended upon the fact that, until 1969, the chief executive was General de Gaulle, who regarded himself (and was regarded) as an institution that eclipsed all others; that he had reinforced the special legitimacy of his position by periodic popular mandates; and that there was usually a cooperative majority of Gaullists in the Assembly. This majority collapsed after the parliamentary election of March 1973 and was replaced by a "presidential" majority composed of Gaullists, Independent Republicans, Centrists, and Radical Socialists. The newly elected speaker, Edgar Faure, announced that soon there would be important "structural decisions . . . relating to the proper

40. Cf. Alain Duhamel, "Quel est le rôle du Parlement dans les démocraties modernes?" *Le Monde*, 19 November 1970.
41. *New York Times*, 3 October 1972.

competence of the legislator."[42] Similar announcements, avowing respect for Parliament and holding out promises for a strengthened role of that institution, have been made by all premiers since the departure of de Gaulle—Chaban, Messmer, Chirac, and Barre—particularly at the beginning of their terms of office. Perhaps they did so for the sake of public relations, for the sake of obtaining "investiture" without difficulty, or for the sake of ensuring that their inaugural government programs would receive a resoundingly affirmative vote. But lest the premiers generate illusions among deputies—and irritate the President of the Republic—they have accompanied their assurances to Parliament with the reminder that it was the President who was the chief decision maker.

The inauguration of Giscard d'Estaing as President in 1974 raised new hope that Parliament—and in particular the Opposition in it— would be called upon to participate more meaningfully in legislative activity than it had done under the first two Presidents. The blatant contraventions of the Constitution in regard to Parliament that had occurred under de Gaulle[43] have not been repeated under Giscard. On the contrary, the restricted options available in an economy beset by difficulties, coupled with a narrowing gap between government and Opposition parties, have rendered many policy initiatives politically risky and have tempted Giscard to share the onus with Parliament. Indeed, between mid-1974 and mid-1975 the formal input of the legislature on important government bills—divorce, abortion, budget, educational reforms, and conditions of employment in the public sector—was significant. A recent "balance sheet" of parliamentary work indicates that in the spring and fall sessions of 1975, Parliament adopted about 1,200 amendments to government bills. Moreover, of the 67 bills adopted, 10 (or 14.9 percent) were private members' bills—a proportion that marks an improvement over previous years, and is not out of line in comparison with other parliamentary regimes.[44]

However, deputies have not been persuaded that this burst of

42. Raymond Barrillon, "Une réalité et un tournant," Le Monde, 4 April 1973. Faure is the third Speaker of the Assembly since the inauguration of the Fifth Republic—his predecessors being Chaban-Delmas (1958–69) and Achille Peretti (1969–73).

43. E.g., in 1960, the government's refusal to convoke a special session demanded by Parliament in accordance with Art. 29; and in 1962, the government's refusal (in violation of Art. 49) to permit a vote on foreign policy.

44. Francès, "Leçons et promesses." Comparative figures for the percentage of private members' bills among the total passed are: Britain, 1957–69, 23%; West Germany, 1949–69, 24%; France, 1961–66, 7%. Based on John E. Schwarz and L. Earl Shaw, The United States Congress in Comparative Perspective (Hinsdale, Ill.: Dryden Press, 1976), p. 199.

activity has transformed them into genuine co-decision makers, particularly on financial matters. Although nearly half of the hours of discussion in both chambers were devoted to an examination of the budget, M. Ballanger, the chairman of the Communist parliamentary party, complained that "the budget [still] leaves the Assembly in practically the same condition in which it entered"; and even Assembly Speaker Faure admitted that Parliament does little more than perform an "autopsy" on the budget.[45] Furthermore, in a situation in which deputies are given "five days for examining a score of government bills"—and an Opposition faction is allowed two minutes each for a discussion of farmers' benefits, the problems of artisans, and the economic plan—the deputies cannot make informed contributions. A less perfunctory parliamentary involvement would require a prolongation of ordinary legislative sessions beyond the annual limit of five and a half months (rather than merely longer hours, which tend to "overheat" the deputies); but even Giscard does not favor this solution, because it might set a precedent tending to undermine the preeminence of the President.[46]

45. Francès, "Leçons et promesses." In December 1974, the chairman of the Senate Finance Committee introduced a bill to amend Art. 28, 47, and 48 of the Constitution which, respectively, restrict the annual length of parliamentary sessions; provide for a 70-day limit on parliamentary examination of budget bills; and give priority to government bills over private members' bills. See L'Année politique 1974, p. 124; and Edouard Bonnefous (the Senate Finance Committee chairman), "Travail parlementaire: une réforme s'impose," Revue politique et parlementaire 77 (May–June 1975): 23–28.
46. Patrick Francès, "Le Parlement est menacé de surchauffe," Le Monde, 4 June 1975.

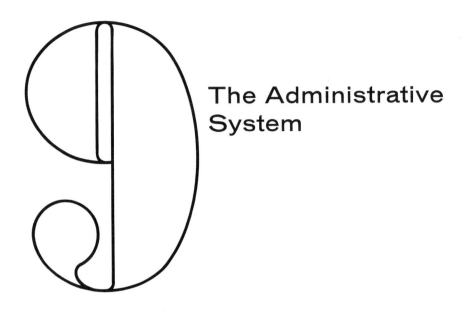

The Administrative System

BACKGROUND, STRUCTURE, AND RECRUITMENT

In contrast to Parliament, and in compensation for the legislature's weakness, the French civil service has increased its importance in decision making during the Fifth Republic and recaptured the role it played in earlier regimes. In fact, the bureaucratic tradition in France, as in Italy and Germany, antedates the republican system. In the fifteenth century, the Bourbon monarchs appointed officials who served the king as tax collectors or commissioners (*intendants*—the precursors of the modern prefects) in the provinces. The sixteenth century witnessed the establishment of technical corps, such as the Forest Administration and the Bridges Authority. The function of this bureaucracy was to some extent "modern" in that it was an instrument of "forceful national integration."[1] But the basis of its recruitment was distinctly traditional, i.e., ascriptive. Since they had to buy or inherit their positions, most high administrative recruits came from the nobility. Under the Bourbon monarchs, civil servants had no right of permanent tenure and could be dismissed at the pleasure of the king or his ministers. As a result of the Revolution of 1789, hereditary office was abolished, and

1. John A. Armstrong, "Old Regime Administrative Elites: Prelude to Modernization in France, Prussia and Russia," *International Review of Administrative Sciences* (hereafter cited as *IRAS*) 38, no. 1 (1972): 21–40. See also Marceau Long, "The Civil Service in France," in *Civil Service Systems*, ed. Louis Fougère (Brussels: International Institute of Administrative Sciences, 1967), pp. 67–68.

during Napoleon's reign the criteria of professionalism and merit were introduced, under the dictum of "careers open to talent"; during the July Monarchy, the principles of political independence and permanent tenure of bureaucrats became more generally accepted. Still, bureaucrats were expected to be supporters of the regime and proponents of its ideology. Each change of political system was accompanied by a "purge" of the civil service, for which there existed no overall national organization and no coherent recruitment criteria. Hence, each minister had complete discretion in matters of appointment, promotion, and dismissal of civil servants. In the 1830s the Bourbon bureaucracy, composed mainly of landed aristocrats, was replaced by an Orleanist one, consisting largely of the upper bourgeoisie; and in 1848, middle-class prefects were chosen to help fight revolutionary activities in the provinces.

In the Third Republic, the social base of recruitment was somewhat expanded. The growth of public education provided greater opportunities for the petite bourgeoisie to find places, particularly in the middle echelons of the civil service. Many prestige positions did remain the preserve of the upper and upper-middle classes, especially in the foreign service and finance; and even middle-echelon bureaucrats tended to reflect the traditional values of etatism and conservatism.[2] But the bureaucracy gradually accepted the two dominant values of laicism and republicanism. With the assertion of supremacy by Parliament, the civil service ceased, in theory, to be a significant decision maker. In practice, however, it was as powerful as ever. Since Parliament was too disparate in its composition and too disorganized and since the ministers responsible to it held too brief a term to familiarize themselves with their departmental domains, higher civil servants were often left to their own devices. The less France was governed, the more it was "administered."[3] Parliament recognized its own weaknesses, and its unwillingness to make detailed administrative decisions, by the custom of passing framework laws (lois cadres) under which ministers were given vast powers to issue decrees and regulations. Such powers in fact devolved upon the civil servants.

Many Frenchmen did not view this lack of political supervision as an evil. In contrast to the American notion of a federal bureaucrat as a "hired hand," that is, an individual employed to implement public policy, the French have considered the civil servant as one who pursues a respected vocation and who is a member of a superior class, who may

2. David Thomson, *Democracy in France: The Third and Fourth Republics* (2nd ed.; London: Oxford University Press, 1958), pp. 58–61.
3. Herbert Luethy, *France Against Herself* (New York: Meridian, 1957), p. 40.

be following a family tradition, and whose job, especially at the higher levels, includes policy making.[4] French higher civil servants have represented an awesome entity known as the State—at one time equated with the monarch, and later with the Republic.

Until 1945, relatively little uniformity and cohesion existed in the civil service. The division of grades was imprecise and differed somewhat from one ministry to another, because each ministry was in charge of its own organization and recruitment. The Council of State, the pinnacle of the bureaucracy, provided only general supervision. In 1945, the civil service received the form which it has today: it was unified; a Civil Service Commission (*Direction de la fonction publique*) was established and put under the supervision of the prime minister; hierarchial grades were set up; training and recruitment methods were standardized; and fiscal responsibility for the bureaucracy was delegated to the Ministry of Finance.

Today more than 2.5 million people are employed by the state— about 15 percent of the total labor force. The civil service proper, i.e., the regular national bureaucracy and its local agents, accounts for about 1.25 million. This number may seem excessive, but it includes nearly 700,000 teachers from elementary to university levels, about 300,000 telecommunications employees, and about 140,000 officials in the Finance Ministry, as well as all the local prefects and their staffs. In addition, about 1,200,000 work for nationalized industries, e.g., railroads, mines, gas and electricity.

There are four basic categories of regular civil servants, which are roughly similar to those that prevail in the British Civil Service:

Category	Percentage	Class
A	20	Administrative (*fonctionnaire de conception*)
B	40	Executive (*fonctionnaire d'application*)
C	30	Clerical (*fonctionnaire d'exécution spécialisée*)
D	10	Custodial (*fonctionnaire d'exécution*)

Within each category there are corps (e.g., *grand corps* or prefectoral corps), indicating the type of service or agency of the civil servant; and echelons, determining the nature of the position, the rank, and the salary received. The most complicated differentiation prevails in the upper ranks—the administrative civil service. This class includes the following, in ascending order of importance and status: (1) *fonction-*

4. Roger Grégoire, *The French Civil Service* (Brussels: International Institute of Administrative Sciences, 1954), pp. 17–27.

naires principaux (e.g., attachés to central administrative offices, to the revenue service and to prefectures); (2) *fonctionnaires supérieurs* (e.g., engineers, and most of the civil administrators); (3) *hauts fonctionnaires* (e.g., inspectors of finance, officials of the Court of Accounts, members of the diplomatic and prefectoral corps); and (4) *grands fonctionnaires* (e.g., secretaries-general of ministries, ambassadors, the director of the budget, the chief of the Planning Commission, and the top members of the Council of State).

As elsewhere in Europe, recruitment to the various categories of the French civil service is tied to the educational system. Thus for category *D*, very little formal schooling is required; for *C*, the requirement is completion of elementary school; for *B*, a *baccalauréat* (secondary school diploma) is necessary; and for category *A*, a university education. Prior to 1945, training for the civil service generally was provided by the *Ecole Libre de Science Politique* (a private institution founded in 1871) and by the law faculties of universities. These institutions prepared the bulk of the recruits either for immediate entry into the higher bureaucracy, or for "postgraduate" studies in the *Ecole Polytechnique* or other *grandes écoles*. Most of these schools are attached to, and run by, individual ministries. Thus the Ministry of Finance has maintained the *Ecole Nationale des Impôts* for training tax officials; and the *Ecole des Mines* has been maintained by the Ministry of Industry for the training of geologists. After World War II, a number of additional *grandes écoles* were founded in order to prepare civil servants for the specialized technocratic functions that were becoming increasingly important in a growing welfare state.

By far the most interesting postwar innovation in the education of the bureaucracy is the National School of Administration (*Ecole Nationale d'Administration*, or ENA), established in 1946. The purpose of this "superinstitution" has been to deemphasize the legal curriculum traditional for the vast majority of civil servants in favor of more modern subjects such as sociology, economics, statistics, and public administration. (However, about two-thirds of the entrants to ENA between 1947 and 1969 were graduates of law faculties.)[5] The curriculum provides for a unique combination of the practical and the theoretical. The three-year program includes first a year of work in an administrative office, usually in the provinces. The second year is devoted to academic study in Paris. The third year consists of further on-the-job training in the particular ministry that the student hopes

5. See Jean-Luc Bodiguel, "Sociologie des élèves de l'Ecole Nationale d'Administration," *IRAS* 40, no. 3 (1974): 230–44.

to enter. ENA is in many other ways unique. Unlike ordinary university faculties (which are supervised by the minister of education), it is under the authority of the premier; it is politically neutral, in contrast to the ideological tendencies often found in various law faculties; it conducts mostly seminars rather than the large lectures (*cours magistraux*) typical of the ordinary institution of higher education; and it has virtually no permanent faculty, professors being lent to ENA from universities, from the civil service, and occasionally from business.[6] Finally, ENA graduates choose their own career, that is, determine by themselves which part of the civil service they wish to enter. As a result, ENA has a virtual monopoly of training for the Council of State, the Inspectorate of Finances, the Diplomatic Services, and the prefectoral corps. The largest number of ENA graduates—there are now nearly 2,500—have gone to prestige ministries; some have gone into the planning technocracy; others into business. ENA is the main source of members of category *A* of the civil service (followed by the *Ecole Polytechnique*).

During the Third and Fourth republics, most graduates of the *grandes écoles* had been from the upper classes and hailed from Paris. ENA was intended to provide for less ascriptive and more democratic recruitment not only by means of competitive entrance examinations but also by a system of financial subsidies—in effect salaries—paid to students. (At the end of 1975, the monthly stipend was about $600.) The attempt to broaden recruitment did not succeed. In the early 1970s little more than 1 percent of ENA graduates were from the working class. ENA entrants, too, have been largely Parisians, or at least graduates of a Parisian *lycée* and a Parisian university, and have been children of civil servants or other professionals.[7]

THE POLITICAL COMPLEXION OF CIVIL SERVANTS

Such social selectivity has led to the impression that *Enarques* ("Enarchs") have in common not only high intelligence and technical competence, but also accent and manners, and feel a certain degree of contempt for other members of the political apparatus. *Enarques* may

6. François Gazier, "L'Ecole Nationale d'Administration: apparences et réalités," *IRAS* 31, no. 1 (1965): 31–34.
7. On the social and geographical origins of entrants to ENA, see statistical tables in Ezra Suleiman, *Politics, Power and Bureaucracy in France* (Princeton: Princeton University Press, 1974), pp. 54–63. For recent attempts to make entrance to ENA more democratic and to modernize its curriculum, see Pierre Racine, "L'Ecole Nationale d'Administration et son évolution," *Revue Administrative* 26 (March–April 1973): 131–41. See also Alain Darbel and Dominique Schnapper, "Les structures de l'administration française," *IRAS* 40, no. 4 (1974): 335–49.

not be Gaullists, but they probably share the Gaullist disdain of Parliament, because it is composed of nonexperts and tends to interfere with the handiwork wrought by administrative technicians. Even though the educational and cultural backgrounds of parliamentarians and *Enarques* are often similar, the professional orientation of the latter leads them to exaggerate the distinctions commonly made in a modern democratic system between politics and administration. In a democracy, the elected representatives are expected to make the political decisions, and the civil servants to implement them. The former are by necessity partisan, while the latter are (ideally) politically neutral; the former are instruments of change, while the latter provide stability and continuity—but always remain somehow responsible to the politicians and hence responsive to demands for change.

However, while the French civil service—like its counterparts elsewhere—has constituted an "objective" counterweight to a "nonobjective" parliamentary and party system, it has never been completely dissociated from the ideological arguments that usually inform politicians. The higher civil servant in France—unlike his colleague in Britain—is not expected to be politically neutral. He may join the political party of his choice, express his ideological preferences, and even run for a seat in Parliament (in which case he receives a leave of absence without loss of his seniority). Occasionally there may be some restrictions regarding the civil servant's partisan commitments, as in 1945, when there was a purge of collaborationist bureaucrats, but the purge occurred because those bureaucrats had adhered to the ideology of a regime regarded as illegitimate. During the middle years of the Fourth Republic, some ministers attempted to block the appointment or promotion of Communist civil servants; however, in 1954 the Council of State ruled such discrimination illegal. Nonetheless, certain political parties have almost always enjoyed a preferred status in the civil service.

In the Third and Fourth republics the staffs of national ministries tended to reflect the ideological diversity of parliaments and coalition cabinets, and there were always a good number of bureaucrats who identified themselves as "leftist" irrespective of the etatist outlook implicit in their roles. In the Fifth Republic, the diminished position of Parliament has tended to fortify both the conservative and the technicist orientation of civil servants. They have attained a higher status and greater autonomy in relation to Parliament than they had possessed in previous republics; but their political dependence on the executive has increased, because the premiers have asserted their authority more effectively by virtue of the fact that most have themselves had civil service backgrounds. Under de Gaulle's Presidency, many civil service

positions were politicized by ascriptive recruitment: he often preferred
his Resistance companions (*anciens fidèles*) to young ENA graduates
whose political reliability was an unknown factor.[8]

Moreover, there has been a continuation of the Fourth Republic
practice of appointing parliamentarians of the favored party, after they
have failed in their attempts at reelection, to official positions in quasi-
public sectors (e.g., the nationalized industries), although, to be sure,
many of these appointees have a background in the civil service. Many
higher civil servants—including about half the directors of the central
administration—have owed their positions to political collaboration with,
and fidelity to, a minister, and their appointments and promotions have
not been justified merely by merit or seniority.[9] Partisan criteria have
been particularly important in the staffing of certain "delicate" agencies,
such as the Foreign Ministry and the radio and television networks,
because great importance has been attached to the civil servant's reliability in voicing the official viewpoints. Until 1974, with a strong
Gaullist executive and a weakened (and in any case Gaullist) Parliament, many higher civil servants (including prefects) were blatantly
Gaullist and participated actively in UDR activities.[10]

Since the mid-1960s there has been a gradual implantation of rival
ideologies, when increasing numbers of civil servants began to identify
with the Socialist party and even the PSU, and when, in 1970, the
CFDT established a section for higher civil servants. There may be a
more meaningful political diversity in the (nonpolicy making) middle
and lower echelons of the civil service, which are characterized by
ideologically fragmented unionization. (Of the approximately one million unionized civil servants in 1970, 27 percent relied upon the laicist
(and mildly "socialist") Teachers' Union (FEN) to manage the election
of representatives to joint civil service committees, 20 percent upon the
FO, and 20 percent upon the Communist-linked CGT.)[11]

While such orientations influence the civil servant's general political

---

8. Julien Cheverny, "Le mode autoritaire de l'anarchie," *L'Esprit*, special issue,
   January 1970, pp. 61–62.
9. Bernard Gournay, "Un groupe dirigeant de la société française," RFSP 25 (April
   1964): 215–31.
10. Cf. Philip Williams and Martin Harrison, *Politics and Society in de Gaulle's
    Republic* (New York: Doubleday Anchor, 1973), p. 242. Officially, partisan in-
    volvement on the part of higher civil servants is condemned. In October 1975, a
    circular issued by the premier's office reaffirmed the illegality of such involve-
    ment.
11. Georges Langrod, ed., *La consultation dans l'administration contemporaine*
    (Paris: Cujas, 1971), p. 77.

"conceptions," they do not determine his bureaucratic behavior. "Once in a high post, the administrative civil servants have all accepted the [political] hierarchy."[12] Conservative attitudes are fortified by extra-bureaucratic influences, particularly from the law schools and *grandes écoles* and their faculties, with whom higher civil servants are bound to have continuing contact.[13] Although "in France the aroma of political reaction which aspirants for the higher administrative career acquired during their preparation for entrance [into prestige schools] as late as the 1930's has gone out of style," and although ENA has fostered the idea of opposition to government that acts in behalf of special interests,[14] there cannot be any question that the civil service is constantly influenced by interest groups and indeed even seeks their input. But this influence is unequal, because the civil service does not represent the kind of broad cross section of the population that is organized into competing socio-economic associations, and hence does not reflect the most progressive or democratic ideologies. Higher civil servants tend to be rather close to the business sector because they are both bound to the existing order (the former for professional reasons and the latter because the system has favored the economic advantages of the owning classes). Moreover, the higher civil service has shared a general economic philosophy with business. During the Third Republic, the influence of business on the *grand corps* was important because both shared a belief in laisser-faire, and during the Fourth and Fifth republics, because both shared a commitment to rationalized economic decisions (including planning) that have emphasized productivity and expansion. This shared commitment has strengthened the institutional ties between big business and the higher civil service, especially in the modernization commissions of the planning machinery—and both sectors have in fact used that machinery to head off the "unrealistic" demands of the trade unions. The emphasis on productivity is as characteristic of the *Enarques* of the *grand corps* as of the civil servants in the technical services (e.g., gas, electricity, railroads, and nationalized manufacturing industries). Many of the specialized civil servants who staff these technical services are trained in the *Ecole Polytechnique*, which was originally established in 1795 as a military school and was to be open to the talented of all

12. André Passeron, "La Bastille administrative" (pt. 1), *Le Monde*, 12 March 1975.
13. Alfred Diamant, "Tradition and Innovation in French Administration," *Comparative Political Studies* 1 (July 1968): 255–56. See also Cathérine Lalumière, "Les fonctionnaires et le service public," *Le Monde*, 6 March 1976.
14. F. M. Marx, "The Higher Civil Service as an Action Group in Western Political Development," in *Bureaucracy and Political Development*, ed. J. La Palombara (Princeton: Princeton University Press, 1963), p. 79.

social classes, as long as they were "attached to Republican principles."[15] The polytechnicians, like the *Enarques*, have a respect for efficiency and for entrepreneurial and technological (rather than legal or partisan) approaches to problems. They, too, entertain the hope of someday being able to cross over (*pantoufler*) into remunerative positions in big business. "One is often told in French business circles that a Polytechnician who is among the top ten or twenty graduates of his year can, after he has first spent some ten years in government service in order to solidify his qualifications, choose the private firm into which he wishes to be 'parachuted'!"[16] In addition, rapport between the technical civil servants and private entrepreneurs is strengthened by the fact that occasionally there are close ties between private manufacturing and nationalized industries—and sometimes virtual mergers of production and marketing, as, for example, between the public Renault and private Peugeot automobile manufacturing firms.

To what extent, then, is the French civil service an instrument of democracy? Administrative careers are not quite so open to the masses as are political careers. The sons of bakers (like Daladier) or of café owners (like Laval) could become prime ministers in the Third and Fourth republics (and theoretically still in the Fifth),[17] but such people are not likely to enter the higher civil service since they would be unlikely to climb the educational ladder—and achieve admission to the prestigious *grandes écoles*—required for an administrative career. While Parliament was supreme, this upper-class bias of the civil service was moderated by the lower-class ideological orientation of many parliamentarians and cabinet ministers, who theoretically furnished the "political" input into the bureaucracy and also provided an antidote to the conservative and antipopulist extraadministrative influence of law professors and business leaders.

Now the only effective counterforce to bureaucratic conservatism is the President, who appoints the politicians who supervise the civil service. Presidents are products of popular majorities; but it is questionable whether any of the three Presidents of the Fifth Republic, given their elitist and administrative backgrounds, has been willing to alter bureaucratic attitudes and interpret the "public interest" in a democratic fashion. It has been argued that the notion of public interest is largely a myth, used by administrators (and by the government) to

---

15. See Michalina Vaughan, "The Grandes Ecoles," in *Governing Elites*, ed. Rupert Wilkinson (New York: Oxford University Press, 1969), p. 86.
16. David Granick, *The European Executive* (Garden City, N.Y.: Doubleday Anchor, 1964), p. 74.
17. Thomson, *Democracy in France*, p. 58.

perpetuate the existing nonegalitarian social order.[18] Nevertheless, the internal reshuffling of civil service positions does show a certain democratic trend, in that the staffs of ministries concerned with upward mobility and egalitarian resource allocation have been enlarged at the expense of other ministries. To cite examples, from 1952 to 1967, the number of people employed by the Ministry of Education increased from 263,000 to 616,000, and the number employed in the Social Affairs, Public Health, and Labor ministries increased from 19,000 to 25,000. Conversely, there was a decrease in the personnel employed in the Foreign Affairs and Defense ministries.[19]

CONTROLS OVER THE CIVIL SERVICE

The French civil service is not unlimited in its power. In the first place, civil servants can administer only on the basis of laws. During the heyday of parliamentary supremacy, particularly during the Third and Fourth republics, the laws on which administrative regulations were based had emanated from Parliament, and therefore it could be said that Parliament exercised control over bureaucratic behavior. This is less true today, since parliamentary activities are controlled by the government (itself a product of presidential discretion), and since under the present Constitution the executive is given sweeping decree powers.

The second limitation on bureaucratic absolutism traditionally resulted from the "checks and balances" provided by the ideological diversity of civil servants. This diversity was fed by the impact of a multiplicity of parties in Parliament, and therefore of coalition governments—which insisted that bureaucrats of certain parties be rewarded for loyal service, placed in responsible positions, and promoted. But today this check is no longer adequate, given the parliamentary majority of a "presidential" coalition and the relatively free hand of the President in appointing higher civil servants. With the increased chance of a higher civil servant being appointed a cabinet minister, the rewards for being a loyal supporter of the President are obvious.

The third limitation is provided by the input of expertise from social and economic sectors via the ever-expanding consultative ma-

---

18. Jacques Chevallier, "L'intérêt général dans l'Administration française," *IRAS* 41, no. 4 (1975): 325–50.
19. Gabriel Mignot and Philippe d'Orsay, *La machine administrative* (Paris: Seuil, 1968), p. 8. See also Jean Montheu, "Un château-fort médiéval: le ministère de l'économie et des finances," *L'Esprit*, n.s., special issue, January 1970, p. 147. According to this source, the staff of the tax office (Ministry of Finance) grew from 48,900 in 1963 to 59,600 in 1970, but there were still not enough inspectors to resolve the continuing problem of tax evasion.

chinery. This consultative machinery is of three distinct types. The most widespread are the advisory councils attached to ministries and composed of representatives of interest groups, technicians, and prominent personalities chosen by the government. The second type are the multipartite boards attached to national and local social security organisms, and composed of trade unionists, employers' representatives, and others. The third type of consultative machinery is found in the regional economic development commissions. There are today over 15,000 councils, committees, and commissions with which the bureaucracy deals, and they are of widely divergent character.[20] These have included the Superior Council on Education, the Central Commission for Marketing, the National Committee for the Control of Real Estate, and regional employment and retraining committees. It is, however, unclear whether many of these consultative bodies provide significant checks on the administration since most of them are either ad hoc in nature or have restricted competence.

Bureaucratic regulations are based on framework laws, and the input of interest groups on these laws (except indirectly via the Social and Economic Council) may not be decisive. Such an input is limited by several factors: the administrative ego of civil servants, which does not easily lend itself to the notion that nonprofessional outsiders can make a significant contribution to administrative decisions; the inequitable representation of social sectors; and the principle of central governmental responsibility and supervision (tutelle), which permits civil servants to restrict the parameters of consultative input. Moreover, a committee's recommendations may be ignored by the civil servants (even in cases where consultation is obligatory); may merely provide the façade of public participation; or may be cited to promote unpopular regulations—to permit the civil servants to escape the blame for these.

A fourth check on bureaucratic absolutism is provided by the administrative court system, in which a citizen may challenge the legality of bureaucratic regulations or behavior. The pinnacle of this system is the Council of State (Conseil d'Etat). This body is not "independent" in the Anglo-American sense, since it is officially a component of the civil service. The Council of State was established in 1799 by Napoleon as a mechanism for resolving disputes within the civil service, to advise the government on legal matters, and to protect it from unpleasant challenges on the part of citizens by hearing (and heading off) griev-

20. Mignot and d'Orsay, Machine administrative, p. 92. See also Langrod, La consultation. Langrod's massive work on "consultative administration" lists more than 300 comités, commissions, and conseils on the national level.

ances. One important reason for the creation of the Council of State was the need to have a means for preventing interference by ordinary courts in administrative acts, i.e., shutting off juridical and political surveillance of the civil service.[21]

The independence of the Council of State was strengthened when, in 1875, its members obtained security of tenure, and when, subsequently, appointments to it were based not on political considerations but on competence and competitive examinations. These changes led to the transformation of the nature of the Council of State. Throughout the early part of the Third Republic, the Council was one of the main pillars of authority, while Parliament was the arena of partisan controversy and opposition to authority. Gradually the Council developed a degree of detachment from the executive, and became concerned with protecting citizens against administrative arbitrariness.[22] But since the Council is formally still part of the executive elite (in the social as well as juridical sense), there is considerable lateral movement between it and a variety of political positions. Some councilors run for Parliament (obtaining a leave of absence when elected); others are detailed to service as ambassadors, ministers of state or cabinet secretaries; and still others serve as officials in public corporations.

The Council still resolves intrabureaucratic disputes and advises the government on the language of draft bills and on the legality of regulations, and it is presided over by the minister of justice (see figure 2). But the latter is only the nominal head—the actual chairman, the vice president, is chosen from among the councilors—and does not interfere in the Council's activities. Nearly half of the councilors are members of the judicial or redress section, which operates separately from the other four sections dealing with administrative and advisory matters. (There are altogether 186 higher civil servants in the Council of State, of whom only about one-third are Councilors of State, the remainder being the subordinate *maîtres de requêtes* and auditors.)

21. Charles E. Freedeman, *The Conseil d'Etat in Modern Times* (New York: Columbia University Press, 1961), p. 4. See also Jean-Paul Negrin, *Le Conseil d'Etat et la vie politique en France depuis 1958* (Paris: PUF, 1968), pp. 30–37, 44–45, 140–41; Margherita Rendel, *The Administrative Functions of the French Conseil d'Etat* (London: Weidenfeld & Nicolson, 1970), pp. 28–40; and F. Ridley and J. Blondel, *Public Administration in France* (London: Routledge & Kegan Paul, 1964), pp. 125, 129 f.
22. Most of the work of the Council of State concerns *excès du pouvoir*—i.e., overstepping of responsibilities by an official in such a way as to damage a private citizen's interest. There are actually four grounds of challenge to bureaucratic action: (1) lack of authority (*ultra vires*), (2) failure to observe procedures called for by an existing law, (3) abuse of power (*détournement de pouvoir*), (4) violation of the law.

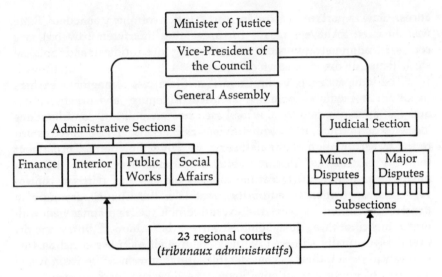

Figure 2. The Council of State

SOURCE: Based on Ambassade de France, Service de Presse et d'Information, *France*, May 1975, pp. 4–6.

Despite the size of the redress section of the Council of State and despite the fact that only five councilors are required to sit in judgment on a case, it may take several years for a case to be decided by the Council, since the docket is often full, and auditors and *maîtres de requêtes* may need a great deal of time to complete an investigation. In the early 1950s, the burden of the Council of State was lightened when the original jurisdiction of the two dozen inferior courts (*tribunaux administratifs*) was enlarged, and when the Council of State was transformed into a largely appellate court. Although councilors have come mainly from the upper-middle class, there has not been in France the kind of class justice one frequently finds in the administrative courts of Germanic countries; and although in the past several decades the Council of State has been at least as likely to find in favor of the citizen as of the government, the Council is not completely effective as an instrument for safeguarding the individual against governmental excesses or arbitrariness. Many a seemingly harsh or undemocratic decision or regulation is based on laws whose constitutionality can hardly be challenged at all, and whose lack of wisdom can be questioned only by Parliament.

It was perhaps for that reason that the French became interested in instituting an "ombudsman," or mediator (*médiateur*), system. In accordance with a law of January 1973 the government appointed the first mediator (Antoine Pinay, a former Fourth Republic premier) to a six-year, nonrenewable term. Unlike the Swedish ombudsman, the mediator receives complaints not directly from the citizen, but through the "filter" of a deputy or senator. The mediator's competence extends to all administration—ordinary, nationalized industries, social security, and justice. According to the law, he can request from administrative agencies any information he considers pertinent and can initiate proceedings against malfeasant civil servants. He submits an annual report to the President and Parliament. The office of mediator, which was modeled largely on that of the British parliamentary commissioner, represents an institutional grafting that is not entirely appropriate to the French context. Theoretically, the administrative court system already provides the French citizen with a redress mechanism against illegal bureaucratic actions, while checks against maladministration (the proper province of the mediator) are already provided by the government itself in the form of commissions of inspection and inquiry. Thus far the mediator has not been spectacularly successful, because neither civil servants nor their ministers have been very cooperative in revealing information.[23]

The less than perfect redress machinery is a minor matter compared with what many perceive to be the structural deficiencies and lack of modernity of the civil service. Some of the problems of the French civil service are endemic to government bureaucracies everywhere, such as the rivalry among different agencies; the conflict between the Finance Ministry which allocates money and the ministries which are on the fiscal receiving end; the tendency to duplication of services; the political interference in administrative work; and the question of the efficiency of bureaucrats.

There is relatively little corruption among higher administrative bureaucrats, not only because of their professional self-esteem, but also because they are well paid and therefore are not tempted to supplement their incomes by taking bribes. Traditionally, certain civil servants— particularly those recruited to the administrative staff of a minister (*cabinet ministériel*)—have retained their connections with, and derived additional incomes from, their private business or professional activities,

23. At the end of the first year of office (December 1973), the mediator had received 1,773 complaints. Of these, 564 were declared unacceptable; 740 were still being examined early in 1974. Of the 469 files examined, 287 were considered partly justified and only 70 were accepted as completely justified. See Louis-Jérome Chapuisat, "Le médiateur français ou l'ombudsman sacrifié," *IRAS* 40, no. 2 (1974): 109–29.

but recently (owing to scandals) there has been a tightening of regulations concerning such connections.[24]

The prestige of the lower-echelon civil servants is not so high as to counterbalance their relatively low pay, and consequently their unions engage in tough bargaining and occasionally call strikes.[25] But even among administrative civil servants, there is sometimes the question of salary inequities. A "pecking order" exists not only between administrative grades, but also within a particular grade; thus an ENA graduate who works for the Ministry of Finance receives 40 percent more pay than one who works for the Ministry of Culture.[26] Despite the postwar organizational reforms it is very difficult to move a higher civil servant from one ministry to another against his will, or from one corps to another—a situation that inevitably results in the overstaffing of some ministries and the understaffing of others. The proliferation of administrative staff is related not only to a growth of welfare-state *dirigisme* (referred to earlier), but must be attributed also to the pressure to create enough positions to employ civil servants in the service grades to which their educational attainments entitle them—without a clear regard to work needed.[27]

SUBNATIONAL ADMINISTRATION

During the last three generations of the *ancien régime*, local government was severely circumscribed by the Bourbon monarchy's policy of centralizing control over localities and provinces in the hands of the Crown and its emissaries. After a brief interlude of decentralization between 1789 and 1799, Napoleon established the pattern of centralization of administrative functions which prevails to the present day. Under this system, the communes, cantons, districts (*arrondissements*), and counties or departments (*départements*) are not independent decision-making centers so much as subnational units existing for national administrative convenience. Each of the units has, presumably, a rationale and an administrative function: in the commune the citizen is dealt with most directly; the canton contains a police squad of the

24. Cf. Victor Silvera, "Incompatibilité, fonction publique, et affairisme," *Revue Administrative*, November–December 1971, pp. 642–47.
25. In 1946, civil servants obtained the right to join unions. Their right to strike has remained unclear; striking is not forbidden, but neither is it specifically permitted by law.
26. Yves Roulet, "La rémunération du fonctionnaire," in *L'Esprit*, n.s., special issue, January 1970, p. 96.
27. Marceau Long, "Réflexions sur la fonction publique en 1985," in *Revue Administrative*, May–June 1965, p. 242.

national gendarmerie, and in addition functions as the district for elections to departmental councils; the *arrondissement* serves as the basic (single-member) constituency for parliamentary elections; and the department is the immediate subdivision of the national government and the *locus operandi* of its chief agent, the prefect. Although some units—the commune with its council and mayor, and the department with its assembly—have elected bodies, there is very little in the way of locally generated decision-making power. The prefects, who administer the ninety-five departments and are the chief subnational executive officers, are neither elected by the local constituency nor directly responsible to it. Rather, the prefect is a national civil servant appointed by the minister of the interior and responsible to him. The prefect is assisted by a subprefect and a cabinet composed of specialists for public works, agriculture, water supply, public health, housing, finances, and so on. Until 1960, the prefect's task of supervising *all* local services was rendered difficult because the specialists had not only to take orders from him, but also to clear their activities with the relevant national ministries. Since then, the prefect has been empowered to deal with these ministries himself, a change that facilitates his coordinating efforts.

As the chief liaison between the national government and local administrative units, the prefect should maintain good relations with mayors and members of regional and local councils, and process local complaints and demands. Prefects can fulfill their roles as liaisons only as long as they enjoy the confidence of the minister of the interior, who can shift them from one department to another, or even dismiss them. After the end of the "purges" of the immediate post-World War II years, the suspension of prefects became a rare occurrence. However, between the inauguration of Giscard d'Estaing in May 1974 and April 1975, twenty-seven prefects were suspended by his interior minister, Poniatowski, for "inadequate" performance of their functions.[28]

THE COMMUNE

The commune is the basic administrative unit. Based on the old, prerevolutionary parish, the commune was established in 1789. Each commune has a municipal council elected for a six-year term. The number of councilors varies with the size of the commune: for localities of 500 souls or fewer, there are 9 councilors; for towns of over 60,000

---

28. In April 1975, Poniatowski suspended a prefect because he had lacked the requisite coolness in negotiations with a group of kidnappers in a holdup. *Le Monde*, 8 April 1975.

there are at least 37; and for Lyons there are 61, for Marseilles, 63, and for Paris, 90. The council's main function is to select one of its members as mayor and to supervise his governmental activities. Just as the prefect is the chief executive of the department, so the mayor is the chief executive of the commune; and just as the prefect is the government's chief representative in the department, so the mayor is the government's chief representative in the commune—in addition to being the elected spokesman of the people. The mayor has a number of responsibilities, not all of which can be associated with local self-government: he is charged with implementing national laws; the registration of births, marriages, and deaths; the maintenance of electoral lists; and the issuing of building permits. He keeps order, but the police he calls upon is financed and controlled by the national government. He drafts the budget, but many of the expenditures of the commune have been made mandatory by the national government. Just as the laws pertaining to the election of municipal councilors and to the selection of the mayor are made by the national government (which bears the costs of printing ballots and posters in the elections of most communes), so the national government may veto acts of the mayor and may even dismiss him from his post—although this step is resorted to rarely. (It was done in November 1970 in the case of the mayor of Saint-Laurent-du-Pont [Isère] after 145 young people were killed when a dance hall caught fire.)

One scholar emphasizes the strong leadership of the mayor: his control over the political machine, his initiative in local improvement projects, and his role in obtaining for his community the necessary financial assistance from the central government. He insists that "local governments are in fact free to make numerous choices," that they "determine policy," and that "the particular choices made by a local government have consequences for the commune." But he also admits that local governments "are relatively inactive and do not play a vital role in meeting local needs."[29] After the family, the commune is still perhaps the most important socialization agent in France, but it is certainly not an important decision-making unit. Rather it is a subnational administrative unit created and maintained for the convenience of the national government. Its legal powers are determined by the government in Paris; and to the extent that the mayor has significant political power he derives it not merely from the fact that he is the mayor or local notable, but because—especially if his commune is

29. Mark Kesselman, *The Ambiguous Consensus* (New York: Knopf, 1967), p. 8. See Appendix B, pp. 171–84, for a description of legal powers of communes.

large—he uses his position in order to exert influence on a political party on the national level and get himself elected to Parliament.

According to another scholar, the fact that mayors are often also deputies does not seem to reduce their dependence on the prefect. In interviews conducted in 1973, it was revealed that 47.9 percent of the mayors received special favors through the prefectoral system, as against 11.1 percent through ministerial offices.[30] The position of the mayor in his relationship to the prefecture may be strengthened if he has an additional public office, such as the chairmanship of a mixed (public-private) construction agency or housing or social aid office. Furthermore, the prefecture may sometimes be bypassed, particularly in large towns, whose mayors may have direct dealings with the Finance Ministry via the Delegation for Space Planning and Regional Action (*délégation à l'aménagement du térritoire et à l'action régionale*— DATAR), which helps secure funds for regional and local economic projects. Finally, the mayor of a large town may have less need for the intercession of the prefecture if he is himself appointed to the cabinet. A classic example is former Premier Chaban-Delmas, mayor of Bordeaux since 1947.

The government of Paris has always been exceptional, and the national government has taken a special interest in it because the capital is the pride and property of the French nation. By special statute promulgated by Napoleon in 1800, the City of Paris was divided into twelve administrative districts (*arrondissements*). During the Second Empire eight more districts were added, to form the twenty subdivisions existing to this day. Each *arrondissement* has its own mayor (but no separate council). His responsibilities are quite restricted, hardly encompassing more than the maintenance of personal registers and electoral rosters, and the performance of marriages. There is an elected municipal council for all twenty *arrondissements* that has the power to change street names, to recommend budgets, and to issue traffic regulations. The real government is concentrated in the executive, which in the case of Paris consists of two prefects: the prefect of the Seine and the prefect of police, both of whom are under the authority of the Ministry of the Interior, and whose jurisdictions sometimes overlap. Such a centralized administration has proved somewhat inadequate in view of the urban sprawl around the capital. To take into account suburban growth and population shifts, some departments surrounding Paris were subdivided in the early 1960s. In addition, there was established a Paris

30. Sidney Tarrow, "Local Constraints and Regional Reform: A Comparison of France and Italy," *Comparative Politics* 7 (October 1974): 1–36.

"regional government"—with its own (appointed) council—which is concerned with certain types of public services and urban planning. In December 1975, the Assembly passed a bill providing (for the first time since 1870) for a mayor for all of Paris—to be elected for a six-year term—and for an enlargement of the capital's municipal service bureaus. The two prefects, however, are to remain, and the mayor will have no more power than his colleagues in other towns.[31]

To a very large extent the administrative powerlessness of local governmental units is caused by their relative poverty. Budgetary options are limited by the lack of financial resources of the locality and by its underdeveloped revenue-generating powers. Some of the locally collected taxes, voted on by the municipal council, are quite petty, such as dog license taxes, hunting and fishing fees, and surtaxes on the income tax. Other, and more important, taxes—e.g., assessments on property, on rents, and on shops, which are collected by the local government—are based upon the national government's calculation of the taxable worth of each community, a calculation that local economic developments have rendered unrealistic in many communes. Such revenues cover little more than half the expenses that must be incurred in the administration of required services—the rest coming from the national government in the form of grants-in-aid. Much of this national subsidy comes from the value-added tax which is collected locally, transferred to the national government, and then reallocated to local governmental units. There has been a progressive increase in the amount of money allocated by the central government to local communities (from $700 million in 1958 to $1.5 billion in 1964 to $2 billion in 1970). In 1975, about 85 percent of the personal income taxes collected by the national government were in fact paid out to localities; but their share of the total governmental expenditures is quite small (in 1967, it was 13 percent in France as compared to 24 percent in West Germany and 43 percent in the United States[32]—and was still below 20 percent in 1970).

The ineffectiveness of municipalities has been due also to the character of their locally recruited administrative personnel, which has been described as "top-heavy, bureaucratic and archaic," and as "reproducing and often multiplying the faults of the national bureaucracies." In many of the smaller towns, the municipal employee is "aged, not well-educated, lethargic," and has little job mobility.[33]

31. Cf. François Luchaire, "Faut-il un préfet à la capitale?" Le Monde, 11 November 1975.
32. Mignot and d'Orsay, Machine administrative, p. 48. Cf. Jean de Savigny, L'Etat contre les communes? (Paris: Seuil, 1971), p. 64, which cites 8% for departments and 20% for communes.
33. Pierre Gaudez, "La réforme des collectivités locales," Le Monde, 4 June 1975.

Finally, the lack of viability of local communities stems from the excessive multiplicity and archaic nature of local units. There are still some 37,000 communes in France, as compared to 1,350 in Britain, 8,000 in Italy, and 24,000 in West Germany. This large number was perfectly realistic about 150 years ago when France was essentially agrarian and the extent of local services was limited. Today many communes are inadequate as administrative units because of their depopulation, their loss of an economic base, and their consequent inability to maintain essential services efficiently. Only 12 percent of the communes are "urban" settlements of more than 2,000 inhabitants.[34] In 1971, 24,000 communes (i.e., nearly two-thirds of the total) had fewer than 500 inhabitants, and only 37 had more than 100,000. Many residents of rural communes have moved to the cities, a move that has spurred the growth of metropolitan areas which spill over into several traditional administrative subdivisions. Grenoble, for example, increased in population from 80,000 in 1950 to 185,000 in 1970, and its metropolitan area to well over 250,000.

Raymond Marcellin, who was minister of the interior until 1973, seemed to be interested in giving greater authority to the communes. In the spring of 1970 he declared at a meeting of the National Association of Mayors: "The city hall (la mairie) is the most perfect symbol of an administration accessible to those who are being administered and the most responsive to the concerns of man. The commune is also the most natural arena for civic training."[35] That civic training is, unfortunately, likely to result in anticentralistic, evaluative, and antistate attitudes as long as local administrative units possess only phantom powers.

ADMINISTRATIVE REFORM AND "REGIONALIZATION"

Since the end of World War II, French governments, for a variety of reasons, have been concerned with the reform of subnational administration: (1) population movements and inequalities;[36] (2) the need for new forms of functional administration for which old units were insufficient; (3) the problems of duplication and inefficiency; (4) the recognition of the fact that regional provincial attitudes have survived strongly in some areas (e.g., Alsace, Brittany, and Provence) and that these attitudes—as well as the localism of political parties—may be inconsistent with existing patterns of overcentralization; and (5) the

---

34. Kesselman, *Ambiguous Consensus*, p. 4.
35. *Le Monde*, 8 April 1970.
36. An example of such inequality: at the end of the 1960s the department of Basses-Alpes had a population of 83,354, and Nord, 1,917,452.

popular desire to participate in a more meaningful type of grass-roots politics. Similar developments can of course be found in other Western European countries with unitary governments; and it is quite probable that the attempts by France's neighbors—e.g., Italy and the Low Countries—to devise novel administrative formulas inspired French politicians and technocrats.

Originally the centralization of the French administrative structure served the purpose of national unification, but today this centralization is viewed as somewhat dysfunctional. The word "regionalization" is now on the lips of many politicians and technocrats; regionalization, however, does not mean federalization, i.e., the creation of viable subnational decision centers, for that would constitute too drastic a departure from French administrative tradition.[37] Moreover, different political parties are opposed to regionalization: the Communists for ideological reasons, and the Gaullists for fear lest too much power accrue to local or regional assemblies that tend to be controlled by anti-Gaullist politicians.[38] Furthermore, the establishment of meaningful regional autonomy might deprive the national government of the opportunity to grant payoffs to local politicians as a means of securing support for its policies. Regionalism does, however, imply the creation of better and more realistic instruments for the regional or local execution of centrally conceived policies. One way in which local government has been modernized has been the passing of laws permitting the merger of communes which have become too small and inefficient to perform mandatory services by themselves. As an alternative to merger, a law passed in July 1971 permitted the establishment of commune associations for the joint administration of selected public services, and laws passed subsequently extended the communes' powers in financial matters.[39]

Another approach to administrative reform has been the creation of economic regions. These were first established during the Fourth Republic, in order to provide the means for local, and therefore more

37. See Suleiman, *Politics, Power and Bureaucracy*, pp. 24–29, 33.
38. In March 1976, following the cantonal elections, the UDR had less than 10% of the department council seats, and controlled only 11 of the 95 councils. *Le Monde*, 17 and 20 March 1976.
39. "L'allègement de la tutelle administrative," *Revue Administrative*, July 1971, pp. 459–62. See also *L'Année politique 1971*, p. 45; and Yves Madiot, *Fusions et regroupements de communes* (Paris: LGDJ, 1973). The commune associations are not "interest groups" in the proper sense; rather, they are gatherings of municipal councilors whose recommendations must still be approved by the national government. Elisabeth Zoller, "La création des syndicats de communes: une décision des communes ou de l'état?" *Revue du droit public* 92 (July–August 1976): 985–94.

relevant, input of economic information necessary for economic planning, and also to have more realistic units to which to apply regional plans (*plans nationaux d'aménagement du territoire*)—containing a catalogue of needs and resources in order to deconcentrate industry and population. In 1964, the government gave greater recognition to these regions by creating the office of "superprefect" (one of the departmental prefects) for each region (see figure 3). This superprefect does not replace the departmental prefect; rather, he is a coordinator; he "stimulates, encourages, and holds conferences."[40] The superprefect was assisted in his task by Regional Economic Development Commissions (*commissions de développement économique régional*—CODERs), bodies in which local politicians, deputies and senators, interest-group spokesmen, and technicians participated not in the making of policy, but in advising the superprefect about regional needs and prospects (cf. page 251). The hope that the CODERs would provide an arena of provincial economic policy inputs was not fulfilled; they were abolished at the end of 1974, and their tasks were vested in the regional councils, which were to be assisted by lower-powered socioeconomic advisory committees. The regional councils, which had been established by Parliament in July 1972, are composed of locally elected politicians and an equal number of members of Parliament, who belong to the councils ex officio. The councils were given the power to obtain revenues from drivers' license fees and taxes on real estate transfers, to be used to finance regional investments. But the 1972 reforms fell short of providing meaningful provincial self-government. The region has not been recognized as a formal territorial unit of government; the nationally appointed department prefect remains the effective executive; and regional economic development is still largely promoted by means of the national economic plans and investment contracts between the Ministry of Finance on the one hand, and the nationalized industries or the private business sector, on the other.[41]

Regionalization, as instituted thus far, has been criticized as pro-

40. P. B. M. Jones, "The Organization of Regional Economic Planning in France," *Public Administration* (London) 45 (Winter 1967): 358. For a more detailed discussion, see François Damiette, *Le térritoire français et son aménagement* (Paris: Editions sociales, 1969).
41. Jacques Baguenard, "L'organisation régionale (loi du 5 juillet 1972)," *Revue du droit public* 89 (November–December 1973): 1405–65. See also Dominique Henry, "La région et l'aménagement du térritoire," *Revue Administrative*, January–February 1976, pp. 73–75; and, for a general treatment, Jerome Monod and Philippe de Castelbajac, *L'aménagement du térritoire* (Paris: PUF, 1971); and (on regional reform), William G. Andrews, "The Politics of Regionalization in France," in *Politics in Europe*, ed. Martin Heisler (New York: McKay, 1974), pp. 293–322.

Figure 3. The Regions in France

Source: Ambassade de France, Service de Presse et d'Information, *France*, October 1973, p. 5. In 1975, Corsica (*Corse*) was constituted as a separate region and divided into two *départements*.

viding for only a symbolic transfer of financial resources to subnational units and as constituting merely a "caricature of decentralization."[42] As President Giscard d'Estaing has said, "the role of the region is not to administer, but to provide an [additional] coordinating echelon. France is not rich enough to have four echelons of administration— local, departmental, regional and national. It is too divided to wish to introduce new political games."[43] Moreover, meaningful regional reform has been opposed by local politicians, who are against the creation of rival subnational centers of power and who are often themselves part of the national elite.[44]

Meanwhile, the French continue to talk about regional administrative reform; and the government, too, has appeared to make a commitment to such reform by the establishment of a specific portfolio for it. Already in the Fourth Republic there was a minister of civil service and administrative reform. Such a position was retained in the beginning of the Fifth Republic, but its first incumbent, Guy Mollet, being a non-Gaullist, could not be expected to pursue bureaucratic changes. In 1963, the office was downgraded to a Ministry of State (or subministry); and in 1967 there remained only the subministry for the Civil Service. In 1970 that was upgraded to a full Ministry for Administrative Reform, which seemed to indicate that the government had become more serious about reform.[45] After the election of Giscard, Jean-Jacques Servan-Schreiber functioned briefly as the new minister for administrative reform. Since his dismissal, there has remained only the secretary of state for the civil service, who is attached to the premier's office and whose main concern is, presumably, the protection of the existing status of the bureaucracy.

In a study published in 1968, it was pointed out that administrative reform, which goes beyond regionalization, has preoccupied virtually every regime since the end of World War I. There has been an intellectual commitment by governments to address themselves to the fol-

42. François Grosrichard, "Renouvellement politique et ouverture régionale," Le Monde, 28 March 1973. See also Bernard Brigouleix, "La réforme régionale un an après," Le Monde, 20 December 1974; and (on the lack of "legitimacy" of the regions), F. Grosrichard, "Le crépuscule des régions," Le Monde, 28 November 1975.
43. Le Monde, 26 November 1975. See also Alain Peyrefitte, "Régionalisation ou décentralisation?" Le Monde, 22 November 1975.
44. See Sidney Tarrow, "Local Constraints on Regional Reform," Comparative Politics 7 (October 1974): 1–36.
45. Cf. Victor Silvera, "Le prémier remaniement de la structure du septième gouvernement de la cinquième République," Revue Administrative, May 1971, pp. 277–80. See also Mignot and d'Orsay, Machine administrative, p. 104.

lowing "constant themes": the reduction of the number of ministries; better training and more democratic recruitment of civil servants; better coordination of administrative work; the deconcentration of administrative responsibilities; and the reduction of tensions between administrator and administered.[46] In that study, the existence in France of multiple obstacles to reform is noted: the lack of financial resources, the rivalries among administrative offices, and the automatic advancement of civil servants which renders them resistant to change. Moreover, there is the obstacle of a centralizing tradition, which weighs more heavily in France than in other modern countries.[47] This tradition has been directly responsible for the refusal to change existing departmental boundaries (except for the Paris region and, more recently, Corsica), without which meaningful administrative regionalization is very difficult.

For all these reasons, the intellectual commitment to reform has not culminated in serious decentralization of decision-making powers. Many reforms are not effectively carried out because of bureaucratic inertia, and there is a lag of a few years between the proposal of a reform and its implementation. For example, the regulations for setting up the regional councils were produced fifteen months after the 1972 legislation which authorized such councils.

The main tendency of the national government is to pass administrative power not to local communes, but to a "technostructure."[48] In some areas, in fact, the supervision of the central government has even increased, as in the administration of social security, where the Treasury has progressively encroached upon purely technical concerns of regional

46. Albert Lanza, *Les projets de réforme administrative en France de 1919 à nos jours* (Paris: PUF, 1968), pp. 22, 30, 76, and 97 ff. In November 1975, civil servants established the *Association pour l'amélioration des rapports entre administration et le public*, whose task is to be the simplification of procedures and language, the sensitizing of officials to the needs of the public, and the improvement of the public image of officialdom. *Le Monde*, 27 November 1975.
47. It is argued that the following prevailing ideologies (shared by local politicians) have militated against meaningful regionalization: individualism (which does not tolerate geographical intermediaries between citizen and state); and the "logic of capitalism" and the "ethnocentrism of the bourgeoisie" (both of which have justified the traditional suppression of the provinces). Claude de Vos, "La région: à la recherche d'un sens," in "Urbanisation, développement régional et pouvoir public," *Annales de la Faculté des Lettres et Sciences Humaines de Nice*, no. 26 (1975): 137–51. See also Club Moulin, *Les Citoyens au pouvoir* (Paris: Seuil, 1968).
48. Cf. Pierre Viansson-Ponté, "L'Année zéro de l'après-Gaullisme" (pt. 3), *Le Monde*, 7 October 1969.

administrative agencies.[49] The various agencies for the administration of health insurance, family subsidies, and retirement benefits are based on functional and quasi-federal subdivisions, perhaps because their establishment was modeled upon the social security apparatus of a federal West Germany. These agencies, or funds (caisses), which are essentially mutual-aid societies that have acquired legal personalities because they have been coopted for certain administrative tasks and put under the supervision of a national ministry, operate on various subnational levels that do not exactly match the usual administrative units. Thus while there are 22 ordinary "regions" in France, there are only 16 regional social security offices (caisses régionales de sécurité sociale); and while there are 95 departments in metropolitan France, there are 114 family allowance offices and 121 primary social security offices.

Another kind of "functional decentralization" has been the establishment of twenty-four university regions, in which the rector of a particular university is responsible for the administration of the region's entire educational system, including secondary and elementary schools. The university reform laws (lois d'orientation) of Edgar Faure, passed in 1968, and of Olivier Guichard, passed in 1970, have empowered these university regions—and regional councils of education—to make many decisions without direct prior approval by the national Ministry of Education, e.g., in the areas of changing curricula, restructuring academic departments, and the disbursement of certain day-to-day expenditures; but in practice, this kind of decentralization is being implemented with hesitation. The overlapping of geographical and functional administrative subdivisions is symptomatic of the problems of the French administrative system. This overlapping may provide flexibility, but the duplication it introduces must be a nightmare for the specialist in administrative law.

One scholar has spoken of the phenomenon of "overinstitutionalization," that is, the existence of an excessive number of agencies that are resistant to internal organizational adaptation as well as to external pressures for political change.[50] The civil service, with its old legal features and multiplicity of echelons, exemplifies this overinstitutionalization, perhaps in order to compensate for tendencies in France toward individualism, anomic action, and ascriptive recruitment. Political inter-

49. Cf. Doreen Collins, "The French Social Security Reform of 1967," Public Administration (London) 47 (Spring 1969): 91–111.
50. Mark Kesselman, "Overinstitutionalization and Political Constraint: The Case of France," Comparative Politics 3 (October 1970): 21–44.

vention is now less likely to come from a weakened and partly bureau-cratized Parliament,[51] especially since Giscard, himself a professional bureaucrat, exercises tight surveillance over the administrative system.

BUREAUCRACY, TECHNOCRACY, AND ECONOMIC ADMINISTRATION

The personnel involved in economic administration, i.e, that part of the administrative system concerned with nationalized industries and public corporations, fall outside the ordinary civil service categories. The economic-industrial sector of the administrative apparatus has been important in France for several generations; its increased significance since the end of World War II is a manifestation not only of French *dirigisme*, but also of the importance of left-wing political parties during the Fourth Republic that committed France to a policy of nationalization of industries and a plethora of welfare state schemes whose administra-tion required the establishment of novel, technocratic agencies. Recruit-ment of personnel to these agencies is according to technical and nonpolitical criteria, at least in theory, which gives the nationalized industries considerably greater flexibility in hiring than is found in the ministries. In the administration of this economic-industrial sector there are, however, a number of problems. First of all, there is a lack of uniformity even greater than that which now prevails in the regular bureaucracy. There is a multitude of legal forms and institutional typologies—ranging from the (commercial or industrial) *établissement public* to the *régie autonome* (e.g., the Parisian transport network). Although many of these concerns are supposed to be "autonomous" in their administration and to follow purely business or technological rather than political methods in their management, each of the enter-prises is in fact under the control and supervision of a particular minister. Nevertheless, there is very little democratic supervision of these public corporations. Whereas in the Fourth Republic there were special parliamentary "watchdog" committees in charge of ˙specific public corporations, today there is no effective parliamentary control. More-over, there is not the redress mechanism that one finds in the ordinary civil service; the Council of State has virtually no jurisdiction in cases involving the nationalized industries.

51. The percentages of higher civil servants (and teachers at all levels) in the Na-tional Assembly have been as follows: 1936, 3.5 (and 10.5); 1956, 4.0 (15.0); 1958, 8.0 (10.0); 1972, 10.0 (14.0). Based on Philip Williams, *The French Parlia-ment* (New York: Praeger, 1968), p. 34; and André Passeron, "L'administration en question," *Le Monde*, 10 February 1972.

The government's policy on strikes, already confusing with respect to civil servants, appears to be even more unclear for the economic sectors of the public service. It is true that in the Fifth Republic various laws or ordinances have been passed forbidding strikes: in 1964, strikes by airline controllers were forbidden; and in 1963, *grèves tournantes* ("staggered" strikes of short duration by successive segments of the work force in a particular plant or office) were forbidden to all sectors of the nationalized economy. But such laws have not been strictly enforced.

A certain kind of formal "democratic" input is provided by the multipartite advisory councils attached to the various nationalized industries and composed of representatives of consumers, officials, business managers, and trade unions—but these councils have little power, owing to their disparate compositions, their lack of expertise and information, and their purely consultative nature (see chapter 6). The loosening and "modernization" of the administrative structure that have occurred have often been the consequence of pressure from the business sector and have been in the interest of economic expansion. One example of this modernization is the Institute for Industrial Development (IDI), which was established in July 1970 to facilitate company mergers, to secure loans to firms, and to help industries modernize production processes. The IDI is an "autonomous" public corporation and although it is under the supervision of both the minister for industrial and scientific development and the minister of the economy and finance (as it must be since funds are partly obtained from the government), much of its personnel consists of people who have special relations with the business world. Its first head had been director-general of *Crédit Lyonnais*, one of the largest nationalized banks in France.[52]

Finally, there is the technocracy of the French Planning Commission, which is in many ways quite different from the traditional civil service. Like many higher civil servants, most of the planning technocrats are graduates of ENA, and are subject to supervision by a guardian ministry: in this case the Ministry of Economy and Finance. But the relatively small number of economic planning officials (about 150–200 in all) are economists and statisticians; they are likely to be younger than higher civil servants elsewhere, and they work under an aura of "scientific mystique." While ministerial civil servants tend to be etatist and *dirigiste*, many of the planners are nonideological, and are willing to accept both interventionist and liberal principles if these help to

---

52. The IDI differs from the Italian Institute for Industrial Reconstruction (IRI) in that unlike the latter it is *not* a "holding company" for nationalized industries.

promote the objectives of growth and efficiency. But, like the traditional civil servants, French planners have distrusted Parliament because of its "vagaries and vulgarities" and have welcomed the decline of interference from that quarter in the Fifth Republic. The administration of economic policy therefore tends to remain a "partnership between the managers of big business and the managers of the state,"[53] rather than a partnership between government and a diversity of social and economic sectors (see chapter 11). This fact renders technocratic alternatives or supplements to the traditional civil service far less democratic than they might be.

53. Stephen S. Cohen, *Modern Capitalist Planning: The French Model* (Cambridge, Mass.: Harvard University Press, 1969), pp. 35, 39, 52, 163.

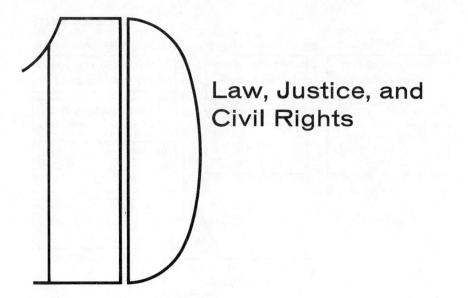

Law, Justice, and Civil Rights

THE JUDICIAL SYSTEM

The French judicial system shares many features with those of Britain and the United States: the belief in procedural due process, the principle that no action is punishable except on the basis of law (*nulla poena sine lege*), the rejection of ex post facto law, the presumption of the innocence of the accused, and the independence of the judiciary. The French system of legal norms is based upon abstract principles (code law) as against the Anglo-American notion of judicial precedents (common law or case law), although such a distinction has in reality become somewhat obscured. Much common law in Anglo-American democracies has been superseded by statute law; conversely, French code law allows for rules of custom and precedent in cases where codes are insufficient. French civil and criminal codes date back to the Romans, but were revised by the Napoleonic Civil Code of 1804, followed by the Penal Code of 1810. Code law has the merit of providing uniformity—of ensuring that in a given case the same principles apply throughout the country and that decisions are not dependent on diverse judicial temperaments. Code law, however, may also be considered more rigid than common law, and its principles might quickly become antiquated. The French Parliament began to modernize the Criminal Code in 1959, and the modernization is still proceeding.

The French judicial system has been widely imitated because it has many admirable features. There is, first, a wide geographical distribution

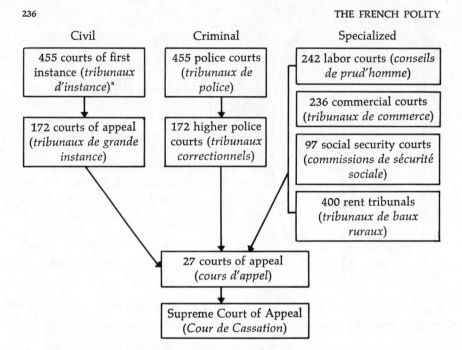

Figure 4. The French Court Structure (Metropolitan France)

[a] Until 1958, there were about 3,000 justices of the peace—one for each canton—whose functions have since been taken over by the courts of first instance.

SOURCES: Ambassade de France, Service de Presse et d'Information, *France*, June 1974, pp. 5–8; and Daniel Rondi, "L'organisation de la justice en France," *Après-Demain*, no. 122 (March 1970): 20–21 (adapted and simplified).

of courts at various levels and therefore easy accessibility to justice for most of the population. Courts of first instance are found in every district (*arrondissement*), and there is a large number of higher courts (see figure 4). In addition to the civil and criminal courts, a network of functionally specialized tribunals exists. The best known are the administrative courts, in which citizens can bring a suit against civil servants for violations of laws and regulations and for arbitrary behavior (see chapter 9). There are also separate regional tribunals for labor relations, social security matters, commercial disputes, and conflicts between tenant farmers and landlords (*baux ruraux*), the decisions of which can be appealed to the ordinary courts of appeal. Some of these specialized tribunals date back to the First Empire and even to the *ancien régime*, but they are especially relevant for highly technical disputes engendered by the administration of the contemporary welfare state. Traditionally, these regional tribunals were structurally separate from the civil and criminal courts. In 1970, legislation was passed to bring these tribunals into the ordinary appellate court system. The law provided for the setting up of "social chambers" within every court of appeal, which were to deal with labor relations and collective contracts. These chambers are each composed of one judge and four lay assessors— two from trade unions and two representing employers—chosen by the government from lists submitted by the appropriate associations. (This method differs from that of the *conseils de prud'homme*, where the assessors are *elected* by trade unions and employers' associations.)

The corps of judges in France represents a distinct segment of the legal profession. A privately practicing attorney cannot, after he is well established, decide to become a judge. A person who is interested in a judicial career must, after completing his studies at a faculty of law, enter a special school, the National Center of Judicial Studies (*Centre National d'Etudes Judiciares*—CNEJ), which was set up in Bordeaux in 1958, and which, in terms of its three-year study program and its social selectivity, is patterned somewhat on the ENA (see chapter 9).[1] Before he completes his studies at the CNEJ, the student must opt for a specific part of the national judiciary: either the magistrature or the *parquet*, the former comprising the judges; the latter, the prosecuting attorneys (*avocats généraux* or *procureurs*) working in behalf of the Ministry of Justice.[2]

Career judges are technically part of the civil service, at least in terms of their security of tenure, pay, promotions, and retirement benefits. Original appointments of judges are made not by the minister of justice, but by the President, on the basis of recommendations by the High Council of the Magistrature. This body consists of the President of the Republic, the minister of justice, plus nine others, appointed by the President, of whom two are appointed at his discretion, six from twelve nominees of the Court of Cassation, and one from three nominees of the Council of State. However, the High Council is no longer in charge of promotions. Although in theory the judiciary is independent

1. In 1963, 24% of the entrants to CNEJ had fathers who were magistrates or members of other legal professions; 24% were descended from civil servants; and only 3.5% from the working class. Charles Laroche-Flavin, "Le magistrat, la justice et l'Etat," *Après-Demain*, no. 122 (March 1970): 11.
2. F. Ridley and J. Blondel, *Public Administration in France* (London: Routledge & Kegan Paul, 1964), p. 136.

of the executive, it tends in practice to be subordinated to the government. Judges are virtually irremovable, but the discretion enjoyed by
the minister of justice in promoting them, or in transferring them to
more desirable locations, tends to politicize the bench.

The organization of the French legal profession appears inordi-
nately complex when compared to the American one, with its single
class of lawyers, or the British one, with its two categories, the barristers
and the solicitors. The French have a half dozen types of legal professions aside from judges: (1) *avocats*, who can plead in most trial courts;
(2) *avoués*, who sometimes plead in lower courts, in minor cases, but
more usually are concerned with the preparation of legal briefs; (3)
agréés, who plead before certain commercial tribunals; (4) *notaires*,
whose main responsibility is the preparation of contracts, wills, and
property settlements;[3] (5) *fiduciaires*, who are concerned with tax matters; and (6) *conseillers juridiques*, who give general legal advice. Recently, there has been a tendency toward simplification of the legal
profession, with the categories of *avocat*, *avoué*, and *agréé* in the
process of merger.

At the top of the legal profession's hierarchy are the *avocats aux
conseils*, of whom there are about sixty, who may appear before the
Court of Cassation, the highest court of appeal for civil, criminal, and
socioeconomic cases, or the Council of State, its counterpart for administrative cases.[4] At the bottom there are the *greffiers* (court clerks) and
the *huissiers* (ushers). This excessive functional differentiation goes
back several centuries. The "medieval" aspects of the profession are
also manifested by the special gowns the *avocats* and *avoués* are required
to wear in court; by the hereditary nature of some of the categories
(e.g., *greffiers*, *huissiers*, and *agréés*); and by the retention of the practice of setting fees by law for all but the *avocats*.[5]

The judicial procedure itself, which differs in some important
respects from Anglo-American patterns, presents certain problems.
There is the "inquisitorial" system of trial procedure whereby the
presiding judge intervenes actively in the trial by examining the defendant, the witnesses, and the lawyers on both sides (as contrasted
with the "accusatorial" or "adversary" system common in the United
States and Britain, where the judges' primary duty is to ensure the

3. The *notaire* is the typical "village lawyer" who in more traditional preindustrial
   times used to be one of the chief liaisons between the (often illiterate) peasant
   and the legal authorities, and he was therefore—together with priest, village
   teacher, and prefect—a part of the rural elite.
4. Ridley and Blondel, *Public Administration in France*, pp. 138–39.
5. See *New York Times*, 15 June 1971.

orderly progress of the trial). Most verdicts in the lower courts are given—in typical Roman-law fashion—by a panel of judges, the number needed to decide a case varying according to the level of the court and the nature of the charges. However, trial by jury is becoming more common, particularly in courts of appeal (where typically nine jurors and three judges sit together to decide a case, and where a two-thirds majority is needed to uphold a conviction).

There is a much greater tendency in French courts than in Anglo-American ones to convict a defendant, a phenomenon that has given rise to the notion that in France the innocence of the accused is not safeguarded so well as in the United States or Britain, and that in a criminal trial, procedures favor the state.[6] While it is true, that most trials end in conviction, not all of the cases go to trial; there is a lengthy pretrial investigation by police magistrates, in which the various due-process guarantees are applied and in which the suspect may be able to use counsel.

The pretrial investigation of a crime has two stages: the second stage, the *instruction par le juge*, follows the police inquiry, which is often so protracted that an accused is held for a long time in pretrial detention. (In the summer of 1974, the cabinet approved a bill that would limit such detention to six months for minor transgressions.) There is no writ of habeas corpus; although the Penal Code Reform of 1959 (Article 137) specified that "preventive detention is an exceptional measure" (in conformity with Article 66 of the 1958 Constitution, which provides that "no person may be detained arbitrarily"), in 1968 French prisons held 13,223 pretrial inmates, many of whom were ultimately not brought to trial because of lack of sufficient presumption of guilt.[7]

The question arises whether or not judges in France, who so strongly influence the course of a trial, render justice democratically. Some years ago, a magistrate made the following observation:

Justice recognizes three classes of man: the superman, which includes officers, policemen and politicians; human, which includes ordinary members of society and members of the learned professions; and subhuman, which comprises sections of the population which vary according to the circumstances of the time: Arabs,

6. Henry Abraham, *Courts and Judges* (New York: Oxford University Press, 1959), p. 11.
7. Paul Arrighi, "La liberté de l'homme face à la justice," *La Nef* 27 (January–March 1970): 23. In 1972, the number of Frenchmen under preventive detention was about 10,000.

Jews (during the Occupation), the working class, or Communists (during the McCarthy period in the United States).[8]

The above statement is probably too sweeping. Many French judges have become more sympathetic to the common man as their own self-image as members of an elite has been blurred. Due in part to an expansion of the judiciary and insufficient appropriations for the magistrature (which at the end of the 1960s amounted to only about 1 percent of the government budget), there has been an increase in the unionization of judges; most of them are members of the *syndicat de la magistrature*. The judges' and lawyers' associations have, since the late 1960s, not only agitated for better pay; they have also expressed concern for a liberalization of the penal code; the overhauling of the labyrinthine court structure; and the simplification of the legal language, which is often incomprehensible to the average citizen.[9] Nonetheless, traditional class attitudes—even after the loosening of interclass relations since the rebellions of May 1968—have continued to be reflected in the fact that a trial judge often addresses a bourgeois defendant as *monsieur*, a workingman merely by his last name, and an Algerian more familiarly as *tu*.[10]

There is no doubt that in France, as in most highly stratified societies where legal counsel costs money and where the judiciary tends to be recruited from the bourgeoisie and hence to reflect bourgeois values, the judicial system favors the established regime and the established classes, and one may cite notorious cases to illustrate this point.[11] Discrimination against the poor will undoubtedly continue—despite a reform in 1972 that provides for free legal counsel to indigent defendants.[12]

Class justice is apparent in particular in the application of what Anglo-Americans might call "cruel and unusual punishment." The death penalty (by guillotine) is still valid in France (whereas capital punishment has been abolished in West Germany) and is administered mainly against members of the lower classes. Since the end of the Third Re-

---

8. Quoted in Pierre Vidal-Naquet, *Torture: Cancer of Democracy* (Baltimore, Md.: Penguin, 1963), p. 125.
9. See Laroche-Flavin, "Le magistrat," pp. 9–14.
10. *New York Times*, 15 December 1971. See also Raoul Dargent, "La crise judiciaire en France," *Le Monde*, 17 September 1969; and *Le Monde*, 13 April 1973.
11. For example, the Dewevre case of 1972, in which despite circumstantial evidence pointing to a prominent notary in the murder of a 15-year old girl in a northern provincial town, a young inmate of a reformatory was indicted and convicted, even though the veracity of his confession was doubted.
12. "L'oeuvre législative de l'Assemblée Nationale," *Le Monde*, 22 December 1972.

public there have been no public executions and Presidents have exercised with increasing frequency their right of pardon in capital crimes; there were eleven executions between 1956 and 1961, six between 1962 and 1967, and only one between 1968 and 1971. Two men were executed in November 1972, the first application of the death penalty in three and a half years. It is quite likely that before long the death penalty will be abolished, although 63 percent of Frenchman favor its retention.[13]

Until recently, the laws concerning abortion appeared to be much more discriminatory against the poor than the well-to-do. Abortion was considered a crime for which the patient was punished by a heavy fine; the physician was subjected to a fine, a prison sentence, or the loss of his license. In recent years, however, sentences had been suspended because of a public outcry and a manifesto issued by several hundred physicians confessing to having performed abortions.[14] As a result, the government, in one of the first steps undertaken by the Giscard Presidency to liberalize aspects of French society, successfully introduced a bill in 1974 to legalize abortion. The government of Pompidou had already promoted two related measures: the introduction of sex education in public schools, and the granting of equal rights of inheritance to illegitimate children.[15]

THE POLICE

The poor are also particularly exposed to the vagaries of the police, who have significant power in the judicial process. There have been many reports of police brutality, especially against workers, farmers, and leftists. These categories of people not only form the most immediate underclass to the police force, which is recruited primarily from the petite bourgeoisie, but they are also the most likely to confront the police in situations judged by the latter to be provocative—in demonstrations and strikes. Moreover, the police must take orders from the government—the Ministry of the Interior and the prefectures, which have been very conscious about "law and order."

The French concern for law and order, which is understandable in a society given to periodic challenges to the regime, is reflected in the

13. Michel Foucault, "The Guillotine Lives," *New York Times*, 8 April 1973.
14. Claude Servan-Schreiber, "France and the Abortion Struggle," *New York Times*, 10 March 1973.
15. "L'oeuvre législative de l'Assemblée Nationale," *Le Monde*, 22 December 1972. For a somewhat pessimistic discussion of penal code reforms since the early 1970s, see Roger Errera, *Les libertés à l'abandon* (3rd ed.; Paris: Seuil, 1975).

size and complexity of the police system. It comprises about 100,000 uniformed men, of whom one-third, the *Sûreté Nationale*, operate in communes with more than 10,000 inhabitants; the rest, the *gendarmerie*, operate in the smaller communes but also have departmental, regional, and military police functions. In addition, there is the Paris police, comprising about 28,000 men, which is specially organized and under the immediate direction of the prefect of police. Furthermore, there is the CRS (*Compagnies républicaines de sécurité*), a mobile reserve police force of some 15,000, which (like the American National Guard) can be called upon to quell riots. This impressive police establishment has, however, not transformed France into a police state: the structural subdivisions; the jurisdictional competition between the Ministry of Interior and the Ministry of Defense; the possibility of redress in administrative tribunals; and the watchful eye of the French Left, the intellectuals, and other sectors—all these have contibuted to moderating the power of the police.

Moreover, the police have become concerned about their public image; a few years ago, the policemen's union (*Fédération autonome de Syndicats de Police*) held public interviews and protest demonstrations to counter the police's unpopularity and to inform the public about inadequate pay and working conditions.[16] A spokesman for the association of policemen declared that "policemen wish to be neither the footmen (*valets*) of power nor the garbagemen (*éboueurs*) of society."[17] The sensitivity of policemen to being the "unbeloved" (*mal aimés*) of society has occasionally affected their performance, and in 1970 prompted Raymond Marcellin, then interior minister, to initiate libel actions against several newspapers of the extreme Left that had been particularly critical of the police.

There have been times, however, when the police have acted in sympathy with society's victims: during the Events of May 1968, there was evidence of fraternization between the police and the striking workers.[18] In 1971 the prefect of police of Paris was dismissed for not being tough enough on leftist demonstrators. In the same year the case of a French youth who was imprisoned for having attacked a policeman became a political issue. When the youth was released by a court of appeals in Paris, René Tomasini, the secretary-general of the Gaullist party (UDR), attacked the laxity of the judiciary, a charge for which he had to apologize.[19]

16. *L'Année politique 1971*, p. 22.
17. *Le Monde*, 23 January 1973.
18. *New York Times*, 24 May 1968.
19. *New York Times*, 20 February 1971.

FREEDOM OF SPEECH AND PRESS

Many of the infringements of a citizen's substantive rights are caused not so much by the police as by existing legislative provisions and the governmental attitudes that give rise to them. Although France is committed, in terms of both natural and statute law, to the right of free speech, she has found it necessary to infringe upon this freedom occasionally. Such infringement occurred especially when, after the Liberation, the government had to deal with World War II collaborationists and during the Algerian crisis with seditious elements. Between 1960 and 1962 a number of Algerian plotters, who had been arrested without warrant, were tried by special tribunals under the Ministry of the Armed Forces, rather than by ordinary courts, and the usual rights of the defendants (including protection against self-incrimination) were severely restricted.[20] In 1963 such an approach was institutionalized by the establishment of the controversial State Security Court, for cases of conspiracy and treason. Under the existing law, any case that involves persons accused of subversion can be transferred, by decision of the minister of justice, from the ordinary courts to the State Security Court. This power has been used in more than two hundred instances— particularly in order to prosecute Maoists and other revolutionary leftists. The Security Court's constitutionality has been frequently questioned, and in recent years that court has not been especially active. Moreover, in 1970 the Anti-Breakers' Law was enacted, under which participants in public disorders (and members of organizations instigating them) can be punished. Under this law, the government has been able to ban public meetings of leftists, to suspend radical teachers, and to censor Maoist (but not Communist) publications.[21]

In addition, there is a somewhat older tradition of infringement on freedom of speech and press. Freedom of the press was guaranteed by a law passed in 1881, but the same law made it a felony to publish statements damaging to the President of the Republic (*lèse majesté*) or to public authorities in general. This law seemed in the process of desuetude for many years, but the Gaullists revived it. In the Third Republic the law was applied fewer than ten times; in the Fourth Republic, three times; but in the Fifth Republic (more exactly, between

---

20. Jerome B. King, "The Canal Affair and the OAS Cases," in *Politics and Civil Liberties in Europe*, ed. Ronald F. Bunn and William G. Andrews (New York: Van Nostrand, 1967), pp. 38–59.
21. See J. Deedy, "Repression in France: New Anti-Destroyer Law," *Commonweal* 92 (12 June 1970): 282.

1958 and 1970) about 100 times.[22] As if this law were not enough, Article 30 of the Penal Code of 1959 gives departmental prefects (and the prefect of police in Paris) the right to "undertake all acts necessary with a view to preventing crimes and violations of the . . . security of the state."[23] These laws have been used as the basis for seizures of newspapers and occasionally even the harassment and temporary detention of newspaper vendors. The most notorious instance of governmental intervention, the seizure of a Maoist journal, La Cause de Peuple, and the arrest of its editor, occurred in 1970. The case backfired on the government, however, when Jean-Paul Sartre, the famous philosopher, immediately took over the journal's editorship and, to the great embarrassment of the government, transformed the seizure into a cause célèbre. Another recent instance of governmental interference concerned Le Canard Enchaîné, a mass-circulation weekly of political satire. Early in 1974, following a typical "revelation" by the paper about scandals involving Gaullists, the journal's offices were raided and its staff phones wiretapped by government agents. According to a law of 1970, wiretaps (generally placed by French security services or interministerial committees) can be used, with the premier's approval, only for reasons of national security. But the law has been widely abused. In fact, about 1,500 Paris telephones of union leaders, journalists, left-wing politicians, and even government officials were bugged during the last year of Pompidou's Presidency.[24] (After Giscard d'Estaing assumed the Presidency, most wiretapping abuses were discontinued.)

Despite such instances, the French press has remained relatively free and unobstructed. There is a great diversity and independence of opinion, and there are a number of highly respected newspapers (see table 21). Most of the important newspapers are published in Paris (although there are some distinguished provincial newspapers). Journals are not the forums of the common man they are (ideally) presumed to be in the United States. Letters to the editor are rare in French newspapers. The average person can contribute to the weekly newsmagazine, L'Express, but Le Monde, which is noted for the regular commentaries written by France's foremost intellectuals (and for its general

22. In 1965, a right-wing author, Jacques Laurent, was sentenced to prison by a criminal court for having written a book, Mauriac sous de Gaulle (Paris: Table Ronde) that was critical of de Gaulle. The publisher, too, was fined. Between 1965 and 1970, the law was applied "only" three or four times a year. Cf. François Sarda, "Offenses aux chef d'état," Le Monde, 8–9 March 1970. See also Philip Williams, The French Parliament (New York: Praeger, 1968), p. 36n.
23. Frede Castberg, Freedom of Speech in the West (Oslo: Oslo University Press, 1960), p. 47.
24. Le Nouvel Observateur, 7 March 1973.

Table 21
Parisian Daily Newspapers

Newspaper	Circulation in 1976	Political Orientation
L'Aurore	290,000	Conservative
La Croix	135,000	Catholic
Les Echos	62,500	Financial
Le Figaro	402,000	Conservative
France-Soir	727,000	Conservative
L'Humanité	151,000	Communist party
Le Monde	432,000	Liberal
Le Parisien Libéré	785,000	Conservative (lower-middle class)
Libération	20,000	Extreme Left

SOURCE: Europa Yearbook 1976 (London: Europa Publications Ltd., 1976), p. 639.

excellence), accepts letters or responses only from "established" individuals.

There are, theoretically, certain limits to a newspaper's independence insofar as the newspaper depends for many of its new sources on a government-controlled news agency (Agence-France-Presse) that is under the supervision of the Ministry of Information; and more importantly, insofar as the newspaper depends upon the government's indirect financial subsidies. These subsidies involve reduced postal and railroad transportation charges and reduced tax rates (including a waiver of value-added tax). These reductions may together amount to 10–15 percent of the total budget of a typical newspaper, and may make the difference between the continuation or termination of publication.[25] Although there is little concrete evidence that the government has used its fiscal powers to control the content of newspaper articles, it is noteworthy that many important newspapers have been hesitant about attacking government policy. Two of the top Parisian bourgeois

25. Jacques Sauvageot, "L'Etat, la presse et le citoyen," Le Monde, 22 June 1972.

dailies, *Le Figaro* and *France-Soir*, are generally pro-government; a third one, *Le Monde*, while often critical of the government, tends in most cases to endorse it on foreign policy and other crucial issues.[26] Several important newspapers have in recent years had to cease publication, including the Socialist party's *Populaire* and the Gaullist-oriented *Paris-Jour* and *La Nation*. Newspapers are beset by rising costs of newsprint (much of it imported) and rising wages of reporters and printers. The decline in the number of dailies in France—paralleled in other countries—has been significant: from 414 in 1892 to 84 in 1966. The typical French newspapers—with such notable exceptions as *L'Humanité*, which has solid Communist party backing, and *Le Monde*, which has an international and elite subscribership—cannot depend any longer on support by a political party because the latter's own coffers are empty. Newspapers lacking such support are occasionally maintained as a "hobby" by business interests (e.g., *L'Aurore* and *Le Figaro*, which are owned by textile magnates). Newspapers, moreover, cannot rely much on advertising, because since 1968 the main medium for advertisers has been the television network.

Despite the fact that TV ownership is now widespread among Frenchmen, newspapers are not likely to be completely eclipsed by television because of the suspicions that people harbor about the latter medium. The radio and television networks are a government monopoly in France, as in many other countries. But while in West Germany they are regionalized, in France they are centralized; while in Britain the BBC is an autonomous corporation rarely subject to government interference, in France all broadcasting was until recently controlled by the ORTF (*Office pour la télévision et la radiodiffusion françaises*), which was never free of intervention by the ruling authorities. Cabinet control over radio and television during the Fourth Republic did not materially infringe upon the independence and diversity of these media, since there were so many cabinet reshuffles and there were several political parties in a position to exert influence over broadcasts. Although technically an autonomous agency, ORTF in the Fifth Republic was a mouthpiece of the Gaullist regime and of the President in particular.

Since the beginning of the Fifth Republic, TV and radio news broadcasts of *France-Inter*, especially, have been highly selective and one-sided—except for the limited time made available to Opposition candidates during election campaigns and the occasional TV and radio

---

26. See Michel Legris, *Le Monde tel qu'il est* (Paris: Plon, 1976), for a sharp critique of that newspaper's excessively pro-establishment position.

programs in which political differences have been aired by means of a dialogue (e.g., *Aux Armes Egales*). News has been frequently doctored by distortion or omission, and the government almost always presented in a favorable light. In 1964, the role of the government was strengthened when ORTF was put under the control of an interministerial committee including the premier and an advisory committee composed mainly of Gaullists.

During the May Events of 1968, the failure to provide full and accurate information led to resentment by the public and by the reporting staff. Many of the latter struck and were dismissed from their jobs. Periodic attempts by Parliament (or rather, by the Senate) to provide a truer measure of independence for radio and television have failed.[27]

This is not to say the ORTF was ever monolithic; in fact, several "feudal fiefdoms" tried to make their influence felt and to provide an input in broadcasting: the Ministry of Posts, Telephones and Telegraphy (PTT), which collects the annual subscribers' fees; the Foreign Ministry, whose views must be taken into account in the presentation of international news; the ENA; big business (which provides fees for advertising); the Ministry of Information; and the Ministry of Culture. But in the opinion of one newspaper, this diversity did not lead to real independence; rather, it made the ORTF into a "blocked society."[28]

In the summer of 1972, Parliament passed a bill providing for the reorganization of ORTF. The network was divided, with each of the three television channels and the radio (*France-Inter* and *France Musique*) being granted a separate budget and its own authority concerning finances. The system was to be "advised" by a board composed of two representatives of views and listeners, three representatives of the press, and six representatives of the state. The latter six, as well as the director (chairman of the board), were appointed by the cabinet.[29] The representatives of the listeners were named by the Assembly and Senate committees on Cultural Affairs. As before, the ORTF was under the guardianship (*tutelle*) of the premier.

A new director, Arthur Conte, was chosen. Although an orthodox

---

27. Cf. Williams, *French Parliament*, pp. 91–93. Some commentators are skeptical about the desire of Parliament to foster a genuinely free information policy; they argue that the "timidity" of journalists is paralleled by "a fundamental intolerance on the part of the political forces [including opposition parties] . . . regarding information." Jean Legres and Claude Sales, "L'information: fin des monopoles?" *Etudes*, February 1976, pp. 163–79.
28. "Les Féodalités," *Le Monde*, 4 May 1972.
29. Ambassade de France: Service de Presse et d'Information, *Bulletin*, August–September 1972. For text of the government bill, see *Le Monde*, 11–12 June 1972.

Gaullist who perceived the ORTF as a handmaiden of the government, M. Conte soon ran afoul of Pompidou and was dismissed. Under President Giscard, further reforms have been undertaken, ostensibly to provide for more meaningful autonomy and decentralization for the radio and television networks. In January 1975, ORTF as such was eliminated, and replaced by six independent units, each with its own budget: one unit for broadcasting facilities, four national program networks (one for radio and three for television), and one unit to provide for production facilities. This decentralization was intended to facilitate greater technical innovation and greater internetwork competition; but since the state continues to maintain a monopoly over broadcasting, it is uncertain whether these structural reforms will result in more genuine freedom to criticize the government.[30]

30. In October 1974, Giscard announced proposed liberalization measures for the networks. In the same month the government dismissed the director-general of Europe No. I, because in his broadcasts he had not been "obsequious" enough to the government. Cf. Le Figaro, 25 October 1974. Europe No. I is technically a "private" station, in which the government has 37% of the shares.

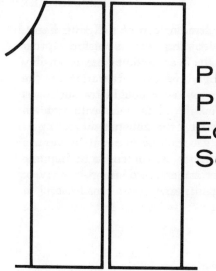

Processes and Problems of Economic and Social Policy

The governments of postwar France have been committed to three distinct economic policies: reconstruction and industrial expansion, the improvement of the material and social conditions of the majority, and the redistribution of wealth. The main approaches used were an active and innovative social policy, mainly enacted by Parliament; the nationalization of crucial industries; and economic planning.

During the early years of the Fourth Republic, extensive social security schemes—whose legislative basis had been laid by the Popular Front government of 1936—were implemented and expanded to include statutory medical coverage, old-age insurance, paid vacations, family income supplements, subsidies for students and, somewhat later, a minimum-wage policy. In order to move France closer to a "mixed economy," the first postwar government pursued a policy of extensive nationalizations, which culminated in the public or quasi-public ownership of railroads, gas and electric companies, seaports and airfields, urban transport, civil aviation, mines, several banks and insurance companies, and petroleum prospecting and marketing.

Some of the nationalization had been ideologically motivated; during the Popular Front regime, munitions manufacturing had been nationalized, since it was hoped, naively, that war would become less likely once the profit-oriented "merchants of death" were expropriated. Throughout the period of tripartism (1944–47), the Socialist and other "collectivist" parties applied pressure to bring the major sectors of production under public control. Some nationalization was externally conditioned, episodic, or punitive. After World War II, the Renault auto works were taken over by the government because the firm's private owners had been collaborators with the Nazi regime; the railroads in Alsace were nationalized when that area reverted to France after World War I; and the railroads in central France were bought by the government because under private ownership they had become unprofitable. A number of industries were acquired by the government because of their monopolistic character, such as gas and electricity.[1] Whatever its origin, the nationalized sector in France is one of the most important among the Western industrialized countries, accounting in a typical year for more than half of all investments, and serving as a useful tool for comprehensive economic planning.[2]

THE MEANING OF PLANNING

Immediately following World War II, when the need arose for an overall plan to reconstruct the war-ravaged economy, the government rejected the Soviet planning model, which is imperative and which depends exclusively on a totally nationalized economy. However, in accordance with the French etatist tradition and in the interest of accommodating to left-wing demands for welfare statism and social redistribution, the French authorities also rejected the free market model. They compromised by devising an economic plan that is "indicative" or "voluntaristic" in that it tries to combine governmental fiscal intervention and official policy preferences with the decisions, commitments, and projections of the free market.

Economic planning in France is based on several assumptions and processes: (1) the notion of a total set of goals for society, (2) a rational and empirical orientation to problem solving, (3) a process of information gathering, (4) a matching of information on available resources with a number of "options," and (5) the belief that the self-interest of the private sector can be merged with a common interest promoted by the public authorities. On the basis of a complex system of stock-taking and forecasting, the government makes long-range decisions affecting employment, production, consumption, allocation of resources, growth, social security, public-works projects, and the like. The system does not impose a set of decisions that are absolutely binding upon all private

---

1. *Les entreprises publiques nationales* (Paris: Documentation française, 22 November 1963). See also Mario Einaudi et al., *Nationalization in France and Italy* (Ithaca, N.Y.: Cornell University Press, 1955), esp. pt. 2, for types of nationalized industry and their organization.
2. Pierre Gonod, *Le plan français* (Paris: Ministère de la Cooperation, 1962), p. 212.

sectors; rather, it offers guidelines, based on economic data, which the government coordinates with the decisions of private firms, the agricultural sector, and even the trade unions.

Planning involves a variety of governmental, quasi-public, and private institutions (see figure 5). At the apex is the General Commission on Planning (*Commissariat général au Plan*—CGP), which is staffed by economists, statisticians, sociologists, and other specialists, and which is attached to the premier's office. The government provides a catalogue of general objectives or aims to the CGP, which produces several alternative blueprints containing basic economic data, short- and long-range projections, and recommendations for resource allocation. These preliminary blueprints are then submitted to subnational and functional units for discussion and for additional inputs. In the course of years, a large number of such units or agencies has developed, in which, in a typical year, more than 2,000 technicians, local and regional politicians, industrialists, trade unionists, representatives of agricultural and other interests, and independent experts provide information supplementary to that already obtained by the CGP.

The oldest and most complex of these functional-representation devices are the economic "modernization" commissions. The number of such commissions has ranged from twenty-five to thirty, depending upon the plan. The commissions have been functionally divided among several sectors, such as general economy, employment, research, education, housing, and social security. In addition, after France was divided into twenty-two economic development regions, each of these regions was equipped with a Committee for Regional Economic Development (CODER).[3] The CODERs, which existed from 1961 to 1974, consisted half of interest-group representatives, one-quarter of local and regional politicians, and one-quarter of "experts" and "personalities" appointed by the premier. The CODERs were concerned with geographically deconcentrating the French industry, while the modernization commissions, each consisting of between thirty and fifty representatives of the government and the private sector, have been concerned with aggregating the conflicting demands of business, labor, and the "public." A further aggregative process takes place during the final phases of the planning enterprise, when the plan is discussed and dissected in the Social and Economic Council, the national arena of interest-group representatives, before it is approved by the Cabinet.

The public authorities are involved in the planning process at

3. In addition to these regions, France was divided into eight ad hoc geographical units in the late 1960s: the *zones d'étude pour la préparation du VIe Plan*.

1. Preliminary Stage: Information Gathering

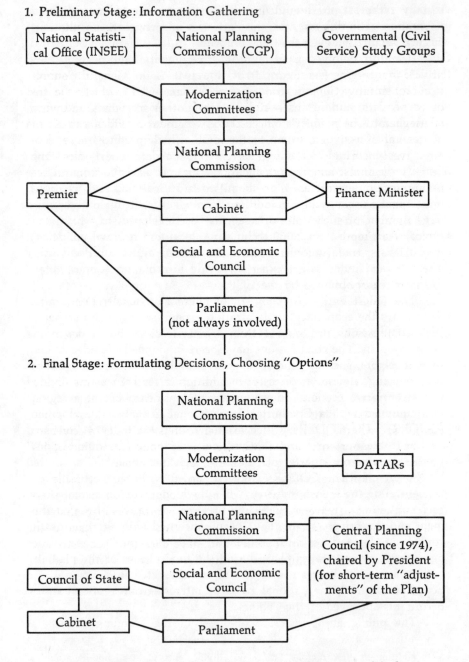

2. Final Stage: Formulating Decisions, Choosing "Options"

Figure 5. The Formulation of Economic Plans (Simplified)

virtually every stage. Thus during the first stage, the technocratic and information-gathering one, there are intimate and ongoing consultations with the Finance Ministry, the Central Bank, and the National Statistical Office (*Institut national de la statistique et des études économiques*—INSEE), the government's collector of aggregate data. During the subsequent consultative phases, the Finance Ministry continues to be involved, while in addition there are the Delegations for Spatial Planning and Regional Action (DATARs), established in 1963, which consist of civil servants assigned by the premier's office to the various economic regions. The DATARs work closely with regional bodies—the (elected) regional councils and the socioeconomic advisory committees (see page 227)—influencing their policy directions via the regional prefect (and probably also influencing local elections). Technically, the DATARs are under the authority of the premier, who has delegated control over them to the minister of the interior. In practice, however, space planning—which embraces land use, urban planning and environmental improvement policies—heavily involves the finance minister, who is in charge of the largest of the various national development funds, the *Fonds du développement économique et social* (FDES).[4]

METHODS AND ORIENTATIONS OF PLANNING

The planning methods of the governmental authorities are, first, the traditional "Keynesian" ones of fiscal intervention: the manipulation of interest rates, the use of governmental contracts, tax allowances, export guarantees, import licenses, tariffs, wage policies, and price controls; second, the granting of investment funds for industrial, urban, and rural development;[5] and third, the use of nationalized industries in order to influence the price structure of private industry.

The question whether the fiscal methods of the public authorities—the "imperative" component of the plan—are conservative or progressive is not easy to answer. On the one hand, it is probably true that the public authorities, represented by the higher civil servants, have been suspicious of private-sector activities and have therefore been striving to direct and control them in behalf of the state's purposes and in behalf

4. French Embassy, Press and Information Division, *France*, July 1975, pp. 5–7. On the confusion of orientations within DATAR, see François Grosrichard, "La DATAR à bout de souffle," *Le Monde*, 3 March 1976.
5. One of the most important of these funds is the *Institut de développement industriel* (IDI). In 1972, this fund had a capitalization of 400 million francs, which was used by the government to keep firms afloat by means of loans or the acquisition of shares.

of official notions of the public interest.[6] On the other hand, it is equally true that many higher civil servants are excessively receptive to the business viewpoint, not only because they originate from the same social and educational milieu as many business leaders, but also because of the employment opportunities in private industry that await a higher civil servant when he retires or resigns. It is estimated that by the mid-1960s about one-fourth of the graduates of ENA who had begun their careers in the government bureaucracy had transferred to elite positions in private business and banking.

The initial fears of the business community that the plan might become a socialistic device were successfully overcome with the appointment of the first planner, Jean Monnet, himself a businessman, who convinced the business community that French-style planning would help save capitalism and stave off further nationalization of industries.[7] Indeed, most chief planners have been chosen either because of their affinity for capitalist management or because of their ideological acceptability to business-oriented premiers: Monnet's successors were Etienne Hirsch, who had once been director of a private chemical firm; Pierre Massé, a director of the French Electricity Board; and François-Xavier Ortoli and Pierre Montjoie, both of whom were friends of Premier Pompidou. (It is curious that two of the chief planners subsequently assumed leading roles in the European Community, which is often viewed as a multinational or supranational "neo-capitalist" enterprise: Monnet was to become the guiding personality of the Coal and Steel Community, and Ortoli, the chief of the Fifth Plan, became the president of the Common Market Commission in 1974.)[8]

The industrialist outlook of the planning directors has been heavily reflected in the composite objectives of each of France's development plans. Thus the First Plan (1946–53) concentrated on reconstruction and quantitative growth; the Second Plan (1954–57), on the modernization

6. Michel Crozier, *The Stalled Society* (New York: Viking, 1973), p. 97. Gaullist ministers have generally endorsed the notion of the primacy of the public authorities over the private sector in economic affairs. However, as Ezra Suleiman points out (*Politics, Power and Bureaucracy in France* [Princeton: Princeton University Press, 1974], pp. 173-77), certain ministers (such as Albin Chalandon, minister of housing and equipment between 1967 and 1972) felt that the hold of the higher civil service over the business community was excessive and favored a more rapid devolution of economic initiatives to the private sector.
7. Stephen S. Cohen, *Modern Capitalist Planning: The French Model* (Cambridge, Mass.: Harvard University Press, 1969), p. 4.
8. Jean Ripert, the planning commissioner since October 1974, is an agricultural engineer who had been briefly involved in the setting up of the Coal and Steel Community before becoming professionally associated with the CGP some twenty years ago. For seven years he was director-general of INSEE.

of industrial and agricultural production; the Third Plan (1958–61), on fiscal stability and the improvement of the balance of payments; the Fourth Plan (1962–65), on regional development and the creation of a million new jobs; the Fifth Plan (1966–70), on a rise in productivity; and the Sixth Plan (1971–75), on a strong annual growth rate, the raising of the level of foreign currency reserves, and an improved highway system.[9] The Seventh Plan (1976–80) is an austerity plan, whose main emphasis is on the reduction of unemployment and the fight against inflation.

All these plans have contained a number of social elements, such as vocational training, increased social benefits, housing, and education.[10] But in view of the closeness between the planners and the business community, the trade unions have had persistent doubt whether the social features of the plan would be actively promoted. To the trade unionist (or the socialist), whose ideal plan is more imperative and less voluntaristic, and is primarily an instrument of a redistributive policy, the capitalist nature of the plan is manifested not only by the recurrent stress on productivity, but also by the underrepresentation of organizations speaking for the beneficiaries of progressive social policies in the various discussion committees. The average representation of the participating sectors in the modernization committees for the First through the Fourth Plan was as follows: labor, 10 percent; farmers, 2.25 percent; business and management, 38.25 percent; and civil servants, 25.75 percent.

But even if unions were equitably represented in these bodies, they would still be at a disadvantage vis-à-vis the government and the business sectors, since the unions have been impecunious and ideologically fragmented and have lacked the technical expertise and industrial information possessed by their antagonists. To be sure, the attitudes of the various trade unions are not uniform. The CGT has been most consistently negative about the plan, because it is designed to preserve the capitalist structure; the attitude of the CFDT has been moderately negative, because in its view the planning process does not provide for genuine industrial democracy; while the FO tends to be favorably inclined and has what its rivals consider an excessively "collaborationist" attitude. (In 1965 labor prepared a "counter-plan" embodying social

9. See Commissaire général au Plan, *Rapport sur les principales options qui commandent la préparation du VIe Plan* (Paris: Imprimerie des Journaux officiels, 1970), esp. pp. 63–87.
10. Pierre Bauchet, *Economic Planning: The French Experience* (New York: Praeger, 1964), pp. 65–75. See also Ambassade de France: Service de Presse et d'Information, *Bulletin*, April 1973.

investment ideas—but this served only for purposes of public debate.)[11]

The agricultural sector has looked upon planning with reserve; to the extent that planning has focused on the consolidation of land holdings and has favored highly mechanized and competitive sectors of farming, the plan has been supported by the large landholders but viewed with misgivings by the small family farmer. In the same way, small business has been suspicious about the plan while big business and its main spokesman, the CNPF, has generally favored it. Occasionally certain interests have boycotted some or all of the modernization commissions—the CGT in 1948–59 and in 1975, agricultural associations in 1965, and the CFDT in 1970—in order to protest against underrepresentation or against the general "options" preferred by the government and the business community, such as a low farm price structure and the neglect of an "incomes policy" for the workers. In January 1976, the CFDT and CGT announced that they would refuse to participate in the second (elaborative) phase of the Seventh Plan unless the government responded affirmatively to the demands of unions regarding the place in the plan for a commitment to raising purchasing power, increasing social benefits, lowering the workers' retirement age, and improving working conditions.[12]

THE PLAN, THE PARLIAMENT, AND THE PUBLIC

Theoretically, whenever Parliament deals with the plan itself or is called upon to participate in decisions relating to it, the various mass-oriented political parties could provide an input favorable to such neglected sectors as workers, small farmers, and small businessmen to "balance" the pro-business bias of the executive branch. However, the left-wing parties—that is, those likely to be most critical of the business orientation of the plan—have had inadequate representation in Parliament since 1958. Moreover, at the first stage of parliamentary involvement, when the broad options of the plan are presented, Parliament cannot make any meaningful contribution because deputies possess little expertise and less precise factual information.

Parliamentary legitimation is required for the imperative, or "carrot and stick," aspects of economic policy—since these involve taxing and spending; in addition the government may in some cases take into account minor parliamentary inputs such as space planning or agricultural policy. But Parliament has been in a poor position to tamper

11. John Sheahan, *An Introduction to the French Economy* (Columbus, Ohio: Merrill, 1973), p. 80.
12. *Le Monde,* 29 January 1976.

with the fiscal parts of the plan, because whenever Parliament is called upon to approve credits for a plan it has not yet adopted it is confronted with the same kind of no-choice situation that the American Congress experiences when it is asked to approve appropriations to pursue a war it has not declared. During the second parliamentary phase, when the final plan is submitted to Parliament, the contribution of the parliamentary parties is not much more effective than during the preliminary phase, because the plan is then already considered a *fait accompli*. Parliament hesitates to intervene in the plan for an additional reason: the plan, when it emerges in "final" form, has already been democratically legitimated—there is the notion (or myth, in the eyes of critics) promoted by the government and the business community that the plan, whatever its imperfections, reflects the aggregation of demands of trade unions, business, agriculture, and the government experts.[13]

Parliamentary submission of the formal plan is a matter of courtesy in any case, because the plan itself is not a government bill or policy that constitutionally requires parliamentary processing. The First and Third plans were not submitted to Parliament at all; the Second Plan was submitted to, and approved by, Parliament more than two years after it had already gone into effect; the Fourth, Fifth, and Sixth plans were all discussed and approved by Parliament, but this participation produced little change in the social content of the plan, owing to the predominance of Gaullist parties in the Assembly and owing, equally, to the institutional devaluation of that body. As for the Seventh Plan, its "preliminary orientation" draft was approved by Parliament in June 1975, and its final version a year later. Whatever the role assigned to Parliament by the Constitution, or whatever its party composition, parliamentary decision making is incompatible with planning, since the budget enacted by Parliament is an annual affair and hence influenced by short-term political considerations, while the plan—if it is to be worthy of that name—must be multiannual.[14]

In theory, planning as a process has never stood in the way of parliamentary decision making; rather, it has made the circumvention of Parliament easier. In the Fourth Republic, economic planning was an ideal way of proposing policy alternatives. Despite the politicians' insistence on the supremacy of Parliament, the relationship between Left and Right parliamentary factions was often so delicately balanced that Parliament was hesitant to advocate any economic policy that might upset that balance. The resulting policy immobility could be overcome

13. Cohen, *Modern Capitalist Planning*, pp. 58–59, 228–37.
14. Pierre Corbel, *Le parlement français et la planification* (Paris: Cujas, 1969), p. 81.

by a specific set of choices—in favor of either business or labor—but the price to be paid for this might be too steep, i.e., the collapse of the government. By imposing economic policy directives that derived from intergroup bargains as well as from the "objective" criteria introduced by planning technocrats, the parties escaped the obligation to match their own programs with their ideologies and were left free to "maintain the Republic" (that is, to maintain themselves in power). Planning, then, had a certain regime-stabilizing function.[15]

The attitude of the Gaullists (and of de Gaulle himself) toward planning had always been somewhat ambivalent. On the one hand, aggregation of conflict outside the framework of Parliament accommodated itself easily to the Gaullists' disdain for that institution, and made political parties appear to be irrelevant intermediaries. On the other hand, the institutionalized (though often illusory) participation of trade unions, agricultural associations, and other interests in the process of recommending economic decisions enhanced the legitimacy of *these* intermediaries, many of which were ideologically oriented (and sometimes anti-Gaullist) and hence tended to challenge presidential decision-making authority. Nonetheless, economic decision making outside the plan—and in contradiction to it—has been easier in the Fifth Republic than in the Fourth, because it has involved less political risk; de Gaulle and his successors could not be so easily "punished" by Parliament as could prime ministers during the Fourth Republic, whose tenure in office was often shortened as a consequence of unpopular economic decisions. The executive's freedom of maneuver during the Fifth Republic, more than anything else, has accounted for the fact that there has been far less hostility in recent years to parliamentary involvement in the plan.

In view of the purely consultative nature of the Social and Economic Council, and the inequitable representation of the less privileged sectors of the population in the functional (vertical) commissions, as well as the business bias of the technocrats, these institutions tend to be less significant as arenas of bargaining and demand aggregation than as devices for social mobilization and cooptation. This social mobilization is achieved to the extent that commitments are secured from business to invest in certain areas, to relocate plants to sparsely populated provinces, or to practice modesty in pricing decisions, and to the extent that promises are extracted from trade unions to refrain from striking and

15. Ibid., p. 216. See also Antoine Légres, "Le parlement et les choix économiques," *Revue politique et parlementaire* 72 (October 1970): 27–38.

to be reasonable in making wage demands. The plan sparks a public discussion among unions, business firms, clubs, political parties, and academic circles about economic policy, thereby raising public consciousness and contributing to a "cognitive" political culture, and (as Michel Crozier argues) bringing about the kind of face-to-face contact that is normally made difficult by the pervasive distrust that exists in France between government and the citizenry.[16]

Ultimately, the success of every plan depends upon the public authorities' promoting "civic" and responsible economic behavior on the part of the important economic antagonists. The government has had little difficulty in harnessing the business sectors to the plan, although occasionally it has been necessary to manipulate the tax and credit systems, and to use nationalized industries, in order to prevent prices from being raised too irresponsibly. In October 1961, Premier Debré appeared to be threatening further nationalization when he introduced the Fourth Plan to Parliament, asking that body to authorize the government "to substitute itself for private companies when the objectives set out in the Plan, in sectors which are essential for economic expansion and for the Plan's social program, are not being achieved by private enterprise."[17] Such a threat was probably a reaffirmation of the orthodox Gaullist principle of the primacy of the state—and incidentally also a sop to trade unions and left-wing parties—rather than a clear commitment to an economic policy, given the fact that the "economic" ministers, with Finance Minister Giscard d'Estaing at the head, were generally inclined to give the widest possible scope to private enterprise. In any case, the threat did little to allay the suspicions of the trade unions about the antilabor bias of the executive authorities.

The weakness of the social component of the plan—apart from housing—is reflected in the fact that the first four plans ignored the question of income distribution while concentrating on wage and price stabilization. But in order to reduce strikes and other forms of group pressure, the government has often been forced to be concerned with social investments and other redistributive measures, particularly before presidential and parliamentary elections, and during periods of political uncertainty. For if it is true that "the plan has inserted itself into a parliamentary regime in crisis,"[18] the reverse may also be true: Parliament

16. Michel Crozier, "Pour une analyse sociologique de la planification française," *Revue française de sociologie* 6 (April–June 1965): 147–63.
17. John and Anne-Marie Hackett, *Economic Planning in France* (London: Allen & Unwin, 1963), p. 348.
18. Corbel, *Parlement et planification*, p. 216.

and other political decision makers may insert themselves into the economic decision process when the *plan* is in crisis: when external and internal economic pressures are such that they could not have been foreseen by the planners.

In 1949, Parliament passed a minimum-wage law largely because of the predominance of left-wing parties in that body. In the early 1960s, Premier Debré, not having to worry about political opposition from the Left, badgered the business community to keep wages down. In 1964, the National Association of Milk Producers managed to secure a significant increase in dairy price supports by exerting pressures on the Ministry of Agriculture and on Gaullist deputies from rural constituencies, and ultimately by striking. At the same time, the dissatisfaction of workers with their wages led to the establishment of a committee of investigation on an "incomes policy." Although it was headed by Pierre Massé, the planning commissioner, the committee was in effect a supplementary instrument for dialogue and "aggregation," since it consisted of representatives of trade unions, employers' associations and agricultural organizations, in addition to planners and government officials. In 1965 Gilbert Grandval, a Gaullist deputy, introduced a bill to force employers to inform workers about a firm's investment plans and to provide for trade union representation on "works' councils." The scope of the bill was enlarged by the Vallon amendment, which provided profit sharing for workers. The bill, as amended, was passed, but was not implemented for several years, owing to pressures from the CNPF. In 1967, the government, in anticipation of the parliamentary elections, prepared and successfully promoted legislation aimed at minimizing class antagonisms and, hopefully, reducing the electoral prospects of left-wing parties. The legislation required private companies to introduce stock-ownership plans for workers. This policy of *intéressement* was extended to the nationalized industries. In 1968, by means of legislation, government decrees, and "Central Accords" between government, industry, and labor, workers' wages were raised by some 30 percent and trade unions were accorded the right to organize on factory premises. In 1970, Premier Chaban-Delmas, in order to weaken pressures from the Left and in order to secure firmer support from the Center, inaugurated his "new society" program, replete with promises of increased attention to working conditions, the aged, and young people. In 1972, 500,000 low-cost housing units were built in France, in contrast to an annual average of 128,000 units between 1945 and 1958.[19] In 1974, social security coverage was extended, as were

19. *Le Monde Hebdomadaire*, 4–10 January 1973.

payments for the unemployed. These measures were undertaken largely outside, or alongside, the current Economic Plan, but most of them were "incorporated" into subsequent plans.

The success of the French plan has depended not only on the closeness of its reasoning, but also on a plethora of policies that are supplementary to the plan, "rectify" its internal thrust and reintroduce a balance of economic priorities, thereby redounding to the credit of the plan itself. The Fifth Plan was almost completely upset by the disturbances of 1968, when it had to be supplemented by various ad hoc policies and finally by an "interim" plan in which the social content of economic policy was greatly enlarged.

With the accession of Giscard d'Estaing to the Presidency, many more economic decisions have been arrived at outside the plan: Giscard's "advanced liberalism" has inclined him to a preference for economic-policy decisions made as much as possible by market forces. However, even a "liberal" President of France must adhere to the *idea* of planning, regardless of how little stock he puts in its efficacy. It is a paradox of French political culture that the majority of French citizens, their individualism notwithstanding, have lost faith in the self-regulating capacity of the market, and that, despite their lack of confidence in a particular government, they have favored one or another kind of comprehensive plan (see table 22). It is not clear whether the acceptance of planning stems from the belief that a highly intellectualized exercise by technocrats is preferable to decisions made by mere politicians; whether it is only a theoretical preference that implies no clear position regarding a particular plan; or whether the Frenchman feels that unjust economic choices made by the planners are in any case rectified by the politicians. (A poll conducted in 1969 revealed that 40 percent of Frenchmen thought that economic policy is made by the government, 38 percent by the President, and 13 percent by Parliament. According to the same poll, 49 percent thought that economic decisions *should* be made by the government, 30 percent by Parliament, and only 15 percent by the President.)[20]

In view of Giscard d'Estaing's economic professionalism *and* the etatism that he must represent as chief executive, it is not surprising that he should attempt to politicize (or "governmentalize") the planning process even more than had hitherto been the case. The CGP has been demoted to a coordinating body under the direct control of the premier. In September 1974, a new Planning Council (*Comité central de planification*) was established, chaired by the President of the Republic, and

20. Jack Hayward, *The One and Indivisible French Republic* (New York: Norton, 1973), p. 97.

Table 22
Attitudes Regarding State Economic Intervention
(in percent)

	All Categories	Farmers	Workers	Big Business	Shop-keepers
Nonintervention: Laisser-faire	2	2	4	1	2
Selective intervention (corrective)	33	31	29	38	35
Comprehensive intervention indicative	20	22	16	32	26
imperative	36	32	42	27	33
No opinion	9	13	9	2	4

Source: Adapted from SOFRES, *Les Français et l'Etat*, 1970, p. 59.

including the planning commissioners, and the ministers of finance and of labor. It has been argued that this composition insures a "symmetrical presence" of opposing ministers—an equilibrium between a minister presumably speaking for business and a minister speaking for organized labor—and provides a balance between economic and social criteria. But the main purpose of the new Council seems to be to recommend adjustments to the plan, and to suggest short-term "adaptations" and a "redeployment of resources," that is, to slow down capital expenditures for schools, agriculture, and housing, and to take the onus for these unpopular decisions away from the planners.[21] In conformity with his penchant for governmentalizing economic decisions, Giscard has continued the practice of his predecessors of having cabinet ministers make collective agreements (*contrats de progrès*) with workers in the nationalized industries—agreements which set the pace for the private sector and are subsequently taken into account by the planners. At the same time—and in conformity with his liberalism—he has encouraged meetings (*rencontres paritaires*) between trade unions and the associations of the private business sector that are designed to produce the

21. Pierre Massé, "Disparition et resurgence du plan," *Le Figaro*, 12 October 1974.

kinds of social-welfare concessions that are not yet found in the plan.[22]

Irrespective of Giscard's orientation regarding planning, the implementation of the Sixth Plan (1971–75) was seriously affected, if not ruined, by the fuel crisis that began in the fall of 1973. The nearly fourfold increase in the price of crude petroleum made unrealistic whatever growth rate the plan had envisaged. The balance-of-payments deficit could be reduced only by a decrease in consumption; and the rise of unemployment and the problem of falling incomes could be resolved only by political decisions outside the plan: the former by more progressive taxation and by a belt-tightening policy capable of effective implementation only by authoritarian means; and the latter, by raising unemployment compensation as well as by relieving France of some of her guest workers and hence by an exportation of the problem. Such emergency measures must be inspired and promulgated by the President rather than the professional planners. In the spring of 1975, the government announced a two-pronged policy of fighting lagging industrial production by means of tax incentives for business investments, and of fighting inflation by means of price controls. This policy (which was criticized by the trade unions for not addressing itself directly to the problem of growing unemployment) was initiated by President Giscard d'Estaing and his finance minister, Jean-Pierre Fourcade, rather than by the planners, although it ultimately became a component of the new economic plan.

The Seventh Plan has been frequently criticized by Frenchmen for its modesty of scope. It is true that in comparison with several preceding plans, the Seventh Plan is less comprehensive, and that it merely articulates "a list of pious hopes" in the sense that it relies on voluntary action by the private sector for the achievement of some of its aims— such as the maintenance of an annual economic growth rate of 5–6 percent, an increase of the workers' purchasing power by 3 percent annually, and the reduction of the inflation rate from 17 percent (in 1974) to 6 percent.[23] Nonetheless, despite Giscard's admiration for the "Anglo-American" way of promoting economic goals, the Seventh Plan is much more than a British "Royal Address" to Parliament or an American President's "State of the Union" message to Congress (and more than a mere outline of policy whose future implications can only be guessed at). The Seventh Plan contains twenty-five highly detailed programs—

22. *Le Monde,* 21 June 1975.
23. Clyde Farnsworth, "Paris Has Design to Spur Economy," *New York Times,* 25 April 1976.

indicating the sums to be spent on them over a number of years. Many of these programs would, in Giscard's words, require an "offensive strategy" and commit the fiscal resources of the government.[24]

In addition to the planners and the Presidency, the "offensive strategy" may involve other nonparliamentary devices in aggregating economic conflicts and proposing policy alternatives. The most prominent among these devices have been ad hoc commissions dealing with specific economic problems. Although interest groups are usually represented in, or consulted by, these commissions, the fact that they are led by distinguished personalities gives the recommendations emanating from these committees an aura of objectivity and helps to depoliticize the economic struggle—thereby contributing to the plan's success. Examples of such commissions (in addition to the Massé Commission mentioned above) have been the Toutée Commission on wage negotiations in the nationalized industries (1963); and the Mathey Commission on workers' participation in industrial management (1966). The most recent was the Sudreau Commission, launched in late 1974 in order to study the reform of management of private and public firms. The commission consisted of representatives of private and nationalized enterprise, three trade unions (CFDT, FO, and CGC), professional organizations, and the civil service. The commission's preliminary report, which was widely disseminated to the public and then submitted to the cabinet in February 1975, recommended the appointment at factory levels of worker-management committees (comités paritaires) that would participate in decisions about production and the allocation of resources.[25] The report also contained suggestions regarding asset-sharing by workers, the improvement of factory working conditions, the expansion of welfare-state legislation, and the further democratization of the educational system. It was hoped that the public discussion sparked by the report would influence the options of the planners and the decisions of the government. Unfortunately, since the final version of the Sudreau report stopped far short of recommending the kind of compulsory "co-determination" found in West Germany, many construed it as a blatantly "defensive" political strategy designed to retain the support of

24. Among the public fiscal commitments are ca. $20 billion for the expansion of the telephone system, $800 million for the expansion of hospitals and the improvement of medical care, $350 million for the development of new energy resources, and $700 million for the creation of new jobs. See Assemblée Nationale, no. 2346, Le VIIe plan de développement économique et social, 1976–1980 (session of 1 June 1976).
25. Le Monde, 13 February 1975 and 14 February 1975.

the small or medium-scale entrepreneur who is part of Giscard's centrist electorate—and as a means of compensating for the interventionist features of the Economic Plan.[26]

French planning has been generally hailed as a success, has aroused interest in other countries and is the subject of numerous analyses. Since the inception of the First Plan in 1946, the annual growth rate has averaged about 5 percent (except in 1968 and 1974) while the inflation rate was held down to less than 5 percent annually (except, again, during these years of crisis). Economic infrastructures, notably the transport system, were modernized; the franc was stabilized; France became the fourth largest exporting nation; and the country became oriented to mass consumption levels. There were certain failures, notably in the redistribution of incomes, the reduction of social inequities, the equalization of the tax burden, and the "regionalization" of industrial production.[27] At the same time, however, the outlay, in absolute terms, for social purposes increased, particularly in housing, education, and municipal transport services. Real income was raised, and fringe benefits were extended; but in terms of the gross national product France's welfare spending declined from second place in 1960 to fourth place in 1970 among Western European industrial democracies.[28] Whether the successes and failures of economic policy could be attributed directly to the plan itself is a matter of controversy. Between 1950 and 1960, the economic growth rates of West Germany and Italy (then non-planning countries) were higher than that of France; but between 1960 and 1968, they were lower. To some extent, economic policy outcomes have depended also on external and internal political factors over which professional planners have had no control. The expansion of growth rates was surely influenced by the competitive environment which the Common Market created, by the modernization and prosperity of cer-

26. The government's own interpretation of the report by Sudreau (himself a Centrist deputy) envisages that *co-gestion* would be based largely on voluntary collective contracts rather than government decree; would entail "information sessions" rather than significant worker participation in industrial decisions; and would not apply to firms employing fewer than one or two thousand workers. See Jacques Chirac, *Déclaration du gouvernement sur la réforme de l'entreprise*, Assemblée Nationale, no. 2275, *procès-verbal* of session of 11 May 1976.

27. Between 1955 and 1971 only about 375,000 new jobs were created in provincial areas—mainly as a consequence of decisions by 2,600 private firms. *A Look at France* (Paris: La Documentation française, 1973), p. 29.

28. For an analysis of the achievements and failures of recent French plans, see Jean-Pierre Dubarry, "L'activité économique française en 1972," *Revue d'économie politique* 83 (September-October 1973): 737–68.

tain segments of agriculture, and by a hard-nosed French position with respect to the Common Agricultural Policy of the European Economic Community. Similarly, the expansion of welfare-state coverage must be attributed to such non-plan factors as emerging supranational social-legislative norms to which France has had to adhere, as well as to the dynamic of social accommodation forced upon governments whenever internal political stability was threatened by mass unrest. In any event, the success of the plan within the context of an incremental economy was real enough at the onset of the present decade for planners to devote increasing attention to raising the cultural level of the masses, as well as to environmental problems.

THE ENVIRONMENT AND THE QUALITY OF LIFE

For many years, neither the Parliament nor the political parties had appeared to be greatly concerned about the environment. The Malthusianism prevalent in the political culture of the petit-bourgeois Frenchman failed to translate itself into noticeable concern with ecology in the course of France's efforts at becoming a mass-consumption society. When France became prosperous in the 1960s, she began to devote some attention to luxury items not related directly to production and consumption, but these items had less to do with environmental matters than with cultural and aesthetic ones. In France, whose citizens have viewed the state as a custodian not only of "law and order," but also of the nation's civilization, governments have attached great importance to a *politique de culture* that goes far beyond the support of school systems and scientific research centers. Unlike the United States, where the establishment of a symphony orchestra is often a spinoff of corporate opulence, France has lacked the tradition of reliance on business for the support of the arts. Moreover, the French elite has viewed culture as being separate from the marketplace. "Cultural politics" has, first of all, included the governmental subsidization of theaters, symphonies, and museums. Second, it has been reflected in an official concern with the purity of the French language, because the latter is a tool of domestic political socialization and an instrument of foreign policy, and—particularly in the past two decades—because of the need to counteract the Americanization of taste and expression that has accompanied the spread of mass culture.

Each of the Fifth Republic Presidents has put his particular stamp on the politics of culture. In collaboration with André Malraux, his minister of state for cultural affairs, de Gaulle laid stress on the restoration of architectural treasures, especially in Paris, where a massive project was inaugurated to sandblast buildings and to restore the *Marais* and other old sections of the capital to their former glory. President Pompidou was primarily concerned with the visual arts and literature. In 1971, he appointed a "Council on Cultural Development"— it was chaired by a member of the *Académie Française*—which advised the government on films and television programs, fought the commercialization of the government-controlled media, and suggested ways of disseminating good literature.[29]

For years the demand for housing was so great that large housing projects, especially in urban centers, had to be built quickly, at the cost of the uglification of the landscape. Moreover, the use of the automobile became so widespread that the Paris region and the countryside were ribboned with superhighways. The consequences of rapid industrialization and urbanization were especially apparent in the Paris region, which remains the center of 25 percent of the nation's economic activities. That region—with 3 percent of the geographic area—is the home of 20 percent of the nation's population.

As housing and transportation problems became less critical, government concern for the environment moved up on the priority scale. As early as 1961 the government decreed a limit for all industries on the maximum emission of waste particles into the atmosphere. This decree was not enforced because of the power of the industrial lobbies, the lack of trained personnel, and jurisdictional confusions: both the Ministry of the Interior and the Ministry for the Protection of the Environment and Nature have had responsibilities for environmental matters. Similarly, an ordinance of the mid-1960s concerning height limitations in Paris has been enforced in an erratic fashion. In this case, however, a conflict could be seen between the proponents of efficient use of the space available and the lovers of the traditional Paris skyline. Pompidou himself considered high-rise structures (and fast cars) as necessary aspects of a modernizing civilization. In the late 1960s France began to supplement her excellent national railroad system by building a high-speed rail network in the environs of Paris, with the aim of reducing automobile congestion.

The Sixth Plan devoted some attention to "the quality of life," but like previous plans, it emphasized facilities for leisure-time activities and

29. In 1972, the government—reflecting Pompidou's humanistic professional background—decided to have mayors throughout France provide all newly wed couples with five books, chosen from a list including Victor Hugo, Balzac, Stendhal, Fromentin, Flaubert, and Chateaubriand.

sports. The plan paid some lip service to "spatial planning" and mentioned the need for the deconcentration of industry, the promotion of public transport, and the protection of water resources. However, few details were given, and pollution was mentioned last. In 1973 the government announced forthcoming measures aimed at the cleaning of rivers (initially through contracts with paper manufacturers); a 30 percent reduction of the lead content in gasoline by 1976; noise abatement; and the introduction of speed limits on highways. In 1971, a six-nation intergovernmental committee was formed to protect the shared Alpine region against such environmental nuisances as the snowmobile. Furthermore, in recent years France has been pressured by her Common Market partners to act on river pollution, since rivers cross borders and no European country wants to have its drinking water flavored by the industrial effluents of its neighbors.

Under the Presidency of Giscard d'Estaing, much greater concern for the environment has been expressed than during preceding regimes. The construction of superhighways around Paris has been slowed down, and the number of national parks has been increased. Recently, Giscard forced the shelving of an elaborate project to convert the old wholesale market in the capital (les Halles) into a cultural center and decided that a much-needed city park be built there instead. He established a full Ministry for the Quality of Life that, early in 1975, prepared legislation that would constitute a "code for the quality of life for 1977." This legislation included provisions for the protection of nature, regulations regarding the destruction of wildlife and flora, stipulations that all public works projects be preceded by an environmental impact report, the regulation of hunting, the control over the dumping of chemicals into the sea, and the establishment of a national committee on the environment.[30] The concern for environmental protection is now embodied in the Seventh Plan, which commits the government to an expenditure of about $500 million for pollution control, the protection of' shorelines, and the expansion of public land. Additionally, the plan envisages an outlay of nearly $200 million for the rehabilitation of "architectural treasures."[31]

The growing concern about the environment also found political expression in the ecologist movement (les écologistes). This movement was at once a manifestation of protest against plans to build nuclear energy units in various parts of France and a reaction to technocratism

30. See Ambassade de France, Service de Presse et d'Information, France, October 1973, pp. 6–8; and Le Monde, 28 February 1975.
31. Le VII Plan, pp. 137–41.

and "productivism."[32] The ecologist movement fielded candidates in the municipal elections of 1977 and the parliamentary elections of 1978. Although it did not succeed in electing a single deputy to the Assembly, the movement did manage to make the other parties sufficiently aware of environmental concerns to include environmental plants in their platforms.

Much of the visual and atmospheric pollution of France has been the result of spreading affluence: for example, the destruction of the natural beauty of parts of the Mediterranean coast where speculators have built vacation resorts for the masses and "second homes" for the newly rich. It is probable that much of this problem will be resolved not so much by environmental legislation as by the high cost of gasoline and the declining living standards that threaten France today.

32. See *Les écologistes*, "présenté par eux mêmes" (Paris: Flash-Actualité Marabout, 1977), esp. pp. 65 ff.

Themes and Problems of Foreign Policy

The role of international diplomacy in France's political development may be adduced from the list of foreign policy misadventures that led to the inauguration of new regimes. For example, the Napoleonic defeat in the war with Prussia in 1870 was instrumental in the collapse of the Second Empire; the French defeat in 1940 resulted in the Vichy regime; the "victory" of France on the side of the Allies in 1945 permitted France to restore her parliamentary republic; and the humiliation of France in Southeast Asia in 1954, at Suez in 1956, and in Algeria in the late 1950s undermined the credibility of the Fourth Republic and led to the establishment of the Fifth Republic.

Moreover, the affective relationship of the citizen to his regime has been heavily influenced by France's position in the international system, her internal self-image having depended upon the image she could project to the world outside. To the extent that the average Frenchman views the *ancien régime* in a favorable light, he does so mainly because under the Bourbon kings, and notably under Louis XIV, France had become one of the foremost nation-states; French culture had been imitated in foreign lands; and the French language had become the lingua franca of international diplomacy. It was also during the *ancien régime* that the boundaries of metropolitan France were approximately fixed, and that France began to lay the foundations for a policy that, by the beginning of the twentieth century, was to make her the second largest colonial empire in the world.

During the nineteenth century, France's foreign policy was concerned primarily with retaining her role as one of the most important diplomatic powers in Europe. From 1815 to 1940, France pursued, often together with Britain, a policy of alliances to keep the Germans, the Austrians, the Russians, and the Ottoman Turks from gaining undue strength and upsetting the European equilibrium. This Europocentric foreign policy was frustrated by the rise of Germany, which undermined the dominance of France in Europe; France could not match Germany's rapid industrialization and population increase, and consequently could put up no effective resistance in the Franco-Prussian War. France defeated Germany in World War I—and regained the province of Alsace, which she had lost to Germany in 1870—but only with the help of her allies. France then attempted, by means of the Treaty of Versailles and the Little Entente, both to keep Germany in check and to reassert her own European dominance, but the attempt ended in failure.

The collapse of the Little Entente and Locarno Treaty systems and the rise of the Hitler regime proved that France had lost her capacity to preserve the European status quo. The German defeat of France in 1940 confirmed France's military weakness, which the Gaullists were later to attribute to the weakness of parliamentarism. Similarly, France's liberation by the Americans in 1944 underscored her renewed dependence on the United States. After World War II, Europe as a whole had become a political and military vacuum, and the "European system" had been effectively replaced by a bipolar balance in which the two main actors—the United States and the Soviet Union—were extra-European, continental giants. To be sure, France was permitted the appearance of great-power status by winning a permanent seat on the United Nations Security Council, by being given an occupation zone in Germany, and by regaining control over her colonies. But such prestige proved soon to be ephemeral, because the United Nations was immobilized; because the occupation of Germany ended; and because France, like Britain and the Low Countries, was unable to retain her colonies.

In the mid-1950s, France began the slow process of decolonization; under the leadership of Pierre Mendès-France, she granted independence to Morocco and Tunisia, and at the same time disengaged herself from Indochina. Algeria was a somewhat different matter because about 1.5 million settlers (*colons*) in that territory regarded themselves as fully French and wished to retain a permanent political connection with the mainland. These settlers and the French military establishment were

embroiled in a protracted war against the indigenous Algerian population, and this conflict was the proximate cause for the collapse of the
Fourth Republic in 1958.

When General de Gaulle returned to power as President of the
new Fifth Republic, he set out to accomplish two main goals: the solution of the Algerian problem and the restoration of France to a position
of importance in the international system. Under the Evian Accords of
1962, Algeria was granted complete independence. As for her sub-
Saharan colonies, France in 1958 asked them to elect one of several
options: to remain dependencies of France as before, to become
provinces (or overseas departments) of France, to opt for membership
in a "French Community" (somewhat analogous to the British Commonwealth), or to become completely independent. Although virtually all
ultimately chose independence—and the French Community therefore
never developed in a meaningful sense—France's former African colonies
retain a degree of economic dependence upon their former protector.

The problem of enhancing France's global role—the crux of Gaullism in the international context—was a more complex one. At the end
of World War II, a condition of inequality existed between France and
the other two major Western powers, a condition that de Gaulle felt
the Americans and the British had brought about and wished to perpetuate. During the Fourth Republic, France had been content with her
role as a client state of the United States; her need for aid under the
Marshall Plan and her military weakness in the face of a still-credible
Soviet aggressiveness made her a willing junior partner in the North
Atlantic Alliance inaugurated in 1949. Moreover, the recognition of her
economic weakness make her amenable to European integration.

By 1958, France was well on the way to economic recovery and
had made a start toward the development of a national nuclear weapons
system. It is possible that the Atlantic collaborative spirit might have
been maintained had de Gaulle felt that France's national ego had been
accommodated by changes in the structure of the Atlantic Alliance—
specifically, the establishment of a military leadership triumvirate consisting of the United States, Britain, and France. But the United States
rejected this idea because it was not willing to slight a revived West
Germany.

Since the Atlantic Alliance frustrated French aspirations for prestige, de Gaulle increasingly pursued a policy of independence of the
two blocs. In 1966, he withdrew French military forces from the
integrated command of NATO and expelled the European NATO
headquarters from French soil. Moreover, he pursued a policy of
rapprochement with Communist regimes, in particular the Soviet Union

(while simultaneously warning his compatriots of the danger of communism within France). In a further attempt to free France—and Europe —from American domination, he twice vetoed the British application for membership in the Common Market because he considered Britain as a potential American "Trojan horse" in Europe, and because he feared that spreading Anglo-American influences would undermine a traditional French linguistic hegemony. To some extent, de Gaulle's visits to Latin America, Rumania, and to Canada—where, to the dismay of many Canadians, he proclaimed the slogan "Long Live Free Quebec"—must have been inspired by pan-Gallic pretensions to capitalize on a common Latin heritage.

De Gaulle felt that a nation's diplomatic independence was predicated on its ability to defend itself, that is, its possession of deterrent capabilities. De Gaulle was not satisfied by the fact that the nuclear umbrella over the NATO nations was controlled solely by the United States, not only because there was no assurance that nuclear weapons would be used to protect primarily European interests, but also because there was imperfect—if any—consultation on a joint Western policy. He therefore expended much effort on building France's own nuclear deterrent. France's *force de frappe* has been frequently criticized, by both Americans and Frenchmen, as an expensive toy that cut too deeply into the domestic budget while providing neither adequate defense nor significant spillover for nonmilitary technology. The question whether France can afford her "nuclear" diplomacy is controversial. During the 1960s, while France built up the *force de frappe*, she also significantly increased the educational budget. Moreover, from 1960 to 1970 the percentage of the national budget allocated to defense actually *decreased.*[1] The nuclear deterrent may be useful as a prestige weapon, in that France is now a member of the nuclear club; and it may even be "usable" as a last-ditch weapon for French self-defense in case a neighboring minor power (Germany?) should think of attacking France; but she is not yet equipped with a powerful enough delivery system or stockpile for counterstrikes against the Soviet Union.

While the likelihood of a new world war was receding, de Gaulle pursued a strictly "national" foreign policy. This policy was reflected in France's refusal to sign the test-ban and nonproliferation agreements as well as the European Human Rights Convention. It expressed itself in a pronounced hostility to the "so-called United Nations" and in a

1. The 1960 figures for defense expenditures were 25.1% of the national budget, and 6.4% of the GNP; for 1970, 17.6% and 3.4% respectively. Cited in Edward L. Morse, *Foreign Policy and Interdependence in Gaullist France* (Princeton: Princeton University Press, 1973), p. 163.

reluctance to foster the evolution of the European Common Market toward greater supranationality. It was, finally, reflected in France's attempt, by means of systematic gold purchases, to bring about a dethronement of the American dollar as an international currency.

Despite de Gaulle's abhorrence of nonpragmatic, purely ideological considerations in the conduct of foreign policy, the latter was subject to occasional intrusions of ideologism (and even irrationalism) that cannot be clearly related to the promotion of national interest. Thus, in the late 1960s, de Gaulle demonstrated a rather surprising friendship for nondemocratic regimes. He declined to endorse the Council of Europe's denunciation of Greece's military dictatorship, he refused to join a United Nations condemnation of South Africa's apartheid policy, and he advocated the membership of fascist Spain in the Common Market.

Four great achievements in French foreign policy have been ascribed to de Gaulle or Gaullism: the liberation and economic restoration of France; her decolonization; a reconciliation with Germany; and, finally, the attempt to find an alternative to the bipolar conflict and to moderate it by the establishment of a "third force." But it can be argued that these were not achievements of Gaullism at all, or at best phantom achievements; that France was liberated by the United States rather than by France's own efforts; and that the economic restoration of France, for which the foundations were laid in the Fourth Republic, was made possible by the Marshall Plan. Decolonization was begun in the Fourth Republic and was continued by de Gaulle because he had little choice; continued involvement in Algeria proved an unbearable economic and psychological strain on the French people. Reconciliation with Germany, too, was begun when France committed herself to the Schuman Plan and signed the Treaty of Rome that set up the Common Market; the Franco-German Treaty of Friendship of 1963, which formally ratified this reconciliation, was in a sense made necessary by de Gaulle's exclusion of Britain from the Common Market.

De Gaulle's reminder that Europe consisted of separate nations and national interests that could not simply be submerged into an Atlantic civilization was realistic, but his evocation of a Europe "from the Atlantic to the Urals"—embracing Western and Eastern European countries—ignored the permanence of the postwar satellization of Eastern Europe. The attempt to find an alternative to the bipolar conflict and to create an atmosphere of détente in Europe was a worthy one, but there is doubt that the attempt succeeded, if at all, by means of French efforts. It is ironic that to the extent that there has been an East-West *rapprochement* in Europe, it was brought about not by French efforts, but by Germany's *Ostpolitik* in the late 1960s on the one hand, and

Soviet-American bilateral efforts on the other; that the growing "aliena-tion" of Canada from the United States has been a consequence not of Gaullist policy but of an inter-American conflict over the control of scarce natural resources; that the war in Vietnam, against which de Gaulle had railed so vehemently, was terminated not through French diplomacy, but by a concatenation of domestic developments in the United States; that the loss of American power in the United Nations was occasioned not by French efforts at building a "third force," but by the skillful use of the oil weapon by Middle Eastern countries of which France, too, has been a victim; and that the Middle East crisis is still, by turns, encouraged and "controlled" by the two superpowers, despite the long-held French illusion that the crisis would be resolved by a four-party agreement in which France would have a prominent role. Despite doubts regarding the long-range significance of de Gaulle's foreign policy, there is no question that he restored the pride of Frenchmen and left an imprint on the world scene by dint of his personality.

Pompidou continued the basic course of his predecessor's foreign policy. However, one of Pompidou's first acts upon assuming the Presi-dency was to devalue the franc, thereby admitting that the hope of a stable French currency, upon which de Gaulle had rested his challenge to the dollar-based international monetary system, had been ill-founded. But Pompidou continued the Concorde project, a joint British-French venture, costing several billion dollars, to design and build supersonic aircraft, despite growing doubts whether the international prestige accruing to France was worth the expense. Pompidou's overall style, though, was less stridently anti-American and more pragmatic than de Gaulle's, a change that can be explained by the fact that Pompidou had not experienced the same (real and imagined) slights at the hands of the "Anglo-Saxons" as his predecessor. A certain acerbity of public discourse returned when, after the parliamentary election of 1973, Michel Jobert took over the foreign minister's portfolio from the mild-mannered Maurice Schumann. The outspokenness of Jobert, who regarded himself as a true Gaullist and displayed intense personal competition with Henry Kissinger, temporarily strained the dialogue between the two countries, particularly after the Middle East war of 1973, but it did not affect the substance of Franco-American relations.

While under Pompidou no move was made to rejoin NATO's inte-grated command structure, and the development of France's nuclear striking force was continued, there was at the same time a more openly voiced recognition of France's (and Europe's) dependence on the Ameri-can deterrent and opposition to further withdrawal of American troops from Europe. The idea of an independent Quebec, annoying both to Canada and the United States, was dropped, and replaced by expanded bilateral cultural and economic arrangements with Canada. Pompidou also abandoned de Gaulle's opposition to the United Nations in favor of open support of the world organization. France could well afford this move, since the United Nations had been transformed from what had been viewed as an appendage of the United States into a forum of opposition to it, and France could hope to play a visible role at once as a mediator between the two superpowers and as a spokesman for the Third World countries. France's new interest in the United Nations underscored a continuation of her *rapprochement* with the Soviet Union —with which commercial and political relations were expanded—because in many crucial United Nations votes France supported the USSR against the United States. Pompidou relinquished de Gaulle's opposition to British entry into the Common Market both in order to add a counter-weight against a stronger Germany and to weaken "Atlanticism" and reduce American political influence in Europe by splitting the United Kingdom from America.

In Africa, Pompidou strengthened France's relations not only by means of highly publicized state visits to her former colonies but also by expanded economic and technical aid. But a protracted military involvement in Chad to shore up a conservative, pro-French regime and the continued linkage of the financial edifices of France's former colonies to the French Finance Ministry and the Bank of France were viewed by an increasing number of Africans as manifestations of a neo-colonialist policy.[2]

In the Middle East, the policy of de Gaulle was continued. France maintained her embargo on the shipment of military equipment to Israel, even refusing to release airplanes and missile boats already paid for. Conversely, in the spring of 1970 France signed a contract for the sale of more than a hundred warplanes to Libya. France's pro-Arab policy became more categorical during the most recent Mideast war and immediately thereafter, as France refused to help Israel and the United States diplomatically and pressured her Common Market associates to develop a unified "European" policy with respect to the Middle East, independent of, and often hostile to, the United States. France's Middle East policy was largely determined by economic considerations. France has been much more dependent than the United States on oil imports from Arab countries and has been forced to pay virtually any price for them demanded by these countries.

2. *Le Monde*, 2 December 1972.

Many French foreign policies have foundered because of the inability of France to bridge the gap between Gaullist aspirations to grandeur and her economic weakness—between her desire to play a "balancing" role between opposing blocs and the continued reality of Soviet-American duopoly. Because France lacks the power to challenge the United States alone, she needs Europe. Unfortunately, however frequent the pro-European official statements have been since the departure of de Gaulle, the continuing French distaste for supranationality and France's recognition that she can no longer aspire to unchallenged leadership in a united Europe caused her to pursue nationalistic policies in relation to the rest of the Common Market countries. France fought against the American monetary policy by refusing to abandon the gold standard and by insisting on a joint European monetary approach to the United States, but because of her own balance-of-payments difficulties she had to float the franc despite the opposition of other European countries. Outside Europe, France has, regardless of her "neutrality," been losing influence, especially in Africa, because, owing to economic weakness, she has been unable to compete effectively with China, the United States, Germany, Japan, and even Libya for an influential role. One indication of this weakness is the fact that the flow of government revenues to the developing countries decreased from 2.16 percent of France's GNP in 1960 to 1.24 percent in 1969.

One French scholar has insisted that French foreign policy differs from that of, say, the United States or Britain in that there has been a "primacy of political factors over economic."[3] Specifically, French policy has been motivated much less by a desire for economic advantage than by a quest for cultural prestige. But such a tradition has hardly been maintained consistently. It may be argued that some French foreign policies have had little to do with economics, and have even been economically counterproductive, such as the original exclusion of Britain from the Common Market, the development of the French nuclear striking force, the pursuit of cultural imperialism in Africa, or the construction of the Concorde—although such policies were not devoid of expectations of ultimate economic side benefits. However, the early Franco-American collaboration which culminated in the Marshall Plan, and the French promotion of European unity beginning with the Schuman Plan, were almost entirely inspired by economic considerations.

The official announcements following the election of the first non-Gaullist President of the Fifth Republic in May 1974 indicated a

3. J. B. Duroselle, in *In Search of France*, ed. Stanley Hoffmann (New York: Harper & Row, 1965), p. 313.

continuation of the broad outline of Gaullist foreign policy, in the proclaimed stress on national independence, a French nuclear deterrent, and friendly collaboration with all major countries and regions.[4] Moreover, Giscard has fully subscribed to presidential primacy in foreign and defense affairs.

The daily tasks relating to foreign policy are performed by career civil servants and diplomats at the *Quai d'Orsay* (the Foreign Ministry), professionals who take scant account of public opinion. It so happens that since de Gaulle's accession to the Presidency, French foreign policy has reflected a broad spectrum of public opinion. In the past, France's Europeanism was supported by the Centrists and many Socialists; her policy of decolonization by the Left; her anti-Americanism by the Gaullists and Communists; and her opposition to American involvement in Indochina by virtually all parties. At present, France's quest for a policy of nonalignment is endorsed by well over half the population.[5] But the Foreign Office remains institutionally fairly immune to political intervention. Members of Parliament must content themselves with receiving periodic reports from the Foreign Minister, and the occasional foreign policy debates in the two chambers' committees of foreign relations—and the less frequent floor debates—are little more than shadowboxing. The background of the foreign ministers has not made for a high level of tolerance for parliamentary involvement. Of the six foreign ministers in the Fifth Republic, only one (Maurice Schumann, 1969–73) had an independent parliamentary career and had been clearly identified with leadership in a political party, while the five others have been technicians, diplomats, or civil servants.[6]

Nevertheless, despite the obvious institutional immunity of the

4. Press Conference of Giscard, 24 October 1975; and statement of Jean Sauvagnargues to Assembly, on Foreign Policy, 6 November 1974.
5. A public-opinion poll in 1969 revealed that although 24% of Frenchmen considered the United States as France's best friend, 52% favored a policy of nonalignment between the two superpowers. *Sondages*, nos. 1–2 (1969): 47.
6. That does not mean that a particular technician may not also be chosen for a "political" (or personal) reason. Couve de Murville (1958–68) had a reputation for the cold-blooded technical application of de Gaulle's ideas; Michel Debré (1968–69) was a most reliable disciple of de Gaulle and had served for several years as his defense minister; and Michel Jobert (1973–74) had been the chief secretary of Pompidou's office during most of the latter's term as Premier. Jean Sauvagnargues, the foreign minister under Chirac, had been ambassador to Bonn, and his appointment doubtlessly served to emphasize the importance Giscard attached to Franco-German relations. His replacement in August 1976 by Louis de Guiringaud, likewise a career diplomat (and former ambassador to the United Nations), may well reflect Giscard's desire to deflate the significance of the German connection.

foreign policy establishment to Parliament, the Gaullist aspects of Giscard's policies are at least partly influenced by electoral considerations; in the face of his narrow victory over the Socialists and the growing strength of the parties of the Left, he does not wish needlessly to antagonize the deputies of the UDR, which remains the largest party in the Assembly. In order to propitiate this party—and incidentally also in order to moderate the impact of Michel Jobert's New Democratic Movement, which claims true fidelity to de Gaulle's foreign policy ideals—Giscard regularly proclaims his adherence to certain general principles. Foremost among them is the safeguarding of France's pride, which can be translated as an attempt to convey the impression that France can pursue a policy independent of the United States and that France remains the most important power in Western Europe. However, the realities of general international interdependence and the gravity of France's economic situation have made Giscard and his advisers question the assumption that France is ultimately capable of defending herself without help from the United States. Consequently, the old hostilities vis-à-vis the "Anglo-Saxons" have been muted and a greater tolerance toward the United States has developed. De Gaulle and (to a lesser extent) Pompidou had emphasized the role of America as an obstacle to détente and as a challenger to Europe's economic modernization and its control over its own industrial processes. Under Giscard, the imputation to America of such motives has lost much of its compelling force: given America's own interest in détente, the branding of the United States as a cold-war monger is no longer credible; given its own economic difficulties the United States is no longer viewed as "threatening" the Western European economic system. Consequently, the French have rediscovered America as a protector.

Under Giscard, France is still committed to the retention and improvement (but not expansion) of the *force de frappe*; at the same time, she has been insisting on the importance of the maintenance of significant troop levels in Europe, and—without intending to rejoin the integrated command of NATO—has even indicated a desire to consult and collaborate with the Eurogroup military structure within NATO. Nevertheless, Giscard appears to have as little use for the Atlantic concept as his predecessors had. The American dream of reviving the Atlantic partnership, as articulated in the spring of 1973, was rejected by Pompidou precisely because to the French it looked like a revival of America's Atlantic hegemony of the late 1940s and mid-1950s, and continues for that reason to be rejected by Giscard. Moreover, Giscard is convinced that irrespective of whether or not a formal alliance system exists, it would be in the best interest of the United States to help France in the event of Soviet aggression.[7] In the absence of such aggression, the international policies of lesser powers are largely histrionics—and in this field Giscard, lacking de Gaulle's stature and flair, could not match the theatricalism of American Secretary of State Kissinger. Giscard is willing to engage in a sustained dialogue with the United States, but is at the same time attempting to widen the *rapprochement* with the Communist world by visits to the USSR and Eastern Europe. In December 1974, French and American aircraft manufacturers competed over the sale of Mirage versus YF-16 and YF-17 jet fighters to several small European members of NATO—that is, over the prospect of earning between $15 and $20 billion.[8] This contest must, therefore, be seen less in old-fashioned Gaullist prestige terms than in the light of economic considerations: the need to protect the French aircraft industry, one of the largest employers and foreign currency earners. Moreover, the contest did not unduly aggravate general Franco-American relations.

A similar pragmatism has informed Giscard's policies regarding Europe. While the present government holds to a traditional Gaullist view of a Europe of nations, it has argued in favor of further European political integration, primarily by means of an institutionalized summitry—the meeting, at least three times a year, of European heads of government. Giscard has continued to pursue agricultural integration in the European Community—not primarily in order to promote French power and irritate the British or Germans, but rather to protect the high price structure for French farm products, which figure importantly in the French trade balance. However, Giscard has reacted with commendable equanimity to British attempts at renegotiating the terms of her Common Market membership. Moreover, in contrast to de Gaulle's Anglophobia, Giscard uses the English language freely, particularly in his regular contacts with Helmut Schmidt, the West German chancellor.[9]

7. This belief is not likely to be shaken by the apparent failure of the United States to live up to her "commitments" in Indochina. Rather than being viewed as a portent of what the United States might do to her Atlantic allies, the American abandonment of Southeast Asia is seen as enabling her to concentrate her attention once more on Europe.
8. One interesting consequence of this competition was that the late Gaullist deputy, General Stehlin, was demoted from his leadership position in the parliamentary Gaullist party because he had publicly held the American jet to be superior to the French one.
9. In 1976, the relationship between France and West Germany became somewhat strained, owing to the close contacts between François Mitterrand and Chancellor Helmut Schmidt, the tendency of the latter to criticize France's management of her economy, and France's envy of Germany's relatively strong economy.

While France maintains a pro-Arab policy, and was in fact instrumental in arranging a dialogue between European Common Market and the Arab League countries in the spring of 1974, she has been less moralistic than previously in her pronouncements against Israel. She has permitted the first official visit of a French foreign minister to that country and has recognized France's lack of power to contribute materially to a solution of the Middle East conflict. She rejected an American-sponsored proposal to establish an oil consumer consortium that might confront the OPEC countries, preferring instead bilateral regional understandings and French-Arab commercial deals in order to secure an adequate supply of petroleum, entice "petrodollars" to France, and secure a market for French military and industrial products. But she has not closed the door to future collaboration with the United States in the face of the oil crisis.

While France continues to foster close relations with African countries, such relations are bound to be adversely affected by the worldwide economic crisis. France has been sending teachers abroad—there were 31,000 in 1974, most of them instructors of French—but it is difficult to determine whether this activity represents a policy of prestige or whether it reflects economic considerations: the need to find employment for the excessive number of French university graduates. In the face of a growing French balance-of-payments deficit, France may be hard pressed to maintain, let alone augment, the virtual army of civil servants, teachers, and technicians—which in 1973 numbered about 250,000 —in her former colonies, particularly since this venture has entailed annual subsidies of more than $200 million.[10] Furthermore, as a consequence of growing unemployment, many African "guest workers" in France are likely to be sent home, thus further aggravating the relations between France and her former colonies.

It is almost inevitable that France will abandon the Gaullist conviction that she can conduct her own foreign policy; her relative lack of economic and military power is bound to draw her further into a state of de facto dependence on both the European Community (in particular her richer neighbor, West Germany) and the United States. Nevertheless, France has frequently subverted American efforts to mobilize a common Western response to the worldwide economic crisis. France's short-range policy of selling military equipment to unstable regimes— a policy unfortunately practiced by several other countries as well— is bound to increase the likelihood of local wars in the Third World.

10. Cf. Burnett Anderson, "France's Linguistic Imperialism," *Guardian Weekly*, 1 February 1975.

A collective Western approach to international politics was also undermined by France's reluctance to participate in talks concerning mutual balanced force reduction (MBFR), which took place in 1974 in the context of a "European Security Conference." Her position was due not so much to opposition to the reduction of military forces as to the French perception that the negotiations were largely a Soviet-American affair. French distrust of the United States is at least partly based on uncertainty about the degree of American commitment to Europe: not only whether the United States would come to the defense of Europe in an all-out conflict, but also whether Americans would tighten their own belts and share their fuel resources in the event of another Middle East war and another oil embargo—an uncertainty increased when, at the end of 1974, the U.S. government began to "re-examine" her policy of selling enriched uranium to Common Market countries.

Thus despite Giscard's basic friendliness to—and awareness of ultimate military dependence on—the United States, he is forced to pursue a "national" foreign policy for the sake of economic interest, rather than to conduct an assertive French diplomacy for its own sake. Under Pompidou, the "primacy of foreign policy" had continued to prevail because he was ideologically identified with de Gaulle and because the economic prosperity of the industrialized countries permitted the view that many domestic problems would be solved as a consequence of an expanding economy. Since Giscard's election, such optimism has evaporated; moreover, he is subject to great pressure from the Left Opposition to turn his attention to domestic problems. Such pressure is more important than that emanating from the orthodox Gaullists for the pursuit of a foreign policy of grandeur. The stability and prestige of the French regime will, in short, clearly be measured not by international "achievements," which must be severely limited, but rather by the government's domestic economic accomplishments.

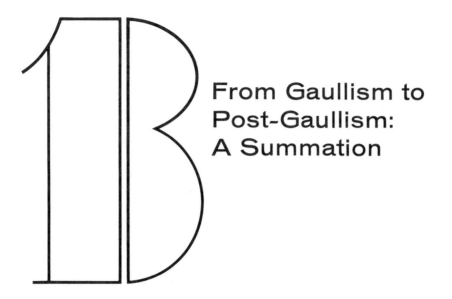

From Gaullism to Post-Gaullism: A Summation

THE HERITAGE OF DE GAULLE

A final assessment of the Fifth Republic is difficult, and a judgment would depend upon whichever features and accomplishments the reader considers important. There is no argument that the Fifth Republic has thus far worked more stably than its predecessor and has lasted longer. It has provided France with the prosperity, international prestige, and peace that had often eluded the previous regime, although it should be borne in mind that the foundations of that prosperity had been laid in the Fourth Republic and that the international achievements of France tended often to be chimerical. During the Fifth Republic, the government initiated reforms of the penal code and modernized the court system; promoted structural changes of the educational system, provided for a vast expansion of university enrollments, and modernized the curriculum by stressing technical education; and promoted the consolidation of farms and industries. It has emphasized, more than previous regimes, youth and sports; constructed housing projects and superhighways; and extended social security coverage. Above all, under the Fifth Republic the decision process has been made more efficient by the "rationalization" of Parliament and the reduction of the executive's dependence on the vagaries of clashing personal ambitions and shifting ideologies of deputies.

The modernizing tendencies of de Gaulle's regime were in some measure reflected also in the recognition that the traditional overconcentration of political and other activities in Paris had led to imbalances in economic development, and in a growing feeling that more should be done to enliven the provinces. The creation of "regions" as a superimposition on the departments, the experiment with CODERs, and even the ill-fated referendum of the spring of 1969 were steps in this direction. But although little was done beyond granting minor revenue-generating and decision-making powers to local communities, there has been at least an animated discussion about "regionalization."

Modernization was also the goal of de Gaulle's attempt to develop a government elite on the basis of expertise and training rather than party connections. De Gaulle's efforts at separating the political parties from the elite recruitment process (partly by means of Article 23) were invalidated by the gradual replacement of technicians in the cabinet by parliamentary deputies; and his attempt to factor parties out of presidential politics was abandoned when he became more openly and publicly identified as the leader of the UDR. Moreover, he did not manage to make elite recruitment more democratic than it had been before; and there has been little change in the "political stratum," which is still composed of middle and upper-middle-class products of prestigious schools. There developed a new criterion of "ascriptive recruitment" constituting a throwback to premodern patterns: wartime and postwar personal loyalty to de Gaulle. The depolitization of the masses—about which so much has been written—and their commitment to the regime turned out to be partial myths, especially since institutional stability could not compensate for what many perceived to be de Gaulle's failure to promote adequate policies of social and economic justice.

Like many great political leaders, de Gaulle was not particularly interested in economics. The modernization of the economy, the greater emphasis on technology, and the stabilization of the franc are achievements associated with the political stability that existed under de Gaulle, although built on foundations laid earlier. De Gaulle's own economic ideas were conservative, somewhat myopic, and often unworkable, such as the notion that he could eliminate the class struggle by "associating" workers and business by means of profit-sharing schemes rather than by a genuine attempt at a redistribution of economic benefits. For a while, he managed to keep disaffection of the masses in check—on the one hand, by captivating them with large global visions, prestige projects, and image building; and on the other hand, by undermining the orderly expression of demands of the disprivileged in restricting the role of intermediaries between the "elected monarch" and the people. As a consequence, he stimulated the growth of extraparliamentary movements, mass demonstrations, and antisystem behavior that gradually demythologized him, threatened to bring down his regime in 1968, led to his departure in 1969, and subsequently contributed to the revival and the impressive electoral gains of the Left in 1973 and 1974.

THE POMPIDOU PRESIDENCY

When Pompidou assumed the Presidency, he attempted to maintain his leadership image—a difficult task after de Gaulle's giant presence— by simultaneously invoking the name of de Gaulle and extending his own political support base. This balancing act kept him too busy to concentrate on meaningful structural reforms or policy innovations. Pompidou's program focused on the maintenance of the institutions of the Fifth Republic, while not neglecting the development of cooperation between the executive and the legislature.[1] Like his predecessor, Pompidou stressed growth and neglected to promote a policy of social and economic equalization. The pace of innovation, the building of hospitals and schools, the construction of middle-income housing, and the rise of real minimum wages for workers and farmers, which began in immediate reaction to the May Events of 1968, were slowed down. In education, many of the advances made in curriculum development and administrative decentralization were slowed, too, or left unenforced—while the government's financial support of parochial schools increased. The "de-blocking" of French society[2] that many had anticipated did not occur: there was no systematic reform of the tax structure that would have forced the independent entrepreneur to assume his fair fiscal burden; entry to the administrative bureaucracy was not made more accessible to the lower-middle classes; the monopoly of the *grandes écoles* was not weakened; and the opportunities for collective bargaining among groups were not expanded significantly. Contrary to promises, governmental control over the media was not relaxed. In foreign policy there was a departure from de Gaulle's style if not substance, as seen in the appointment of a moderate and a "good European," Maurice Schumann, as foreign minister. But while French policy toward Britain became more positive, and that toward America less acerbic, the main Gaullist lines were retained.

Pompidou was largely an orthodox Gaullist in his views concerning

1. Cf. Michel-Antoine Burnier et al., *La chute du Général* (Paris: Editions et Publications Premières, 1969), pp. 24–25; and Gilles Martinet, *Le système Pompidou* (Paris: Seuil, 1973).
2. Cf. Stanley Hoffmann, *Decline or Renewal: France Since the 1930's* (New York: Viking, 1974), p. 472; and Michel Crozier, *The Stalled Society* (New York: Viking, 1973), pt. 2.

political institutions. But he was a moderate in his domestic policies to the extent that electoral strategy required and the continuing dominance of the Gaullist party in the Assembly permitted. His campaign platform contained policies that most of the Centrists would find unobjectionable: an increase in the number of telephones, the support of the farmer, the raising of minimum industrial wages, the protection of noncompetitive industries, and worker participation in enterprises.[3] Pompidou's moderate outlook was reflected in his appointment of Chaban-Delmas as premier. In his first speech before Parliament as premier, on June 16, 1969, Chaban announced his program for a "new society," in which he committed himself to the implementation of Pompidou's electoral platform.

An assessment of Chaban's reforms is difficult. On the one hand, he succeeded in having generous binding contracts made between the trade unions and the nationalized industries, in slightly increasing tax rates for business, and in having several hundred thousand housing units built, especially for the aged and for young workers. On the other hand, his promises for the elimination of shantytowns (particularly for guest workers) were unfulfilled, as were those relating to meaningful "regionalization" and the weakening of the tutelage of the national government. Prices of public transport, telephones, electricity, and postage were sharply increased, and the inequities of the tax structure were, by and large, allowed to remain. Much of Chaban's program remained confined to the realm of rhetoric, probably because of an insufficiency of fiscal resources.[4] Nevertheless, Chaban's Radical Socialist background, his genuine interest in modernizing French society, and his open-mindedness enabled him to draw the support of many who had hitherto been alienated from the regime: leftist civil servants, intellectuals, and a flock of reformers, progressives, and pragmatists. Chaban initiated a dialogue with the trade unions, assuring them that henceforth socioeconomic policy would be based on consultation with them, and promised the Social and Economic Council that it, too, would have a large role to play. As a former speaker of the Assembly, he had kind words for Parliament, cultivated good relations with the Senate, and reversed the practice of previous premiers of not allowing cabinet ministers to appear before the upper chamber. The Assembly in particular was well-disposed to Chaban. Although, having been elected with a "backlash" vote following the May Events of 1968, the Assembly was

3. *Le Monde*, 14 June 1969.
4. Jean-Henri Briguel, "La nouvelle société: un slogan ou une politique?" *Revue politique et parlementaire*, 72 (September 1970): 6–23. See also P. Viansson-Ponté, "De l'ouverture à la fidélité," *Le Monde*, 7 July 1972.

very conservative and hence hardly in favor of the "progressive" elements of Chaban's program, that body gave him two massive votes of confidence—a vote of 369–85 in September 1969, and 369–96 in July 1972—because it saw in Chaban's outlook a departure from the institutional rigidities of Gaullism and an enlarged role for the Assembly.

Pompidou was never able to overcome widespread doubts about his Gaullist credentials despite certain aspects of Gaullist continuity in his policies. His hesitant moves toward centrism, which included the appointment of formerly oppositionist PDM deputies to the cabinet, did not enhance his power base in a reliable fashion, because the moderately progressive orientation of his regime was belied by many of his policies, and was identified therefore at least as much with Chaban-Delmas as with Pompidou. Moreover, the Center politicians—in particular the local notables—continued to have too many liaisons with anti-Gaullist moderates and Radicals. Pompidou finally returned to a more orthodox Gaullism, particularly during the latter half of his presidential tenure, when he appointed Pierre Messmer as premier and later Michel Jobert as foreign minister. Messmer's program was conservative, although not devoid of the usual references to educational reforms, the restructuring of the radio and television networks and the elaboration of de Gaulle's favorite profit-sharing schemes for workers. Messmer viewed himself as little more than a tool of the President; he had been a technician with little parliamentary experience, and his only significant foray into partisan politics had come when, in 1969, he led *Présence et Action*, a small movement concerned with the guarding of orthodox Gaullist principles.

But this return to Gaullist orthodoxy came, unfortunately, at a time when the UDR was suffering from fragmentation and incipient decay. The seeds of corruption, such as the real estate speculations of deputies, tax evasion by ministers, excessive politicization of the media, wiretapping and other scandals, had been sown during the stewardship of de Gaulle, but the latter was able to cover them up with symbolic outputs and appeals to the patriotic sentiments of Frenchmen. Pompidou was unable to do this, and thereby to arrest the decline of the UDR. His lack of stature, his petit-bourgeois background, his indecisiveness regarding economic problems, and finally his illness, all contributed to the erosion of the Gaullist parliamentary majority, the growth of left-wing parliamentary forces, and a greater assertiveness of Parliament. This assertiveness began after the spring 1973 parliamentary elections, which resulted in the loss of absolute majority status for the UDR, and the subsequent choice of Edgar Faure, a strong personality, as speaker of the Assembly. The changed composition of Parliament was duly reflected in Messmer's first postelectoral program, which he presented to the Assembly in April 1973. The program promised an increase in wages and pensions, an improvement of industrial working conditions, the lowering of the retirement age, and a stepped-up drive against tax fraud.[5] But neither these promises nor Pompidou's cabinet reshuffles during the last year of his presidency sufficed to shore up the President's authority. There was, moreover, increasing doubt about the utility of such constitutional provisions as Article 16 (Emergency Powers), Article 23 (the Incompatibility Clause), and the seven-year presidential term, which Pompidou himself wished to see reduced to five years. Although Pompidou adhered to the end to an orthodox Gaullist conception of presidential power, he could not exercise that power effectively. The public became increasingly bored with the tenets and personalities of Gaullism, and with Pompidou in particular. His sudden death, brought on by an illness whose seriousness had not been fully revealed to the public, came, in the political sense, at an opportune moment, because by the time of his demise he had lost much of the credibility he had once enjoyed while serving as de Gaulle's premier, and because the economic crisis which followed in the wake of the Mideast war of 1973 showed France to be less than a complete mistress of her own fate and thereby put into question a basic assumption of Gaullism.

GISCARDISM

The struggle for the succession began immediately after Pompidou's death—if not a few weeks before. The original list of presidential candidates contained twenty-two names, and was later reduced to twelve. Many orthodox Gaullists at first supported Pierre Messmer for the nomination, but finally endorsed the more dynamic Chaban-Delmas for first-ballot candidacy. The Center was divided: the CDP—the centrist coalition partners of Pompidou's presidential majority—supported Chaban; Servan-Schreiber's moderate Radical Socialists tended to prefer Giscard d'Estaing, who ran under his own Independent Republican label; while Lecanuet's Democratic Center remained uncertain.[6]

5. Ambassade de France, Service de Presse et d'Information, *France*, May 1973. On the confusion about the socioeconomic policies during Pompidou's Presidency, and the question whether the President or his premiers were responsible for progressive or retrogressive measures, see René Mouriaux, "Le bilan social d'un quinquennat," *Etudes*, July 1974, pp. 869–78.
6. *Le Monde*, 22 April 1974.

After Chaban's decisive defeat by Giscard on the first ballot, the Gaullists reluctantly threw their support to the latter, who had become the favorite of a united Center. The Left, which included the Communists, the Socialists, and the left wing of the Radical Socialists, was solidly behind Mitterrand.[7]

The victory of Giscard can be attributed to a variety of factors: the "desanctification" and departure of de Gaulle; the decline of the UDR in the parliamentary election of 1973; the unexpected illness and death of Pompidou; the deficiencies of Giscard's rivals for the presidential nomination; the emergence of a united Left and, simultaneously, the growing importance of a reorganized Center. In addition to these largely accidental factors, there is the personality of Giscard himself, and his nearly ideal background for the presidential office. Born in 1926, he was the son of a higher civil servant, the grandson of a deputy, and the great-grandson of a cabinet minister.[8] He achieved an excellent scholastic record at a good Parisian *lycée*; was involved, in a minor capacity, in the Parisian Resistance, and after Liberation joined the army to fight the Germans. He graduated from two *grandes écoles*: the *Ecole Polytechnique* and ENA, and married into an upper-class family. He began his public career as an inspector of finances, and subsequently, in 1955, he was appointed deputy director of the cabinet of Premier Edgar Faure. In contrast to de Gaulle and Pompidou, neither of whom had been involved in Fourth Republic politics, Giscard entered Parliament during that Republic. He was elected a deputy in 1956 under the label of Independents and Peasants (CNIP), and soon thereafter became a founder of the Independent Republican party.

The composition of Giscard's first government clearly reflected the pragmatic centrism of his party, and thereby constituted a sharp break with Gaullism. Jacques Chirac, the first premier, was a member of the Gaullist party, but he resembled Giscard in that he combined a number of politically desirable traits and experiences. Taking office at forty-one, he was one of France's youngest premiers (and the youngest in the twentieth century). A graduate of ENA, he served in the civil service as an auditor in the Court of Accounts. After his election to Parliament in 1967, he became a protégé of Pompidou, who appointed him to a cabinet position as secretary of state for social affairs. In 1968,

7. The Mitterrand supporters also included the CGT, the CFDT, the FEN and other unions. The PSU campaigned separately for Mitterrand.
8. Noel-Jean Bergeroux, "Du château de Varvasse au palais de l'Elysée," *Le Monde Hebdomadaire*, 16–22 May 1974. The article notes that Giscard's lineage goes back to the Bourbon kings.

he was named secretary of state in the Ministry of Economics and Finance, becoming thereby the immediate subordinate of Giscard. In 1971, under the premiership of Chaban, he was the cabinet's "delegate" in charge of relations with Parliament and, a year later, under the premiership of Messmer, briefly headed the Ministry of Agriculture (where, together with Jobert, he pursued a hard line on agricultural policies at Common Market discussions). After Pompidou's death, Chirac defected from the UDR by supporting Giscard against Chaban for the first-ballot candidacy for the Presidency.

Chirac's background, which combined Gaullism, "Pompidolianism," technocratism, and Giscardian pragmatism had, to some critics, made his commitment to true Gaullism suspect. He had repeatedly affirmed that, although a member of the UDR, his first loyalty was not to the party, but to the President. At the end of 1974 the latter, in an attempt to "Giscardize" the UDR, successfully promoted Chirac's election as secretary-general of that party over the opposition of Chaban, Debré, and Messmer.[9]

The Gaullist background of Chirac—a political convenience in view of the fact that the Gaullist party was the largest single group in the Assembly—was more than counterbalanced by the complexion of the cabinet as a whole. Among the fifteen full ministers (June 1974) there were only five Gaullists (as against ten under Messmer), three Independent Republicans, three Reformers, and four non-partisan technocrats. The latter occupied some of the most important portfolios: Foreign Affairs (Jean Sauvagnargues), Health (Simone Veil, a woman and a Jew), Education (René Haby), and Economics and Finance (Jean-Pierre Fourcade, who had been a civil servant and was subsequently involved in private banking). The new cabinet included four women—one full minister and three secretaries of state—more than in any other cabinet in French history. Moreover, three cabinet members were chosen from among senators, a record number for the Fifth Republic.

Some of the structural innovations in the cabinet may have been more symbolic than substantive. This appeared to be true of the Ministry of the Quality of Life, which combined the portfolios for Culture (which had been "demoted" earlier to a subcabinet position) and Environment (which had been merged earlier with responsibilities for Youth and Sports as well as Tourism). It was equally true of the new Ministry for the Condition of Women, the precise responsibilities of which were unclear,[10] and which was abolished in August 1976. Nonetheless, the

9. *Le Monde*, 29 May 1975.
10. *Le Monde*, 30 May 1974.

new cabinet conveyed an aura of modernity and, at least institutionally, Giscard's commitment to "rejuvenation and change."

This commitment has been reflected in an innovation of style, which is significant in a country addicted to formalized social relations and a ceremonialized approach to the public authorities. Although Giscard is a man steeped in traditional French aristocratic and elitist values, he appears to be sympathetic both to the views of the business world and to the demands of the masses for social progress. His presidential behavior is outwardly different from that of his predecessors in that it evinces a combination of modernity, "sportiness," and elegance. He tends to dress informally and makes a point of circulating freely among ordinary people. He does not seem to be much concerned with the old idea of the President being a quasi-institutionalized embodiment of elected royalty, and views the Presidency as "a career rather than a divine mission."[11] He has not followed the example of de Gaulle and Pompidou in moving his family to the Elysée Palace.

Inevitably, there are Frenchmen who see in the accession of Giscard the inauguration of a Sixth Republic.[12] Yet it is not clear to what extent the evolution of institutional relationships has constituted a departure from Gaullism. While de Gaulle was inclined toward contempt for Parliament and often tried to oppose it and undermine its power, Giscard has demonstrated no such contempt, but rather has mobilized Parliament more subtly in order to harness it for cooperation. Relations with the legislature have clearly improved, despite the hostility with which Chirac's initial government declaration had been received by leftists in the Senate and Gaullist deputies in the Assembly (though the latter approved the declaration by a vote of 297–181). There has been a new parliamentary assertiveness since mid-1974, which has expressed itself in a variety of ways. Edgar Faure, the speaker, proposed several structural and procedural changes which would make Parliament stronger, including the creation of additional standing committees and a large number of committees of inquiry into governmental activities. It was envisaged that some of these committees would be able to meet when Parliament was not in session. Giscard probably favors this parliamentary assertiveness[13]—or at least does not oppose it—not only because the UDR has lost its unity and parliamentary majority (and is therefore

11. Thomas Ferenczi, "Solitary Exercise of Power," *Le Monde Weekly*, 7 December 1974.
12. For example, Michèle Cotta, *La VIe République* (Paris: Flammarion, 1974), esp. chap. 8.
13. Giscard d'Estaing, "Les rapports entre l'éxécutif et le législatif," *Revue politique et parlementaire* 76 (May–June 1974): 19.

less able than previously to obstruct presidential programs), but also because he wishes to provide an institutional buffer between himelf and the growing number of rebellious socioeconomic sectors.

While none of the developments discussed above signified a relinquishment of the executive's dominance, there were those who contended that a realignment of relationships *within* that branch had taken place. Premier Chirac said, in a speech in the spring of 1976, that "there cannot be a divergence between the President and the Premier."[14] But the liaison function fulfilled by Chirac, as a Gaullist and as a long-time collaborator of Giscard, led a French commentator to suggest that the premier had reached a position almost equivalent to that of the President; that the one could "immobilize" or "veto" the other; and that decisions had become joint enterprises of the President, the premier, and the rest of the cabinet—in sum, that real meaning had been invested in Article 20 of the Constitution, which provides that "the government determines and leads national policy."[15] If this were true, it would be possible to speak of a "depresidentialization" of the regime—a development highly desirable precisely to those Gaullist parliamentarians who, under the Presidency of de Gaulle, would have considered it anathema. In fact, Chirac concentrated not so much on "decisions" as on the difficult task of persuading the Gaullist deputies that he took them seriously while avowing his obedience to the President. The resentment with which Chirac's appointment as premier had been received by Gaullist deputies did not abate in subsequent months; the premier's Gaullist affiliation appeared meaningless in view of the fact that Giscard himself had become a nonpartisan figure,[16] and in view of the latter's insistence that he alone decided the composition of the government and considered Chirac merely as a "coordinator" of the composite presidential majority.[17]

The primacy of the President was tellingly reemphasized on August 25, 1976, when Premier Chirac submitted his resignation. For several weeks prior to that event, rumors had circulated concerning disagreements between Chirac and Giscard. The President (following the advice of his friend Poniatowski) wanted to continue his efforts at moving his majority in a "liberal" direction—i.e., toward the Center and even the moderate Left—and to that end promoted progressive land-transfer tax policies for which the UDR had little enthusiasm. Conversely, Premier

14. *Le Monde,* 14 April 1976.
15. R. G. Schwartzenberg, "Deux scénarios," *Le Monde,* 6 May 1976.
16. In the summer of 1976, Giscard confirmed that he was no longer a member of *any* political party.
17. *Le Monde,* 26 March 1976; and *New York Times,* 17 June 1976.

Chirac, in order to maintain himself as a *persona grata* with the Gaullist deputies, wished to safeguard for the UDR the major place in the presidential system. Believing that most Frenchmen were "conservative, nationalistic, cautious and parsimonious,"[18] Chirac favored earlier parliamentary elections (to be held in 1977); Giscard, in the conviction that his economic policies would ultimately vindicate his presidential leadership and help split the Left alliance, preferred to let Parliament run its normal course. Giscard favored the use of Chirac's good offices to enlist the support of Gaullist legislators for the President's economic programs, while Chirac preferred executive policy making by means of decrees, in which the premier would play a significant role. The President did not wish to grant such a role to the premier—perhaps because, like his predecessors, Giscard feared that Chirac (whose popularity was on the rise) might use his office as a steppingstone to the Presidency. Furthermore, Chirac was reportedly angered by the fact that he had to share his preeminence in the cabinet (limited as it was) with Poniatowski: according to one source, "every time [Chirac] appeared at the Elysée Palace, 'Ponia' was there, too."[19]

The new cabinet appeared to be constructed for the purpose of emphasizing the orthodox Gaullist view of the totally dependent role of the premier and, at the same time, the subordinate position of the Gaullist party. Raymond Barre seemed to be ideally suited to preside over such a cabinet. A professional economist—he held the Ministry of Finance along with the premiership—Barre graduated from the University of Paris Law School, subsequently teaching there and at the *Institut d'Etudes Politiques*. Later he became a staff director of the Ministry of Industry (where he cultivated good relations with the trade unions); a member of the Common Market Executive Commission; a general counsel of the Bank of France; a participant in various governmental study commissions; and finally minister of foreign trade. Never having been elected to political office, and lacking any party base, he gave the impression of being entirely "nonpolitical" and was expected to function as "a private secretary of Giscard d'Estaing."[20] Nevertheless, his relationship with the parliamentary Gaullists has been cordial because he has agreed with certain aspects of their economic nationalism.[21]

The replacement of Chirac led to a strain in the relationship between Giscard and his supporters on the one hand, and the Gaullists on the other, the latter having lost both the Presidency and the premiership.

18. *Le Nouvel Observateur*, 30 August 1976, p. 22.
19. Ibid., p. 17.
20. Ibid., p. 18.
21. On Barre's background, see *L'Express*, 30 August–5 September 1976, pp. 24–29.

Chirac made no secret of his ambition to succeed to the Presidency in 1981; in an effort to foster this ambition, he assumed control over the Gaullist party, which in December 1976 was relabeled the *Rassemblement du peuple pour la République* (RPR). A few months later, Chirac became the first mayor of Paris in a century—a position to which the city council of the capital, with the reluctant support of Giscard's Independent Republicans, elected him.

The two major parties of the majority promised to support each other in the parliamentary elections of March 1978. Chirac did so with little enthusiasm because Giscard's conception of the "presidential majority" did not envisage a dominant role for the Gaullist party. On the contrary, Giscard had been busy since the fall of 1977 creating his own non-Gaullist political alliance system, which would permit him to reduce his dependence on Chirac. In January 1978 the *Union pour la démocratie française* (UDF) was established; it grouped Giscard's own party—renamed the *Parti républicain* (PR)—together with the Radical Socialists, the Centrists, the CNIP, and a number of related political clubs.[22]

This alliance building was facilitated by the fusion, more than a year earlier, of the "oppositionist" Democratic Centrists and the "majoritarian" CDP into a new party, the *Centre des démocrates sociaux* (CDS). The program of the new party contained a certain progressive rhetoric, with its emphasis on social justice, increased aid for France's underprivileged sectors, as well as demands for a greater role for Parliament and more viable local government.[23] The founding of the CDS had not resolved all the problems of the Centrists, for among their activists differences of opinion persisted about leadership, and, more important, about the strategy to be adopted. Some Centrists favored a closer identification with the Republicans; others, somewhat prematurely, held out the hope of a *rapprochement* with the Socialists.[24]

In any case, the creation of the UDF was not welcomed by the RPR. As the UDF had agreed on single candidates in numerous constituencies in the first election round—now frequently termed a "primary" election—the new formation was construed by Chirac as a blatantly anti-Gaullist device.

---

22. The CNIP, because of its obviously conservative identification, did not fit comfortably into a grouping that proclaimed itself to be "progressive-centrist."
23. See *L'Autre Solution* (Paris: CDS, October 1977).
24. For an attempt to trace the scissions and fusions of Centrist parties, cf. William Safran, "Centrism in the Fifth Republic: An Attitude in Search of an Instrument" (paper delivered at a conference on Two Decades of Gaullism, Brockport, N.Y., June 1978).

The disunity within the majority considerably enhanced the prospects of the Common Program allies. Indeed, from late 1977 to early 1978, most public-opinion polls confidently predicted victory for the Left. Unfortunately, the unity of the Left began to be shaken when, in late 1976, disagreements broke out between the Communist and Socialist parties about the meaning of the Common Program (see chapter 5). The Common Program had made references to the nationalization of industries but had not been specific about the extent of nationalization nor about a timetable for its implementation. Now that the possibility of the Left's achieving control of the Assembly had become more realistic, the PCF demanded that the missing details be agreed upon. Specifically, the PCF demanded that 1,000 firms be nationalized; the PS wanted to limit the list to 9 firms. Both parties favored a raise in the minimum wage, but the PCF wanted to reduce the existing income gap between the highest and lowest categories of wage earners much more sharply than the PS (which included in its ranks a significant element of the bourgeoisie) was prepared to do. Furthermore, there were differences of opinion regarding foreign and defense policies: the PCF had suddenly reversed itself by agreeing with the Gaullists in favoring an independent French nuclear striking force. Finally, the PCF demanded that Mitterrand, who was expected to become prime minister in the event of a victory of the Left alliance, commit himself to allocating a number of important ministerial portofolios to the PCF (e.g., interior, justice, defense, or foreign affairs). Mitterrand was unwilling to make such a commitment in advance. In spite of numerous meetings between the leaders of the two major parties of the Left, their compromise proposals were insufficient to bridge the gap between the parties, and the PCF refused to guarantee the second-ballot withdrawal of its candidates in favor of Socialists. It was widely speculated that programmatic considerations were far less important than tactical ones: that the PCF wanted to scuttle the victory of the Left at this time largely because the PS, which had replaced the PCF as the foremost party of the Left, would be the principal beneficiary. Such disagreements raised doubts among many voters that the parties of the Left would be cohesive enough to provide clear policy leadership and contributed heavily to the Left's election defeat (see table 23).

The PS, which had tasted power on previous occasions and had obtained the largest proportion of the popular vote in the March 1978 elections, was particularly frustrated. These frustrations led the PS, immediately after the elections, to a reexamination of the outlook and premises of the party, and to put in question not only the utility of the

Table 23
The Parliamentary Elections of 1978

	First Ballot (March 12)		Second Ballot (March 19)		Total Seats (491)[b]	Change from Previous Elections
	Popular Vote (in percent)[a]	Seats	Popular Vote (in percent)[a]	Seats		
Common Program Alliance						
Communists (PFC)	20.5	4	18.6	82	86	+12
Socialist (PS)	22.5	1	28.3	103	104	+9
Left Radicals (MRG)	2.3		2.3	10	10	−3
Extreme Left	3.3					0
Miscellaneous opposition	1.1			1	1	1
Gaullists (RPR)	22.6	31	26.1	119	150	−23
UDF						
Republicans (RP)		16		55	71	+10
Centrists (CDS)		6		29	35	+7
Radicals		3	23.2	4	7	0
Social-Democrats (MDSF)[c]	21.5			1	1	−5
Independents and Peasants (CNIP)		1		8	9	+1
"Presidential majority"[d]	2.4	6	1.6	10	16	−1
Ecologists	2.1					
Miscellaneous[e]	1.9			1	1	−3

[a] Rounded off.

[b] After the convocation of the Assembly in April, the parliamentary groups were broken down as follows: RPR, 153 (143 regular + 10 apparentés [associated]); UDF, 123 (108 + 15); 115 (103 + 12); PCF, 86; and Independents (non-inscrits), 14.

[c] Mouvement démocrate-socialiste français, a Socialist (ex-SFIO) splinter group with centrist inclinations.

[d] Candidates identified as supporters of Giscard but not formally associated with the UDF or its major components.

[e] Largely conservatives, about equally divided between supporters and nonsupporters of Giscard.

SOURCE: "Les élections législatives de mars 1978," Le Monde, Dossiers et Documents, p. 89. Le Monde 14, 15, 21, and 22 March and 5 April 1978.

old alliance tactics but also the continued leadership of Mitterrand. Most Socialists agreed in assigning the major blame for the election defeat to the PCF, but they also wondered what the PS could do in the future to attain power. One minority faction, led by CERES,[25] advocated a quick patching up of the Left alliance, if necessary by greater acquiescence in the PCF's demands; others contended that the reconstitution of the Left alliance for future elections could take place only under a substitute joint platform, or perhaps no platform at all. Still others suggested a tactical departure—that is, a *rapprochement* with the Radical Socialists and other progressive Centrists. Jacques Attali, an economist prominent in the PS leadership and a principal adviser of Mitterrand, might have hinted at such a tactic when he said that "the Left is no longer ideologically dominant" and that the PS faced a widespread "neo-capitalist sentiment" among the masses.[26] Such a departure might have to be accompanied by a replacement of Mitterrand as leader of the PS. Indeed, at least two possible successors were on the horizon: Michel Rocard and Pierre Mauroy. But neither was considered a perfect choice;[27] moreover, changes in the leadership could be undertaken only after a decent interval. In any event, a PS-Centrist *rapprochement* was out of the question as long as the Centrists remained tied to the "presidential majority"; furthermore, the overwhelming sentiment within the PS seemed to be in favor of maintaining the party's Left oppositionist stance, and the shelving of alliance options for the time being.

Within the PCF, too, a reexamination was in progress as several prominent leaders of the party acknowledged that the PCF's preelection behavior—and Marchais's leadership—had not been faultless. Jean Elleinstein, a co-director of the PCF's research bureau, called for greater de-Stalinization and "Italianization" of the party, freer internal discussion, and less organizational rigidity.[28] Conversely, Louis Althusser, another important party personality, called for a return to revolutionary Leninism and the abandonment of all "reformist" tendencies.

25. CERES—the *Centre d'Etudes, de Recherche et d'Education Socialistes*—was founded in 1967, contained a number of intellectuals and technocrats, and pretended to a position of "revolutionary reformism." See Michael Charzat et al., *Le CERES: Un combat pour le socialisme* (Paris: Calmann-Lévy, 1975), esp. pp. 61–65, 144 ff., and 244–60.
26. *Le Monde*, 14 April 1978.
27. Rocard was said to possess a dynamic personality, but both his previous connection with the rival PSU and his technocratic orientation made him suspect to many Socialist activists. Mauroy, prominent in the old SFIO and an anticommunist, seemed to be much more acceptable to the party's professional politicians, but he was said to lack mass appeal.
28. See Jean Elleinstein, "La mutation necéssaire," *Le Monde*, 14 April 1978; and idem, "Aller au fond des choses," *Le Monde*, 15 April 1978.

One of the most interesting results of the elections has been the apparent revival of political Centrism under the organizational aegis of the UDF, a development that has exploded the myth of the semipermanent bipolarization of French political life. Most Frenchmen are "centrist" by inclination, but such inclinations had been imperfectly reflected in the party system as it evolved from the early 1960s to the early 1970s. It is of course a matter of controversy whether Giscardism or the UDF has been an ideal, or even a genuine, embodiment of Centrist sentiment. It is true that the UDF has been a collecting point for the remainders of the Fourth Republic's Centrist parties. But it may be equally true that the growing success of the PS has been in part attributable to that party's being perceived by many as tending to moderation—a perception that has attracted many bourgeois elements to the PS. (If that is the case, the PCF's frequent charge that PS leaders have been toying with moderate reformism—"playing a centrist game"—is not entirely unjustified.) Finally, the partial revival and continued appeal of Gaullism, or "neo-Gaullism," must reflect in some measure the RPR's being viewed as programmatically Centrist at least as much as mystically nationalist. Whether such a view is justified is hard to say. When Giscard presented the UDF's Blois program, the RPR did not offer more conservative counterproposals, much as it might have liked to do. On the contrary, some Gaullist legislators even suggested that the UDF program was not "progressive" enough. The program (made public in January 1978) contained 30 "objectives" and 110 detailed "propositions," many of which bespoke the Giscardians' commitment to institutional liberalization as well as social justice, and largely reflected the President's ideas as embodied in his book *La Démocratie française*.[29] These ideas included an extension of citizens' rights, a strengthening of the powers of municipalities, an expanded role for the small shopkeepers in economic planning, a reduction of the workweek, an increase in retirement and widows' pensions and family subsidies, a raise in the pay of the most impoverished unskilled workers, and surtaxes on large fortunes.

When Premier Barre presented parts of that program to the Assembly several weeks after the parliamentary elections, most of the Gaullist deputies supported them—in particular since the program also contained features they viewed as "financially sound" or likely to appeal to the *grande bourgeoisie*.[30] The features the Gaullists found most

29. Paris: Fayard, 1976.
30. Some anti-Chiraquian Gaullists have even shared Giscard's neo-liberal institutional views and his admiration for "Anglo-American" political culture. See, for example, Alain Peyrefitte, *Le mal français* (Paris: Plon, 1976), esp. pp. 21–29, 303 ff.

acceptable included raising interest rates and lowering of taxes on savings; establishing ceilings on other taxes, including social security contributions, value-added, and corporate taxes; increasing fees for public services; and gradually abolishing price controls. Most Gaullists have accepted the argument of Giscard and his premier that in a period of economic stringency, the spending options of the government have been narrowed, and its first priority is to bring about a situation characterized by a stable currency, economic growth, and modernization that will ultimately result in higher wages and greater prosperity for the masses. Obviously, both majority groups consider such a "trickle-down" policy a responsible one, whereas the parties of the Left, viewing it as a shelving of the great promises of the Blois program and an abdication of presidential responsibility, are convinced that this policy will perpetuate the existing economic inequalities.

The UDF and the Gaullists have disagreed on a number of matters. The UDF has favored a more active involvement in European integration including French support for direct elections to the European Parliament; the RPR has opposed it. The UDF has been calling for a more active role by the United States in the management of the international financial system; the RPR has continued to be suspicious of American motives. The UDF has reiterated its commitment to the decentralization of the French administrative system; the RPR still views such a policy as detrimental to the unity of the French state.

It should be noted that some disagreements between the Gaullists and Giscardists have been inspired by tactical rather than ideological considerations. Thus, Giscard has favored a "statute for the opposition" (entailing possibly the allocating of one or two legislative committee chairmanships to the Left parliamentary parties), while the Gaullist leadership has questioned the utility of such an innovation. Giscard's approach has sprung not only from his attempt to bring about a "reasonable cohabitation" with the parliamentary opposition (especially with the Socialists) as a matter of democratic principle but also—if not primarily—from a desire to decrease his dependence on Chirac and improve his presidential options.

Similar tactical considerations have inspired the UDF's view of the electoral system. Two of the components of the UDF, the Centrist and Radical-Socialist parties, had consistently favored a return to an election system based on proportional representation, in their conviction that it would help break up the "artificial" and "unnatural" division of France into two political camps and hence contribute to the revival of the moderate Centrist parties. Some Republicans shared this view, and so, apparently, did Giscard before the elections, and the UDF officially embraced it when that coalition was founded. Since the elections, Giscard and other prominent leaders have had second thoughts: the reintroduction of proportional representation might lead to a refragmentation of the UDF and endanger Giscard's relative autonomy vis-à-vis the Gaullists.

A complicating factor is the existence of differences of opinion about the future role of the UDF. Lecanuet, as the official leader of that formation, has been envisaging it as the nucleus of a new, progressive party to which individuals might adhere directly (thus dispensing with the "intermediation" of its component groups). Some Radicals see in the UDF an instrument for the reintegration of the Left Radicals (the *Mouvement des radicaux de gauche*—MRG), the minor partner of the Left's electoral alliance and the first after the elections of 1978 to disengage itself from the Common Program, and hope to move the UDF in a more leftward direction. However, Poniatowski and other leaders of the Republican component are primarily concerned about safeguarding their own party's dominance[31] and promoting as much socioeconomic conservatism as possible, and view the UDF as little more than an instrument for securing and expanding the support for Giscard in future elections and thus reducing the political chances of Chirac.

Such tactical considerations explain a number of postelection developments. In mid-1977, Chirac, as mayor of Paris, had tried by unilateral action to reduce the capital's financial contribution for the maintenance of its police from 25 percent to 12.5 percent. However, the budget submitted by Giscard's government after the election provided for no governmental increase for the Paris police—a development that forced Mayor Chirac to increase local assessments.[32]

The convocation of the newly elected Assembly in April 1978 provided another occasion for a contest between Giscardians and "Chiraquians." The Gaullist parliamentary group had nominated Edgar Faure, the incumbent Speaker, as its candidate, while the UDF (unofficially) endorsed Jacques Chaban-Delmas, who had been the Speaker between 1958 and 1969. Both were members of the RPR, and both had, when the occasion demanded, projected a "centrist" image. But because Chaban was viewed as more adamantly anti-Chiraquian,[33]

---

31. In the spring of 1978 the Republican party claimed a membership of 90,000, at least as much as the combined membership of the CDS and the Radical party.
32. Note that in this contest between Chirac and Giscard, which was transformed into a contest between Paris and the state, the Left parties represented in the municipal council sided with the Gaullists! *Le Monde*, 29 April 1978.
33. When Chaban was Speaker, he was considered an orthodox supporter of Gaullism and faithfully reflected the General's view of the Assembly as a docile tool of the government; but when he became premier in 1969, he exploited his background as a

the UDF and the anti-Chirac Gaullist deputies now provided enough votes to secure Chaban's election.

Another manifestation of the Giscard-Chirac contest is the composition of the postelection cabinet (see table 24). Still headed by Raymond Barre, the cabinet of 38 members contains 10 Gaullists— roughly the same proportion as the cabinet of August 1976 (see page 161). But the Gaullist ministers adhere without exception to the anti-Chiraquian (i.e., "Centrist") faction. It may be noted that in at least one respect the new Barre government resembles the governments in the first four years of the Fifth Republic: more than a third of the ministers were chosen from among the civil servants, and most of these had not been holding parliamentary mandates at the time of their appointment. Furthermore, about two-thirds of the members had held ministerial positions in previous governments, including those established under Gaullist Presidents.

Table 24
Political Composition of the Government, April 1978

	Full Ministers (serving in the cabinet)	Ministers Not in the Cabinet and Secretaries of State	Total
Gaullists (RPR)	6	4	10
Republicans (PR)	5	7	12
Centrists (CDS)	3	1	4
Radicals		2	2
"Presidential majority"[a]	6	3	9
CNIP[b]		1	1
Total	20	18	38

[a]This includes Premier Barre and one secretary of state "affiliated" (apparenté) to the UDF, as well as two "nonpolitical" technocrats.

[b]This individual, an undersecretary for agriculture, is a veterinarian who once sat in Parliament apparenté, by turns, to the Democratic Center, the PDM, and the Independent Republicans.

SOURCE: Le Monde, 8 April 1978.

former Radical to project a "centrist" image. It is useful to recall that in the 1974 presidential elections, Chaban was the official candidate of the Gaullists; Chirac, no less Gaullist, supported Giscard for the Presidency. Faure, who had served in numerous cabinets in the Fourth and Fifth republics, had tried to combine his support of Gaullism with simultaneous membership in the Radical party and had, in fact, once tried to assume the Presidency of that party while still supporting Gaullism.

The foregoing developments do not, unfortunately, resolve the controversial question whether the Giscardian system represents a continuation of the Gaullist system under a different label or differs from that system only in matters of style, or whether it represents a significant departure from Gaullism.

The theme of continuity is clearly best reflected in the institutional setting. The basic relationships among the President, the government, and the Parliament have not been significantly altered, and the electoral, judicial, and administrative systems have not undergone meaningful reforms. Moreover, the "changes" in parliamentary leadership, the composition of the cabinet, and the management of political parties have been such as to illustrate the staying power and adaptability of prominent politicians—a phenomenon not confined to the Fifth Republic.

Nevertheless, since 1974 there have been significant policy innovations that have reflected Giscard's liberal and pragmatic views of institutions and social relations. The voting age (and the age of legal majority) has been lowered from twenty-one to eighteen. The rights of women (particularly regarding property settlements) are in the process of being improved; policies regarding birth control, abortion, and divorce have been liberalized; and the right of political asylum has been extended. Prison conditions have been improved, and the rights of prisoners have been enlarged. Excesses of the police have been curbed, and in contrast to the situation prevailing under the presidencies of de Gaulle and Pompidou, there has been little governmental interference with the freedom of the press. In addition, further attempts have been made to modernize the educational system. Under the reform proposals initiated by René Haby (minister of education from 1974 to 1977), uniform elementary education was to be extended from five to six years; "streaming" into technical, general, or academic orientations, which had commenced at age eleven, was to begin at twelve; and study for secondary school diplomas was to be made more flexible by the introduction of a two-stage (general and specialized) baccalauréat. Annual meetings between teachers and parents of elementary and secondary school pupils were inaugurated, a development that spurred the growth of parent-teacher organizations.

Some of these reforms are not so much innovations as extensions of measures already initiated in earlier regimes, and are thus part of the dynamics of continuity. Other reforms are more structural than they are substantive; for example, the "reorganization" of ORTF, while providing for greater administrative flexibility (see chapter 10), will not seriously affect the governmental monopoly over broadcasting.[34] Still other reforms—such as Giscard's promise to shorten the term of the Presidency and progress toward regionalization—may remain verbal commitments for a long time to come, because French traditions, bureaucratic immobility, or political counter-pressures may be too much for one person to overcome.

Giscard's critics have contended that most of these reforms, while laudable, have had little effect on the pattern of economic redistribution. Both before and immediately after the presidential election of 1974 and the parliamentary election of 1978, Giscard reiterated his promise to reduce the socioeconomic gap and promised to lend a sympathetic ear to all sectors of French society. It is true that Giscard has had more meetings than his predecessors with spokesmen of trade unions, farmers, shopkeepers, and opposition parties, and has consulted them on pending legislation. Nevertheless, his critics doubt whether Giscard's commitment to social justice and modernization—articulated in such slogans as "advanced liberalism" and "society of participatory management"—is credible. In view of Giscard's own capitalist background (from which he cannot liberate himself), and considering that his presidential majority is composed of privileged elements (that oppose social justice) and provincial shopkeepers (who oppose modernization), these critics feel that his visits to hospitals, prisons, or centers for the handicapped are merely symbolic actions befitting a titular chief of state rather than a determined decision maker.[35]

It is possible to argue that nowadays, as a result of bureaucratic constraints and limited economic resources, leaders of most industrial democracies can be little more than figureheads, and that Giscard is no exception. Even before the accession of Giscard, it was asserted that the presidential leadership system had been replaced by a bureaucratic republic, in which the *grand corps* had become the real decision maker—or rather, the administrator of a budget, 80 percent of which consisted of items that had been previously built into the system and had to be continued, and in which, consequently, the options were in

34. A report issued in June 1976 by an "information watchdog committee," set up a year earlier by the Opposition parties, charged that the government coalition got three times more radio and TV time than the Opposition parties. Pierre Vianssone-Ponté, "Changement sans risque," *Le Monde*, 8 July 1976.
35. See P. Viansson-Ponté, *Lettre ouverte aux hommes politiques* (Paris: Albin Michel, 1976), pp. 26–27 and 34–35; Jacques Robert, "Le giscardisme existe-t-il?" *Le Monde*, 25 March 1976; Jean-Pierre Chevénement (a Socialist deputy), "Perspective et réalité du giscardisme," *Le Monde*, 13 May 1976; and H. Madelin, "Le libéralisme de Giscard," *Projet*, December 1975, pp. 1157–70.

most cases too restricted for an incrementalist approach, "leaving the President, the Prime Minister, and the Minister of Finance with very little room to initiate or change policy to suit themselves."[36]

Such a statement would apply above all to foreign policy, in which Giscard has not been strikingly original. He has perpetuated Gaullist foreign policy because of a continued need for overall support from Gaullist deputies, because certain policies—such as those regarding NATO and the Middle East—seem to be approved by a broad spectrum of French opinion or greeted with popular indifference, or because circumstances (including France's limited power) render post-Gaullist innovation difficult.

Conversely, it may be argued that Giscard has shown himself capable of promoting certain reforms that have been more than symbolic. Among these has been the austerity program introduced in June 1974, which was designed to control inflation and curb consumption, particularly of fuel. The program provided for an 18 percent increase in corporate taxes, a surtax on the incomes of top earners, a 10 percent capital-gains tax on real-estate transactions, and an increase in gasoline taxes. Giscard's pro-business reputation was also belied by a governmental decision to grant nearly full wages as unemployment compensation for an entire year. It is interesting to note that in spite of Giscard's commitment to economic liberalism, and in spite of the existence of the "old-boy network" of ENA graduates that links government and big business, the president of the CNPF asserted several months after Giscard's election that he had not succeeded in getting an audience with Giscard and complained about a lack of harmonization between the public authorities and the private business sector. By contrast, Giscard and his prime ministers met directly with trade-union leaders in an attempt to "sell" their economic program to them, even before it was reflected in government bills. Although Giscard favored holding down wages, he did not wish to force such a policy on organized labor; rather, he preferred a "neo-capitalist" approach, somewhat analogous to the "social contract" espoused by Harold Wilson when he was prime minister of Britain. In this approach, wage restraint would be voluntarily agreed to by the unions in exchange for a governmental commitment to progressive social legislation.

36. Monica Charlot, "The Language of Television Campaigning," in *France at the Polls: The Presidential Election of 1974*, ed. Howard R. Penniman (Washington, D.C.: American Enterprise Institute, 1975), p. 241. On Giscard's "progressivism," see Valéry Giscard d'Estaing, "Progrés économique et justice sociale," *Revue politique et parlementaire* 74 (September 1972): 1–12; on Mitterrand's pragmatism and moderation, see his interesting if somewhat verbose "political diary," *La paille et le grain* (Paris: Flammarion, 1975), esp. pp. 242–51.

But many of Giscard's reforms occurred in the wake of two events: the energy crisis, which is continuing; and the consolidation and strengthening of the Left opposition parties, which were expected to mount a serious challenge to Giscard's leadership. The defeat of the Left in the most recent parliamentary elections reduced that challenge and gave the President a freer hand: either to pursue measured reforms relatively unencumbered by the pressures of the "revolutionary" Left or—as many leftists would contend—to ignore the plight of the underprivileged.

In the early 1970s it was still possible for the government to argue that the opposition was out to abolish the "system," and hence that the protection of the system had to take precedence over various social reforms. In the tripolar presidential election of 1974, it had already become apparent that all the major candidates accepted the system: the ideological pronouncements of Mitterrand and Giscard had been kept to a minimum, and there had even been a certain (largely verbal) convergence with respect to social and economic issues.   The 1978 elections signaled an end to the Manichaean approach that had characterized French politics in the 1960s; in the arguments about the nature of political institutions there was little that reminded the French voters of the "legitimacy crises" that had figured so prominently in the elections of the Fourth and early Fifth republics.

It is too early to predict whether the emergence of a four-party system will give rise to a middle-of-the-road politics in which the noncommunist Left in Parliament will be a partner in policy making, and in which the ideological preoccupations of hard-line communists and ultra-orthodox Gaullists will play a reduced role. If such a new politics is put in place, then France will be truly launched into a "post-Gaullist" era.

Appendix

The French Constitution of 1958

This is an abridged version of the 1958 Constitution, containing only the most important provisions, and including all parts mentioned in the book.[1]

Preamble

The French people hereby solemnly proclaims its attachment to the Rights of Man and the principles of national sovereignty as defined by the Declaration of 1789, reaffirmed and complemented by the Preamble of the Constitution of 1946.

. . .

Title I—On Sovereignty

Article 2. France is a Republic, indivisible, secular, democratic and social. It shall ensure the equality of all citizens before the law, without distinction of origin, race or religion. It shall respect all beliefs.

The national emblem is the tricolor flag, blue, white and red.

The national anthem is the "Marseillaise."

The motto of the Republic is "Liberty, Equality, Fraternity."

Its principle is government of the people, by the people and for the people.

Article 3. National sovereignty belongs to the people, which shall exercise this sovereignty through its representatives and by means of referendums.

No section of the people, nor any individual, may attribute to themselves or himself the exercise thereof.

---

1. Based on English translation furnished by French Embassy, Press and Information Division, New York.

Suffrage may be direct or indirect under the conditions stipulated by the Constitution. It shall always be universal, equal and secret.

All French citizens of both sexes who have reached their majority and who enjoy civil and political rights may vote under the conditions to be determined by law.

Article 4. Political parties and groups shall be instrumental in the expression of the suffrage. They shall be formed freely and shall carry on their activities freely. They must respect the principles of national sovereignty and democracy.

Title II—The President of the Republic

Article 5. The President of the Republic shall see that the Constitution is respected. He shall ensure, by his arbitration, the regular functioning of the governmental authorities, as well as the continuance of the State.

He shall be the guarantor of national independence, of the integrity of the territory, and of respect for Community agreements and treaties.

Article 6.[2] The President of the Republic shall be elected for seven years by direct universal suffrage.

The procedures implementing the present article shall be determined by an organic law.

Article 7.[3] The President of the Republic shall be elected by an absolute majority of the votes cast. If no such majority is obtained on the first ballot, there is a second ballot on the second Sunday following the first ballot. Only the two candidates who received the most votes on the first ballot, not taking into account those candidates who had placed better but withdrawn, may run on the second ballot.

The election of the new President of the Republic shall take place not less than twenty days and not more than thirty-five days before the expiration of the powers of the incumbent President.

In the event that the Presidency of the Republic has been vacated for any cause whatsoever, or impeded in its functioning as officially noted by the Constitutional Council, to which the matter has been referred by the Government, and which shall rule by an absolute majority of its members, the functions of the President of the Republic, with the exception of those provided for by Articles 11 and 12 below, shall be temporarily exercised by the President of the Senate, or, if the latter is, in turn, prevented from functioning, by the Government.

In the case of a vacancy, or when the inability to function is de-

2. Amendment by referendum of October 1962.
3. Ibid.

clared definitive by the Constitutional Council, the vote for the election of the new President shall take place, except in case the Constitutional Council declares the existence of *force majeure*, not less than twenty nor more than thirty-five days after the beginning of the vacancy or the declaration of the definitive character of the inability to function.

Articles 49, 50 or 89 of the Constitution may not be invoked during the period of vacancy of the Presidency of the Republic, or during the period between the declaration of presidential incapacity and the election of a successsor.

Article 8. The President of the Republic shall appoint the Premier. He shall terminate the functions of the Premier when the latter presents the resignation of the Government.

On the proposal of the Premier, he shall appoint the other members of the Government and shall terminate their functions.

Article 9. The President of the Republic shall preside over the Council of Ministers.

Article 10. The President of the Republic shall promulgate the laws within fifteen days following the transmission to the Government of the finally adopted law.

He may, before the expiration of this time limit, ask Parliament for a reconsideration of the law or of certain of its articles. This reconsideration may not be refused.

Article 11. The President of the Republic, on the proposal of the Government during [Parliamentary] sessions, or on joint motion of the two assemblies, published in the *Journal Officiel*, may submit to a referendum any bill dealing with the organization of the governmental authorities, entailing approval of a Community agreement, or providing for authorization to ratify a treaty that, without being contrary to the Constitution, might affect the functioning of [existing] institutions.

When the referendum decides in favor of the bill, the President of the Republic shall promulgate it within the time limit stipulated in the preceding article.

Article 12. The President of the Republic may, after consultation with the Premier and the Presidents of the assemblies, declare the dissolution of the National Assembly.

General elections shall take place twenty days at the least and forty days at the most after the dissolution.

The National Assembly shall convene by right on the second Thursday following its election. If this meeting takes place between the periods provided for ordinary sessions, a session shall, by right, be held for a fifteen-day period.

There may be no further dissolution within a year following these elections.

Article 13. The President of the Republic shall sign the ordinances and decrees decided upon in the Council of Ministers.

He shall make appointments to the civil and military posts of the State.

.   .   .

Article 15. The President of the Republic shall be commander of the armed forces. He shall preside over the higher councils and committees of national defense.

Article 16. When the institutions of the Republic, the independence of the nation, the integrity of its territory or the fulfillment of its international commitments are threatened in a grave and immediate manner and when the regular functioning of the constitutional governmental authorities is interrupted, the President of the Republic shall take the measures commanded by these circumstances, after official consultation with the Premier, the Presidents of the assemblies and the Constitutional Council.

He shall inform the nation of these measures in a message.

These measures must be prompted by the desire to ensure to the constitutional governmental authorities, in the shortest possible time, the means of fulfilling their assigned functions. The Constitutional Council shall be consulted with regard to such measures.

Parliament shall meet by right.

The National Assembly may not be dissolved during the exercise of emergency powers [by the President].

.   .   .

Article 18. The President of the Republic shall communicate with the two assemblies of Parliament by means of messages, which he shall cause to be read, and which shall not be followed by any debate.

Between sessions, Parliament shall be convened especially for this purpose.

.   .   .

Title III—The Government

Article 20. The Government shall determine and direct the policy of the nation.

It shall have at its disposal the administration and the armed forces.

It shall be responsible to Parliament under the conditions and according to the procedures stipulated in Articles 49 and 50.

Article 21. The Premier shall direct the operation of the Government. He shall be responsible for national defense. He shall ensure the execution of the laws. Subject to the provisions of Article 13, he shall have regulatory powers and shall make appointments to civil and military posts.

He may delegate certain of his powers to the ministers.

He shall replace, should the occasion arise, the President of the Republic as chairman of the councils and committees provided for under Article 15.

He may, in exceptional instances, replace him as chairman of a meeting of the Council of Ministers by virtue of an explicit delegation and for a specific agenda.

Article 22. The acts of the Premier shall be countersigned, when circumstances so require, by the ministers responsible for their execution.

Article 23. The office of member of the Government shall be incompatible with the exercise of any Parliamentary mandate, with the holding of any office at the national level in business, professional or labor organizations, and with any public employment or professional activity.

An organic law shall determine the conditions under which the holders of such mandates, functions or employments shall be replaced.

The replacement of members of Parliament shall take place in accordance with the provisions of Article 25.

Title IV—The Parliament

Article 24. The Parliament shall comprise the National Assembly and the Senate.

The deputies to the National Assembly shall be elected by direct suffrage.

The Senate shall be elected by indirect suffrage. It shall ensure the representation of the territorial units of the Republic. Frenchmen living outside France shall be represented in the Senate.

Article 25. An organic law shall determine the term for which each assembly is elected, the number of its members, their emoluments, the conditions of eligibility and ineligibility and the offices incompatible with membership in the assemblies.

It shall likewise determine the conditions under which, in the case of a vacancy in either assembly, persons shall be elected to replace the deputy or senator whose seat has been vacated until the holding of new complete or partial elections to the assembly concerned.

.   .   .

Article 27. All binding instructions [upon members of Parliament] shall be null and void.

The right to vote of the members of Parliament shall be personal.

Article 28. Parliament shall convene, by right, in two ordinary sessions a year.

The first session shall begin on the first Tuesday of October and shall end on the third Friday of December.

The second session shall open on the last Tuesday of April; it may not last longer than three months.

Article 29. Parliament shall convene in extraordinary session at the request of the Premier, or of the majority of the members comprising the National Assembly, to consider a specific agenda.

When an extraordinary session is held at the request of the members of the National Assembly, the closure decree shall take effect as soon as the Parliament has exhausted the agenda for which it was called, and at the latest twelve days from the date of its meeting.

Only the Premier may ask for a new session before the end of the month following the closure decree.

.   .   .

Title V—On Relations Between Parliament and the Government

Article 34. All laws shall be passed by Parliament.

Laws shall establish the regulations concerning:

—civil rights and the fundamental guarantees granted to the citizens for the exercise of their public liberties; the obligations imposed by the national defense upon the persons and property of citizens;

—nationality, status and legal capacity of persons, marriage contracts, inheritance and gifts;

—determination of crimes and misdemeanors as well as the penalties imposed therefor; criminal procedure; amnesty; the creation of new juridical systems and the status of magistrates;

—the basis, the rate and the methods of collecting taxes of all types; the issuance of currency.

Laws shall likewise determine the regulations concerning:

—the electoral system of the Parliamentary assemblies and the local assemblies;

—the establishment of categories of public institutions;

—the fundamental guarantees granted to civil and military personnel employed by the State;

—the nationalization of enterprises and the transfer of the property of enterprises from the public to the private sector.

Laws shall determine the fundamental principles of:

—the general organization of national defense;

—the free administration of local communities, the extent of their jurisdiction and their resources;

—education;

—property rights, civil and commercial obligations;

—legislation pertaining to employment, unions and social security.

The financial laws shall determine the financial resources and obligations of the State under the conditions and with the reservations to be provided for by an organic law.

Laws pertaining to national planning shall determine the objectives of the economic and social action of the State.

The provisions of the present article may be developed in detail and amplified by an organic law.

Article 35. Parliament shall authorize the declaration of war.

Article 36. Martial law shall be decreed in a meeting of the Council of Ministers.

Its prorogation beyond twelve days may be authorized only by Parliament.

Article 37. Matters other than those that fall within the domain of law shall be of a regulatory character.

Legislative texts concerning these matters may be modified by decrees issued after consultation with the Council of State. Those legislative texts which may be passed after the present Constitution has become operative shall be modified by decree, only if the Constitutional Council has stated that they have a regulatory character as defined in the preceding paragraph.

Article 38. The Government may, in order to carry out its program, ask Parliament to authorize it, for a limited period, to take through ordinances measures that are normally within the domain of law.

The ordinances shall be enacted in meetings of the Council of Ministers after consultation with the Council of State. They shall come into force upon their publication, but shall become null and void if the bill for their ratification is not submitted to Parliament before the date set by the enabling act.

At the expiration of the time limit referred to in the first paragraph of the present article, the ordinances may be modified only by law in those matters which are within the legislative domain.

Article 39. The Premier and the members of Parliament alike shall have the right to initiate legislation.

Government bills shall be discussed in the Council of Ministers after consultation with the Council of State and shall be filed with the Secretariat of one of the two assemblies. Finance bills shall be submitted first to the National Assembly.

Article 40. Bills and amendments introduced by members of Parliament shall not be considered when their adoption would have as a consequence either a diminution of public financial resources, or the creation or increase of public expenditures.

Article 41. If it appears in the course of the legislative procedure that a Parliamentary bill or an amendment is not within the domain of law or is contrary to a delegation [of authority] granted by virtue of Article 38, the Government may declare its inadmissibility.

In case of disagreement between the Government and the President of the assembly concerned, the Constitutional Council, upon the request of either party, shall rule within a time limit of eight days.

Article 42. The discussion of Government bills shall pertain, in the first assembly to which they have been referred, to the text presented by the Government.

An assembly, given a text passed by the other assembly, shall deliberate on the text that is transmitted to it.

Article 43. Government and Parliamentary bills shall, at the request of the Government or of the assembly concerned, be sent for study to committees especially designated for this purpose.

Government and Parliamentary bills for which such a request has not been made shall be sent to one of the permanent committees, the number of which shall be limited to six in each assembly.

Article 44. Members of Parliament and of the Government shall have the right of amendment.

After the opening of the debate, the Government may oppose the examination of any amendment which has not previously been submitted to committee.

If the Government so requests, the assembly concerned shall decide, by a single vote, on all or part of the text under discussion, retaining only the amendments proposed or accepted by the Government.

Article 45. Every Government or Parliamentary bill shall be examined successively in the two assemblies of Parliament with a view to the adoption of an identical text.

When, as a result of disagreement between the two assemblies, it has become impossible to adopt a Government or Parliamentary bill after two readings by each assembly, or, if the Government has declared the matter urgent, after a single reading by each of them, the Premier shall have the right to have a joint committee meet, composed of an equal number from both assemblies and instructed to offer for consideration a text on the matters still under discussion.

The text prepared by the joint committee may be submitted by the Government for approval of the two assemblies. No amendment shall be admissible except by agreement with the Government.

If the joint committee fails to approve a common text, or if this text is not adopted under the conditions set forth in the preceding paragraph, the Government may, after a new reading by the National Assembly and by the Senate, ask the National Assembly to rule definitively. In this case, the National Assembly may reconsider either the text prepared by the joint committee or the last text adopted [by the National Assembly], modified, when circumstances so require, by one or several of the amendments adopted by the Senate.

Article 46. The laws that the Constitution characterizes as organic shall be passed and amended under the following conditions:

A Government or Parliamentary bill shall be submitted to the deliberation and to the vote of the first assembly to which it is submitted only at the expiration of a period of fifteen days following its introduction.

The procedure of Article 45 shall be applicable. Nevertheless, lacking an agreement between the two assemblies, the text may be adopted by the National Assembly on final reading only by an absolute majority of its members.

The organic law relative to the Senate must be passed in the same manner by the two assemblies.

Organic laws may be promulgated only after a declaration by the Constitutional Council on their constitutionality.

Article 47. Parliament shall pass finance bills under the conditions to be stipulated by an organic law.

Should the National Assembly fail to reach a decision on first reading within a time limit of forty days after a bill has been filed, the Government shall refer it to the Senate, which must rule within a time limit of fifteen days. The procedure set forth in Article 45 shall then be followed.

Should Parliament fail to reach a decision within a time limit of seventy days, the provisions of the bill may be enforced by ordinance.

Should the finance bill establishing the resources and expenditures of a fiscal year not be filed in time for it to be promulgated before the beginning of that fiscal year, the Government shall immediately request Parliament for the authorization to collect the taxes and shall make available by decree the funds needed to meet the Government commitments already voted.

The time limits stipulated in the present article shall be suspended when Parliament is not in session.

The Audit Office shall assist Parliament and the Government in supervising the implementation of the finance laws.

Article 48. The discussion of the bills filed or agreed upon by the Government shall have priority on the agenda of the assemblies in the order set by the Government.

One meeting a week shall be reserved, by priority, for questions asked by members of Parliament and for answers by the Government.

Article 49. The Premier, after deliberation by the Council of Ministers, may pledge the responsibility of the Government to the National Assembly with regard to the program of the Government, or with regard to a declaration of general policy, as the case may be.

The National Assembly may question the responsibility of the Government by the vote of a motion of censure. Such a motion shall be admissible only if it is signed by at least one tenth of the members of the National Assembly. The vote may only take place forty-eight hours after the motion has been filed; the only votes counted shall be those favorable to the motion of censure, which may be adopted only by a majority of the members comprising the Assembly. Should the motion of censure be rejected, its signatories may not introduce another motion in the course of the same session, except in the case provided for in the paragraph below.

The Premier may, after deliberation by the Council of Ministers, pledge the Government's responsibility to the National Assembly on the vote of a text. In this case, the text shall be considered as adopted, unless a motion of censure, filed in the succeeding twenty-four hours, is voted under the conditions laid down in the previous paragraph.

The Premier shall be entitled to ask the Senate for approval of a general policy declaration.

Article 50. When the National Assembly adopts a motion of censure, or when it disapproves the program or a declaration of general policy of the Government, the Premier must submit the resignation of the Government to the President of the Republic.

·   ·   ·

Title VI—On Treaties and International Agreements

Article 52. The President of the Republic shall negotiate and ratify treaties.

He shall be informed of all negotiations leading to the conclusion of an international agreement not subject to ratification.

Article 53. Peace treaties, commercial treaties, treaties or agreements relative to international organization, those that imply a commitment for the finances of the State, those that modify provisions of a legislative nature, those relative to the status of persons, those that call for the cession, exchange, or addition of territory may be ratified or approved only by a law.

They shall go into effect only after having been ratified or approved.

No cession, no exchange, no addition of territory shall be valid without the consent of the populations concerned.

Article 54. If the Constitutional Council, the matter having been referred to it by the President of the Republic, by the Premier, or by the President of one or the other assembly, shall declare that an international commitment contains a clause contrary to the Constitution, the authorization to ratify or approve this commitment may be given only after amendment of the Constitution.

Article 55. Treaties or agreements duly ratified or approved shall, upon their publication, have an authority superior to that of laws, subject, for each agreement or treaty, to its application by the other party.

Title VII—The Constitutional Council

Article 56. The Constitutional Council shall consist of nine members, whose term of office shall last nine years and shall not be renewable. One third of the membership of the Constitutional Council shall be renewed every three years. Three of its members shall be appointed by the President of the Republic, three by the President of the National Assembly, three by the President of the Senate.

In addition to the nine members provided for above, former Presidents of the Republic shall be members ex officio for life of the Constitutional Council.

The President shall be appointed by the President of the Republic. He shall have the deciding vote in case of a tie.

Article 57. The office of member of the Constitutional Council shall be incompatible with that of minister or member of Parliament. Other incompatibilities shall be determined by an organic law.

Article 58. The Constitutional Council shall ensure the regularity of the election of the President of the Republic.

THE FRENCH POLITY

It shall examine complaints and shall announce the results of the vote.

Article 59. The Constitutional Council shall rule, in the case of disagreement, on the regularity of the election of deputies and senators.

Article 60. The Constitutional Council shall ensure the regularity of referendum procedures and shall announce the results thereof.

Article 61. Organic laws, before their promulgation, and regulations of the Parliamentary assemblies, before they come into application, must be submitted to the Constitutional Council, which shall rule on their constitutionality.

To the same end, laws may be submitted to the Constitutional Council, before their promulgation, by the President of the Republic, the Premier, the President of one or the other assembly, sixty deputies or sixty Senators.[4]

In the cases provided for by the two preceding paragraphs, the Constitutional Council must make its ruling within a time limit of one month. Nevertheless, at the request of the Government, in case of emergency, this period shall be reduced to eight days.

In these same cases, referral to the Constitutional Council shall suspend the time limit for promulgation.

Article 62. A provision declared unconstitutional may not be promulgated or implemented.

The decisions of the Constitutional Council may not be appealed to any jurisdiction whatsoever. They must be recognized by the governmental authorities and by all administrative and juridical authorities.

. . .

Title VIII—On Judicial Authority

Article 64. The President of the Republic shall be the guarantor of the independence of the judicial authority.

He shall be assisted by the High Council of the Judiciary.

. . .

Magistrates may not be removed from office.

Article 65. The High Council of the Judiciary shall be presided over by the President of the Republic. The Minister of Justice shall be

4. As amended by joint session of Parliament in October 1974.

its Vice President ex officio. He may preside in place of the President of the Republic.

．　．　．

Article 66. No one may be arbitrarily detained.

The judicial authority, guardian of individual liberty, shall ensure respect for this principle under the conditions stipulated by law.

．　．　．

Title X—The Economic and Social Council

Article 69. The Economic and Social Council, whenever the Government calls upon it, shall give its opinion on the Government bills, ordinances and decrees, as well as on the Parliamentary bills submitted to it.

．　．　．

Article 70. The Economic and Social Council may likewise be consulted by the Government on any problem of an economic or social character of interest to the Republic or to the Community. Any plan, or any bill dealing with a plan, of an economic or social character shall be submitted to it for its advice.

．　．　．

Title XIV—On Amendment

Article 89. The initiative for amending the Constitution shall belong both to the President of the Republic on the proposal of the Premier and to the members of Parliament.

The Government or Parliamentary bill for amendment must be passed by the two assemblies in identical terms. The amendment shall become definitive after approval by a referendum.

Nevertheless, the proposed amendment shall not be submitted to a referendum when the President of the Republic decides to submit it to Parliament convened in Congress; in this case, the proposed amendment shall be approved only if it is accepted by a three-fifths majority of the votes cast. The Secretariat of the Congress shall be that of the National Assembly.

No amendment procedure may be undertaken or followed when the integrity of the territory is in jeopardy.

The republican form of government shall not be subject to amendment.

.   .   .

Select Bibliography

The following list includes a sampling of books that have been specifically relied upon by the author, as well as a number of additional works of interest to the student of French politics. The periodical literature cited in the footnotes is not listed separately below, nor are a number of French-language titles, of use primarily to the specialist. However, the reader's attention is directed to the following periodicals that have been found most useful: *Année politique*; *Documentation française*; Ambassade de France, Service de Presse et d'Information, monthly and irregular bulletins; *Le Monde*, daily and (occasionally) weekly editions; *Sondages*; *Revue française de science politique*; *Revue politique et parlementaire*; *Revue de droit public et de science politique*; *Revue administrative*; and *Revue française de sociologie*.

The Historical Background

Brogan, Denis W. *The Development of Modern France*. London: Hamish Hamilton, 1940.

Cobban, Alfred. *A History of Modern France*. New York: George Braziller, 1965.

Hoffmann, Stanley. *Decline or Renewal? France Since the 1930's*. New York: Viking, 1974.

Shirer, William L. *The Collapse of the Third Republic*. New York: Simon and Schuster, 1969.

Thomson, David. *Democracy in France Since 1870*. 5th ed. New York: Oxford University Press, 1969.

Wright, Gordon. *France in Modern Times*. Chicago: Rand-McNally, 1960.

The Economic and Social Context

Ardagh, John. *The New France*. London: Penguin, 1970.

Boudon, Raymond. *L'inégalité des chances*. Paris: Colin, 1973.

Chenot, Bernard. *Organisation économique de l'état*. Paris: Dalloz, 1965.

Coffey, Peter. *The Social Economy of France*. London: Macmillan, 1973.

Einaudi, Mario; Byé, Maurice; and Rossi, Ernesto. *Nationalization in France and Italy*. Ithaca, N.Y.: Cornell University Press, 1955.

Hoffmann, Stanley, ed. *In Search of France*. New York: Harper & Row Torchbooks, 1965.

Sheahan, John. *An Introduction to the French Economy*. Columbus, Ohio: Merrill, 1973.

Wright, Gordon. *Rural Revolution in France: The Peasantry in the Twentieth Century*. Stanford, Calif.: Stanford University Press, 1964.

Perspectives on Political Culture

Aron, Raymond. *The Opium of the Intellectuals*. New York: Norton, 1962.

Crozier, Michel. *The Stalled Society*. New York: Viking, 1973.

Curtius, Ernst Robert. *The Civilization of France*. New York: Vintage, 1962.

Fougeyrollas, Pierre. *La conscience politique dans la France contemporaine*. Paris: Denoel, 1963.

Gramont, Sanche de. *The French: Portrait of a People*. New York: Bantam, 1970.

Luethy, Herbert. *France Against Herself*. New York: Meridian, 1957.

Morazé, Charles. *The French and the Republic*. Ithaca, N.Y.: Cornell University Press, 1958.

Morin, Edgar. *Rumor in Orleans*. New York: Pantheon, 1971.

Rudorff, Raymond. *The Myth of France*. New York: Coward-McCann, 1970.

Touraine, Alain. *The May Movement*. New York: Random House, 1971.

Wylie, Laurence. *Village in the Vaucluse*. 2nd ed. New York: Harper & Row, 1964.

―――. *Chanzeaux: A Village in Anjou*. Cambridge, Mass.: Harvard University Press, 1967.

The Constitution and Its Background

Duval, Hervé, et al. *Référendum et plébiscite*. Paris: Colin, 1970.

Duverger, Maurice. *Institutions politiques et droit constitutionnel*. 11th ed. Paris: Presses Universitaires de France, 1970.

Fabre, Michel-Henri. *Principes républicains de droit constitutionnel*. 2nd ed. Paris: Librairie Générale de Droit et de Jurisprudence, 1970.

Gaulle, Charles de. *Major Addresses, Statements and Press Conferences of General Charles de Gaulle, May 19, 1958–January 31, 1964*. New York: French Embassy, Press and Information Division, 1964.

Macridis, Roy C., ed. *De Gaulle: Implacable Ally*. New York: Harper & Row, 1966.

Maier, Charles S., and White, Dan S., eds. *The Thirteenth of May: The Advent of de Gaulle's Republic*. New York: Oxford University Press, 1968.

Pickles, Dorothy. *The Fifth French Republic*. 3rd ed. New York: Praeger, 1966.

Tay, Hughes. *Le régime présidentiel et la France*. Paris: Librairie Générale de Droit et de Jurisprudence, 1967.

Wahl, Nicholas. *The Fifth Republic: France's New Political System*. New York: Random House, 1959.

Werth, Alexander. *De Gaulle: A Political Biography*. Baltimore: Penguin, 1967.

Wright, Gordon. *The Reshaping of French Democracy*. Boston: Beacon, 1970.

Political Parties

Anderson, Malcolm. *Conservative Politics in France*. London: Allen & Unwin, 1974.

Bizot, Jean-François, et al. *Au parti des socialistes*. Paris: Grasset, 1975.

Charlot, Jean. *The Gaullist Phenomenon*. New York: Praeger, 1971.

Duverger, Maurice. *La démocratie sans le peuple*. Paris: Seuil, 1967.

Hartley, Anthony. *Gaullism: The Rise and Fall of a Political Movement*. New York: Outerbridge & Lazard, 1972.

Hoffmann, Stanley. *Le mouvement Poujade*. Paris: Colin, 1956.

Johnson, Richard. *The French Communist Party Versus the Students*. New Haven, Conn.: Yale University Press, 1972.

Kriegel, Annie. *The French Communists: Profile of a People*. Chicago, Ill.: University of Chicago Press, 1972.

Laurens, André, and Pfister, Thierry. *Les nouveaux communistes*. Paris: Stock, 1973.

Leites, Nathan. *On the Game of Politics in France*. Stanford, Calif.: Stanford University Press, 1959.

McRae, Duncan. *Parliament, Parties and Society in France, 1946–1958*. New York: St. Martin's, 1967.

Micaud, Charles. *Communism and the French Left*. New York: Praeger, 1963.

Philip, André. *Les socialistes*. Paris: Seuil, 1967.

Remond, René. *The Right Wing in France from 1815 to de Gaulle.* 2nd ed. Philadelphia: University of Pennsylvania Press, 1969.

Savary, Alain. *Pour le nouveau parti socialiste.* Paris: Seuil, 1970.

Simmons, Harvey. *French Socialists in Search of a Role.* Ithaca, N.Y.: Cornell University Press, 1970.

Tarr, Francis de. *The French Radical Party: From Herriot to Mendès-France.* London: Oxford University Press, 1961.

Waterman, Harvey. *Political Change in Contemporary France: The Politics of an Industrial Democracy.* Columbus, Ohio: Merrill, 1969.

Williams, Philip. *Crisis and Compromise.* New York: Doubleday Anchor, 1966.

Wilson, Frank L. *The French Democratic Left.* Stanford, Calif.: Stanford University Press, 1971.

Interest Groups

Adam, Gérard. *La négotiation collective en France.* Paris: Editions ouvrières, 1971.

Adam, Gérard, et al. *L'ouvrier français en 1970.* Paris: Colin, 1970.

Barjonet, André. *La CGT.* Paris: Seuil, 1968.

Bockel, Alain. *La participation des syndicats ouvriers aux fonctions économiques et sociales de l'Etat.* Paris: Librairie Générale de Droit et de Jurisprudence, 1965.

Capdevielle, Jacques, and Mouriaux, René. *Les syndicats ouvriers en France.* Paris: Colin, 1970.

Clark, James M. *Teachers and Politics in France.* Syracuse, N.Y.: Syracuse University Press, 1967.

Ehrmann, Henry W. *Organized Business in France.* Princeton, N.J.: Princeton University Press, 1957.

Hamon, Léo, ed. *Les nouveaux comportements politiques de la classe ouvrière.* Paris: Presses Universitaires de France, 1962.

Maire, Edmond, and Juilliard, Jacques. *La CFDT d'aujourd'hui.* Paris: Seuil, 1975.

Meynaud, Jean. *Nouvelles études sur les groupes de pression en France.* Paris: Colin, 1962.

Tavernier, Yves. *Le syndicalisme paysan.* Paris: Colin, 1969.

Tavernier, Yves, et al. *L'univers politique des paysans dans la France contemporaine.* Paris: Colin, 1972.

The Executive and the Legislature

Alexandre, Philippe. *The Duel: De Gaulle and Pompidou.* Boston: Houghton Mifflin, 1972.

Anderson, Malcolm. *Government in France: An Introduction to the Executive Power*. Oxford: Pergamon, 1970.

Antoni, Jean-Dominique and Pascale. *Les ministres de la Cinquième République*. Paris: Presses Universitaires de France, 1976.

Avril, Pierre. *Le régime politique de la Ve République*. Paris: Librairie Générale de Droit et de Jurisprudence, 1967.

————. *Politics in France*. Baltimore: Penguin, 1969.

Cayrol, Roland; Parodi, Jean–Luc; and Ysmal, Colette. *Le député français*. Paris: Colin, 1973.

Lamy, Jean-Claude, and Kunstlé, Marc. *Au petit bonheur la chambre*. Paris: Julliard, 1972.

Maoût, Jean-Charles, and Muzellac, Raymond. *Le Parlement sous la Ve République*. Paris: Colin, 1971.

Marichy, Jean-Pierre. *La deuxième chambre dans la vie politique française*. Paris: Librairie Générale de Droit et de Jurisprudence, 1970.

Viansson-Ponté, Pierre. *The King and His Court*. Boston: Houghton Mifflin, 1965.

Williams, Philip. *The French Parliament: Politics in the Fifth Republic*. New York: Praeger, 1968.

Woshinsky, Oliver H. *The French Deputy*. Lexington, Mass.: Lexington, 1973.

Administration and the Judicial Process

Crozier, Michel. *The Bureaucratic Phenomenon*. Chicago: University of Chicago Press, 1964.

Kesselman, Mark. *The Ambiguous Consensus: A Study of Local Government in France*. New York: Knopf, 1967.

Langrod, Georges, ed. *La consultation dans l'administration contemporaine*. Paris: Cujas, 1971.

Lord, Guy. *The French Budgetary Process*. Berkeley: University of California Press, 1973.

Madiot, Yves. *Fusions et regroupements de communes*. Paris: Librairie Générale de Droit et de Jurisprudence, 1973.

Rendel, Margherita. *The Administrative Functions of the French Conseil d'Etat*. London: Weidenfeld & Nicolson, 1970.

Ridley, F., and Blondel, J. *Public Administration in France*. 2nd ed. London: Routledge & Kegan Paul, 1969.

Suleiman, Ezra. *Politics, Power and Bureaucracy in France: The Administrative Elite*. Princeton, N.J.: Princeton University Press, 1974.

Economic Planning

Bauchet, Pierre. *Economic Planning: The French Experience*. New York: Praeger, 1964.

Carré, Jean-Jacques, et al. *La croissance française*. Paris: Seuil, 1972.

Cohen, Stephen S. *Modern Capitalist Planning: The French Model*. Cambridge, Mass.: Harvard University Press, 1969.

Hackett, John and Anne-Marie. *Economic Planning in France*. London: Allen & Unwin, 1963.

Hayward, Jack. *Private Interests and Public Policy: The Experience of the French Social and Economic Council*. New York: Barnes & Noble, 1966.

Hayward, Jack, and Watson, Michael, eds. *Planning, Politics and Public Policy*. Cambridge: Cambridge University Press, 1975.

Shonfield, Andrew. *Modern Capitalism: The Changing Balance of Public and Private Power*. New York: Oxford University Press, 1965.

Foreign Policy

Andrews, William G. *French Politics and Algeria*. New York: Appleton-Century-Crofts, 1962.

Furniss, Edgar S., Jr. *France, Troubled Ally*. New York: Praeger, 1960.

Grosser, Alfred. *French Foreign Policy under de Gaulle*. Boston: Little, Brown, 1967.

Morse, Edward L. *Foreign Policy and Interdependence in Gaullist France*. Princeton, N.J.: Princeton University Press, 1973.

Serfaty, Simon. *France, de Gaulle and Europe*. Baltimore: Johns Hopkins Press, 1968.

From Gaullism to Post-Gaullism

Burnier, Michel-Antoine, et al. *La chute du Général*. Paris: Editions et Publications Premières, 1969.

Cotta, Michèle. *La VIe République*. Paris: Flammarion, 1974.

Macridis, Roy C. *French Politics in Transition: The Years after de Gaulle*. Cambridge, Mass.: Winthrop, 1975.

Martinet, Gilles. *Le système Pompidou*. Paris: Seuil, 1973.

Penniman, Howard R., ed. *France at the Polls: The Presidential Election of 1974*. Washington, D.C.: American Enterprise Institute, 1975.

Viansson-Ponté, Pierre. *Lettre ouverte aux hommes politiques*. Paris: Albin Michel, 1976.

Miscellaneous

Ambler, John S. *Soldiers Against the State: The French Army in Politics.*
New York: Doubleday Anchor, 1968.

Gaulle, Charles de. *The Complete War Memoirs.* 3 vols. New York:
Simon and Schuster, 1972.

Williams, Phillip. *French Politicians and Elections, 1951–1969.* Cambridge: Cambridge University Press, 1970.

————. *Wars, Plots and Scandals in Postwar France.* Cambridge: Cambridge University Press, 1970.

Index